ESSENTIALS OF NEGOTIATION

Third Edition

Roy J. Lewicki
The Ohio State University

David M. Saunders
Queen's University

Bruce Barry
Vanderbilt University

John W. Minton
Havatar Associates

Boston Burr Ridge, IL Dubuque, IA Madison, WI New York
San Francisco St. Louis Bangkok Bogotá Caracas Kuala Lumpur
Lisbon London Madrid Mexico City Milan Montreal New Delhi
Santiago Seoul Singapore Sydney Taipei Toronto

We dedicate this book to all negotiation and mediation professionals who try to make the world a better place.

ESSENTIALS OF NEGOTIATION
Published by McGraw-Hill/Irwin, a business unit of The McGraw-Hill Companies, Inc., 1221 Avenue of the Americas, New York, NY, 10020. Copyright © 2004, 2001, 1997 by The McGraw-Hill Companies, Inc. All rights reserved. No part of this publication may be reproduced or distributed in any form or by any means, or stored in a database or retrieval system, without the prior written consent of The McGraw-Hill Companies, Inc., including, but not limited to, in any network or other electronic storage or transmission, or broadcast for distance learning. Some ancillaries, including electronic and print components, may not be available to customers outside the United States.

This book is printed on acid-free paper.

4 5 6 7 8 9 0 DOC/DOC 0 9 8 7 6 5

ISBN 0-07-254582-8

Publisher: John E. Biernat
Sponsoring editor: Ryan Blankenship
Editorial coordinator: Trina Hauger
Executive marketing manager: Ellen Cleary
Producer, Media technology: Mark Molsky
Senior project manager: Christine A. Vaughan
Production supervisor: Gina Hangos
Designer: Kami Carter
Supplement producer: Joyce J. Chappetto
Senior digital content specialist: Brian Nacik
Typeface: 10/12 Times Roman
Compositor: Electronic Publishing Services, Inc., TN
Printer: R. R. Donnelley

Library of Congress Cataloging-in-Publication Data

Essentials of negotiation / Roy J. Lewicki ... [et al.].— 3rd ed.
    p. cm.
    Rev. ed of: Essentials of negotiation / Roy J. Lewicki. 2nd ed. c2001.
    Includes bibliography references and index.
    ISBN 0-07-254582-8 (alk. paper)
    1. Negotiation in business. 2. Negotiation. I. Lewicki, Roy J. II. Lewicki, Roy J.
Essentials of negotiation.
HD58.6.L49 2004
658.4'052—dc21
                                                    2003051035

www.mhhe.com

About the Authors

Roy J. Lewicki is the Dean's Distinguished Teaching Professor and Professor of Management and Human Resources at the Max M. Fisher College of Business, The Ohio State University. He has authored or edited 24 books, as well as numerous research articles. Professor Lewicki has served as the President of the International Association of Conflict Management, and received the first David Bradford Outstanding Educator award from the Organizational Behavior Teaching Society for his contributions to the field of teaching in negotiation and dispute resolution.

David M. Saunders is Dean of the Queen's School of Business at Queen's University, Canada. He has coauthored several articles on negotiation, conflict resolution, employee voice, and organizational justice. Prior to accepting his current appointment, he was Dean of the Haskayne School of Business at the University of Calgary and Director of the McGill MBA Japan program in Tokyo. He has traveled extensively throughout Asia, Europe, and South America.

Bruce Barry is Associate Professor of Management and Sociology at Vanderbilt University, and also Director of the Ph.D. program at Vanderbilt's Owen Graduate School of Management. His research on negotiation, influence, power, and justice has appeared in numerous scholarly journals and volumes. Professor Barry served a term as President of the International Association for Conflict Management (2002–2003), a professional society of researchers, teachers, and practitioners specializing in the fields of conflict, dispute resolution, and negotiation.

John W. Minton is the President and CEO of Havatar Associates, Inc., a management consultation, development, coaching, and recruiting firm specializing in meeting the needs of small and medium-sized organizations. He has taught in the business schools of Appalachian State and Duke Universities, and at Pfeiffer University where he was the Jefferson-Pilot Professor of Management. He is currently an Adjunct Professor at Gardner-Webb University, and has served as a volunteer mediator and arbitrator.

Preface to the Third Edition

Welcome to the Third Edition of *Essentials of Negotiation*. Again, this book represents our response to many faculty who wanted a brief version of the longer text, *Negotiation* (Fourth Edition). The objective of this shorter volume is to provide the reader with the core concepts of negotiation in a more succinct version. Many faculty requested such a book for use in shorter academic courses, executive education programs, or as an accompaniment to other resource materials for courses in negotiation, labor relations, conflict management, human resource management, and the like.

We welcome to the author team Prof. Bruce Barry of Vanderbilt University. Bruce has impressive professional credentials as a researcher in the fields of negotiation and conflict management, a newspaper columnist, a die-hard Mets fan, and an experienced teacher of negotiation at the Owen Graduate School of Management.

OVERVIEW OF THIS BOOK

The organization of this volume generally follows the more complete Fourth Edition of *Negotiation*. The fundamental difference between this and the Fourth Edition text is that this book contains only 9 chapters, while the complete Fourth Edition contains 13 chapters. The first four chapters have only been minimally shortened for this volume, because we believe that the content is essential to any negotiation course. (The shortening process includes editing out some of the more research-oriented references and descriptions, deleting many of the boxes and sidebars, and occasionally some secondary sections.) Five more chapters have been included, but shortened by 25–40 percent each. Finally, the four chapters which were excluded—chapters on Relationships, Multiparty Negotiations, Individual Differences, and Third-Party Approaches—have been shortened and placed on the book's McGraw-Hill website.

For the instructor who was not familiar with *Essentials* (First and Second Editions) or *Negotiation* (Fourth Edition), a brief overview is in order. The first four chapters introduce the reader to "Negotiation Fundamentals." The first chapter introduces the field of negotiation and conflict management, describes the basic problem of interdependence with other people, and briefly explores the problems of managing that interdependence. The second chapter introduces the concepts of strategy (the overall plan for a negotiation), "framing" (how parties come to decide what a negotiation is all about), and planning (how parties need to prepare for an upcoming negotiation). Chapters 3 and 4 then present the two core approaches to negotiation: the basic dynamics of competitive (win-lose) bargaining (Chapter 3) and the basic dynamics of integrative (win-win) negotiation (Chapter 4).

The next three chapters present three key subprocesses of negotiation: communication, persuasion, and ethical judgment. In Chapter 5, we review basic processes of cognition and communication in negotiation; we specifically examine communication dynamics, and a number of common cognition and judgment biases made by negotiators. In Chapter 6, we look at the tools negotiators can use to "pressure" the other side, using the tools of persuasion and power to get the other to change their perspective or give in to our arguments. Finally, in Chapter 7, we examine the ethical standards and criteria that surround negotiation, and create unique challenges for negotiators in deciding how fully and completely they are going to disclose their bargaining positions.

Chapter 8 explores the complex ways that negotiation processes change as one moves around the globe, from one culture to another. The last chapter emphasizes strategies that can be used by the parties to resolve breakdowns in the negotiation process.

Finally, as noted above, the four chapters deleted from *Negotiation* to form *Essentials* have also been edited and shortened. These chapters are:

- Supplementary Chapter 1: Social Context: Relationships and Representatives *(Negotiation* Chapter 8)
- Supplementary Chapter 2: Coalitions, Multiple Parties and Teams (*Negotiation* Chapter 9)
- Supplementary Chapter 3: Individual Differences (*Negotiation* Chapter 10)
- Supplementary Chapter 4: Managing Difficult Negotiations: Third-Party Approaches (*Negotiation* Chapter 13)

Instructors who want to use these chapters can download them from the website at www.mhhe.com/lewickinegotiation.

COMPARISON OF THIS BOOK TO THE SECOND EDITION OF *ESSENTIALS*

While we made major renovations in the Second Edition, the changes from the second to this third edition have been relatively minor. The content has been extensively revised and updated. Every chapter was completely revised for the third edition. The chapter organization now parallels more closely the organization of the longer text. We continue to enhance the readability and interest level of the book by leaving in several boxes (taken from current events and contemporary media) and occasional cartoons. We hope you find that these additions make the book less dry and more engaging, although we have had to use them sparingly in the *Essentials* volume, in order to keep the presentation concise.

The organization of the book also parallels more closely the organization of a third companion volume, *Negotiation: Readings, Exercises, and Cases (Fourth Edition)*, by Roy J. Lewicki, David M. Saunders, Bruce Barry, and John W. Minton, also published by Irwin/ McGraw-Hill (2003). An excellent *Instructor's Manual* for this volume is also available from the publisher. The *Essentials* and *Readings* books can be used together or separately, and we encourage instructors to contact the publisher for an examination copy.

SUPPLEMENTARY MATERIALS

A test bank and PowerPoint transparencies have been prepared for the Fourth Edition of *Negotiation,* and can be adapted for use with *Essentials.* Instructors should request these materials from your McGraw-Hill/Irwin representative. The CD-ROM also contains a number of instructional tools for the effective organization and instruction of a Negotiation course.

APPRECIATION

Once again, this book could not have been completed without the assistance of many other people. We would specifically like to thank

- Many of our colleagues in the negotiation and dispute resolution field, whose research efforts have made the growth of this field possible, and who have used earlier editions and told us what they liked and did not like.

- The staff of McGraw-Hill/Irwin: publisher John Biernat and editor John Weimeister, for their ongoing confidence and patience as we completed the works; Trina Hauger, Editorial Coordinator, for solving any problem and fixing any disaster; Christine Vaughan, Senior Project Manager, for turning a jumble of words into readable text and finding (almost) every spelling and copyediting mistake; Marketing Manager Ellen Cleary, for continuing to promote the volume; and Joyce Chappetto, for preparing our new supplements.

- Our families, who continue to provide us with the time and support that we require to finish this project.

Thank you one and all!

Roy J. Lewicki
David M. Saunders
Bruce Barry
John W. Minton

Contents in Brief

Contents

CHAPTER 1

The Nature of Negotiation

JOE AND SUE CARTER

The day started early, as usual. Over breakfast, Sue Carter raised the question of where she and her husband, Joe, would go for their summer vacation. She wanted to sign up for a tour of the Far East being sponsored by her college's alumni association. However, two weeks on a guided tour with a lot of other people was not what Joe had in mind. He needed to get away from people, crowds, and schedules, and he wanted to charter a sailboat and cruise the New England coast. In addition, they were still not sure whether the children would go with them. The two kids really wanted to go to camp, and Joe and Sue couldn't afford both summer camp and a vacation for the four of them. The Carters had not argued (yet), but it was clear that they had a real problem here. Some of their friends handled problems like this by taking separate vacations. With both of them working full-time, though, one thing Joe and Sue did agree on was that they would take their vacation together.

As Joe drove to work, he thought about the vacation problem. What bothered Joe most was that there seemed to be no good way to manage the conflict productively. With some conflicts, they could compromise; but given what each wanted this time, compromise didn't seem possible. At other times they would flip a coin; that might work for choosing a restaurant, but it seemed unwise in this case because of how much money was involved and how important vacation time was to them. In addition, flipping a coin might be more likely to make one of them feel like a loser and the other feel guilty than to help both feel really satisfied.

Walking through the parking lot, Joe met his company's purchasing manager, Ed Laine. Joe was the head of the engineering design group for MicroWatt, a manufacturer of small electric motors. Ed reminded Joe that they had to settle a problem created by the engineers in Joe's department: The engineers were contacting vendors directly rather than going through MicroWatt's purchasing department. Joe knew that purchasing wanted all contacts with a vendor to go through them; but he also knew that his engineers badly needed technical information for design purposes, and waiting for the information to come through purchasing slowed things considerably. Ed Laine was aware of Joe's views about this problem, and Joe thought the two of them could probably find some way to resolve this if they really sat down to work on it. Joe and Ed were also both aware that upper management expected middle managers to settle differences among themselves; if this problem "went upstairs" to senior management, it would make both of them look bad.

Shortly after reaching his desk, Joe received a telephone call from an automobile salesman with whom he had been talking about a new car. The salesman asked how Sue felt about the car and whether she wanted to drive it. Joe wasn't quite sure that Sue would go along with his choice; Joe had picked out a luxury import, and he expected Sue to say it is too expensive. Joe was pleased with the latest offer the salesman had made, but thought he might still get a few more concessions out of him, so he introduced Sue's concerns to put more pressure on the salesman to lower the price.

As soon as Joe hung up the phone, it rang again. It was Sue, calling to vent her frustration to Joe over some of the procedures at the local bank where she worked as a senior loan officer. Sue was frustrated working for an old "family-run" bank that was not very automated, was heavily bureaucratic, and was slow to respond to customer needs. The competition would approve certain types of loans within three hours that took Sue a week to get approved. While the bank staff was oriented to the public and polite to customers, they were losing clients to large state and multinational banks that had entered the city and were providing more efficient services. It seemed that every week Sue was losing more and more of her clients to the larger banks. Whenever she tried to discuss this with senior management, she was met with resistance and a lecture on traditional values.

Most of Joe's afternoon was taken up by the annual budget meeting. Joe hated these meetings. The people from the finance department came in and arbitrarily cut everyone's figures by 30 percent, and then all the managers had to argue endlessly to try to get some of their new-project money reinstated. Joe had learned to work with a lot of people, some of whom he did not like very much, but these people from finance were the most arrogant and arbitrary number crunchers imaginable. He could not understand why the top brass did not see how much harm these people were doing to the engineering group's research and development efforts. Joe considered himself a reasonable guy, but the way these people acted made him feel like he didn't want to give them an inch. He was prepared to draw the line and fight it out for as long as it took.

In the evening, Sue and Joe attended a meeting of their town's Conservation Commission, which, among other things, was charged with protecting the town's streams, wetlands, and nature preserves. Sue is a member of the Conservation Commission, and Sue and Joe both strongly believe in sound environmental protection and management. This evening's case involved a request by a real estate development firm to drain a swampy area and move a small creek to build a new regional shopping mall. All projections showed that the new shopping mall would attract jobs and revenue to the area and considerably fatten the town's treasury. The new mall was badly needed to replace several others that had closed, putting a sizable number of people out of work and reducing the town's tax revenues. But the plan might also do irreparable damage to the wetlands and the wildlife in that area. The initial plan proposed by the development firm had serious problems, and the commission had asked Sue to see if an acceptable solution could be developed. Eventually a site plan had been worked out that would have considerably more benefits than drawbacks. But now Sue was having difficulties with some members of the commission who were ardent conservationists and argued against *any* change in the wetlands on that lot. In addition, word about the application had leaked out, and even some members of the town council had decided to join the conservationists in the fight.

Joe and Sue discussed their respective days as they drove home from the council meeting. Each thought that life is kind of strange, because sometimes things go very smoothly and other times things seem much too complicated. As they went to sleep later, they each thought about how they might have approached certain situations differently during the day and were thankful that they had a relationship where they could discuss things openly with each other.

INTRODUCTION

People negotiate all the time. Friends negotiate where to have dinner. Children negotiate which television program to watch. Businesses negotiate to purchase materials and to sell their products. Lawyers negotiate to settle legal claims before they go to court. The police negotiate with terrorists to free hostages. Nations negotiate to open their borders for free trade. Negotiation is not a process reserved only for the skilled diplomat, top salesperson, or ardent advocate for organized labor; it is something that *everyone* does, almost daily. Although the stakes are not usually as dramatic as peace accords or large corporate mergers, everyone, like Joe and Sue Carter, negotiates; sometimes people negotiate for major things like a new job, other times for relatively minor things, such as who will wash the dishes. The structure and processes of negotiation are fundamentally the same at the personal level as they are at the diplomatic and corporate levels.

Negotiations occur for one of two reasons: (1) to create something new that neither party could do on his or her own, or (2) to resolve a problem or dispute between the parties. A large number of perspectives can be used to understand different aspects of negotiations, including theory and research from economics, psychology, political science, communication, labor relations, law, sociology, and anthropology. The same negotiation outcome may also be explained simultaneously from several different perspectives.[1] Because people can negotiate about so many different things, understanding the fundamental processes of negotiation is essential for anyone who works with other people. We will draw from several different research traditions throughout the book, but our focus will always be on promoting a deeper understanding of the negotiation process.

Sometimes people fail to negotiate because they do not recognize that they are in a bargaining situation. By choosing options other than negotiation, they may fail to identify a good opportunity and not achieve their goals, or they may not manage their problems as smoothly as they might like to. People may also recognize the need for bargaining but do poorly because they misunderstand the process and do not have good negotiating skills.[2] After reading this book, people should be well prepared to recognize negotiation situations; understand what the process of bargaining involves; know how to analyze, plan, and implement successful negotiations; and, perhaps most important, be able to obtain better negotiation outcomes than before.

We will use the words *bargaining* and *negotiation* interchangeably throughout the book. In most conversations the words mean the same thing, but sometimes they are used as if they mean different things. For example, bargaining is like the competitive haggling over price that happens during a yard sale or flea market, whereas negotiation is a more formal process that occurs when parties are trying to find a mutually acceptable solution to a complex conflict. In Chapters 3 and 4, when we describe the differences between two very different forms of negotiation, we will call one *bargaining* and the other *negotiation* to make the comparisons between the two clearer.

To illustrate further what this book is about, and the breadth and scope of negotiation in our professional and personal lives, we will return to the hypothetical, but not unrealistic, Joe and Sue Carter story that opened this chapter.

CHARACTERISTICS OF A NEGOTIATION SITUATION

The Joe and Sue Carter story highlights the variety of situations that can be handled by negotiation. Any of us might encounter one or more of these situations over the course of a few days or weeks. We identify them as *negotiation situations* because they have fundamentally the same characteristics as peace negotiations between countries at war, business negotiations between two corporations, or a standoff between police and hostage takers. There are several characteristics common to all negotiation situations:[3]

1. There are two or more parties—that is, two or more individuals, groups, or organizations. Although people can "negotiate" with themselves—as when someone debates whether to spend the afternoon studying, playing tennis, or going to the football game—we will discuss negotiation as an *interpersonal, intragroup,* or *intergroup* process. In the Carter story, Joe negotiates with his wife, the purchasing manager, and the auto salesman, and Sue negotiates with her husband, senior management at the bank, and the Conservation Commission, among others.

2. There is a conflict of interest between two or more parties—that is, what one wants is not necessarily what the other one wants—and the parties must search for a way to resolve the conflict. Joe and Sue negotiate over vacations, budgets, automobiles, and company procedures.

3. The parties negotiate because they think they can use some form of influence to get a better deal that way than by simply taking what the other side will voluntarily give them or let them have. Negotiation is largely a voluntary process. It is a strategy pursued by choice; seldom are we required to negotiate (see Box 1.1 for examples of when we should *not* negotiate).

4. The parties, at least for the moment, prefer to search for agreement rather than to fight openly, have one side capitulate, permanently break off contact, or take their dispute to a higher authority to resolve it. Negotiation occurs when there is no system—no fixed or established set of rules or procedures—for resolving the conflict, or when the parties prefer to work outside of the system to invent their own solution. If we keep a rented movie too long, the store will charge us a fee, but we might be able to negotiate that fee if we have a good excuse as to why the tape is being returned late. Similarly, attorneys negotiate or plea-bargain for their clients who would rather be assured of a negotiated settlement than take their chances with a judge and jury in the courtroom. In the Carter story, Joe pursues negotiation rather than letting his wife decide on the vacation, accepting a fixed price for the car, or accepting the budget cut without question. Sue uses negotiation to try to change the bank's procedures rather than accepting the status quo, and she works

BOX 1.1
When You Shouldn't Negotiate

There are times when you should avoid negotiating. In these situations, stand your ground and you'll come out ahead.

When you'd lose the farm
If you're in a situation where you could lose everything, choose other options rather than negotiate.

When you're sold out
When you're running at capacity, don't deal. Raise your prices instead.

When the demands are unethical
Don't negotiate if your counterpart asks for something that you cannot support because it's illegal, unethical, or morally inappropriate. When your character or your reputation is compromised, you lose in the long run.

When you don't care
If you have no stake in the outcome, don't negotiate. You have everything to lose and nothing to gain.

When you don't have time
When you're pressed for time, you may choose not to negotiate. If the time pressure works against you, you'll make mistakes, and you may fail to consider the implications of your concessions. When under the gun, you'll settle for less than you could otherwise get.

When they act in bad faith
Stop the negotiation when your counterpart shows signs of acting in bad faith. If you can't trust their negotiating, you can't trust their agreement. In this case, negotiation is of little or no value. Stick to your guns and cover your position, or discredit them.

When waiting would improve your position
Perhaps you'll have a new technology available soon. Maybe your financial situation will improve. Another opportunity may present itself. If the odds are good that you'll gain ground with a delay, wait.

When you're not prepared
If you don't prepare, you'll think of all your best questions, responses, and concessions on the way home. Gathering your reconnaissance and rehearsing the negotiation will pay off handsomely. If you're not ready, just say "no."

SOURCE: J. C. Levinson, M. S. A. Smith, and O. R. Wilson, *Guerrilla Negotiating: Unconventional Weapons and Tactics to Get What You Want* (New York: John Wiley, 1999), pp. 22–23. This material is used by permission of John Wiley & Sons, Inc.

to influence the outcome of the shopping mall plan rather than letting others decide how to resolve the problem or watching it go to court.

5. When we negotiate, we expect give and take. We expect that both sides will modify or give in somewhat on their opening statements, requests, or demands. Although the parties may at first argue strenuously for what they want, each pushing

the other side for concessions, usually both sides will modify their positions and each will move toward the other. As we will discuss, however, truly creative negotiations may not require compromise; instead the parties may invent a solution that meets the objectives of all sides.

6. Successful negotiation involves the management of *intangibles* as well as the resolving of *tangibles* (e.g., the price or the terms of agreement). Intangible factors are the underlying psychological motivations that may directly or indirectly influence the parties during a negotiation. Some examples of intangibles are (*a*) the need to "look good" to the people you represent, (*b*) the desire to book more business than any other salesperson in your office, and (*c*) the fear of setting precedent in the negotiations. Intangibles can also include core beliefs and values. Intangible factors can have an enormous influence on negotiation processes and outcomes, and need to be managed proactively during negotiations. For example, Joe may not want to make Ed Laine angry about the purchasing problem because he needs Ed's support in the upcoming budget negotiations, but Joe also doesn't want to lose face to his engineers, who expect him to back them up.

INTERDEPENDENCE

In negotiation, both parties need each other. A buyer cannot buy unless someone else sells, and vice versa. This situation of mutual dependency is called *interdependence*. Interdependent relations are complex and have their own special challenge. They are more complex than situations in which one party is independent of the other or in which one is simply dependent on the other. Independent parties can, if they choose, have a relatively detached, indifferent, uninvolved outlook. One who is dependent on another must accept and accommodate that other party's demands and idiosyncrasies. For example, if an employee is totally dependent on an employer for a job, the employee will have to either do the job as instructed or quit. Interdependent parties, however, have an opportunity to influence each other, and many options are open to both. Managing and dealing with those options can be difficult, however, because of the complexity of the interdependent relationship.

Interdependent relationships are characterized by interlocking goals—the parties need each other in order to accomplish their goals. For instance, in a business project management team, no single person could complete a complex project alone within the time limit imposed by the organization. For the group to accomplish its goals, each person needs to rely on the other project team members. In that sense, the goals of the project team members are interdependent. Note that having interdependent goals does not mean that everyone wants or needs exactly the same thing. Different project team members may need different things, but they must work together. This mix of personal and group goals is typical of interdependent situations. Another example of interdependence is two people playing a competitive game of squash. On the one hand, both players want to win the game, so their goals are in conflict (only one person can win). On the other hand, both want to play the game, so their goals converge (one cannot play squash alone). This mix of convergent and conflicting goals characterizes many interdependent relationships.

Interdependent goals are an important aspect of negotiation. The structure of the interdependence between different negotiating parties determines the range of possible outcomes of the negotiation and suggests the appropriate strategies and tactics that the negotiators should use. For instance, if the interdependence is a "win-lose" situation—that is, the more one party gains, the more the other party loses—then the negotiation will focus on how to divide a fixed amount of outcomes. An example of this type of negotiation is determining the price of a major appliance or vehicle. (Such situations, known as distributive bargaining, are discussed in detail in Chapter 3.) Another type of interdependence occurs in a "win-win" situation—that is, solutions exist so that both parties can do well in the negotiation. An example of this type of negotiation is determining the relationship between two companies in a joint venture. (Such situations, known as integrative negotiation, are discussed in detail in Chapter 4.) The type of interdependence between the negotiating parties will determine both the range of possible negotiation solutions and the type of strategies the negotiators should use.

The interdependence of people's goals is the basis for much social interaction. By examining the ways in which the goals are interdependent, we can estimate what type of behavior is most likely to emerge. When the goals of two or more people are interconnected so that only one can achieve the goal—such as winning a gold medal in a race—we have a competitive situation, also known as a zero-sum or distributive situation, in which "individuals are so linked together that there is a negative correlation between their goal attainments."[4] To the degree that one person achieves his or her goal, the other's goal attainment is blocked. In contrast, when parties' goals are linked so that one person's goal achievement *helps* others to achieve their goals, we have a mutual-gains situation, also known as a non–zero-sum or integrative situation, where there is a positive correlation between the goal attainment of both parties. The nature of the interdependence will have a major impact on the nature of the relationship, the way negotiations are conducted, and the outcomes of a negotiation.[5]

Fisher, Ury, and Patton, in their popular book *Getting to Yes: Negotiating Agreement without Giving In,* also stress the importance of understanding the nature of interdependence.[6] They suggest that knowing and developing alternatives to reaching an agreement with the other party in a negotiation is an important source of power. They note that, "whether you should or should not agree on something in a negotiation depends entirely upon the attractiveness to you of the best available alternative."[7] They call this concept BATNA (an acronym for *Best Alternative To a Negotiated Agreement*) and suggest that each negotiator needs to understand both parties' BATNAs when they negotiate. The value of a person's BATNA is always relative to the possible settlements available in the current negotiation, and the possibilities within a given negotiation are heavily influenced by the nature of the interdependence between the parties.

MUTUAL ADJUSTMENT

Interdependent relationships—those in which people are mutually dependent—are complex. Both parties know that they can influence the other's outcomes and that their outcomes can, in turn, be influenced by the other.[8] This mutual adjustment continues throughout the negotiation as both parties act to influence the other.[9] It is important to recognize that negotiation is a *process* that transforms over time, and mutual adjustment is one of the key causes of the changes that occur during a negotiation.[10]

Let us explore Sue Carter's job situation in more detail. Rather than accepting a layoff or reduced pay, Sue would like to leave her present employer and take a job that is available in a large multinational bank in her town. Her prospective manager, Bob, perceives Sue as a desirable candidate for the position and is ready to offer her the job. Bob and Sue are now attempting to establish Sue's salary. The job description announced the salary as "competitive." Sue has, privately, identified a salary below which she will not work ($40,000) but suspects she may be able to get considerably more. Because the bank has a reputation for running "hard and lean," Sue has decided not to state her minimally acceptable salary; she suspects that the bank will pay no more than necessary and that her minimum would be accepted quickly. Moreover, she knows that it would be difficult to raise the level if it should turn out that $40,000 was considerably below what Bob would pay. Sue has thought of stating her ideal salary ($45,000), but she suspects that Bob will view her as either presumptuous or rude for asking that much (see Box 1.2). If this happened, then the interview would probably end with Bob viewing her negatively and making it harder for her to get the best possible salary.

Let's take a closer look at what is happening here. Sue is making her decision based on how she *anticipates* Bob will react to her actions. Sue recognizes that her actions will affect Bob. Sue also recognizes that the way Bob acts toward her in the future will be influenced by the way her actions affect him now. As a result, Sue is assessing the *indirect* impact of her behavior on herself. Further, she also knows that Bob is alert to all this and will look upon any statement by Sue as reflecting a preliminary position on salary rather than a final one. To counter this expected view, Sue will probably try to find some way to state a number as close to her desired final salary as possible. For example, she could refer to salaries that she knows other people with similar qualifications have received in other banks. Sue is choosing among behavioral options with a thought not only to how they will affect Bob but also to how they will then lead Bob to act toward Sue. Further, Sue knows that Bob believes she will act in this way and makes her decision on the basis of this belief.

One may wonder if people really pay attention to all this complexity, or think in such detail in their relationships with others. Certainly people don't do this most of the time, or they would be frozen in inactivity while they tried to think through the possibilities. However, when people face complex, important, or novel situations, they are more likely to think in this way. The effective negotiator needs to understand how people will adjust and readjust what they say during negotiations based on what the other party does and is expected to do.

Behavior in an interdependent relationship is frequently calculated on the premise that the more information one has about the other person, the better. There is the possibility, however, that too much knowledge only confuses, or it may accentuate differences in perceived fairness.[11] For example, suppose Sue knows the average salary ranges for clerical, supervisory, and managerial positions for local, national, and multinational banks in her county, state, and country. Does all this help Sue determine her actions or does it only confuse things? In fact, given all these complexities, Sue may not have reached a decision about what salary she should be paid, other than a minimum figure

BOX 1.2
The Importance of Aligning Perceptions

Having information about your negotiation partner's perceptions is an important element of negotiation success. When your expectations of a negotiated outcome are based on faulty information, it is likely that you will not be taken seriously by the other party. Take, for example, the following story told to one of the authors:

> At the end of a job interview, the recruiter asked the enthusiastic MBA student, "And what starting salary were you looking for?"
>
> The MBA candidate replied, "I would like to start in the neighborhood of $125,000 per year, depending on your benefits package."
>
> The recruiter said, "Well, what would you say to a package of five weeks' vacation, 14 paid holidays, full medical and dental coverage, company matching retirement fund up to 50 percent of your salary, and a new company car leased for your use every two years . . . say, a red Corvette?"
>
> The MBA sat up straight and said, "Wow! Are you kidding?"
>
> "Of course," said the recruiter. "But you started it."

below which she will not go. This is the classic bargaining situation. Both parties have their outer limits for an acceptable settlement (how high or low they are willing to go), but within that range, neither has determined what the exact number should be. The parties have to exchange information and make an effort at influencing each other and at problem solving. They must work toward a solution that takes into account each person's requirements and, hopefully, optimizes the outcomes for both.[12]

Problem solving is essentially a process of specifying the elements of a desired outcome, examining the components available to produce the outcome, and searching for a way to fit them together. It is possible for a person to approach problem solving in negotiation from his or her own perspective and attempt to solve the problem by considering only the components that affect his or her own desired outcome. For instance, going back to the beginning of the Carter story, Sue could decide what was best for her vacation and ignore Joe's needs. When approaching the situation as a joint problem-solving effort, however, the outcomes desired by the other party must be taken into account. In the case of Sue's salary negotiation, Bob may be constrained by company rules that limit how far he can go in negotiating salary with Sue, but the company may allow him to be very flexible in negotiating other aspects of the employment relationship. One difficulty is that opposing parties may not be open about their desired outcomes, or they may not be clear in their own minds about what they actually want. Hence, a necessary step in all negotiation is *to clarify and share information about what both parties really want as outcomes.*

As negotiations evolve, at least some part of the combined set of desired outcomes becomes known, usually through statements of bargaining positions or needs. If the suggested outcomes don't immediately work, the negotiation continues as a series of proposals. Each party's proposals usually suggest alterations to the other party's position, and perhaps contain changes to his or her own position. When one party accepts a change in his or her position, a *concession* has been made.[13] Concessions restrict the range of options within which a solution or agreement will be reached; when a party makes a concession, the bargaining range is confined closer to one or both sides' limits or resistance point. For instance, Sue would like to get a starting salary of $45,000, but she scales her request down to $43,000, thereby eliminating all possible salary options above $43,000. People may recognize that concessions are necessary for a settlement, but they obviously are reluctant to make all or most of them. Before making any concessions below $43,000, Sue probably will want to see some willingness on the part of the bank to add some combination of attractive benefits to the salary package.

Making and interpreting concessions is no easy task, especially when there is little trust between negotiators. Two of the dilemmas that all negotiators face, identified by Harold Kelley, help explain why this is the case.[14] The first dilemma, the *dilemma of honesty*, concerns how much of the truth to tell the other party. (The ethical considerations of these dilemmas are discussed in Chapter 7.) On the one hand, telling the other party everything about your situation may give that person the opportunity to take advantage of you. On the other hand, not telling the other person anything about your needs and desires may lead to a stalemate. Just how much of the truth should you tell the other party? If Sue told Bob that she would work for as little as $40,000 but would like to start at $45,000, it is quite possible that Bob would hire her for $40,000 and allocate the extra money that he might have paid her elsewhere in the budget. We are not suggesting that Bob should do this; rather, because the long-term relationship is important in this situation, Bob should ensure that both parties' needs are met (see Chapter 4 for an expanded discussion of this point). If, however, Sue did not tell Bob any information about her salary aspirations, then Bob would have a difficult time knowing how to satisfy those needs.

The second dilemma that every negotiator faces, the *dilemma of trust*, concerns how much to believe of what the other party tells you. If you believe everything that the other party says, then he or she could take advantage of you. If you believe nothing that the other party says, then you will have a great deal of difficulty in reaching an agreement. To what extent you should trust the other party depends on many factors, including the reputation of the other party, how he or she treated you in the past, and the present circumstances. If Bob told Sue that $38,000 was the maximum he was allowed to pay her for the job without seeking approval "from above," should Sue believe him or not? As you can see, sharing and clarifying information is not as easy as it first appears.

The search for an optimal solution through the processes of giving information and making concessions is greatly aided by trust and a belief that you're being treated honestly and fairly. Two efforts in negotiation help to create such trust and belief—one is based on perceptions of outcomes and the other on perceptions of the process. An outcome effort attempts to change a party's estimation of the perceived importance or value of something. If Bob convinces Sue that a lower salary for the job is relatively unimportant given the high potential for promotion associated with the position, then Sue may feel comfortable making a concession on salary.

In contrast, an effort based on the negotiating process may help convey images of equity, fairness, and reciprocity in proposals and concessions. When one party makes several proposals that are rejected by the other party and the other party makes no alternate proposal, the first party may feel improperly treated and may therefore break off negotiations. When people make a concession, they feel much more comfortable and trusting if the other party responds with a concession. In fact, the belief that concessions will occur in negotiations appears to be almost universal. During training seminars, we have asked negotiators from more than 50 countries if they expect give-and-take to occur during negotiations in their culture; all have said they do. This pattern of give-and-take is not just a characteristic of negotiation; it is also essential to joint problem solving in most interdependent relationships.[15] Satisfaction with a negotiation is as much determined by the process through which an agreement is reached as with the actual outcome obtained. To eliminate or even deliberately attempt to reduce this give-and-take—as some labor–management negotiating strategies have attempted—is to short-circuit the process, and may destroy both the basis for trust and any possibility of joint decision making.[16] Even if the strategy results in maximizing joint outcomes, the other party may express dissatisfaction with the process or with the negotiation as a whole. Following a fair process will contribute to feelings of satisfaction and success for both parties.

INTERDEPENDENCE AND PERCEPTIONS

We have been treating interdependence as a more or less objective phenomenon in negotiation. That is, we have looked at how the structure of the negotiation itself (e.g., win-lose versus win-win situation) plays an important part in determining how two negotiating parties should interact. People frequently perceive economic exchanges, such as the purchase of a new car or a commodity, as win-lose situations. At other times, however, such exchanges may be structured as win-win, in which case there are opportunities for both parties to gain. For example, two companies that are considering a merger could be in a situation where both could be more effective competing with other companies after the merger. A recent trend among consulting companies illustrates this well. Companies that are traditionally strong in one area of consulting (e.g., accounting or taxation) have been merging with companies that are traditionally strong in other areas (e.g., human resource management or corporate strategy) in order to create comprehensive consulting services across several lines of business. The challenge in negotiating in these types of situations is to find solutions where *all* parties can do well.

Understanding the nature of the interdependence of the parties is critical to successful negotiation. Unfortunately, negotiation situations do not typically present themselves with neat labels. Rather, negotiators make judgments about the nature of the interdependence in their negotiation situations, and negotiator perceptions about interdependence become as important as the actual structure of the interdependence.[17]

To examine how perception and structure are critically linked, let us return to the example of the merging consulting companies. Recall that one company, which we'll call Company A, was stronger in accounting and taxation consulting, although they also offered consulting in human resource management and corporate strategy. The other company, which we will refer to as Company B, was stronger in human resource management and corporate strategy consulting, although they also did some consulting in accounting and taxation. Assume that both companies were extremely competitive in the past. If one approaches the other to suggest a merger, the receiver would be likely to view the move skeptically, perhaps even seeing it as a sign of weakness of the other company. Instead, now assume that each company had strong respect for the other company's ability in its primary consulting domain and neither competed head on with each other. In this situation, an offer to merge would likely be viewed in a very different manner.

The point here is that people bring much baggage with them to a negotiation, including past experience, personality characteristics, moods, habits, and beliefs about how to negotiate. These factors will influence how people perceive an interdependent situation, and this perception will in turn have a strong effect on the subsequent negotiation.

Considerable research has been conducted on the role of perception and cognition in negotiation.[18] This research suggests that how people perceive interdependent situations has an important effect on how they will negotiate. (Perception and cognition are discussed in more detail in Chapter 5.) Leigh Thompson and Reid Hastie suggest that negotiators' perceptions and judgments can have important influences on judgments they make about (*a*) the other party, (*b*) themselves, (*c*) the utilities of both parties, (*d*) offers and counteroffers, (*e*) negotiation outcomes, and (*f*) the negotiation process as a whole.[19]

Another line of research has sought to identify systematic biases in negotiators' initial perceptions of the nature of the interdependence between the negotiating parties. Max Bazerman, Thomas Magliozzi, and Margaret Neale labeled one such systematic bias the "mythical fixed pie." Bazerman and his colleagues suggest that most negotiators will assume that there is a fixed pie; that is, the more I get, the less you have.[20] In a laboratory study of negotiation that investigated this hypothesis, Leigh Thompson and Reid Hastie[21] found that more than twice as many negotiators (68 percent) assumed their upcoming negotiations were win-lose situations rather than win-win situations (32 percent). Thompson and Hastie also found that the degree to which negotiators adjusted to the situation during the first five minutes of the negotiation had an important effect on the outcome of the negotiation. Negotiators who better adjusted their assessments of the structure of the negotiation early in the process earned higher profits than those who did not adjust until later.[22]

Researchers continue to identify other systematic perceptual biases that make negotiators less than ideal decision makers (see Chapter 5 for further discussion). It is no simple task to correct the biased perceptions that occur when negotiating, however. Most authors agree that *identifying* the systematic biases in negotiators' perceptions is an important first step. An important unsolved issue is whether the next step, reducing the effect of the biases, is best accomplished through the use of an unfreezing-change-refreezing model, systematic consideration of the other party's position, or some other technique.[23]

Two potential consequences of interdependent relationships are (1) value creation and (2) conflict. Negotiation skills and subprocesses are useful in situations where one wants to create value or needs to manage conflict. There is no simple recipe, however, that guarantees positive outcomes in either situation. Negotiation is a craft that blends art and science, and positive outcomes are a consequence of knowledge, experience, careful planning, and some luck. In the next section we discuss aspects of value creation, and in the following section we examine the extensive literature on conflict management.

VALUE CREATION

At the most fundamental level interdependence has the potential to lead to synergy, which is the notion that "the whole is greater than the sum of its parts." There are numerous business, Non-Government Organizations (NGOs), and personal examples of this. For instance, the recent joint ventures in research by pharmaceutical companies are designed to increase their joint research potential beyond what companies can do individually, as well as controlling their costs. Protests against globalization by various action groups are far more effective when mutually coordinated than run independently. Each of these situations involves interdependence between two or more parties, and the potential of successful value creation is significantly increased with the appropriate application of the negotiation skills discussed throughout this book.

Lax and Sebenius, in their book *The Manager as Negotiator,* describe several sources of where value may be created.[24] One of the main sources of value creation is contained in the differences that exist between negotiators. Negotiators are seldom identical, and according to Lax and Sebenius the key differences among negotiators may include differences in interests, opinions, risk aversion, and time preferences. These differences are fundamental to creating value for each negotiator, and are discussed in turn below:

• *Differences in interests*. Negotiators seldom value all items in a negotiation equally. For instance, in a collective bargaining situation management may be more willing to concede on benefits than salary because the benefits may cost them less. A wholesaler of telephone airtime may be more interested in the total value of the deal than the number of minutes sold or the rate per minute. An advertising company may be quite willing to bend on creative control of a project, but very protective of advertising placement.

• *Differences in opinions.* People differ in their evaluation of what something is worth or the future value of an item. For instance, is a piece of property in the neighborhood a good or bad investment of your hard-earned income? Some people will imagine all types of future potential, while others will see a piece of land that will unlikely increase in value. Real estate developers work hard to identify properties where they see future potential while the current owners undervalue it.

• *Differences in risk aversion.* People differ in the amount of risk that they are comfortable assuming. A young, single-income family with two children can sustain less risk than a middle-aged, dual-income couple without children. A company with a cash flow problem can assume less risk of expanding its operations than one that is cash rich.

• *Differences in time preference.* Negotiators frequently differ in how time affects them. One negotiator may be more patient with the negotiation process than the other, one may need a resolution sooner than the other, and finally there may be differences in preference for cash now versus future investments. All of these differences in time preferences have the potential to create value in a negotiation. For instance, a car salesman may want to close a deal by the end of the month in order to be eligible for a special company bonus, while the potential buyer does not need the car for another month. Or, a potential donor to a charity may need to make the donation by year end in order to realize certain tax advantages, while the charity may need to seek board approval for engaging in the new project that the donor wants and this cannot occur until the following year.

In summary, it is important that negotiators be aware that potential differences between them may be the critical factors that they can use to reach an agreement. It is also possible, however, to create value through shared interests and through scale.[25] For instance, a couple who resolve their yearly vacation dilemma after a pleasant discussion, when it frequently results in arguments and acrimony, will have created positive value in their relationship, a shared interest. Companies often enter into joint ventures to reach the scale required in order to complete a project that any individual company would have trouble reaching alone. For instance, large oil companies develop expensive long-term projects together (e.g., the Alberta, Canada Tar Sands development costs well in excess of $1 billion and is being done in a joint venture), and pharmaceutical companies share capital and human resources to fund their blue sky research and development projects.

CONFLICT

The other potential consequence of interdependent relationships is conflict. Conflict can be due to the highly divergent needs of the two parties, a misunderstanding that occurs between two people, or some other, intangible factor. Conflict can occur when the two parties are working toward the same goal and generally want the same outcome, or when both parties want a very different settlement. Regardless of the cause of the conflict, negotiation can play an important role in resolving it. Because many opportunities for negotiation are a result of conflict, we present a broad overview of the key definitions, concepts, terms, and models in this area.

Definitions

Conflict may be defined as a "sharp disagreement or opposition, as of interests, ideas, etc." and includes "the perceived divergence of interest, or a belief that the parties' current aspirations cannot be achieved simultaneously."[26] Others suggest that conflict results from "the interaction of interdependent people who perceived incompatible goals and interference from each other in achieving those goals."[27]

Levels of Conflict

Conflict exists everywhere. One way to classify conflict is by level, and four levels of conflict are commonly identified.

1. *Intrapersonal or intrapsychic conflict.* At this level, conflict occurs within an individual. Sources of conflict can include ideas, thoughts, emotions, values, predispositions, or drives that are in conflict with each other. We want an ice cream cone badly, but we know that ice cream is very fattening. We are angry at our boss, but we're afraid to express that anger because the boss might fire us for being insubordinate. Depending on the source and origin of the intrapsychic conflict, this domain is traditionally studied by various fields of psychology: cognitive psychologists, personality theorists, clinical psychologists, and psychiatrists. Although we will occasionally delve into the internal states of negotiators (e.g., in Chapters 5 and 8), this book generally doesn't address intrapersonal conflict.

2. *Interpersonal conflict.* A second major level of conflict is between individual people. Conflict that occurs between bosses and subordinates, spouses, siblings, or roommates is all interpersonal conflict. Most of the negotiation theory in this book addresses the resolution of interpersonal conflict, although much of it can also be applied to the levels specified below.

3. *Intragroup conflict.* A third major level of conflict is within a small group—among team and committee members and within families, classes, fraternities and sororities, and work groups.[28]

4. *Intergroup conflict.* The final level of conflict is intergroup—between unions and management, warring nations, feuding families, or community action groups and government authorities. At this level, conflict is quite intricate because of the large number of people involved and possible interactions among them. Conflict can occur within groups and among groups simultaneously. Negotiations at this level are also the most complex.[29]

Functions and Dysfunctions of Conflict

Most people initially think that conflict is bad or dysfunctional. This notion has two aspects: first, that conflict is an indication that something is wrong or that a problem needs to be fixed and, second, that conflict creates largely destructive consequences. Deutsch and others[30] have elaborated on many of the elements that contribute to conflict's destructive image:

1. *Competitive processes.* Parties compete against each other because they believe that their goals are in opposition and that the two of them cannot both achieve their objectives. (As mentioned earlier, however, the goals may not actually be in opposition, and the parties need not compete.) In addition, competitive processes often have their own side effects; thus, the conflict that created the competition may lead to further escalation.

2. *Misperception and bias.* As conflict intensifies, perceptions become distorted. People tend to view things consistently with their own perspective on the conflict. Hence, they tend to interpret people and events as being either on their side or on the other side. In addition, thinking tends to become stereotypical and biased—parties in conflict endorse people and events that support their position and reject outright those that they suspect oppose their position.

3. *Emotionality.* Conflicts tend to become emotionally charged as the parties become anxious, irritated, annoyed, angry, or frustrated. Emotions tend to dominate thinking, and the parties may become increasingly emotional and irrational as the conflict escalates.

4. *Decreased communication.* Communication declines. Parties communicate less with those who disagree with them, and more with those who agree. What communication does occur between disputing parties may be an attempt to defeat, demean, or debunk the other's view or to add additional weight to one's own prior arguments.

5. *Blurred issues.* The central issues in the dispute become blurred and less well defined. Generalizations abound. New, unrelated issues are drawn in as the conflict becomes a vortex that attracts both related issues and innocent bystanders. The parties become less clear about how the dispute started, what it is "really about," or what it will take to solve it.

6. *Rigid commitments.* The parties become locked into positions. As the other side challenges them, parties become more committed to their points of view and less willing to back down from them for fear of losing face and looking foolish. Thinking processes become rigid, and the parties tend to see issues as simple and "either/or" rather than as complex and multidimensional.

7. *Magnified differences, minimized similarities.* As parties lock into commitments and issues become blurred, they tend to see each other—and each other's positions—as polar opposites. Factors that distinguish and separate them from each other become highlighted and emphasized, while similarities and commonalities that they share become oversimplified and minimized. This perceptual distortion leads the parties to believe they are farther apart from each other than they really may be, and hence they work harder to "win" the conflict and work less hard at finding common ground.

8. *Escalation of the conflict.* As the above points suggest, each side becomes more entrenched in its own view, less tolerant and accepting of the other, more defensive and less communicative, and more emotional. The net result is that both parties attempt to win by increasing their commitment to their position, increasing the resources they are willing to put up to "win," and increasing their tenacity in holding their ground under pressure. Both sides believe that by adding a little more pressure (resources, commitment, enthusiasm, energy, etc.), they can force the other to capitulate and admit defeat. As most destructive conflicts tell us, however, nothing could be further from the truth! Still, escalation of the level of the conflict and commitment to winning can increase to levels so high that the parties destroy their ability to resolve the dispute or ever to deal with each other again.

These are the processes that are commonly associated with conflict, but they are characteristic only of *destructive* conflict. In fact, as some authors have suggested, conflict can be productive.[31] Figure 1.1 outlines some *productive* aspects of conflict. In this model conflict is not simply destructive or productive, it is both. The objective is not to

FIGURE 1.1   Functions and Benefits of Conflict

- Discussing conflict makes organizational members more aware and able to cope with problems. Knowing that others are frustrated and want change creates incentives to try to solve the underlying problem.
- Conflict promises organizational change and adaptation. Procedures, assignments, budget allocations, and other organizational practices are challenged. Conflict draws attention to those issues that may interfere with and frustrate employees.
- Conflict strengthens relationships and heightens morale. Employees realize that their relationships are strong enough to withstand the test of conflict; they need not avoid frustrations and problems. They can release their tensions through discussion and problem solving.
- Conflict promotes awareness of self and others. Through conflict, people learn what makes them angry, frustrated, and frightened and also what is important to them. Knowing what we are willing to fight for tells us a lot about ourselves. Knowing what makes our colleagues unhappy helps us to understand them.
- Conflict enhances personal development. Managers find out how their style affects their subordinates through conflict. Workers learn what technical and interpersonal skills they need to upgrade themselves.
- Conflict encourages psychological development. Persons become more accurate and realistic in their self-appraisals. Through conflict, persons take others' perspectives and become less egocentric. Conflict helps persons to believe that they are powerful and capable of controlling their own lives. They do not simply need to endure hostility and frustration but can act to improve their lives.
- Conflict can be stimulating and fun. Persons feel aroused, involved, and alive in conflict, and it can be a welcome break from an easygoing pace. It invites employees to take another look and to appreciate the intricacies of their relationships.

SOURCE: Reprinted with the permission of Lexington Books, an imprint of The Rowman and Littlefield Publishing Group from *Working Together to Get Things Done: Managing for Organizational Productivity* by Dean Tjosvold. Copyright ©1986 by Lexington Books.

eliminate conflict but to learn how to manage it so that the destructive elements are controlled while the productive aspects are enjoyed. Negotiation is a strategy for productively managing conflict.

Factors That Make Conflict Difficult to Manage

There are several useful criteria for analyzing a dispute and determining how easy or difficult it will be to resolve. Figure 1.2 presents the most important ones. Conflicts with more of the characteristics in the middle column will be much more difficult to resolve. Those that have more characteristics in the right-hand column will be easier to resolve.

CONFLICT MANAGEMENT

One of the most popular areas of conflict management research and practice has been to define the different ways that the parties themselves can manage conflict. Many

FIGURE 1.2 Conflict Diagnostic Model

	Viewpoint Continuum	
Dimension	Difficult to Resolve	Easy to Resolve
Issue in question	Matter of "principle"—values, ethics, or precedent a key part of the issue	Divisible issue—issue can be easily divided into small parts, pieces, units
Size of stakes—magnitude of what can be won or lost	Large—big consequences	Small—little, insignificant consequences
Interdependence of the parties—degree to which one's outcomes determine the other's outcomes	Zero sum—what one wins, the other loses	Positive sum—both believe that *both* can do better than simply distributing current outcomes
Continuity of interaction—will they be working together in the future?	Single transaction—no past or future	Long-term relationship—expected interaction in the future
Structure of the parties—how cohesive, organized they are as a group	Disorganized—uncohesive, weak leadership	Organized—cohesive, strong leadership
Involvement of third parties—can others get involved to help resolve the dispute?	No neutral third party available	Trusted, powerful, prestigious third party available
Perceived progress of the conflict—balanced (equal gains and equal harm) or unbalanced (unequal gain, unequal harm)?	Unbalanced—one party feels more harm and will want revenge and retribution whereas stronger party wants to maintain control	Balanced—both parties suffer equal harm and equal gain; both may be more willing to call it a "draw"

SOURCE: Reprinted from "Managing Conflict" by L. Greenhalgh, *Sloan Management Review* (Summer 1986), pp. 45–51, by permission of the publisher. Copyright © 1986 by the Sloan Management Review Association. All rights reserved.

FIGURE 1.3   The Dual Concerns Model

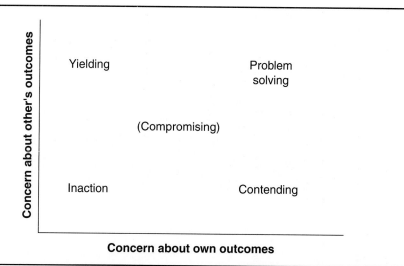

Concern about own outcomes

SOURCE: Reprinted from *Social Conflict: Escalation, Stalemate and Settlement* (2nd ed.) by J. Rubin, D. Pruitt and S. H. Kim by permission of the publisher. Copyright © 1994 by The McGraw-Hill Companies.

approaches to managing conflict have been suggested, and inventories have been constructed to measure negotiators' tendencies to use these approaches.[32] Each approach begins a fundamentally similar two-dimensional framework and then applies different labels and descriptions to five key points. We will describe these different approaches using the framework first proposed by Dean Pruitt and Jeffrey Rubin (Figure 1.3).

This two-dimensional framework is called the dual concerns model. The model postulates that individuals in conflict have two independent levels of concern: *concern about their own outcomes* (shown on the horizontal dimension of the figure) and *concern about the other's outcomes* (shown on the vertical dimension of the figure). These concerns can be represented at any point from none (representing very low concern) to high (representing very high concern). The vertical dimension is often referred to as the cooperativeness dimension, and the horizontal dimension as the assertiveness dimension. The stronger their concern for their own outcomes, the more likely people will be to pursue strategies located on the right side of the figure, whereas the weaker their concern for their own outcomes, the more likely they will be to pursue strategies located on the left side of the figure. Similarly, the stronger their concern for permitting, encouraging, or even helping the other party achieve his or her outcomes, the more likely people will be to pursue strategies located at the top of the figure. The weaker their concern for the other party's outcomes, the more likely they will be to pursue strategies located at the bottom of the figure.

Although we can theoretically identify an almost infinite number of points within the two-dimensional space based on the level of concern for pursuing one's own and the other's outcomes, five major strategies for conflict management have been commonly identified in the dual concerns model:

"My concession speech will be brief. You win."

1. *Contending* (also called *competing* or *dominating*) is the strategy in the lower right-hand corner. Actors pursuing the contending strategy pursue their own outcomes strongly and show little concern for whether the other party obtains his or her desired outcomes. As Pruitt and Rubin state, "[P]arties who employ this strategy maintain their own aspirations and try to persuade the other party to yield."[33] Threats, punishment, intimidation, and unilateral action are consistent with a contending approach.

2. *Yielding* (also called *accommodating* or *obliging*) is the strategy in the upper left-hand corner. Actors pursuing the yielding strategy show little interest or concern in whether they attain their own outcomes, but they are quite interested in whether the other party attains his or her outcomes. Yielding involves lowering one's own aspirations to "let the other win" and gain what he or she wants. Yielding may seem like a strange strategy to some, but it has its definite advantages in some situations.

3. *Inaction* (also called *avoiding*) is the strategy in the lower left-hand corner. Actors pursuing the inaction strategy show little interest in whether they attain their own outcomes, as well as little concern about whether the other party obtains his or her outcomes. Inaction is often synonymous with withdrawal or passivity; the party prefers to retreat, be silent, or do nothing.

4. *Problem solving* (also called *collaborating* or *integrating*) is the strategy in the upper right-hand corner. Actors pursuing the problem-solving strategy show

high concern for attaining their own outcomes *and* high concern for whether the other party attains his or her outcomes. In problem solving, the two parties actively pursue approaches to maximize their joint outcome from the conflict, so that both sides "win."

   5. *Compromising* is the strategy located in the middle of Figure 1.3. As a conflict management strategy, it represents a moderate effort to pursue one's own outcomes and a moderate effort to help the other party achieve his or her outcomes. Pruitt and Rubin do *not* identify compromising as a viable strategy; they see it "as arising from one of two sources—either lazy problem solving involving a half-hearted attempt to satisfy the two parties' interests, or simple yielding by both parties."[34] However, because other scholars (see references above) who use versions of this model believe that compromising represents a valid strategic approach to conflict, we have inserted it in Pruitt and Rubin's framework in Figure 1.3.

Each conflict management strategy has its advantages and disadvantages, and is *more or less appropriate given the type of conflict* and situation in which the dispute occurs. Thus, conflict theory and research have moved away from a normative, prescriptive approach advocating problem solving regardless of the situation and toward a contingency approach advocating that the strategy selected should be based on the objectives of the parties and the nature of their dispute. Although a full-fledged contingency approach to conflict management has yet to be articulated and supported by research, much work has been done to delineate some of the conditions under which each strategy is appropriate or inappropriate (see Figure 1.4).

OVERVIEW OF THE CHAPTERS IN THIS BOOK

   Each chapter in this book can be related to the introductory scenario about Joe and Sue Carter, which incorporates many of the critical elements addressed during negotiations. The book is organized into nine chapters. The first four chapters address the "fundamentals of negotiation." In addition to this first overview chapter, the second chapter explores how parties can frame the negotiation issues, and can plan and prepare for their encounter with the other party. Chapter 3 explores the basic strategy and tactics of distributive bargaining; and Chapter 4 explores the basic strategy and tactics of integrative negotiation. The next two chapters explore two key negotiation subprocesses. In Chapter 5, we explore how a negotiator's cognitions and perceptions tend to shape (and often bias) the way the negotiator views and interprets bargaining interaction. We also explore communication dynamics between negotiators, and the key role played by emotionality. In Chapter 6, we discuss the many ways that negotiators can use power and leverage to influence the other party during bargaining interaction. The next two chapters place the negotiation process in a broader social context, a context that judges the behavior and shapes as appropriate or inappropriate. In Chapter 7, we discuss how different kinds of negotiator behavior can be interpreted within a broader social fabric of ethical standards that dictate "right" and "wrong" behavior. In Chapter 8, we discuss how those same behaviors can be interpreted in a global business environment, which

FIGURE 1.4   Styles of Handling Interpersonal Conflict and Situations Where They Are Appropriate or Inappropriate

Conflict Style	Situations Where Appropriate	Situations Where Inappropriate
Integrating	1. Issues are complex. 2. Synthesis of ideas is needed to come up with better solutions. 3. Commitment is needed from other parties for successful implementation. 4. Time is available for problem solving. 5. One party alone cannot solve the problem. 6. Resources possessed by different parties are needed to solve their common problems.	1. Task or problem is simple. 2. Immediate decision is required. 3. Other parties are unconcerned about outcome. 4. Other parties do not have problem-solving skills.
Obliging	1. You believe that you may be wrong. 2. Issue is more important to the other party. 3. You are willing to give up something in exchange for something from the other party in the future. 4. You are dealing from a position of weakness. 5. Preserving relationship is important.	1. Issue is important to you. 2. You believe that you are right. 3. The other party is wrong or unethical.
Dominating	1. Issue is trivial. 2. Speedy decision is needed. 3. Unpopular course of action is implemented. 4. Necessary to overcome assertive subordinates. 5. Unfavorable decision by the other party may be costly to you. 6. Subordinates lack expertise to make technical decisions. 7. Issue is important to you.	1. Issue is complex. 2. Issue is not important to you. 3. Both parties are equally powerful. 4. Decision does not have to be made quickly. 5. Subordinates possess high degree of competence.
Avoiding	1. Issue is trivial. 2. Potential dysfunctional effect of confronting the other party outweighs benefits of resolution. 3. Cooling off period is needed.	1. Issue is important to you. 2. It is your responsibility to make decision. 3. Parties are unwilling to defer; issue must be resolved. 4. Prompt attention is needed.
Compromising	1. Goals of parties are mutually exclusive. 2. Parties are equally powerful. 3. Consensus cannot be reached. 4. Integrating or dominating style is not successful. 5. Temporary solution to a complex problem is needed.	1. One party is more powerful. 2. Problem is complex enough to need a problem-solving approach.

often dictates appropriate or inappropriate conduct based on the culture in which it occurs. Finally, in Chapter 9, we explore the alternative courses of action available to negotiating parties who are "stuck" or deadlocked, and prescribe a number of things they can do to get negotiations back on track.[35]

ENDNOTES

1. Hochberg and Kressel, 1996; Olekalns, Smith, and Walsh, 1996; Oliver, Balakrishnan, and Barry, 1994; and Weiss, 1997.
2. Weingart, Hyder, and Prietula, 1996.
3. See Lewicki, 1992; Rubin and Brown, 1975.
4. Deutsch, 1962, p. 276.
5. Neslin and Greenhalgh, 1983; Raiffa, 1982.
6. Fisher, Ury, and Patton, 1991.
7. Ibid., p. 105.
8. Goffman, 1969; Pruitt and Rubin, 1986; Raven and Rubin, 1973, and Ritov, 1996.
9. Alexander, Schul, and Babakus, 1991; Donohue and Roberto, 1996; Eyuboglu and Buja, 1993; and Pinkley and Northcraft, 1994.
10. Gray, 1994; Kolb, 1985; and Kolb and Putnam, 1997.
11. Beisecker, Walker, and Bart, 1989; Camerer and Loewenstein, 1993; and Raven and Rubin, 1973.
12. Fisher, Ury, and Patton, 1991; Follett, 1940; Nash, 1950; Sebenius, 1992; Sen, 1970; Walton and McKersie, 1965.
13. Pruitt, 1981.
14. Kelley, 1966.
15. Kimmel, Pruitt, Magenau, Konar-Goldband, and Carnevale, 1980; Putnam and Jones, 1982; Weingart, Thompson, Bazerman, and Carroll, 1990.
16. See Raiffa, 1982; and Selekman, Fuller, Kennedy, and Baitsel, 1964.
17. Bazerman, Magliozzi, and Neale, 1985; Neale and Bazerman, 1985; Neale and Northcraft, 1991; Pinkley, 1992; and Thompson, 1990b.
18. See Bazerman and Neale, 1992; Neale and Bazerman, 1991, 1992b; and Thompson and Hastie, 1990a, 1990b.
19. Thompson and Hastie, 1990a.
20. Bazerman, Magliozzi, and Neale, 1985.
21. Thompson and Hastie, 1990a; a similar study by Dudley, Johnson, and Johnson, 1996 showed this percentage to be even higher in children.
22. Thompson and Hastie, 1990a.
23. See Neale and Bazerman, 1991, and Thompson and Loewenstein, 1992.
24. Lax and Sebenius, 1986.
25. Ibid.
26. See Pruitt and Rubin, 1986, p. 4.
27. Hocker and Wilmot, 1985.
28. At the intragroup level, this affects the ability of the group to resolve disputes and continue to achieve its goals effectively. Within-group negotiation is discussed in the chapter "Coalitions, Multiple Parties, and Teams," which is posted on the McGraw-Hill website at www.mhhe.com/lewickinegotiation.
29. The nature of intergroup negotiations is discussed in the chapters "Social Context" and "Coalitions, Multiple Parties, and Teams" posted on the McGraw-Hill website at www.mhhe.com/lewickinegotiation.

30. Deutsch, 1973; Folger, Poole, and Stutman, 1993; and Hocker and Wilmot, 1985.
31. Coser, 1956, and Deutsch, 1973.
32. Filley, 1975; Hall, 1969; Rahim, 1983a; Thomas, 1992; and Thomas and Kilmann, 1974.
33. Pruitt and Rubin, 1986, p. 25.
34. Ibid, p. 29.
35. Three chapters from the main textbook "Social Context: Relationships and Representatives;" "Coalitions, Multiple Parties, and Teams;" and "Managing Difficult Negotiations: Third-Party Approaches," have not been included in this *Essentials* volume. These chapters may be found on the McGraw-Hill website at www.mhhe.com/lewickinegotiation.

CHAPTER 2

Negotiation: Strategizing, Framing, and Planning

In this chapter, we discuss what negotiators should do before opening negotiations. We believe that effective strategizing, planning, and preparation are the most critical precursors for achieving negotiation objectives. With effective planning and target setting, most negotiators can achieve their objectives; without them, results occur more by chance than by negotiator effort.

We begin the discussion of planning and strategizing by exploring the broad process of strategy development, starting with defining the negotiator's goals/objectives. We then move to understanding the process of developing a strategy to achieve those goals, discussion of the issues at stake, and exploration of how the definition of those issues may change over the course of a negotiation. Next, we address the typical stages and phases of an evolving negotiation, and how understanding them may affect planning. Finally, the critical steps involved in creating a plan to execute a strategy are discussed.

GOALS—THE OBJECTIVES THAT DRIVE A NEGOTIATION STRATEGY

The first step in developing and executing a negotiation strategy is to determine one's goals. Negotiators must anticipate what they want to achieve in a negotiation and prepare for these events in advance. The preparation must include attention to substantive items—including *goals, goal priorities,* and *multigoal packages*—as well as to procedural concerns dealing with *agendas* and *bargaining histories.* Effective preparation requires a thorough, thoughtful approach to these items; negotiators should specify their goals and objectives clearly. This includes stating all goals they wish to achieve in the negotiation, determining the priority among these goals, identifying potential multigoal packages, and evaluating possible trade-offs among them. As noted in Chapter 1, goals are usually *tangibles*—rate, price, specific terms, contract language, fixed packages, and so on—but they can also include *intangibles,* such as maintaining a certain precedent, defending a principle, or getting an agreement regardless of cost.

Direct Effects of Goals on Choice of Strategy

When entering a bargaining relationship, people generally have some idea of what they would like the outcome to be. They often say, "I'd be happy if . . ." and then state something they would really like to have, for example, ". . . I could buy a new car at a price that wouldn't require all of my paycheck as the loan payment." That's not bad as a *wish,* but it's not very good as a goal for negotiation. Four aspects of how goals affect negotiation are important to understand:

1. *Wishes are not goals,* especially in negotiation. Wishes may be related to interests or needs that motivate goals (see Chapter 4), but they are not goals themselves. A wish is a fantasy, a hope that something might happen; a goal is a specific, focused, realistic target that one can specifically plan to achieve.

2. *Our goals are often linked to the other party's goals.* The linkage between the two parties' goals defines an *issue* to be settled (see the discussion of issues later in this chapter). My goal is to get a car cheaply, and the dealer's goal is to sell it at the highest possible price (and profit); thus, the "issue" is the price I will pay for the car. If I could achieve my goal by myself, without the other party, I probably wouldn't need to negotiate. Goals that are not linked to each other often lead the parties either to talk past each other or to intensify the conflict.

3. *There are boundaries or limits to what our goals can be* (see the discussion of alternatives later in this chapter). If what we want exceeds these limits (i.e., what the other party is capable of or willing to give), we must either change our goals or end the negotiation—goals must be reasonably attainable. If my goal— "to buy this car at a cheap price"—isn't possible because the dealer won't sell the car cheaply, I'm going to either change my goal or find a cheaper car to buy (perhaps from a different dealer).

4. *Effective goals must be concrete or specific,* and preferably *measurable.* The less concrete and measurable our goals are, the harder it is (*a*) to communicate to the other party what we want, (*b*) to understand what he or she wants, and (*c*) to determine whether any particular outcome satisfies our goals. "To get a price on a car so that the loan payment does not use all of my paycheck" is not a very clear goal. Is this every week's paycheck or only one check a month? Do I want the payment to be just under 100 percent of the paycheck, or about 50 percent, or perhaps even 25 percent? Today's paycheck only, or the paychecks expected over the life of the loan?

The goals discussed in the preceding paragraph are all quite tangible, and they address directly the questions of the purchase price and the buyer's cash flow. No less important are the many *intangible* goals that typically arise in any negotiation. In the example of the car purchase, intangible goals might include the following: to enhance one's reputation among one's friends by owning and driving an expensive, powerful car; to maintain one's friends' image of oneself as a shrewd, pennywise negotiator; or to pay any price to ensure convenient, reliable transportation. In other negotiations, intangible goals might include: to maintain a reputation as a tough but principled negotiator, to establish a precedent for future negotiations, or to conduct the negotiations in a manner that is fair to all sides and assures each party fair treatment. (Refer back to Chapter 1 for further discussion of intangible goals.)

Which of these many criteria should we use? The answer is that *all* are probably important, for different reasons, and defining them is essential to moving toward a strategy and developing a plan.

Indirect Effects of Goals on Choice of Strategy

Simple and direct goals can often be attained in a single negotiation session. Because such goals may also be pursued infrequently (such as when we buy a car or a home), we tend to view the negotiation as a single episode—a single defined event, without future consequences. This "episodic assumption" affects our choice of strategy; in developing and framing our goals, we may ignore the present or future relationship with the other party in favor of a simplistic concern for achieving *only* the substantive outcome. Thus, the pursuit of a singular, substantive goal often tends to support the choice of a competitive strategy (refer back to the dual concerns model described in Chapter 1).

Other negotiation goals—those that are complex or difficult to define—may require initiating a sequence of negotiation episodes. In these cases progress will be made incrementally, and may depend on establishing a strong relationship with the other party. Examples here include a substantial increase in one's line of credit with a bank or credit union, or the establishment of a privileged status with an important trading partner. Such relationship-oriented goals should motivate the negotiator toward a strategy choice in which the relationship with the other party is valued as much as (or even more than) the substantive outcome. Thus, relational goals tend to support the choice of a collaborative or integrative strategy (refer back to the dual concerns model described in Chapter 1).

STRATEGY—THE OVERALL PLAN TO ACHIEVE ONE'S GOALS

After negotiators articulate goals, they move to the second element in the sequence: selecting and developing a strategy. Experts on business strategy define it as "the pattern or plan that integrates an organization's major targets, policies, and action sequences into a cohesive whole."[1] Applied to negotiations, strategy refers to the overall plan to accomplish one's goals in a negotiation, and the action sequences that will lead to the accomplishment of those goals.

Strategy, Tactics, or Planning?

How are strategy and tactics related? Although the line between strategy and tactics may seem indistinct, one major difference is that of scale, perspective, or immediacy.[2] Tactics are short-term, adaptive moves designed to enact or pursue broad (or higher-level) strategies, which in turn provide stability, continuity, and direction for tactical behaviors. For example, your negotiation *strategy* might be integrative, designed to build and maintain a productive relationship with the other party while using a joint problem-solving approach to the issues. In pursuing this strategy, appropriate *tactics* include maintaining reliable, predictable preferences (to build the other's trust in you) and using open-ended questions and active listening (to foster communication). Tactics, then, are subordinate to strategy; they are structured, directed, and driven by strategic considerations.

How are strategy and planning related? Planning is an integral part of the strategy process—the "action" component. The *planning process* takes in all the considerations and choices that parties in a negotiation make about tactics, resource use, and contingent responses in pursuit of the overall *strategy*—how they plan to proceed, to use what they have to get what they want, subject to their strategic guidelines. We address planning in detail later in this chapter.

Strategic Options—Vehicles for Achieving Goals

In the strictest sense, a unilateral choice of strategy would be wholly one-sided and intentionally ignorant of any information about the other negotiator. In our use of the term, however, a *unilateral* choice is one that is made without the *active* involvement of the other party. A reasonable effort to gain information about the other party and to incorporate that information into the choice of a negotiation strategy is always useful.

In Chapter 1, the dual concerns model was used to describe the basic orientation that people take toward conflict. This model proposes that individuals in conflict have two levels of related concerns: a level of concern for their own outcomes, and a level of concern for the other's outcomes (refer back to Figure 1.3). Savage, Blair, and Sorenson propose a similar model for the choice of a negotiation strategy. According to this model, a negotiator's unilateral choice of strategy is reflected in the answers to two simple questions: (1) How much concern does the actor have for achieving the *substantive outcomes* at stake in this negotiation (substantive goals)? and (2) How much concern does the negotiator have for the current and future quality of the *relationship* with the other party (relationship goals)? The answers to these questions result in the mix of strategic alternatives presented in Figure 2.1.[3]

Alternative Situational Strategies.   The power of this model lies in requiring the negotiator to determine the relative importance and priority of the two dimensions in the desired settlement. As Figure 2.1 shows, answers to these two simple questions suggest at least four types of initial strategies for negotiators: competition, collaboration, accommodation, and avoidance. A strong interest in achieving only substantive outcomes—getting *this* deal, winning *this* negotiation, with little or no regard for the effect on the relationship or on subsequent exchanges with the other party—tends to support a competitive (distributive) strategy. A strong interest in achieving only the relationship outcomes—building, preserving, or enhancing a good relationship with the other party—suggests an accommodation strategy. If both substance and relationship are important, the negotiator should pursue a collaborative (integrative) strategy. Finally, if achieving neither substantive outcomes nor an enhanced relationship is important, the party might be best served by avoiding negotiation. Each of these different strategic approaches also has different implications for negotiation planning and preparation.[4] Avoidance and accommodation strategies are discussed below; competitive (distributive) and collaborative (integrative) strategies will be extensively addressed in Chapters 3 and 4.

Avoidance: The Nonengagement Strategy.   *Avoidance* may serve a number of strategic negotiation purposes. In fact, there are many reasons why negotiators might choose not to negotiate (similar to the reasons for conflict avoidance discussed in Chapter 1). First, if one is able to meet one's needs without negotiating at all, it may make sense to use an avoidance strategy. The other party may not be willing to "cut you in,"

FIGURE 2.1   Considering a Unilateral Negotiation Strategy

	Substantive outcome important?	
	Yes	**No**
Yes	Collaboration	Accommodation
No	Competition	Avoidance

Relational outcome important?

based on a simple request, or your relationship with the other may be so poor that it is not even worth asking for anything. Second, it simply may not be worth the time and effort to negotiate (although there are sometimes reasons to negotiate in such situations; see the section on accommodation below). Third, the decision to negotiate is closely related to the desirability of available alternatives—the outcomes that can be achieved if negotiations don't work out.

Alternatives—that is, the outcomes that can be obtained if this negotiation fails— are a source of power in negotiation. A negotiator with very strong alternatives has considerable power, because he or she doesn't need this negotiation to succeed in achieving at least a satisfactory outcome. But having weak alternatives puts negotiators at a disadvantage. The presence of an alternative can cut both ways in the decision about whether to avoid negotiation. First, if one has a strong alternative, one may wish to avoid negotiation strictly on efficiency grounds—it is simply quicker and easier to take the alternative than to get involved in a negotiation. But having a weak alternative may also suggest that one should avoid negotiation—once negotiations begin, the pressure of the negotiation process may lead one to a poor outcome, which one may feel obligated to accept because the alternative is also very poor.

Active-Engagement Strategies: Competition, Collaboration, and Accommodation.   Competition and collaboration are described extensively in the next two chapters. *Competition* is described throughout this book as distributive or win-lose bargaining, and *collaboration* as integrative or win-win negotiation. *Accommodation* is as much a win-lose strategy as competition, although it has a decidedly different image— it involves an imbalance of outcomes, but in the opposite direction ("I lose, you win" as opposed to "I win, you lose"). As Figure 2.1 shows, an accommodative strategy may be appropriate when the negotiator considers the relationship outcome more important than the substantive outcome. In other words, the negotiator wants to let the other win, keep the other happy, or not endanger the relationship by pushing hard to achieve some goal on the substantive issues. This strategy is often used when the primary goal of the exchange is to build or strengthen the relationship (or the other party) and the negotiator is willing to sacrifice the outcome. An accommodative strategy may also be necessary if the negotiator expects the relationship to extend past a single negotiation episode. The idea is that if "I lose and you win" this time, over multiple negotiations in the relationship the win-lose accounts will balance.

How do these three strategies—competition, collaboration, and accommodation—differ? Table 2.1, on pages 32–33, summarizes the three types of strategies (distributive, integrative, and accommodative), and compares and contrasts them across a number of different dimensions.[5]

In addition to their positive characteristics, as described in the table, each of these three types of negotiation strategies also has certain predictable drawbacks if applied blindly, thoughtlessly, or inflexibly. Distributive strategies tend to create "we-they" or "superiority-inferiority" patterns, which often lead to distortions in judgment regarding the other side's contributions and efforts, and to distortions in perceptions of the other side's values, needs, and positions (see the discussion of cognitive framing biases in Chapter 5). Integrative strategies can also be problematic if used blindly or exclusively. If a negotiator pursues a collaborative strategy without regard to the other's behavior, then the other can manipulate and exploit the collaborator and take advantage of the good faith and goodwill being demonstrated. Excessive integration can also lead negotiators to cease being accountable to their constituencies in favor of pursuit of the negotiation process for its own sake. For example, negotiators who approach the process with an aggressive "we can solve it" attitude may produce an agreement that is unacceptable to their constituency (e.g., their companies). Finally, accommodative strategies also may have drawbacks. They may generate a pattern of constantly giving in to keep the other happy or to avoid a fight. This pattern establishes a precedent that is hard to break. It could also lead the other to a false sense of well-being due to the satisfaction that comes with the "harmony" of a good relationship, which may completely ignore all the giveaways on substance. Over time, this imbalance is unlikely to perpetuate, but efforts to stop the giving or restore the balance may be met with surprise and resentment.

It is also useful to remember that in presenting these strategies we are describing pure forms, typically at odds with the mixture of issues and motivations that actually characterize the evolution of most actual negotiation strategies. Just as most conflicts are neither purely competitive nor purely cooperative, most negotiation strategies reflect a variety of goals, intentions, and situational constraints.[6]

DEFINING THE ISSUES—THE PROCESS OF "FRAMING" THE PROBLEM

The next step in the planning process is determining what issues are at stake. This process is called *framing* the negotiation. Framing is about focusing, shaping, and organizing the world around us. It is about making sense of a complex reality and defining it in terms that are meaningful to us. Frames define a person, event, or process and separate it from the complex world around it. Frames "impart meaning and significance to elements within the frame and set them apart from what is outside the frame."[7] Two people walk into a room full of people and see different things: one (the extrovert) sees a great party, the other (the introvert) sees a scary and intimidating unfriendly crowd. Because people have different backgrounds, experiences, expectations, and needs, they frame people, events, and processes differently. Moreover, these frames can change depending on perspective, or can change over time. What starts out as a game of tag between two boys may turn into an ugly fistfight. A favorite football quarterback is a "hero" when he throws a touchdown, but a "loser" when he throws an interception.

Framing has become a popular concept among social scientists who study cognitive processes, decision making, persuasion, and communication. The popularity of framing has come with the recognition that often two or more people who are involved in the same situation or in a complex problem see it or define it in different ways.[8] Researchers link frames and experience as follows:

> Disputes, like other social situations, are ambiguous and subject to interpretation. People can encounter the same dispute and perceive it in very different ways as a result of their backgrounds, professional training or past experiences. One label that has been placed on this form of individualized definition of a situation based on an interplay of past experiences and knowledge, and the existing situation, is a "frame."[9]

Another view of frames is that of noted management theorist Mary Parker Follett, who was one of the first to write about integrative (win-win) negotiation in organizations. In describing the process by which parties with different views about an issue arrive at a joint agreement, Follett suggests that the parties achieve some form of unity, "not from giving in [compromise] but from 'getting the desires of each side into one field of vision.'"[10] Thus, frames emerge as the parties talk about their preferences and priorities; they allow the parties to begin to develop a shared or common definition of the issues related to a situation, and a process for resolving them.

Why Frames Are Critical to Understanding Strategy

While researchers have only begun to study frames and framing dynamics in depth, there is general agreement that people often use frames to define problems, and that the effects of frames can be identified as we observe negotiations. Whether a frame is "a conception of the acts, outcomes and contingencies associated with a particular choice," an "individualized definition of a situation," or a "field of vision," how parties frame and define a negotiating issue or problem is a clear and strong reflection of what they define as central and critical to negotiating objectives, what their expectations and preferences are for certain possible outcomes, what information they seek and use to argue their case, the procedures they use to try to present their case, and the manner in which they evaluate the outcomes actually achieved.* Frames are inevitable; one cannot "avoid" framing. By choosing to define and articulate an aspect of a complex social

---

*Note that frames themselves cannot be "seen." They are abstractions, perceptions, and thoughts that people use to define a situation, organize information, determine what is important, what is not, and so on. We can infer other people's frames by asking them directly about their frames, by listening to their communication, and by watching their behavior. Similarly, we can try to understand our own frames, by thinking about what aspects of a situation we should pay attention to, emphasize, focus on, or ignore—and by observing our own words and actions. One cannot see or directly measure a frame, however.

TABLE 2.1 Characteristics of Different Engagement Strategies

Aspect	Competition (Distributive Bargaining)	Collaboration (Integrative Negotiation)	Accommodative Negotiation
Payoff structure	Usually a fixed amount of resources to be divided	Usually a variable amount of resources to be divided	Usually a fixed amount of resources to be divided
Goal pursuit	Pursuit of own goals at the expense of those of others	Pursuit of goals held jointly with others	Subordination of own goals in favor of those of others
Relationships	Short-term focus; parties do not expect to work together in the future	Long-term focus; parties expect to work together in the future	May be short term (let the other win to keep the peace) or long term (let the other win to encourage reciprocity in the future)
Primary motivation	Maximize own outcome	Maximize joint outcome	Maximize others' outcome or let them gain to enhance relationship
Trust and openness	Secrecy and defensiveness; high trust in self, low trust in others	Trust and openness, active listening, joint exploration of alternatives	One party relatively open, exposing own vulnerabilities to the other
Knowledge of needs	Parties know own needs but conceal or misrepresent them; neither party lets the other know real needs	Parties know and convey real needs while seeking and responding to needs of the other	One party is overresponsive to other's needs so as to repress own needs
Predictability	Parties use unpredictability and surprise to confuse other side	Parties are predictable and flexible when appropriate, trying not to surprise	One party's actions totally predictable, always catering to other side

Aggressiveness	Parties use threats and bluffs, trying to keep the upper hand	Parties share information honestly, treat each other with understanding and respect	One party gives up on own position to mollify the other
Solution search behavior	Parties make effort to appear committed to position, using argumentation and manipulation of the other	Parties make effort to find mutually satisfying solutions, using logic, creativity, and constructiveness	One party makes effort to find ways to accommodate the other
Success measures	Success enhanced by creating bad image of the other; increased levels of hostility and strong in-group loyalty	Success demands abandonment of bad images and consideration of ideas on their merit	Success determined by minimizing or avoiding conflict and soothing all hostility; own feelings ignored in favor of harmony
Evidence of unhealthy extreme	Unhealthy extreme reached when one party assumes total zero-sum game; defeating the other becomes a goal in itself	Unhealthy extreme reached when one subsumes all self-interest in the common good, losing self-identity and self-responsibility	Unhealthy extreme reached when abdication to other is complete, at expense of personal and/or constituent goals
Key attitude	Key attitude is "I win, you lose"	Key attitude is "What's the best way to address the needs of all parties?"	Key attitude is "You win, I lose"
Remedy for breakdown	If impasse occurs, mediator or arbitrator may be needed	If difficulties occur, a group dynamics facilitator may be needed	If behavior becomes chronic, party becomes negotiationally bankrupt

SOURCE: Adapted and expanded from Robert W. Johnston, "Negotiation Strategies: Different Strokes for Different Folks," *Personnel* 59 (March–April 1982), pp. 38–39. Used with permission of the author.

situation, one has already implicitly "chosen" to use certain frames and to ignore others. This process often occurs without any real intentionality on the part of the negotiator; one can frame a problem because of deeply buried past experiences, deep-seated attitudes and values, or strong emotions. Frames can also be shaped by the type of information that is chosen, or the setting and context in which the information is presented. Understanding framing dynamics helps negotiators to elevate the framing process to one that is more conscious and more under control than it would otherwise be; negotiators who understand how they are framing a problem may be able to understand more completely what they are doing, what the other party is doing, and how to have more control over the negotiation process. Finally, both current theory and a stream of supportive empirical research show that frames may be malleable and, if so, can be shaped or reshaped as a function of information and communication during negotiation (i.e., a third perspective, frames as issue development). The approach here is to introduce the negotiator to the power and prevalence of frames, such that he or she can understand

- Different types of frames.
- How certain frames may be invoked or ignored in a given situation.
- The consequences of framing a conflict in a particular way.
- Approaches that negotiators can use to manage frames more effectively.

Types of Frames

Several researchers have studied different types of frames that parties use in disputes. Examples of frames include:

1. *Substantive*—what the conflict is about. Parties taking a substantive frame have a particular disposition about the key issue or concern in the conflict.

2. *Outcome*—what predispositions the party has to achieving a specific result or outcome from the negotiation. To the degree that a negotiator has a specific, preferred outcome he or she wants to achieve, the dominant frame may be to focus all strategy, tactics, and communication toward getting that outcome. Parties who have a strong outcome frame are more likely to engage primarily in distributive (win-lose or lose-lose) negotiations than in other types of negotiations.

3. *Aspiration*—what predispositions the party has toward satisfying a broader set of interests or needs in negotiation. Rather than focusing on a specific outcome, the negotiator tries to ensure that his or her basic interests, needs, and concerns are met. Parties who have a strong aspiration frame are more likely to be primarily engaged in integrative (win-win) negotiation than in other types.

4. *Conflict management process*—how the parties will go about resolving their dispute. Negotiators who have a strong process frame are less likely than others to be concerned about the specific negotiation issues but more concerned about how the deliberations will proceed, or how the dispute should be managed. When the major concerns are largely procedural rather than substantive, process frames will be strong.

5. *Identity*—how the parties define "who they are." Parties are members of a number of different social groups—gender (male), religion (Roman Catholic), ethnic origin (Italian), place of birth (Brooklyn), current place of residence (Cleveland), etc. These are only a few of the categories people can use to define themselves and distinguish themselves from others.

6. *Characterization*—how the parties define the other parties. A characterization frame can clearly be shaped by experience with the other party, by information about the other party's history or reputation, or by the way the other party comes across early in the negotiation experience. In conflict, identity frames (of self) tend to be positive, characterization frames (of others) tend to be negative.

7. *Loss–gain*—how the parties view the risk associated with particular outcomes. A loss–gain frame is similar to a cognitive-bias frame toward issues of risk but may be more likely to shift as a function of experience and interaction with the other party. This is discussed in more detail in Chapter 5.[11]

Communication plays a central role in this approach to frames. Researchers argue that the language a party chooses to use is a strong reflection of his or her beliefs, experience, and perception of the negotiation.[12] Linguistic analysis of negotiation transcripts has shown a number of important insights about frames:

1. Negotiators can use more than one frame. A land developer discussing a conflict over a proposed golf course that will fill in a wetland can speak about the golf course (the substantive issue), his preferences for how the land should be filled in (an outcome frame), and how much input neighborhood and environmental groups should be able to have in determining what happens to that wetland on his private property (a procedural frame), as well as whether he views these groups favorably or unfavorably (a characterization frame).

2. Mismatches in frames between parties are sources of conflict. Two negotiators may be speaking to each other from different frames (e.g., one has an outcome frame and the other has a procedural frame); using different content in the same frame (e.g., they both have a procedural frame but have strong preferences for different procedures); or using different levels of abstraction (e.g., a broad aspiration frame vs. a specific outcome frame). Such mismatches cause conflict and ambiguity, which may either create misunderstanding, lead to conflict escalation and even stalemate, or lead one or both parties to "reframe" the conflict into frames that are more compatible and that may lead to resolution. For highly polarized disputes, mutual reframing may not occur without the help of a third party. (See Box 2.1 for a discussion of mismatched frames in the Middle East.)

3. Particular types of frames may lead to particular types of agreements. For example, parties who achieve integrative agreements may be likely to use aspiration frames and to discuss a large number of issues during their deliberations. In contrast, parties who use outcome or negative characterization frames may be likely to hold negative views of the other party and a strong preference for specific outcomes, both of which may lead to an intensified conflict with the other.

BOX 2.1
Middle East Experience Frames

Some of the world's most intractable ongoing disputes take place in the Middle East. For many onlookers, the battles are merely political squabbles over land and power. This perspective, however, fails to account for the beliefs and experiences that have shaped the frames of conflict participants. For them, struggles with neighbors are based on deep-seated, long-held beliefs about themselves, their religion, and their rightful entitlements in the region. This intertwining of the daily and the divine is a volatile mix.

Take, for example, the battle between Israelis and Palestinians over land on the West Bank of Israel. Israeli leaders believe their presence in the West Bank has been sanctified because Abraham, the father of the Jewish religion, had intimate connections in the area. Palestinians, meanwhile, argue that they are descended from the Canaanites, who laid claim to the area before Abraham's time. While the dispute is undoubtedly more complex than this brief historical explanation portends, it is important for those attempting to negotiate peace in the area to understand the rationale behind each side's claims.

Religious beliefs in general tend to be strongly held. They create frames and truth perspectives through which believers view the world. When conflict arises, those who view it through a religious framework tend to believe that any compromise on their part represents a compromise of their religious beliefs, which is unacceptable. In these cases, it is important for those attempting to negotiate a peaceful settlement to provide ways for the combatants to shift their frames. They can encourage the disputants to see battles as political struggles, minimizing the religious elements so that compromise can be achieved. However, in places like the Middle East where disputes over land are inherently linked to historical religious claims, such frame shifting is difficult, if not impossible. Understanding the power of religious frames as truth perspectives provides insight into one of the most volatile regions of the world.

SOURCE: Adapted from A. Marcus, "In Mideast Politics, Controlling the Past Is Key to the Present," *The Wall Street Journal,* 77, 244, pp. 1, 13.

---

4. Specific frames may be likely to be used with certain types of issues. Parties talking about salary may be likely to use outcome frames, while parties talking about relationship issues may be likely to use characterization frames.

5. Parties are likely to assume a particular frame because of various factors. Value differences between the parties, differences in personality, power differences, and differences in the background and social context of the negotiators may lead the parties to adopt different frames. Many of these differences are discussed throughout this book, particularly in Chapter 6 (on leverage), and Chapter 8 (on cultural differences).

While the concept of frames seems compelling to those who have witnessed many negotiations, research in this area is difficult to conduct and is still in its infancy. Nevertheless, researchers continue to pursue this approach to frames because it offers great promise for understanding how parties define what a negotiation is about, how they use communication to argue for their own frame or frames and try to shape the other's orientation, and how they resolve differences when they are clearly operating from different frames.

Another Approach to Frames: Interests, Rights, and Power

Another approach to framing disputes suggests that parties in conflict use one of three frames:

Interests. People are often concerned about what they need, desire, or want. People talk about their "positions," but often what is really at stake is their underlying interests. A person says he "needs" a new text messaging cell phone, but what he really *wants* is a new electronic toy because all his friends have one. Parties who focus on interests in a dispute are often able to find ways to resolve that dispute.

Rights. People may also be concerned about who is "right"—that is, who has legitimacy, who is correct, or what is fair. Disputes about rights are often resolved by helping the parties find a fair way to determine who is "right," or that they can both be "right." This resolution often requires the use of some standard or rule such as "taking turns," "split it down the middle," or "age before beauty" to settle the dispute. Disputes over rights are often referred to formal or informal arbitrators to decide whose standards or rights are more appropriate.

Power. People may also wish to resolve a negotiation on the basis of power. Negotiations resolved by power are sometimes based on who is physically stronger or is able to coerce the other, but more often, it is about imposing other types of costs—economic pressures, expertise, legitimate authority, etc. Disputes settled by power usually create clear winners and losers, with all the consequences that come from polarizing the dispute and resolving it in this manner.[13]

Parties have a choice about how they approach a negotiation in terms of interests versus rights versus power; the same negotiation can be "framed" in different ways and will probably lead to different consequences. For example, consider the situation of a student who has a dispute with a local car repair shop near campus over the cost of fixing an automobile. The student thinks she was dramatically overcharged for the work—the garage did more work than was requested, used the most expensive replacement parts, and didn't give her the chance to review the bill before the work was done. The student might "frame" the dispute using one of these three frames:

1. *Interests.* The student might argue, "Well, small businesses have a right to charge a fair price for good quality work. I will go in and try to understand the shop owner's system for pricing repair work; we will talk about what is a fair price for the work and I will pay it, and I will probably go back to the shop again."

2. *Rights.* The student worked in a garage herself one summer and knows that car repairs are priced on what standard manuals state it will generally cost for the labor (hours of work × payment per hour), plus the cost of the parts. "I will ask to see the manual

and the invoice for the parts. I will also go to the garage where I worked myself and ask the owner of that garage if he thinks this bill is out of line. I'll propose to pay for the parts at cost and the labor based on the mechanic's hourly pay rate."

3. *Power.* "I'll go in and start yelling at the owner about gouging, and I'll also threaten to tell all my friends not to use this garage. I'll write letters to the student newspaper about how bad this repair shop is. My dad is a lawyer and I'll have him call the owner. I'll teach them a thing or two!"

Note that the different frames are likely to lead to very different processes of discussion between the student and the garage owner. Moreover, the way the student approaches the problem with the garage owner will probably influence how the garage owner responds. The more the student uses power, the more likely the garage owner is to respond with power of his own (e.g., keep the car until the student pays and not reduce the price at all, and call his own lawyer); the confrontation could become angry and lead the parties into small claims court. In contrast, the more the student uses interests, the more the garage owner may be likely to use interests. The parties will have a discussion about what is fair given the services rendered; while the student may wind up paying more (than if she "won" the power argument), the tone of the discussion is likely to be far different, and the student may be in a much better position to get discounts or considerations in the future.

The Frame of an Issue Changes as the Negotiation Evolves

A final approach to framing argues that the definition of the issues often changes as the conflict evolves. Rather than focus only on the dominant frames that parties hold at the beginning of a negotiation, the issue development approach focuses on the *patterns of change* (transformation) that occur in the issues as parties communicate with each other. For example, in a classic study of legal disputes and grievances, Felstiner, Abel, and Sarat suggested that these disputes tend to be transformed through a process of "naming, blaming, and claiming." Naming occurs when parties in a dispute label or identify a problem and characterize what it is about. Blaming occurs next, as the parties try to determine who or what caused the problem. Finally, claiming occurs when the individual who has the problem decides to confront, file charges, or take some other action against the individual or organization that caused the problem.[14] Thus, as one review of this approach points out,

> Although each side enters the negotiation with some conception or interpretation of an agenda item, the way people talk about a problem influences the way they define it. Frames, then, are not simply features of individual cognition, they are constructed in the ways that bargainers define problems and courses of action jointly through their talk.[15]

Those who focus on issue development note that several factors shape a frame. First, the *negotiation context* clearly affects the way both sides define the issue. For example, in a union–management dispute, the issue will be framed by the history of relations between the parties—grievances, personnel practices, quality of relationships between the chief negotiators, and so on. Second, frames can also be shaped by the *conversations* that the parties have with each other about the issues in the bargaining mix. Although both parties may approach the discussion with initial frames that resemble the categories described earlier, the ongoing interaction between them shapes the discussion as each side attempts to argue from his or her own perspective or counterargue against the other's perspective. At least four factors can affect how the conversation is shaped:

1. Negotiators tend to argue for stock issues or concerns that are raised every time the parties negotiate. For example, wage issues or working conditions may always be on the table in a labor negotiation; thus, the union always raises them, and management always expects them to be raised and is ready to respond. Discussing international negotiations, Spector suggests that conflicts framed as "nationalist, ethnic, or ideological" may be quite difficult to resolve, and a major task for mediators in these types of disputes is to provide creative new frames.[16]

2. Each party attempts to make the *best possible case* for his or her preferred position or perspective. One party may assemble facts, numbers, testimony, or other compelling evidence to persuade the other party of the validity of his or her argument or perspective. Early in a negotiation, as each party presents his or her case, it is not uncommon for the parties to "talk past each other," with each trying to impose a certain perspective as the dominant conversation rather than listening to the other's case and trying to refute it. Each party is interested in controlling the conversation by controlling the focus; however, each party's argument eventually begins to shift as they both focus on either refuting the other's case or modifying their own arguments on the basis of the other's arguments.[17]

3. In a more "macro" sense, frames may also define major *shifts and transitions* in the overall negotiation. Ikle, discussing diplomatic negotiations, suggested that successful bargaining results from a two-stage process he called "formula/ detail."[18] Others describe this process as follows: "Parties first seek a compromise that establishes some formula or framework of broad objectives and principles. Then they draw out a number of detailed points of agreement. The framework defines the subset of points that is debatable, while the detail phase permits the debate and 'packaging' of specific issues to construct a settlement acceptable to both sides."[19] Zartman and his colleagues elaborated on the formula-detail model to create three stages: (*a*) *diagnosis,* in which the parties recognize the need for change or improvement, review relevant history, and prepare positions; (*b*) *formula,* in which the parties attempt to develop a shared perception of the conflict, including common terms, referents, and fairness criteria; and (*c*) *detail,* in which the parties work out operational details consistent with the basic formula.[20]

4. Finally, *multiple agenda items* operate to shape the issue development frames. Although parties usually have one or two major objectives, priorities, or core issues, there are often a number of lesser or secondary items. When brought into the conversation, these secondary concerns often transform the conversation about the primary issues. For example, in her careful analysis of teacher negotiations in two school districts, one researcher showed how issues became transformed throughout a negotiation. For instance, an issue of scheduling was reframed as an issue of teacher preparation time, and an issue on the cost of personal insurance became transformed into an issue about the extent of insurance benefits.[21]

"Now, when we explain this to Mom and Dad, let's make sure we give it the right spin."

One of the most important aspects of framing as issue development is the process of *reframing*, or the manner in which the thrust, tone, and focus of a conversation change as the parties engage in it. Reframing is a dynamic process that may occur many times in a conversation. It comes as parties challenge each other, as they present their own case or refute the other's, or as they search for ways to reconcile seemingly incompatible perspectives. Reframing can also occur as one party uses metaphors, analogies, or specific cases to illustrate a point, leading the other to use the metaphor or case as a new way to define the situation. Reframing may be done intentionally by one side or the other, or it may emerge from the conversation as one person's challenges fuel the other's creativity and imagination. In either case, the parties often propose a new way to approach the problem (see Box 2.2).

Summary. In this section, we have presented three ways to understand frames: as categories of experience; as interests, rights, and power; and as a process of issue development. Research on frames and their impact on negotiation continues to emerge. The way a negotiation problem is defined, and the manner in which a conversation between negotiators leads to a reframing of the issues, are critical elements to consider as negotiators develop a strategy and a plan. We can offer the following prescriptive advice about problem framing for the negotiator:

- Frames shape what the parties define as the key issues and how they talk about them. To the degree that the parties have preferences about the issues to be covered, outcomes to be achieved, or processes to be addressed, they should work to ensure that their own preferred frames are accepted and acknowledged by the others.

- Both parties have frames. When the frames match, the parties are more likely to focus on common issues and a common definition of the situation; when they do not match, communication between the parties is likely to be difficult and incomplete.

BOX 2.2
Transforming the Conversation through Frames

An independent insurance agent in a small town discussed the difficulty of moving some of his agency staff from a straight salary compensation system (at a level of $30,000 per year) to a base salary of $25,000 and performance pay beyond that, with no limits to the amount they could make. The agent was surprised to discover a lot of resistance among the sales representatives. The representatives were afraid of losing the guaranteed base pay and not knowing how much money they would really make under the new system.

One of the authors of this book devised two ways of trying to "sell" the idea: First, the author said, rather than impose the system immediately, phase it in over a multiyear period. Another agent had done this, and stated that as soon as his employees began to trust the system and their ability to earn at-risk income, they not only accepted the plan but began to ask that the transition be completed even before they were finished with the phasing-in process. Second, the author said, maintain the old system but also keep a new set of records, as if you were already on the new system. During this time the staff could see actual results and compare the two systems for actual earned amounts, to allay their fears.

By introducing the system gradually and keeping a comparative set of books, the head agent was able to change the conversation about compensation in that office and to gain rapid acceptance for his new plan.

SOURCE: Adapted from G. T. Savage, J. D. Blair, and R. J. Sorenson, "Consider Both Relationship and Substance When Negotiating Strategically," *Academy of Management Executive* 3 (1989), pp. 37–48.

- Frames are probably controllable, at least to some degree. If negotiators understand what frame they are operating from, and what frame the other party is operating from, they may be able to shift conversation toward the frame they would like to have the other espouse.

- Conversations change and transform frames in ways negotiators may not be able to predict but may be able to control. As parties discuss an issue, introduce arguments and evidence, and advocate a course of action, the conversation changes, and the frame of the problem may change as well. It will be critical for negotiators to track this shift and understand where it might lead.

- Certain frames are probably more likely than others to lead to certain types of processes and outcomes. For example, parties who are competitive are likely to have positive identity frames of themselves, negative characterization frames of each other, and a preference for more win-lose processes of resolving their dispute. Recognizing these biases may empower the parties to be able to reframe their views of themselves, the other, or the dispute resolution mechanism in order to pursue a process that will resolve the conflict more productively.

Understanding frames—which means understanding how parties define the key issues and how conversations can shift and transform those issues—is the first step in effective planning.

FIGURE 2.2   Phases of Negotiation

Phase 1	Phase 2	Phase 3	Phase 4	Phase 5	Phase 6	Phase 7
Preparation →	Relationship building →	Information gathering →	Information using →	Bidding →	Closing the deal →	Implementating the agreement

SOURCE: Reprinted with the permission of The Free Press, an imprint of Simon & Schuster Adult Publishing Group, from *Managing Strategic Relationships: The Key to Business Success* by Leonard Greenhalgh. Copyright © 2001 by Leonard Greenhalgh.

UNDERSTANDING THE FLOW OF NEGOTIATIONS: STAGES AND PHASES

Several researchers who have studied the flow of negotiations over time have confirmed that negotiation, like communication in problem-solving groups and in other forms of ritualistic social interaction, proceeds through distinct phases or stages.[22]

Leonard Greenhalgh has articulated an easy-to-visualize stage model of negotiation, particularly relevant for integrative negotiation. He suggests that there are seven key steps to an ideal negotiation process (see Figure 2.2):

Preparation: deciding what is important, defining goals, thinking ahead how to work together with the other party.

Relationship building: getting to know the other party, understanding how you and the other are similar and different, and building commitment toward achieving a mutually beneficial set of outcomes. Greenhalgh argues that this stage is extremely critical to satisfactorily moving the other stages forward.

Information gathering: learning what you need to know about the issues, about the other party and their needs, about the feasibility of possible settlements, and about what might happen if you fail to reach agreement with the other side.

Information using: at this stage, negotiators assemble the case they want to make for their preferred outcomes and settlement, one that will maximize the negotiator's own needs. This presentation is often used to "sell" the negotiator's preferred outcome to the other.

Bidding: the process of making moves from one's initial, ideal position to the actual outcome. Bidding is the process by which each party states their "opening offer," and then makes moves in that offer toward a middle ground. We describe this process extensively in Chapter 3.

Closing the deal: the objective here is to build commitment to the agreement achieved in the previous phase. Both the negotiator and the other party have to assure themselves that they reached a deal they can be happy with, or at least live with.

Implementing the agreement: determining who needs to do what once the hands are shaken and the documents signed. Not uncommonly parties discover that the agreement is flawed, key points were missed, or the situation has changed and new questions exist. Flaws in moving through the earlier phases arise here, and the deal may have to be reopened, or issues settled by arbitrators or the courts.

Greenhalgh argues that this model is largely prescriptive—that is, this is the way people ought to negotiate, and he creates a strong case for why this is the case. However, examination of the actual practice of negotiators shows that they frequently deviate from this model, and that one can track differences in their practice according to his or her home culture. For example, untrained American negotiators typically view the process more in "win-lose" terms (Chapter 1): their preparation stage is very short, they tend to skip relationship building altogether, spend a lot of time on bidding, gather and share information *after* the bidding, also tend to skip closing altogether, and then implement. In contrast, Japanese negotiators spend a great deal of time on relationship building first, then truncate the steps toward the end of the negotiation process. The influence of culture on negotiation is more thoroughly examined in Chapter 8.[23]

GETTING READY TO IMPLEMENT THE STRATEGY: THE PLANNING PROCESS

On the surface, when one watches the drama and theatrics of tense, conflict-laden, face-to-face confrontation, one can easily get the impression that negotiation success lies in persuasiveness, eloquence, clever maneuvering, and occasional histrionics. Although these tactics make the process interesting (and at times even entertaining), *the foundation for success in negotiation is not in the game playing or the dramatics. The dominant force for success in negotiation is in the planning that takes place prior to the dialogue.* While success in negotiation is affected by how one enacts the strategy, the foundation for success in negotiation is how one prepares.

Identifying potential shortcomings in the planning process is necessary, but it's not enough. Effective planning also requires hard work on several fronts:

- Defining the issues
- Assembling issues and defining the bargaining mix
- Defining interests
- Defining limits
- Defining one's own objectives (targets) and opening bids (where to start)
- Defining the constituents to whom one is accountable
- Understanding the other party and its interests and objectives
- Selecting a strategy
- Planning the issue presentation and defense
- Defining protocol—where and when the negotiation will occur, who will be there, agenda, etc.

The remainder of this chapter discusses each of these steps in detail (see also the planning guide in Table 2.2 that may be used to plan one's own negotiation).[24] In this discussion, we assume that a single planning process can be followed for both a distributive

TABLE 2.2 Negotiation Planning Guide

1. What are the issues in the upcoming negotiation?

2. Based on a review of ALL of the issues, what is the "bargaining mix"? (Which issues do we have to cover? Which issues are connected to other issues?)

3. What are my interests?

4. What are my limits—what is my walkaway? What is my alternative?

5. Defining targets and openings—where will I start, what is my goal?

6. Who are my constituents and what do they want me to do?

7. What are the opposing negotiators and what do they want?

8. What overall strategy do I want to select?

9. How will I present my issues to the other party?

10. What protocol needs to be followed in conducting this negotiation?

and an integrative process. We also assume that the planning process can proceed linearly, in the order in which these steps are presented. Information often cannot be obtained and accumulated quite this simply and straightforwardly, however, and information discovered in some of the later steps may force a negotiator to reconsider and reevaluate earlier steps. As a result, the first iteration through the planning process should be tentative, and the negotiator should be flexible enough to modify and adjust previous steps as new information becomes available.

1. Defining the Issues

The first step in negotiation planning is to define the issues to be discussed. This step itself usually begins with an analysis of the overall situation. Usually, a negotiation involves one or two major issues (e.g., price or rate) and several minor issues. For instance, in buying a house, both parties immediately recognize that the central issues include price, date of sale, and date of occupancy. They might quickly identify other issues, such as appliances to be included or payment for the fuel oil left in the storage tank. During the purchase process, the buyer's lawyer, banker, or real estate agent might draw up a list of other things to consider: taxes to pay, escrow amounts for undiscovered problems, or a written statement that the seller must leave the house in "broom-clean" condition. Note that it does not take long to generate a fairly detailed list. In any negotiation, a complete list of the issues at stake is best derived from the following sources:

1. An analysis of the overall situation.
2. Our own experience in similar negotiations.
3. Research conducted to gather information (e.g., reading a book on how to buy a house).
4. Consultation with experts (real estate agents, bankers, attorneys, accountants, or friends who have bought a house recently).

2. Assembling the Issues and Defining the Bargaining Mix

The next step in planning is to assemble all the issues that have been defined into a comprehensive list. The combination of lists from each side in the negotiation determines the *bargaining mix* (see Chapter 3). In generating a list of issues, negotiators may feel that they put too much on the table at once, or raise too many issues. This may happen if the parties do not talk frequently or if they have lots of business to transact. It often turns out, however, that introducing a long list of issues into a negotiation often makes success more, rather than less, likely—provided that all the issues are real. Large bargaining mixes allow many possible components and arrangements for settlement, thus increasing the likelihood that a particular package will meet both parties' needs and therefore lead to a successful settlement. At the same time, large bargaining mixes can lengthen negotiations because they present many possible combinations of issues to consider, and combining and evaluating all these mixes makes things very complex.

After assembling issues on an agenda, the negotiator next must prioritize them. Prioritization includes two steps:

1. *Determine which issues are most important and which are less important.* Once negotiation begins, parties can easily be swept up in the rush of information, arguments, offers, counteroffers, trade-offs, and concessions. For those who are not clear in advance about what they want (and what they can do without), it is easy to lose perspective and agree to suboptimal settlements, or to get distracted by points that are relatively unimportant. When negotiators do not have priorities, they may be more likely to yield on those points aggressively argued by the other side rather than to yield on the issues that are less important to *them.*

Priorities can be set in a number of ways. One simple way is for the negotiator to rank-order the issues by asking "What is most important?" "What is second most important?" and "What is least important?" An even simpler process is to group issues into categories of high, medium, or low importance. When the negotiator represents a constituency, it is important to involve that group in setting priorities. Priorities can be set for both interests and more specific issues, and for tangibles and intangibles.

In our house example, the buyer may determine that the price is the most important issue and that the closing date is secondary.

2. *Determine whether the issues are connected (linked together) or separate.* If the issues are separate, they can be easily added or subtracted; if connected, then settlement on one will be linked to settlement on the others and making concessions on one issue will inevitably be tied to some other issue. The negotiator must decide whether the issues are truly connected—for instance, whether the price he will pay for the house is dependent on what the bank will loan him—as opposed to simply being connected in his own mind for the sake of achieving a good settlement.

3. Defining Your Interests

After defining the issues, the negotiator must proceed to define the underlying interests and needs. *Positions*—an opening bid or a target point—are what a negotiator wants. *Interests* are why she wants them. $150,000 as a target point for a house would be a position; this is what the negotiator hopes to pay. The interest would be "to pay a fair market price, and one I can afford, for that two bedroom condominium." Although defining interests is more important to integrative negotiation than to distributive bargaining, even distributive discussions can benefit from one or both parties' identifying the key interests. (In Chapter 4, we will discuss in more detail the nature of interests and ways to bring them to the surface.) If issues help us define what we want, then understanding interests requires us to ask why we want it. Asking "why" questions usually brings critical values, needs, or principles that we want to achieve in the negotiation to the surface. Interests may include:

- Substantive, that is, directly related to the focal issues under negotiation.
- Process-based, that is, related to the manner in which the negotiators settle the dispute.
- Relationship-based, that is, tied to the current or desired future relationship between the parties.

Intangibles, including principles or standards to which the parties wish to adhere, the informal norms by which they will negotiate, and the benchmarks they will use to guide them toward a settlement.

4. Knowing Your Limits and Alternatives

What will happen if the other party in a negotiation refuses to accept some proposed items for the agenda or states issues in such a way that they are unacceptable to you? Good preparation requires that you establish two clear points: your *limits* and your *alternatives*.

Limits are the point where you decide that you should stop the negotiation rather than continue, because any settlement beyond this point is not minimally acceptable. Limits are also referred to as resistance points or reservation prices or walkaway points (see Chapter 3). If you are the seller, your limit is the least you will take for the item you have for sale; if you are the buyer, your limit is the most you will pay for the item. Setting limits as a part of planning is critical. Most of us have been involved in buying situations where the item we wanted wasn't available, but we allowed ourselves to be talked into a more expensive model. Moreover, some competitive situations generate intense pressures to "escalate" the price. For example, in an auction, if there is a bidding war with another person, one may pay more than was planned. Gamblers, analogously, may encounter a losing streak and end up losing more money than they had wanted to. Clear limits keep people from agreeing to deals that they later realize weren't very smart.

On the other hand, *alternatives* are other deals negotiators could achieve and still meet their needs. We discussed alternatives earlier in this chapter, when we described the "avoidance" strategy, suggesting that when there are alternative ways to meet needs, it may not be necessary to engage in a negotiation. But alternatives are critical for almost all negotiating situations, not just ones where avoidance may be the best strategy. In any situation, the better your alternatives, the more power you have, because you can walk away from the deal in front of you and still know that you can have your needs and interests met. In the house-purchase example, the more a buyer has searched the real estate market and understands what other comparable houses are available, the more she knows that she can walk away from this negotiation and still have acceptable housing choices.

5. Setting Targets and Openings

After negotiators have defined the issues, assembled a tentative agenda, and consulted others as appropriate and necessary, the next step is to define two other key points: the *specific target point* (where one realistically expects to achieve a settlement) and the *asking price* or *opening bid* (representing the best deal one can hope to achieve).

There are numerous ways to set a target. One can ask, "What is an outcome that I would be comfortable with?" "At what point would I be generally satisfied?" "What have other people achieved in this same situation?" Targets may not be as firm and rigid as limits or alternatives; one might be able to set a general range, or a class of several outcomes that would be equally acceptable.

Similarly, there are numerous ways to set an opening bid. An opening may be the best possible outcome, an ideal solution, something even better than was achieved last time. However, it is easy to get overly idealistic about such a solution, and hence to set an opening that is so unrealistic that the other party immediately laughs, gets angry, or walks away before another word is spoken. While openings are usually formulated around a "best possible" settlement, it is also easy to inflate them to the point where they become self-defeating because they are too unrealistic (in the eyes of the other negotiator).

Target Setting Requires Positive Thinking about One's *Own* Objectives.   When approaching a negotiation, negotiators often attempt to become aware of the other party—how members of that party may behave, what they will probably demand, and how the bargainer feels about dealing with them. It is possible to devote too much attention to the other party, however; that is, to spend too much time trying to discern what the other side wants, how to meet those demands, and so forth. If negotiators focus attention on the other party to the exclusion of themselves, they may plan their entire strategy as a reaction to the other's anticipated conduct. Reactive strategies are likely to make negotiators feel threatened and defensive and to lessen the flexibility and creativity of their negotiating behavior. If negotiators can take a proactive stance, in which they are aware of the range of possible outcomes, they can be flexible in what they will accept and improve the likelihood of arriving at a mutually satisfactory outcome.

Target Setting Often Requires Considering How to Package Several Issues and Objectives.   Most negotiators have a mixture of bargaining objectives, so they must consider the best way to achieve satisfaction across multiple issues. To package issues effectively, negotiators need to understand the definition of the issues, bargaining mix, and the other's bargaining mix. Negotiators propose settlements that will help them achieve their targets on the issues they have defined as important; they may then balance these areas by setting more conservative targets for items less important to them (see also our house-sale example in Chapter 3). Evaluating the bargaining mix may also eventually require the negotiator to invent new options that will permit both parties to achieve their objectives; this process will be extensively described in Chapter 4.

Target Setting Requires an Understanding of Trade-offs and Throwaways.   The discussion of packaging raises another possible problem: What does one do if the other party proposes a package that puts issues A, B, and C in one's optimistic range, puts item D in the realistic range, puts E at the pessimistic point, and does not even mention item F, which is part of one's bargaining mix? Is item F a throwaway item that can be ignored? If it is not a throwaway item, is it relatively unimportant and worth giving up in order to lock in agreement on A, B, and C in the optimal range? Now suppose the other party has proposed two packages, the one described above and a second one that places items A and E in the optimistic range, items B and F in the realistic range, and C at the pessimistic point, while it ignores D. Would the first or the second package be more attractive?

To evaluate these packages, negotiators need to have some idea of what each item in the bargaining mix is worth in terms that can be compared across issues. The negotiator needs some way of establishing trade-offs. This may be a difficult thing to do because different items or issues will be of different value to the negotiator and will often be measured in different terms. When considering the purchase of a used car, a buyer needs to decide the importance of each of the following: (1) the make of the car, (2) the color, (3) the age of the car, and (4) the price.

While it may not be possible to find a common dimension (such as dollar value) to compare issues in the bargaining mix or to compare tangibles with intangibles, many negotiators find it convenient to scale all items on some common dimension. The premise is that even if the fit is not perfect, any guide is better than none. Negotiators who want a different way to compare items and issues may use a point or utility scale to evaluate them. For example, if the value of the entire target package of issues is worth 500 points, then smaller, proportionate numbers of points could be assigned to each issue in the mix reflecting relative priorities and totaling 500. Obviously, such points are only meaningful to the party establishing them, and only for as long as the points reflect the basic values and targets of the negotiator in that situation. As long as they do, such scales are a useful tool for planning and assessing offers and counteroffers.

6. Assessing My Constituents

When people are negotiating for themselves—for example, buying a used racing bicycle or exercise machine—they can determine all of the previous issues on their own. But when people negotiate in a professional context, they most likely will have *constituents*—bosses, parties who make the final decision, parties who will evaluate and critique the solution achieved. Moreover, there may be a number of *observers* to the negotiation who will also watch and critique the negotiation. Finally, negotiation occurs in a context—a social system of laws, customs, common business practices, cultural norms, and political cross-pressures.

One way to assess all of the key parties in a negotiation is to complete a "field analysis." Imagine that you are the captain of a soccer team, about to play a game on the field (see Figure 2.3). Assessing constituents is the same as assessing all of the parties who are in the soccer stadium:

A. Who is, or should be, on the team on my side of the field? Perhaps it is just the negotiator (a 1:1 game). But perhaps we want other help: an attorney, accountant, or other expert assistance; someone to give us moral support or listen closely to what the other side says; a recorder or note taker.

B. Who is on the other side of the field? This is discussed in more detail in the next section.

C. Who is on the sidelines who can affect the play of the game? Who are the negotiation equivalents of coaches and trainers? This includes one's direct superior, or the person who must approve or authorize agreement that is reached.

D. Who is in the stands? Who is watching the game, is interested in it, but can only indirectly affect what happens? This might include senior managers, shareholders, competitors, financial analysts, or others.

E. What is going on in the broader environment in which the negotiation takes place? As we will point out in later chapters of the book, a number of "context" issues can affect negotiation:

FIGURE 2.3   A Field Analysis of Negotiation

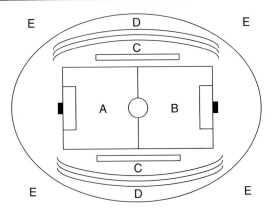

A. The direct actors (who is on the field on our side?)

B. The opposition actors (who is on the field on their side?)

C. Indirect actors (who is on the sidelines?)

D. Interested observers (who is in the stands?)

E. Environmental factors (what is going on in the broad environment of the game—outside the stadium, but shaping and defining what happens in the stadium?)

- What has been the history of the relationship between these parties, and how does it affect the overall expectations they bring to this negotiation?
- What kind of a relationship is expected or desired for the future, and how does it affect the current negotiation?
- How successful has this negotiator been in past deliberations with others?
- What is common and acceptable practice in the legal system in which the deal is being done?
- What is common and acceptable practice in the ethical system in which the deal is being done (Chapter 7)?
- What is common and acceptable practice given the culture in which the negotiation is occurring (Chapter 8)?

7. Analyzing the Other Party

Earlier in this section, we discussed the importance of assigning priorities to one's own goals and objectives. When negotiators have the opportunity to meet with people from the other side, they may be able to learn what issues are important to them. Negotiators may also use this opportunity to discuss their priorities on those issues—which ones are most important, least important, and so on. Finally, negotiators may also have learned something about their interests—why they want what they want. Conversely, if negotiators have not had the opportunity to meet with people from the other side, then they should attempt to see the negotiation from the other party's perspective, or to gather information to learn about their issues, interests, and priorities. Negotiators might call the other party and interview them prior to the actual meeting, or try to take their perspective and anticipate what it is that you would want if you were negotiating from that point of view. Several key pieces of background information will be of great importance:

- The other party's current resources, interests, and needs.
- The other party's objectives.
- The other party's reputation and negotiation style.
- The other party's alternative(s).
- The other party's authority to make an agreement.
- The other party's likely strategy and tactics.

Let us now explore each of these in more detail. In theory, it would be extremely useful to have as much of this information as possible before negotiations occur. In reality, it may not be possible to obtain this information through either direct contact with the negotiator or other research sources. If not, the negotiator should plan to collect as much of this information as possible during the opening stages of the actual deliberations. (Master negotiator Bill Richardson includes gathering information about the other party in his advice to negotiators—see Box 2.3.)

The Other Party's Current Resources, Interests, and Needs.   Negotiators will learn much about the other party while negotiating, but as much information as

---

BOX 2.3
Bill Richardson Interview

Bill Richardson is a master negotiator. When the United States needs to negotiate with hostile governments for the release of political prisoners, they turn to Richardson, a New Mexico congressperson, to represent their interests. His former negotiation adversaries include Iraq's Saddam Hussein, Cuba's Fidel Castro, and Haiti's Raoul Cedras. Richardson offers the following tips for negotiators:

- Be a good listener. In order to negotiate, you must understand your opponent's perspective and know what motivates him or her.
- Use every negotiation technique you know. There is no single "best" strategy.
- Try to come out of every meeting with something, even if it is just a plan for a second meeting.
- Prepare for a negotiation by gathering information from those who are knowledgeable about the situation and the person you will interact with.
- Show humility, but not weakness. You can't back down or let down your guard.

SOURCE: Adapted from J. Martin, "How to Negotiate with Really Tough Guys," *Fortune,* May 27, 1996, pp. 173–74.

---

possible should be gathered in advance through research and homework. Which data are most relevant will depend on what type of negotiation will be conducted and on who the other party is. An analysis of the other party's business history or previous negotiations, successful and otherwise, might provide useful clues. Financial data about the other party might be obtained through channels such as Dun and Bradstreet, financial statements, newspapers, files, company biographies, stock reports, and public records of legal judgments. One might investigate the other party's inventories. Sometimes one can learn a great deal simply by visiting the other party or speaking to his or her friends and peers. Another way to learn is to ask questions of people who have done business with the other party.

In addition to learning about the party's background, one also needs to get information about his or her current interests and needs (see Chapter 4). One can get this information through a variety of routes:

- Conduct a preliminary interview, including a discussion of what the other party would like to achieve in the upcoming negotiations.
- Anticipate the other party's interests.
- Ask others who know or have negotiated with the other party.
- Read what the other party says about himself or herself in the media.

The Other Party's Targets and Openings.   After negotiators have obtained information about the other side's resources and interests, they also need to understand his or her objectives. People often think stereotypically about the other party's interests and targets; they use their own targets and values as a guide and assume that others are like themselves and want similar things. A manager who is always after a bigger paycheck is usually surprised that some of his subordinates are more interested in having a challenging job, schedule flexibility, or increased leisure time than they are in maximizing their salary.

One of the best ways to get this information is directly from the other party. Because information about the other party's targets is so important to the strategy formulation of both parties, professional negotiators will often exchange information about targets or initial proposals days or even weeks before negotiations begin.

The Other Party's Reputation and Style.   As noted earlier, the other party's past negotiating behavior is a good indication of how he or she will behave in the future. Even if a bargainer has had no previous experience with the other person, speaking to those who have dealt with that person in the past can be very valuable. Although gathering information about the other party's past behavior is a reasonable starting point for making assumptions, keep in mind that people do change over time.

One's impression of the other party's reputation may be based on several factors:

1. How the other party's predecessors have negotiated with you in the past.
2. How the other party has negotiated with you in the past, either in the same or in different contexts.
3. How the other party has negotiated with others in the past.

The Other Party's Alternative.   As part of the preparation process, we have stressed that negotiators need to understand their own alternative. The alternative offers the negotiator a viable option for agreement if the current negotiation does not yield an acceptable outcome. Similarly, negotiators should attempt to understand the quality of the other party's alternative. If the other party has a strong and viable alternative, he or she will probably be confident in negotiation, set high objectives, and be willing to push hard for those objectives. In contrast, if the other party has a weak alternative, then he or she will be more dependent on achieving a satisfactory agreement with you, and be less likely to push as hard.

The Other Party's Authority.   When negotiators represent others, their power to make agreements may be limited; in fact, their ability to carry out negotiations may be restricted in many ways. Sometimes a constituency stipulates that negotiators cannot make any agreements; often negotiators can only present proposals from the constituency or collect information and take it back to their superiors.

There are many reasons for limiting a negotiator's authority. Negotiators kept on a short leash cannot be won over by a persuasive presentation to commit their constituency to something that is not wanted. They cannot give out sensitive information carelessly. Although these limitations may actually be helpful to a negotiator, they can also be frustrating. One might ask, "Why should I speak with this person, if she cannot make a decision and may not even be well informed about what I want?" Negotiation under these circumstances can seem like an exercise in futility. When a negotiator always has to check things out with those he represents, the other party may refuse to continue until someone who has the power to answer questions and make decisions is brought to the table. Negotiating teams should therefore think seriously about sending in a negotiator with limited authority. Although that person will not be able to make unauthorized decisions, the limited authority may frustrate the other party and create an unproductive tension in the negotiating relationship. Before negotiations, it might be appropriate to ask the other party specifically about any limits to authority in the impending negotiation; the temptation to lie will be balanced against the likely personal costs and costs to the negotiation of doing so.

The Other Party's Strategy and Tactics.   Finally, it would be most helpful to gain information about the other party's intended strategy and tactics. Although it is unlikely the other party will reveal his or her strategy outright—particularly if he or she is intending to use distributive tactics—one can infer this information from whatever data one collects to answer the previous inquiries in this list. Thus, reputation, style, alternative, authority, and objectives may tell one a great deal about what strategy the other party intends to pursue. As we have noted before, one will have to gather this information on an emergent basis as the negotiation unfolds; if one's expectations have been incorrect, it will be necessary to recalibrate one's own strategic response.

8. What Strategy Do I Want to Pursue?

The four strategic alternatives represented in Figure 2.1 are a good place to start. It may well be that strategy was determined long before this point in the planning process, but by this time, the negotiator should clearly determine which strategy he/she intends to pursue.

9. How Will I Present the Issues to the Other Party?

One important aspect of actual negotiations is to present a case clearly and to marshal ample supporting facts and arguments; another is to refute the other party's arguments with counterarguments.

Because of the breadth and diversity of issues that can be included in negotiations, it is not possible to specify all the procedures that can be used to assemble information. There are, however, some good general guides that can be used. A negotiator can ask these questions:

a. What facts support my point of view? What substantiates or validates this information as factual?

b. Whom may I consult or talk with to help me elaborate or clarify the facts? What records, files, or data sources exist that support my arguments?

c. Have these issues been negotiated before by others under similar circumstances? Can I consult those negotiators to determine what major arguments they used, which ones were successful, and which were not?

d. What is the other party's point of view likely to be? What are his or her interests? What arguments is the other party likely to make? How can I respond to those arguments and seek more creative positions that go further in addressing both sides' issues and interests?

e. How can I develop and present the facts so they are most convincing? What visual aids, pictures, charts, graphs, expert testimony, and the like can be helpful or make the best case?

In Chapter 6, we offer extensive advice to the negotiator on how to use power and how to structure the presentation of information in order to achieve maximum effectiveness.

10. What Protocol Needs to Be Followed in This Negotiation?

There are a number of elements of "protocol" or process that a negotiator should consider:

• *The agenda.* A negotiator may unilaterally draw up a firm list of issues, and even establish specific goals, well before the initial negotiation meeting. This process is valuable because it forces the bargainer to think through his or her position and decide on objectives. The list of issues constitutes the agenda for negotiation. It is what the negotiator wants to discuss, and the order or priority in which he wants to discuss them.

While agendas may be proposed unilaterally by the negotiator, there is also a potential risk. If the negotiator's list differs from a preset agenda or the other side's preferred list, the negotiator may bring issues to the table that the other party is unprepared to discuss, or may define priorities that cannot be achieved realistically. For this reason, many professional negotiators (labor negotiators, diplomats, etc.) often exchange (and negotiate) the agenda in advance. They want first to agree to what issues will be discussed (the agenda) before actually engaging the substance of those issues.

• *The location of negotiation.* Negotiators tend to do better on their home turf—their own office, building, or city. They know the space, they feel comfortable and relaxed, they have direct access to all the amenities—secretaries, research information, expert advice, computers, and so on. In cross-cultural negotiations (see Chapter 8), language and cultural differences may come into play, and the parties may have to travel across many time zones. If negotiators want to minimize the advantage that comes with home turf, then they need to select neutral territory in which neither party will have an advantage. In addition, negotiators can choose the degree of formality of the environment. Formal deliberations are often held in conference rooms or even hotel meeting rooms; informal deliberations can be held in restaurants, cocktail lounges, or rooms that offer an array of furniture such as that found in a typical living room.

• *The time period of negotiation.* If negotiators expect long, protracted deliberations, they might want to negotiate the time and duration of sessions. When do we start? How long do we meet? When do we need to end? When can we call for coffee breaks or time to caucus with our team?

- *Other parties who might be involved in the negotiation.* Is the negotiation between the principals only (refer back to the field analysis, Figure 2.3)? Will one or both sides bring experts or advisers with them? What role will these outsiders play? Will one or both sides be represented by an agent who will negotiate for them? If so, will the principal be there, or will the agent only consult the principal later? Are the media involved, and what role might they play?

- *What might be done if negotiation fails.* What will happen if we deadlock? Will we go to a third-party neutral? Might we try some other techniques? (See Chapter 9 for suggestions on getting negotiations back on track.)

- *How will we keep track of what is agreed to?* Many negotiators don't consider the importance of keeping track of exactly what was discussed and agreed to. Going back to the early days in school when we actively avoided being elected the class or club secretary, note taking is seen as a tedious and uninteresting job. However, experienced negotiators learn that the "secretarial role" is critical. First, the person with the best notes often becomes the "memory" of the session; his or her notes are later consulted to determine what was said and discussed. Second, the person with the best notes may also volunteer to draft the initial agreement; again, this person may be able to take some license in how the agreement is stated, and what points are emphasized or de-emphasized. Finally, if the agreement is highly technical or complex, one certainly wants to have the agreement reviewed by experts and specialists—attorneys, financial analysts, accountants, engineers, and so on. Moreover, if the agreement is between groups who speak different languages, the agreement should be translated and back-translated so that it says and means the same thing in each of the languages.

In new bargaining relationships, discussions about these procedural issues occur before the major substantive issues are raised. The ease or difficulty of resolving these procedural issues can often be used as tests to determine how the negotiation on the larger substantive issues will proceed. If the negotiator enjoys success in these procedural negotiations, he might expect that it may be easier to reach agreement later on the substantive issues.

CHAPTER SUMMARY

In this chapter, we reviewed the key factors that a negotiator needs to know and understand to successfully plan for a negotiation. To recap:

1. Negotiators differ in the goals they select. Goals can be specific (to achieve a particular outcome), or they can be more general (to pursue a broader set of interests). They can also be tangible, such as a particular rate or price or financial outcome; or they can be intangible, such as winning, beating the other, or defending a principle. Goals can shape the frames we adopt, or frames can shape the goals we pursue.

2. There are several major strategies that can be used in a negotiation. Select the strategy that is most likely to achieve one's objectives, and also take into

consideration the long-term relationship with the other party. Two of these major strategies—competition and collaboration—are the focus of the next two chapters of this book.

3. Negotiators differ in how they "frame" the problem, issue, or conflict. Frames may be perspectives on outcomes and the related rewards or penalties that go with those outcomes, or they may be ways to define "the problem" in a negotiation. What is important is that how one or both parties frame the problem will lead them to select some conflict management strategies and ignore others. Therefore, a negotiator needs to attend to the way he or she is defining the problem and specifically be aware that

- There may be other ways to define it that may make the problem more or less amenable to negotiation and resolution.
- The other party may not be defining it in the same way, which may contribute to the ease or difficulty with which the parties can communicate about the problem with each other.

4. Negotiations tend to evolve over time according to certain predictable sequences. These sequences comprise the different stages or phases of a negotiation. The models indicate that negotiation is not a random process but has some predictable elements to it over time.

5. Goals, strategies, frames, and predictable stages set the background for an effective planning process. Again, as we noted, there are a number of different planning templates, which tend to emphasize different elements in slightly different sequences. Nevertheless, we have tried to present the most important steps in the planning process. Effectively attending to each of these steps should allow a negotiator to be very well prepared for the challenges that he or she is going to face in playing out strategy and meeting the other party.

ENDNOTES

1. Mintzberg, H. and Quinn, J. B., 1991.
2. Quinn, J. B., 1991.
3. Savage, Blair, and Sorenson, 1989.
4. See also Johnston, 1982.
5. Ibid.
6. Lax and Sebenius, 1986.
7. Beuchler, 2000, p. 41.
8. Thompson, 1998.
9. Roth and Sheppard, 1995, p. 94.
10. Kolb, 1995; Follett, 1942, quoted in Putnam and Holmer, 1992.
11. Gray, 1997; Gray and Donnellon, 1989; Lewicki, Gray, and Elliott, 2003.
12. Gray, 1991, 1997; Lewicki, Gray, and Elliott, 2003.
13. Ury, Brett, and Goldberg, 1988.
14. Felstiner, Abel, and Sarat, 1980–81.
15. Putnam and Holmer, 1992, p. 138.

16. Spector, 1995.
17. Putnam and Wilson, 1989; Putnam, Wilson, and Turner, 1990.
18. Ikle, 1964.
19. Lewicki, Weiss, and Lewin, 1992, p. 225.
20. Zartman, 1977; Zartman and Berman, 1982.
21. Putnam and Geist, 1985; Putnam, 1994.
22. Douglas, 1962; Greenhalgh, 2001; Morley and Stephenson, 1977.
23. Greenhalgh, 2001.
24. See, for example, Richardson, 1977; Asherman and Asherman, 1990; Burnstein, 1995; Fisher and Ertel, 1995; Lewicki, Hiam, and Olander, 1996; Lewicki and Hiam, 1999; and Greenhalgh, 2001.

CHAPTER 3

Strategy and Tactics
of Distributive Bargaining

Eighteen months ago Larry decided to move closer to where he works. Following this decision to move, he put his house on the market and started to look for a new one—but with no results. Fourteen months later, Larry finally received an offer to buy his house and, after a brief negotiation, settled on the selling price. Because he had not yet found a house to buy, he postponed closing the sale for six months to give himself additional time to look. The buyer, Barbara, was not happy about having to wait that long because of the inconvenience and the difficulty of getting a bank to guarantee an interest rate so far in advance. Larry adjusted the price so that Barbara would accept this postponement, but it was clear that she would be much happier if he could move the date closer.

There were relatively few houses on the market in the area where Larry wanted to live, and none of them was satisfactory. He jokingly said that unless something new came on the market, he would be sleeping in a tent on the town common when the leaves turned in the fall. Two months later a house came on the market that met his requirements. The seller, Monica, set the asking price at $145,000, which was $10,000 above what Larry hoped to pay but $5,000 below the most he would be willing to pay. Larry knew that the more he paid for the house, the less he would have to make some very desirable alterations, buy draperies and some new furniture, and hire a moving company. Monica already had attractive drapes in the house. She was moving to a new house; if she could not use the drapes in the new house, Larry might be able to purchase them or ask Monica to include them with the sale. The same might be true for several rugs, hall tables, and other items. Larry also learned that Monica's new home was supposed to be finished soon, about the time Larry was to close on the sale of his present house.

This illustration provides the basic elements of a distributive bargaining situation. As we've mentioned in Chapters 1 and 2, it is also called competitive, or win-lose, bargaining. In a distributive bargaining situation, the goals of one party are usually in fundamental and direct conflict with the goals of the other party. Resources are fixed and limited, and both parties want to maximize their share of the resources. As a result, each party will use a set of strategies to maximize his or her share of the outcomes to be obtained. One important strategy is to guard information carefully—one party tries to give information to the other party only when it provides a strategic advantage. Meanwhile, it is highly desirable to get information from the other party to improve negotiation power. Distributive bargaining is basically a competition over who is going to get the most of a limited resource (often money). Whether or not one or both parties achieve their objectives will depend on the strategies and tactics they employ.[1]

For many, the strategies and tactics of distributive bargaining are what negotiation is all about. Images come to mind of smoke-filled rooms packed with men arguing and fighting for their points of view. Many people are attracted to this view of negotiation and look forward to learning and sharpening an array of hard-bargaining skills; many others are repelled by distributive bargaining and would rather walk away than negotiate in this manner. They argue that distributive bargaining is old-fashioned, macho, and destructive.

There are two reasons that every negotiator should be familiar with distributive bargaining. First, some interdependent situations that negotiators face *are* distributive, and to do well in them negotiators need to understand how they work. Second, because many people use distributive bargaining strategies and tactics almost exclusively, all negotiators will find it important to know how to counter their effects. While distributive strategies and tactics are useful, they can also be counterproductive and costly. Often they cause the negotiating parties to focus so much on their differences that they ignore what they have in common.[2] These negative effects notwithstanding, *distributive bargaining strategies and tactics are quite useful when a negotiator wants to maximize the value obtained in a single deal and when the relationship with the other party is not important.*

Some of the tactics discussed in this chapter will also generate ethical concerns. (The topic of ethics and negotiation is discussed in detail in Chapter 7.) Do not assume that the other party shares your ethical values when negotiating. Although you may not believe that it is ethical to use some of the tactics discussed in this chapter, other negotiators will be quite comfortable using them. Alternatively, you may be comfortable using some tactics that make other negotiators quite uneasy. Most negotiators accept the difference between "soft" and "hard" distributive bargaining. The discussion of strategies and tactics in this chapter is intended to help negotiators understand the dynamics of distributive situations and thereby obtain a better deal. We also think that a thorough understanding of these concepts will allow negotiators who are by nature not entirely comfortable with distributive bargaining to manage distributive negotiations proactively.

THE DISTRIBUTIVE BARGAINING SITUATION

To describe how the distributive bargaining process works, we will return to our opening example of Larry's new house purchase. Several prices were mentioned: (1) Monica's asking price, (2) the price Larry would like to pay for a new house, and (3) the price above which Larry would not buy the house. These prices represent key points in the analysis of any distributive bargaining situation. Larry's preferred price is the *target point,* the point at which a negotiator would like to conclude negotiations—his optimal goal. The target is also sometimes referred to as a negotiator's *aspiration.* The price beyond which Larry will not go is the *resistance point,* a negotiator's bottom line—the most he will pay as a buyer (for a seller, it's the smallest amount she will settle for). Finally, the *asking price* is the initial price set by the seller; Larry might decide to counter Monica's asking price with his *initial offer*—the first number he will quote to the seller. Using the house purchase as an example, we can treat the range of possible prices as a continuum (see Figure 3.1).

FIGURE 3.1   The Buyer's View of the House Negotiation

	Larry's target point		Monica's asking price	Larry's resistance point
$130,000	$135,000	$140,000	$145,000	$150,000

How does Larry decide on his initial offer? There are many ways to answer this question. Fundamentally, however, to make a good initial offer Larry must understand something about the process of negotiation. In Chapter 1, we discussed how people expect give-and-take when they negotiate, and Larry needs to factor this into his initial offer. If Larry opened the negotiation at his target point ($135,000) and then had to make a concession, this first concession would have him moving away from his target point to a price closer to his resistance point. If he really wants to achieve his target, he should make an initial offer that is lower than his target point to create some room for making concessions. At the same time, the starting point cannot be too far from the target point. If Larry made the first offer too low (e.g., $100,000), Monica might break off negotiations, believing him to be unreasonable or foolish. Although judgments about how to determine first offers can often be quite complex and can have a dramatic influence on the course of negotiation, let us stay with the simple case for the moment and assume that Larry decided to offer $133,000 as a reasonable first offer—less than his target point and well below his resistance point. In the meantime, remember that although this illustration concerns only price, all other issues or agenda items for the negotiation have starting, target, and resistance points.

Both parties to a negotiation should establish their starting, target, and resistance points, at least implicitly, if not explicitly, before beginning a negotiation. Starting points are usually in the opening statements each party makes (i.e., the seller's listing price and the buyer's first offer). The target point is usually learned or inferred as negotiations get under way. People typically give up the margin between their starting points

DILBERT ©UFS. Reprinted by permission.

FIGURE 3.2   The Buyer's View of the House Negotiation (Extended)

Monica's resistance point (inferred)	Larry's initial offer (public)	Larry's target point (private)	Monica's target point (inferred)	Monica's asking price (public)	Larry's resistance point (private)
$130,000	$133,000	$135,000	$140,000	$145,000	$150,000

and target points as they make concessions. The resistance point, the point beyond which a person will not go and would rather break off negotiations, is not known to the other party and should be kept secret.[3] One party may not learn the other's resistance point even after the end of a successful negotiation. After an unsuccessful negotiation, one party may infer that the other's resistance point was near the last offer the other was willing to consider before the negotiation ended.

Two parties' starting and resistance points are usually arranged in reverse order, with the resistance point being a high price for the buyer and a low price for the seller. Thus, continuing the illustration, Larry would have been willing to pay up to $150,000 for the house Monica listed at $145,000. Larry can speculate that Monica may be willing to accept something less than $145,000 and probably would think $140,000 a desirable figure. What Larry does not know (but would dearly like to) is the lowest figure that Monica would accept. Is it $140,000? $135,000? Larry assumes it is $130,000. Monica, for her part, initially knows nothing about Larry's position but soon learns his starting point when he offers $133,000. Monica may suspect that Larry's target point is not too far away (in fact it is $135,000, but Monica doesn't know this) but has no idea of his resistance point ($150,000). This information—what Larry knows or infers about Monica's positions—is represented in Figure 3.2.

The spread between the resistance points, called the *bargaining range, settlement range,* or *zone of potential agreement,* is particularly important. In this area the actual bargaining takes place, for anything outside these points will be summarily rejected by one of the two negotiators. When the buyer's resistance point is above the seller's—he is minimally willing to pay more than she is minimally willing to sell for, as is true in the house example—there is a *positive bargaining range.* When the reverse is true—the seller's resistance point is above the buyer's, and the buyer won't pay more than the seller will minimally accept—there is a *negative bargaining range.* In the house example, if Monica would minimally accept $145,000 and Larry would maximally pay $140,000, then a negative bargaining range would exist. Negotiations that begin with a negative bargaining range are likely to stalemate. They can be resolved only if one or both parties are persuaded to change their resistance points, or if someone else forces a solution upon them that one or both parties dislike. However, because negotiators don't begin their deliberations by talking about their resistance points (they're talking about initial offers and demands instead), it is often hard to know whether a positive settlement range really exists until the negotiators get deep into the process. Both parties

FIGURE 3.3   The Buyer's View of the House Negotiation (Extended with Alternatives)

Monica's resistance point (inferred)	Larry's initial offer (public)	Monica's alternative buyer (private)	Larry's target point (private)	Monica's target point (inferred)	Larry's alternative house (private)	Monica's asking price (public)	Larry's resistance point (private)
$130,000	$133,000	$134,000	$135,000	$140,000	$142,000	$145,000	$150,000

may realize that there was no overlap in their resistance points only after protracted negotiations have been exhausted; at that point, they will have to decide whether to end negotiations or reevaluate their resistance points, a process to be described in more detail later on.

The Role of Alternatives to a Negotiated Agreement

In addition to opening bids, target points, and resistance points, a fourth factor may enter the negotiations: an *alternative* outcome that can be obtained by completing a different deal with a different party. In some negotiations, the parties have only two fundamental choices: (*a*) reach a deal with the other party, or (*b*) reach no settlement at all. In other negotiations, however, one or both parties may have available the possibility of an alternative deal with another party. Thus, in the case of Larry and Monica, another house may come on the market in the neighborhood where Larry wishes to buy. Similarly, if Monica waits long enough (or drops the price of the house far enough), she will presumably find another interested buyer. If Larry picks an alternative house to buy, talks to the owner of that house, and negotiates the best price that he can, that price represents his alternative. For the sake of argument, let us assume that Larry's alternative house costs $142,000 and that Monica's alternative buyer will pay $134,000.

An alternative point can be identical to the resistance point, although the two do not necessarily have to be the same. If Larry's alternative is $142,000, then (taking no other factors into account) he should reject any price Monica asks above that amount. But Larry's alternative may not be as desirable for reasons other than price—let's say that he likes the neighborhood less, that the house is 10 minutes farther away from where he works, or that he likes the way Monica had fixed up her house and wants to enjoy that when he moves in. In any of these situations, Larry may maintain his resistance point at $150,000; he is therefore willing to pay Monica up to $8,000 more than his alternative (see Figure 3.3).

Alternatives are important because they give the negotiator power to walk away from any negotiation when the emerging deal is not very good. The number of realistic alternatives negotiators may have will vary considerably from one situation to another. In negotiations where they have many attractive alternatives, they can set their goals higher and make fewer concessions. In negotiations where they have no attractive alternative, such as when dealing with a sole supplier, they have much less bargaining power. Good distributive bargainers identify their realistic alternatives before beginning negotiations with the other party so that they can properly gauge how firm to be in the negotiation.[4] Good bargainers also look for ways to *improve* their alternatives, even as the negotiation is under way. If Larry's negotiations with Monica are extending over a period of time, he may well keep his eye on the market for another possible (better) alternative. He may also continue to negotiate with the owner of the existing alternative house for a better deal. Both courses of action involve efforts by Larry to maintain and expand his bargaining power by improving the quality of his alternatives. (We discuss power and leverage in bargaining in detail in Chapter 6.)

Settlement Point

The fundamental process of distributive bargaining is to reach a settlement within a positive bargaining range. The objective of both parties is to obtain as much of the bargaining range as possible—that is, to get the settlement as close to the other party's resistance point as possible.

Both parties in distributive bargaining know that they might have to settle for less than what they would prefer (their opening or target point), but they hope that the settlement point will be better than their own resistance point. In order for agreement to occur, both parties must believe that the settlement point, although perhaps less desirable than they would prefer, is the best that they can get. This belief is important, both in reaching agreement and in ensuring support for the agreement after the negotiations. Parties who do not think they got the best agreement possible, or who believe that they lost something in the deal, frequently try to get out of the agreement later or find other ways to recoup their losses. If Larry thinks he got the short end of the deal, he could make life miserable and expensive for Monica by making extraneous claims later on—claiming that the house had hidden damages, that the fixtures that were supposed to come with the house were defective, and so on. Another factor that will affect satisfaction with the settlement point is whether the parties will ever see each other again. If Monica was moving out of the region, then Larry may be unable to contact her later for any adjustments and should therefore ensure that he evaluates the current deal very carefully.

Bargaining Mix

In the house-purchase illustration, as in almost all negotiations, agreement is necessary on several issues: the price, the closing date of the sale, renovations to the house, and the price of items that could remain in the house (such as drapes and appliances). This package of issues for negotiation is the *bargaining mix*. Each item in the mix has its own starting, target, and resistance points. Some items are of obvious importance to both parties; others are of importance to only one party. Negotiators need to know what is important to them and to the other party, and they need to make sure they take these priorities into account during the planning process. (See Chapter 2 for a detailed discussion of planning.)

For example, in the negotiation that we are describing, a secondary issue important to both parties is the closing date of the sale—the date when the ownership of the house will actually be transferred. The date of sale is part of the bargaining mix. Larry learned when Monica's new house was going to be completed and anticipated that she would want to transfer ownership of her old house to Larry shortly after that point. Larry asked for a closing date very close to when Monica would probably want to close; thus, the deal looked very attractive to her. As it turned out, Larry's closing date on his old house—his old target point—was close to this date as well, thus making the deal attractive for both Larry and Monica. If Larry and Monica had wanted different selling dates, then the closing date would have been a more contentious issue in the bargaining mix (although if Larry could have moved the closing date up, he might have been able to strike a better deal with Barbara, the buyer of his house).

FUNDAMENTAL STRATEGIES

The prime objective in distributive bargaining is to maximize the value of *this single deal*. In our example, the buyer has four fundamental strategies available:

1. To push for a settlement close to the seller's (as yet unknown) resistance point, thereby yielding for the buyer the largest part of the settlement range. The buyer may attempt to influence the seller's view of what settlements are possible by making extreme offers and small concessions.

2. To get the seller to change her resistance point by influencing the seller's beliefs about the value of the house. The buyer may try to convince the seller to reduce her resistance point (e.g., by telling her that the house is overpriced) and thereby increase the bargaining range.

3. If a negative settlement range exists, to get the seller to reduce her resistance point to create a positive settlement range or to modify his own resistance point to create an overlap. Thus, Monica could be persuaded to accept a lower price, or Larry could decide he has to pay more than he wanted to.

4. To get the seller to think that this settlement is the best that is possible—not that it is all she can get, or that she is incapable of getting more, or that the buyer is winning by getting more. The distinction between a party believing that an agreement is the best possible (and not the other interpretations) may appear subtle and semantic. However, in getting people to agree it is important that they feel as though they got the best possible deal. Ego satisfaction is often as important as achieving tangible objectives (recall the discussion of tangibles and intangibles in Chapter 1).

In all these strategies, the buyer is attempting to influence the seller's perceptions of what is possible through the exchange of information and persuasion. Regardless of the general strategy taken, two tasks are important in all distributive bargaining situations: (1) discovering the other party's resistance point, and (2) influencing the other party's resistance point.

Discovering the Other Party's Resistance Point

Information is the life force of negotiation. The more you can learn about the other party's outcome values, resistance point, motives, feelings of confidence, and so on, the more able you will be to strike a favorable agreement (see Box 3.1). At the same time, you

---

BOX 3.1
The Piano

When shopping for a used piano, Orvel Ray answered a newspaper ad. The piano was a beautiful upright in a massive walnut cabinet. The seller was asking $1,000, and it would have been a bargain at that price, but Orvel had received a $700 tax refund and had set this windfall as the limit that he could afford to invest. He searched for a negotiating advantage.

He was able to deduce several facts from the surroundings. The furnished basement where the piano sat also contained a set of drums, and an upright acoustic base stood in the corner. Obviously the seller was a serious musician, and probably played jazz. There had to be a compelling reason for selling such a beautiful instrument.

Orvel asked the first, obvious question, "Are you buying a new piano?"

The seller hesitated. "Well, I don't know yet. See, we're moving to North Carolina, and it would be very expensive to ship this piano clear across the country."

"Did they say how much extra it would cost?" Orvel queried.

"They said an extra $300 or so."

"When do you have to decide?"

"The packers are coming this afternoon."

Now Orvel knew where the seller was vulnerable. He could ship the piano cross-country, or sell it for $700 and still break even. Or he could hold out for his asking price and take his chances. "Here's what I can do: I can give you $700 in cash, right now," Orvel said as he took seven $100 bills out of his pocket and spread them on the keyboard. "And I can have a truck and three of my friends here to move it *out of your way* by noon today."

The seller hesitated, then picked up the money. "Well, I suppose that would work. I can always buy a new piano when we get settled."

Orvel left before the seller could reconsider. By the time the group returned with the truck, the seller had received three other offers at his asking price, but because he had accepted the cash, he had to tell them that the piano had already been sold.

If the seller had not volunteered the information about the packers coming that afternoon, Orvel might not have been able to negotiate the price.

SOURCE: From J. C. Levinson, M. S. A. Smith, and O. R. Wilson, *Guerrilla Negotiating* (New York: John Wiley, 1999), pp. 15–16.

---

do not want the other party to have certain information about you. Your real resistance point, some of the outcome values, and confidential information about a weak strategic position or an emotional vulnerability are best concealed.[5] Alternatively, you may want the other party to have certain information—some of it factual and correct, some of it contrived to lead the other party to believe things that are favorable to you. Because each side wants to obtain some information and to conceal other information, and because each side knows that the other also wants to obtain and conceal information, communication can become complex. Information is often conveyed in a code that evolves during negotiation. People answer questions with other questions or with incomplete statements; yet for either side to influence the other's perceptions, they must both eventually establish some points effectively and convincingly.

Influencing the Other Party's Resistance Point

Central to planning the strategy and tactics for distributive bargaining is effectively locating the other party's resistance point and the relationship of that resistance point to your own. The resistance point is established by the value expected from a particular outcome, which in turn is the product of the worth and costs of an outcome. Larry sets his resistance point based on the amount of money he can afford to pay (in total or in monthly mortgage payments), the estimated market value or worth of the house, and other factors in his bargaining mix (closing date, curtains, etc.). A resistance point will also be influenced by the cost an individual attaches to delay or difficulty in negotiation (an intangible) or in having the negotiations aborted. If Larry, who had set his resistance point at $150,000, were faced with the choice of paying $151,000 or living on the town common for a month, he might well reevaluate his resistance point. The following factors are important in attempting to influence the other person's resistance point: (1) the value the other attaches to a particular outcome, (2) the costs the other attaches to delay or difficulty in negotiations, and (3) the cost the other attaches to having the negotiations aborted.

A significant factor in shaping the other person's understanding of what is possible—and therefore the value he or she places on particular outcomes—is the other's understanding of your own situation. Therefore, when influencing the other's viewpoint, you must also deal with the other party's understanding of your value for a particular outcome, the costs you attach to delay or difficulty in negotiation, and your cost of having the negotiations aborted.

To explain how these factors can affect the process of distributive bargaining, we will make four major propositions:[6]

1. *The other party's resistance point will vary directly with his or her estimate of the cost of delay or aborting negotiations.* If the other party sees that you need a settlement quickly and cannot defer it, he or she can seize this advantage and press for a better outcome. Therefore, expectations will rise and the other party will set a more demanding resistance point. The more you can convince the other that your costs of delay or aborting negotiations are low (that you are in no hurry and can wait forever), the more modest the other's resistance point will be.

2. *The other's resistance point will vary inversely with his or her cost of delay or aborting.* The more a person needs a settlement, the more modest he or she will be in setting a resistance point. Therefore, the more you can do to convince the other party that delay or aborting negotiations will be costly, the more likely he or she will be to establish a modest resistance point. In contrast, the more attractive the other party's alternatives, the more that person can hang tough with a high resistance point. If negotiations are unsuccessful, the other party can move to an attractive alternative. In the earlier example, we mentioned that both Larry and Monica have satisfactory alternatives.

3. *A resistance point will vary directly with the value the other party attaches to that outcome.* Therefore, the resistance point may become more modest as the person reduces how valuable he or she considers that outcome. If you can convince

the other party that a present negotiating position will not have the desired outcome or that the present position is not as attractive because other positions are
even more attractive, then he or she will adjust the resistance point.

4. *The other's resistance point varies inversely with the perceived value the
first party attaches to an outcome.* Knowing that a position is important to the
other party, you will expect the other to resist giving up on that issue; thus, there
should be less possibility of a favorable settlement in that area. As a result, you
may lower your expectations to a more modest resistance point. Hence, the more
you can convince the other that you value a particular outcome outside the other's
bargaining range, the more pressure you put on the other party to set a more modest resistance point with regard to that outcome.

TACTICAL TASKS

From the above assessment of the fundamental strategies of distributive bargaining,
four important tactical tasks emerge for a negotiator in a distributive bargaining situation:
(1) to assess the other party's outcome values and the costs of terminating negotiations,
(2) to manage the other party's impression of the negotiator's outcome values, (3) to modify the other party's perception of his or her own outcome values, and (4) to manipulate
the actual costs of delaying or aborting negotiations. Each of these tasks is discussed in
more detail below.

Assess Outcome Values and the Costs of Termination

An important first step for a negotiator is to get information about the other party's
outcome values and resistance points. The negotiator can pursue two general routes:
getting information *indirectly* about the background factors behind an issue (indirect
assessment) or getting information *directly* from the other party about outcome values
and resistance points (direct assessment).

Indirect Assessment.   The process by which an individual sets a resistance point
may include many factors. For example, how do you decide how much rent or mortgage
payment you can afford each month? Or how do you decide what a house is really
worth? There are lots of ways to go about doing this. Indirect assessment is aimed at
determining what information an individual probably used to set target and resistance
points and how he or she interpreted this information. For example, in labor negotiations,
management may infer whether or not a union is willing to strike by how hard the union
bargains or by the size of its strike fund. The union decides whether or not the company
can afford a strike based on the size of inventories, market conditions for the company's
product, and the percentage of workers who are members of the union. In a real estate
negotiation, how long a piece of property has been on the market, how many other potential buyers actually exist, how soon a buyer needs the property for business or living, and
the financial health of the seller will be important factors. An automobile buyer might
view the number of new cars in inventory on the dealer's lot, refer to newspaper articles

on automobile sales, read about a particular car's popularity in consumer buying guides or the Internet (i.e., the more popular the car, the less willing they may be to bargain on the price), or consult reference guides to find out what a dealer pays wholesale for different cars.

Direct Assessment.   In bargaining, the other party does not usually reveal accurate and precise information about his or her outcome values, resistance points, and expectations. Sometimes, however, the other party will provide accurate information. When pushed to the absolute limit and in need of a quick settlement, the other party may explain the facts quite clearly. If company executives believe that a wage settlement above a certain point would drive the company out of business, they may choose to state that absolute limit very clearly and go to considerable lengths to explain how it was determined. Similarly, a house buyer may tell the seller what his absolute maximum price is and support it with an explanation of income and other expenses. In these instances, of course, the party revealing the information believes that the settlement being proposed is within the settlement range—and that the other party will accept the offered information as true rather than see it as a bargaining ploy. An industrial salesperson may tell the purchaser about product quality and service, alternative customers who want to buy the product, and the time required to manufacture special orders.

Most of the time, however, the other party is not so forthcoming, and the methods of getting direct information are more complex. In international diplomacy, various means are used to gather information. Sources are cultivated, messages are intercepted, and codes broken. In labor negotiations, companies have been known to recruit informers or bug union meeting rooms, and unions have had their members collect papers from executives' wastebaskets. In real estate negotiations, sellers have entertained prospective buyers with abundant alcoholic beverages in the hope that tongues will be loosened and information revealed. Additional approaches involve provoking the other party into an angry outburst or putting the other party under pressure designed to cause him or her to make a slip and reveal valuable information. One party may simulate exasperation and angrily stalk out of negotiations in the hope that the other, in an effort to avoid a deadlock, will reveal what is really wanted.

Manage the Other Party's Impressions

Because each side attempts to get information about the other party through direct and indirect sources, an important tactical task for you as a negotiator may be to prevent the other party from getting accurate information about your position, while simultaneously guiding him or her to form a preferred impression of it. Your tasks, then, are to screen actual information about positions and to represent them as you would like the other to believe them. Generally speaking, screening activities are more important at the beginning of negotiation, and direct action is more useful later on. This sequence gives you time to concentrate on gathering information from the other party, which will be useful in evaluating your own resistance point, and on determining the best way to provide information to the other party about your own position.

Screening Activities.   The simplest way to screen a position is to say and do as little as possible. Silence is golden when answering questions; words should be invested in asking questions instead. Selective reticence reduces the likelihood of making verbal slips or presenting any clues that the other side could use to draw conclusions. A look of disappointment or boredom, fidgeting and restlessness, or probing with interest all can give clues about the importance of the points under discussion. Concealment is the most general screening activity.

Another approach, possible when group negotiations are carried on through a representative, is calculated incompetence. Here, the constituents do not give the negotiating agent all of the necessary information, making it impossible for the agent to leak that information. Instead, the negotiator is sent with the task of simply gathering facts and bringing them back to the group. This strategy can make negotiations complex and tedious, and it often causes the other party to protest vigorously at the negotiator's inability to divulge important data or to make agreements. Lawyers, real estate agents, and investigators are frequently used to perform this role. Representatives may also be limited (or limit themselves) in their authority to make decisions. For example, a man buying a car may claim that he must consult his wife before making a final decision.

When negotiation is carried out by a team—as is common in diplomacy, labor–management relations, and many business negotiations—channeling all communication through a team spokesperson reduces the inadvertent revelation of information.[7] In addition to reducing the number of people who can actively reveal information, this allows other members of the negotiating team to observe and listen carefully to what the other party is saying so they can detect clues and pieces of information about the other party's position. Still another screening activity is to present a great many items for negotiation, only a few of which are truly important to the presenter. In this way, the other party has to gather so much information about so many different items that it becomes difficult to detect which items are really important. This tactic, called the snow job or kitchen sink, may be considered a hardball tactic (discussed later in this chapter) if carried to an extreme.[8]

Direct Action to Alter Impressions.   Negotiators can take many actions to present facts that will directly enhance their position or at least make it appear stronger to the other party. One of the most obvious methods is *selective presentation,* in which negotiators reveal only the facts necessary to support their case. Negotiators can also use selective presentation to lead the other party to form the desired impression of their resistance point or to open up new possibilities for agreement that are more favorable to the presenter than those that currently exist. Another approach is to explain or interpret known facts to present a logical argument that shows the costs or risks to oneself if the other party's proposals were implemented. An alternative is to say, "If you were in my shoes, here is the way these facts would look in light of the proposal you have presented." These arguments are most convincing when you have gathered the facts from a neutral source because then the other party will not see them as biased by your preferred outcome. However, even with facts that you provide, selectivity can be helpful in managing the other party's impression of your preferences and priorities. It is not necessary for the other to agree that this is the way things would look if he or she were in your position. Nor must the other agree that the facts lead only to the conclusion you have presented. As long as the other party understands how you see things, then his or her thinking is likely to be influenced.

Displaying *emotional reaction* to facts, proposals, and possible outcomes is another form of direct action negotiators can take to provide information about what is important to them. Disappointment or enthusiasm usually suggests that an issue is important, whereas boredom or indifference suggests it is trivial or unimportant. A loud, angry outburst or an eager response suggests the topic is very important and may give it a prominence that will shape what is discussed. Clearly, however, emotional reactions can be real or feigned.

Taking direct action to alter another's impression raises a number of hazards. It is one thing to select certain facts to present and to emphasize or de-emphasize their importance accurately, but it is a different matter to fabricate and lie. The former is expected and understood in distributive bargaining; the latter, even in hardball negotiations, is resented and often angrily attacked if discovered. Between the two extremes, however, what is said and done as skillful puffery by one may be perceived as dishonest distortion by the other. (The ethical considerations are explored in detail in Chapter 7.)

Modify the Other Party's Perceptions

A negotiator can alter the other party's impressions of his or her own objectives by making the outcomes appear less attractive or by making the cost of obtaining them appear higher. The negotiator may also try to make demands and positions appear more attractive or less unattractive to the other party.

There are several approaches to modifying the other party's perceptions. One approach is to interpret for the other party what the outcomes of his or her proposal will really be. A negotiator can explain logically how an undesirable outcome would result if the other party really did get what he or she requested. This may mean highlighting something that has been overlooked. Another approach to modifying the other's perceptions is to conceal information. An industrial seller may not reveal to a purchaser that certain technological changes are going to reduce significantly the cost of producing the products. A seller of real estate may not tell a prospective buyer that in three years a proposed highway will isolate the property being sold from attractive portions of the city. Concealment strategies may enter into the same ethical hazards mentioned earlier (also see Chapter 7).

Manipulate the Actual Costs of Delay or Termination

Negotiators have deadlines. A contract will expire. Agreement has to be reached before a large meeting occurs. Someone has to catch a plane. Extending negotiations beyond a deadline can be costly, particularly to the person who has the deadline, because that person has to either extend the deadline or go home empty-handed. At the same time, research and practical experience suggest that a large majority of agreements in distributive bargaining are reached when the deadline is near.[9] Manipulating a deadline or failing to agree by a particular deadline can be a powerful tool in the hands of the person who does

"Mr. Mosbacher, are you expecting anything via U.P.S.?"

not face deadline pressure. In some ways, the ultimate weapon in negotiation is to threaten to terminate negotiations, denying both parties the possibility of a settlement. There are three ways to manipulate the costs of delay in negotiation: (1) plan disruptive action, (2) form an alliance with outsiders, and (3) manipulate the scheduling of negotiations.

Disruptive Action. One way to encourage settlement is to increase the costs of not reaching a negotiated agreement. In one instance, a group of unionized food-service workers negotiating with a restaurant rounded up supporters, had them enter the restaurant just prior to lunch, and had each person order a cup of coffee and drink it leisurely. When regular customers came to lunch, they found every seat occupied.[10] In another case, people dissatisfied with automobiles they purchased from a certain dealer had their cars painted with large, bright yellow lemons and signs bearing the dealer's name, and then drove them around town in an effort to embarrass the dealer into making a settlement. Public picketing of a business, boycotting a product or company, and locking negotiators in a room until they reach agreement are all forms of disruptive action that increase the costs to negotiators for not settling and thereby bring them back to the bargaining table. Such tactics can work, but they may also produce anger and escalation of the conflict.

Alliance with Outsiders. Another way to increase the costs of delay or terminating negotiations is to involve other parties in the process who can somehow influence the outcome. In many business transactions, a private party may profess that, if negotiations with a merchant are unsuccessful, he or she will go to the Better Business Bureau and protest the merchant's actions. Individuals who are dissatisfied with the practices and policies of businesses or government agencies form task forces, political action groups, and protest organizations to bring greater collective pressure on the target. For example, professional schools within universities often enhance their negotiation with higher management on budget matters by citing required compliance with external accreditation standards to substantiate their budget requests.

Schedule Manipulation.   The negotiation scheduling process can often put one party at a considerable disadvantage. Businesspeople going overseas to negotiate with customers or suppliers often find that negotiations are scheduled to begin immediately after their arrival, when they are still suffering from the fatigue of travel and jet lag. Alternatively, a host party can use delay tactics to squeeze negotiations into the last remaining minutes of a session in order to extract concessions from the visiting party.[11] Automobile dealers will probably negotiate differently with the customer a half hour before quitting time on a Saturday night than at the beginning of the workday on Monday. Industrial buyers have a much more difficult negotiation when they have a short lead time because their plants may have to sit idle if they cannot secure a new contract for raw materials in time.

The opportunities to increase or alter the timing of negotiation vary widely from field to field. In some industries it is possible to stockpile raw materials at relatively low cost or to buy in large bulk lots; in other industries, however, it is essential that materials arrive at regular intervals because they have a short shelf life (as many manufacturing firms move to just-in-time inventory procedures, this becomes increasingly true).[12]

POSITIONS TAKEN DURING NEGOTIATION

Effective distributive bargainers need to understand the process of taking a position during bargaining (the opening offer or opening stance) and the role of making concessions during the negotiation process.[13] At the beginning of negotiations, each party takes a position. Typically, one party will then change his or her position in response to information from the other party or in response to the other party's behavior. The other party's position will also typically change during bargaining. Changes in position are usually accompanied by new information concerning the other's intentions, the value of outcomes, and likely zones for settlement. Negotiation is iterative. It provides an opportunity for both sides to communicate information about their positions that may lead to changes in those positions.

Opening Offer

When negotiations begin, the negotiator is faced with a perplexing problem. What should the opening offer be? Will the offer be seen as too low or too high by the other and therefore contemptuously rejected? An offer seen as modest by the other party could perhaps have been higher, either to leave more room to maneuver or to achieve a higher eventual settlement. Should the opening offer be somewhat closer to the resistance point, suggesting a more cooperative stance? These questions become less perplexing as the negotiator learns more about the other party's limits and planned strategy. While knowledge about the other party helps negotiators set their opening offers, it does not tell them exactly what to do. The fundamental question is whether the opening offer should be exaggerated or modest. Studies indicate that negotiators who make exaggerated opening offers get higher settlements than do those who make low or modest opening offers.[14]

There are at least two reasons that an exaggerated opening offer is advantageous.[15] First, it gives the negotiator room for movement and therefore allows him or her time to learn about the other party's priorities. Second, an exaggerated opening offer acts as a metamessage and may create, in the other party's mind, the impression that (1) there is a long way to go before a reasonable settlement will be achieved, (2) more concessions than originally intended may have to be made to bridge the difference between the two opening positions, and (3) that the other may have been wrong in estimating their resistance point.[16] Two disadvantages of an exaggerated opening offer are (1) that it may be summarily rejected by the other party, and (2) that it communicates an attitude of toughness that may be harmful to long-term relationships. The more exaggerated the offer, the greater the likelihood that it will be summarily rejected by the other side. Therefore, negotiators who make exaggerated opening offers should also have viable alternatives that they can employ if the opposing negotiator refuses to deal with them.

Opening Stance

A second decision to be made at the outset of distributive bargaining concerns the stance or attitude to adopt during the negotiation. Will you be competitive (fighting to get the best on every point) or moderate (willing to make concessions and compromises)? Some negotiators take a belligerent stance, attacking the positions, offers, and even the character of the other party. In response, the other party may mirror the initial stance, meeting belligerence with belligerence. Even if the other party does not directly counter a belligerent stance, he or she is unlikely to respond in a warm and open manner. Some negotiators adopt a position of moderateness and understanding, seeming to say, "Let's be reasonable people who can solve this problem to our mutual satisfaction." Even if the attitude is not mirrored, the other's response is likely to be constrained by such a moderate opening stance.

To communicate effectively, a negotiator should try to send a consistent message through both opening offer and stance.[17] A reasonable bargaining position is usually coupled with a friendly stance, and an exaggerated bargaining position is usually coupled with a tougher, more competitive stance. When the messages sent by the opening offer and stance are in conflict, the other party will find them confusing to interpret and answer. (Timing also plays a part—see Box 3.2; communication in negotiation is discussed in more detail in Chapter 5.)

Initial Concessions

An opening offer is usually met with a counteroffer, and these two offers define the initial bargaining range. Sometimes the other party will not counter offer but will simply state that the first offer (or set of demands) is unacceptable and ask the opener to come

---

BOX 3.2
The Power of the First Move

In 1997, Mississippi was one of 40 states that initiated legal action against tobacco companies to recover money they spent on health care problems associated with smoking. In July of that year, Mississippi announced that it had reached a settlement with the four largest tobacco companies, guaranteeing that the state would receive $3.6 billion over 25 years and $136 million per year thereafter.

The settlement was a personal battle for Mississippi attorney general Michael Moore, who single-handedly began an effort in 1994 to recoup his state's losses from tobacco-related illness. Over the next three years, he convinced 39 other states and Puerto Rico to join Mississippi in the suit. Their efforts led to a national-level settlement that banned billboard advertising and also forced tobacco companies to include stronger warning labels on cigarettes.

Moore parlayed his efforts into the first successful settlement with the tobacco companies, guaranteeing payment even before federal action was taken. By acting first, he ensured that Mississippi would receive adequate compensation for its losses.

SOURCE: Adapted from M. Geyelin, "Mississippi Becomes First State to Settle Suit against Big Tobacco Companies," *The Wall Street Journal,* July 7, 1997.

---

back with a more reasonable set of proposals. In any event, after the first round of offers, the next question is, what movement or concessions are to be made? You can choose to make none, hold firm and insist on the original position, or you can make some concessions. Note that it is not an option to escalate one's opening offer, that is, to set an offer further away from the other party's target point than the first. This would be uniformly met with disapproval from the other party. If concessions are to be made, the next question is, how large should they be? It is important to note that the first concession conveys a message, frequently a symbolic one, to the other party about how you will proceed.

Opening offers, opening stances, and initial concessions are elements at the beginning of negotiations that parties can use to communicate how they intend to negotiate. An exaggerated original offer, a determined opening stance, and a very small opening concession signal a position of firmness; a moderate opening offer, a reasonable, cooperative opening stance, and a generous initial concession communicate a basic stance of flexibility. By taking a firm position, you attempt to capture most of the bargaining range for yourself so that you maximize your final outcome or you preserve maximum maneuvering room for later in the negotiation. Firmness also creates a climate in which the other party may decide that concessions are so meager that he or she might as well capitulate and settle quickly rather than drag things out. Paradoxically, firmness may actually shorten negotiations.[18] There is also the very real possibility, however, that firmness will be reciprocated by the other. One or both parties may become either intransigent or disgusted and withdraw completely.

There are several good reasons for adopting a flexible position.[19] First, when taking different stances throughout a negotiation, you can learn about the other party's outcome values and perceived possibilities by observing how he or she responds to your proposals. You may want to establish a cooperative rather than a combative relationship, hoping to get a better agreement. In addition, flexibility keeps the negotiations going; the more flexible you seem, the more the other party will believe that a settlement is possible.

Role of Concessions

Concessions are central to negotiation. Without them, in fact, negotiations would not exist. If one side is not prepared to make concessions, the other side must capitulate or the negotiations will deadlock.

People enter negotiations expecting concessions. Good distributive bargainers will not begin negotiations with an opening offer too close to their own resistance point, but rather will ensure that there is enough room in the bargaining range to make some concessions. It appears that people will generally accept the first or second offer that is better than their target point, so negotiators should try to identify the other party's target point accurately and avoid conceding too quickly to that point.[20]

Negotiators also generally resent a take-it-or-leave-it approach; an offer that may have been accepted had it emerged as a result of concession making may be rejected when it is thrown on the table and presented as a *fait accompli*. This latter approach, called Boulwarism,[*] has been illustrated many times in labor relations. In the past, some management leaders objectively analyzed what they could afford to give in their upcoming contract talks and made their initial offer at the point they intended for their final offer (i.e., they set the same opening offer, target point, and resistance point). They then insisted there were no concessions to be made because the initial offer was fair and reasonable based on their own analysis. Unions bitterly fought these positions and continued to resent them years after the companies abandoned this bargaining strategy.[21]

There is ample data to show that parties feel better about a settlement when the negotiation involved a progression of concessions than when it didn't.[22] Rubin and Brown suggest that bargainers want to believe they are capable of shaping the other's behavior, of causing the other to choose as he or she does.[23]

Because concession making indicates an acknowledgment of the other party and a movement toward the other's position, it implies a recognition of that position and its legitimacy. The intangible factors of status and recognition of the right to a position may be as important as the tangible issues themselves. Concession making also exposes the concession maker to some risk. If the other party does not reciprocate, the concession maker may appear to be weak. Thus, not reciprocating a concession may send a powerful message about firmness and leaves the concession maker open to feeling that his or her esteem has been damaged or reputation diminished.

A reciprocal concession cannot be haphazard. If one party has made a major concession on a significant point, it is expected that the return offer will be on the same

---

[*]The term *Boulwarism* is named after the chief labor negotiator for the General Electric Company in the 1950s. Rather than let the union present its contract demands first, the company placed a single "fair" offer on the table and refused to negotiate further. The National Labor Relations Board eventually ruled against G.E. by stating that this practice was unfair because management did not engage in "good faith bargaining."

item or one of similar weight and somewhat comparable magnitude. To make an additional concession when none has been received (or when the other party's concession was inadequate) can imply weakness and can squander valuable maneuvering room. After receiving an inadequate concession, you as a negotiator may explicitly state what you expect before offering further concessions: "That is not sufficient; you will have to give up X before I consider offering any further concessions."

To encourage further concessions from the other side, negotiators sometimes link their concessions to a prior concession made by the other. They may say, "Since you have reduced your demand on X, I am willing to concede on Y." A powerful form of concession making involves wrapping a concession in a package, sometimes described as logrolling.[24] For example, "If you will give A and B, I will give C and D." Packaging concessions also leads to better outcomes for a negotiator than making concessions singly on individual issues.[25] This tactic is discussed further in Chapter 4.

Pattern of Concession Making

The pattern of concessions a negotiator makes contains valuable information, but it is not always easy to interpret. When successive concessions get smaller, the most obvious message is that the concession maker's position is getting firmer and that the resistance point is being approached. This generalization needs to be tempered, however, by pointing out that a small concession late in negotiations may also indicate that there is little room left to move. When the opening offer is exaggerated, the negotiator has considerable room available for packaging new offers, making it relatively easy to give fairly substantial concessions. When the offer or counteroffer has moved closer to a negotiator's hoped-for settlement point, giving a concession the same size as the initial one may take a negotiator past the resistance point. Suppose a negotiator makes a first offer $100 below the other's target price; an initial concession of $10 would reduce the maneuvering room by 10 percent. When negotiations get to within $10 of the other's target price, a concession of $1 gives up 10 percent of the remaining maneuvering room. A negotiator cannot always communicate such mechanical ratios in giving or interpreting concessions, but this example illustrates how the receiver might construe the meaning of concession size, depending on where it occurs in the negotiating sequence.

The pattern of concession making is also important. Consider the pattern of concessions made by two negotiators, Sandra and Linda, shown in Figure 3.4. Assume that the negotiators are discussing the unit price of a shipment of computer parts, and that each is dealing with a different client. Linda makes three concessions, each worth $4 per unit, for a total of $12. In contrast, Sandra makes four concessions, worth $4, $3, $2, and $1 per unit, for a total of $10. Both Linda and Sandra tell their counterparts that they have conceded about all that they can. Sandra is more likely to be believed when she makes this assertion because she has signaled through the pattern of her concession making that there is not much left to concede. When Linda claims to have little left to concede, her counterpart is less likely to believe her because the pattern of Linda's concessions (three concessions worth the same amount) suggests that there is plenty left to concede, even though Linda has actually conceded more than Sandra.[26] Note that we have not considered the words spoken by Linda and Sandra as these concessions were

FIGURE 3.4   Pattern of Concession Making for Two Negotiators

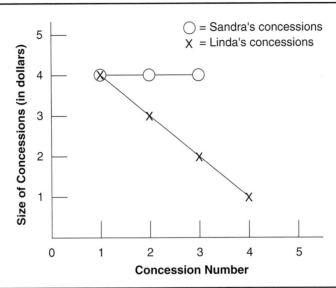

made. Behaviors are interpreted by the other party when we negotiate; it is important to signal to the other party with both our actions and our words that the concessions are almost over.

In multi-issue negotiations, skilled negotiators will also suggest different forms of a potential settlement that are worth about the same to them. They recognize that not all issues are worth the same amount to both parties. For example, a negotiator in a purchasing agreement may be interested solely in the total revenue of a package and not care whether it is paid in full within one month without interest or over six months with a financing fee at current interest rates. The length of the repayment period may, however, be critical to the other party who has a cash flow problem; that party may be willing to pay the financing fee for the right to spread the payments over six months. In fact, different combinations of principal, interest rate, and payback period may have the same value for one party but quite a different value for the other. After trying out different proposals that are worth about the same to them, skilled distributive negotiators will frequently save a final small concession for near the end of the negotiation to sweeten the deal.

Final Offer

Eventually a negotiator wants to convey the message that there is no further room for movement—that the present offer is the final one. A good negotiator will say, "This is all I can do" or "This is as far as I can go." Sometimes, however, it is clear that a simple statement will not suffice; an alternative is to use concessions to convey the point. A negotiator might simply let the absence of any further concessions convey the message in spite of urging from the other party. The other party may not recognize at first that the last offer was the final one and might volunteer a further concession to get the other to respond. Finding that no further concession results, the other party may feel betrayed and perceive that the pattern of concession–counterconcession was violated. The resulting bitterness may further complicate negotiations.

One-way negotiators may convey the message that an offer is the last one to make the last concession substantial. This implies that the negotiator is throwing in the remainder of the negotiating range. The final offer has to be large enough to be dramatic yet not so large that it creates the suspicion that the negotiator has been holding back and that there is more available on other issues in the bargaining mix.[27] A concession may also be personalized to the other party ("I went to my boss and got a special deal just for you"), which signals that this is the last concession the negotiator will make.

COMMITMENT

A key concept in creating a bargaining position is that of *commitment*. One definition of commitment is the taking of a bargaining position with some explicit or implicit pledge regarding the future course of action.[28] An example would be a sports agent who, during negotiation, says to the general manager of a professional sports team, "If we do not get the salary we want, my player will sit out next year." Such an act identifies the negotiator's bargaining position and a pledge of future action if that position is not reached. The purpose of a commitment is to remove ambiguity about the actor's intended course of action. By making a commitment, a negotiator signals his or her intention to take this course of action, make this decision, or pursue this objective—the negotiator says, "If you pursue your goals as well, we are likely to come into direct conflict; either one of us will win or neither of us will achieve our goals." Commitments also reduce the other party's options; they are designed to constrain the other party to a reduced portfolio of choices.

A commitment is often interpreted by the other party as a threat—if the other doesn't comply or give in, some set of negative consequences will occur. Some commitments can be threats, but others are simply statements of intended action that leave the responsibility for avoiding mutual disaster in the hands of the other party. A nation that publicly states that it is going to invade another country and that war can be averted only if no other nation tries to stop the action is making a bold and dramatic commitment. Commitments can also involve future promises, such as, "If we get this salary increase, we'll agree to have all other points arbitrated as you request."

Because of their nature, commitments are statements that usually require a follow-through in action. A negotiator who threatens consequences (e.g., the player will sit out next year), subsequently fails to get what he or she wanted with the threat, and then does not enact the consequences (e.g., the player reports to training camp) is not going to be believed in the future. In addition, a person will likely suffer a loss to self-image after not following through on a publicly made commitment. Hence, once a negotiator makes a commitment, there is strong motivation to hold to it. Because the other party probably will understand this, a commitment, once accepted, will often have a powerful effect on what the other party believes to be possible.[29]

Tactical Considerations in Using Commitments

Like many tools, commitments are two-edged. They may be used to gain the advantages described above, but they may also fix a negotiator to a particular position or point. Commitments exchange flexibility for certainty of action, but they create difficulties if you want to move to a new position. For example, suppose that after committing yourself to a course of action, you find additional information indicating that a different position is desirable, such as later statements showing that an earlier estimate of the other party's resistance point was inaccurate and that there is actually a negative negotiating range. It may be desirable or even necessary to shift positions after making a commitment. For these reasons, when you make commitments you should also make contingency plans that allow you to get out of them if you have to. For the original commitment to be effective the contingency plans must be secret. For example, the player's agent might have planned to retire shortly after the expected completion of negotiations. By advancing retirement, the agent can thereby cancel the commitment and leave a new negotiator unencumbered. A purchaser of a house may be able to back away from a commitment to buy by discovering the hitherto unnoticed cracks in the plaster in the living room or being unable to obtain financing from the bank.

Establishing a Commitment

Given that strong, passionate statements—some of which are pure bluff—are made during negotiation, how does a negotiator establish that a statement is to be understood as a commitment?

A commitment statement has three properties: a high degree of *finality*, a high degree of *specificity*, and a clear statement of *consequences*.[30] A buyer could say, "We are going to get a volume discount, or there will be trouble." This statement is far less powerful than "We must have a 10 percent volume discount in the next contract, or we will sign with an alternative supplier next month." The latter statement communicates finality (how and when the volume discount must be granted), specificity (how much of a volume discount is expected), and a clear statement of consequences (exactly what will happen if the discount is not given). It is far stronger than the first statement and much more difficult to get released from. Several ways to create a commitment are discussed below.

Public Pronouncement.   A commitment statement increases in potency when more people know about it. The sports agent's statement about sitting out the season would have a different impact if given during a television sportscast than if given only at the bargaining table. Some parties in negotiations have called press conferences or placed ads in newspapers or other publications stating what they want and what will or will not happen if they don't get it. In each of these situations, the wider the audience, the less likely it is that the commitment will be changed.

Linking with an Outside Base.   Another way to strengthen a commitment is to link up with one or more allies. Employees who are dissatisfied with management can form a committee to express their concerns. Industry associations may coalesce to set standards for a product. A variation of this process occurs when negotiators create conditions that make it more difficult for them to break a commitment they have made. For example, by encouraging dedicated colonists to settle on the West Bank near Jerusalem, the Israeli government has made it more difficult for Israel to concede this land to the Palestinians, a point the Israelis initially wanted to reinforce.

Increase the Prominence of Demands.   Many things can be done to increase the prominence of commitment statements. If most offers and concessions have been made orally, then writing out a statement may draw attention to the commitment. If prior statements have been written, then using a different size typeface or a different color paper will draw attention to the new one. Repetition is one of the most powerful vehicles for making a statement prominent. Using different communication channels to convey a commitment hammers a point home—for example, telling the other party of a commitment; then handing over a written statement; then reading aloud the statement; then circulating the commitment to others.

Reinforce the Threat or Promise.   When making a threat, there is the danger of going too far—stating a point so strongly that you look weak or foolish rather than threatening. Statements like "If I don't get a concession on this point, I'll see that you don't stay in business another day!" are more likely to be greeted with annoyance or dismissal than with concern or compliance. Long, detailed statements that are highly exaggerated undermine credibility. In contrast, simple, direct statements of demands, conditions, and consequences are more effective.

Several things can be done to reinforce the implicit or explicit threat in a commitment. One is to review similar circumstances and their consequences; another is to make obvious preparations to carry out the threat. Facing the prospect of a strike, companies build up their inventories and move cots and food into their factories; unions build strike funds and give advice to their members about how to get by with less income should there be a strike. Another route is to create and carry out minor threats in advance, thereby leading the other party to believe that major threats will be fulfilled. For example, a negotiator could say, "If the progress of these negotiations does not speed up, I am not going to return to the negotiation table after lunch," and then do just that.

Research on threats in negotiation suggests that negotiators who make threats are perceived as more powerful than negotiators who do not make threats.[31] This perception of greater power does not appear to translate into higher negotiation outcomes for threat users, however. In fact, threat users are also perceived as less cooperative, and their outcomes in integrative situations seem to be lower than those of negotiators who do not use threats.[32]

Preventing the Other Party from Committing Prematurely

All the advantages of a committed position work against a negotiator when the other party becomes committed. Therefore, a general strategy is to try to keep the other from becoming committed. People commonly take committed positions when they become angry or feel pushed to the limit; these commitments are often unplanned and can work to the disadvantage of both parties. Consequently, negotiators should pay careful attention to the other party's level of irritation, anger, and impatience.

One way to prevent the other party from establishing a committed position is to deny him or her the necessary time. In a real estate deal with an option about to run out, a seller may use up the time by being unavailable or requiring extensive checking of deeds and boundaries, thereby denying time to a potential buyer to make a case (if, say, another buyer who would pay more had entered into negotiations). Another approach to keep the other party from taking a committed position is to ignore or downplay the threat by not acknowledging the other's commitment, or even by making a joke about it. A negotiator might lightheartedly say, "You don't really mean that," or "I know you can't be serious about really going through with that," or simply move negotiations along as though the commitment statement was not heard or understood. If the negotiator can pretend not to hear the other party's statement or not to consider it significant, the statement can be ignored at a later point without incurring the consequences that would have ensued had it been taken seriously. Although the other side can still carry out the threat, the belief that it must be carried out (that control of the situation has been given up) may be reduced.

Finding Ways to Abandon a Committed Position

Frequently negotiators want to get the other party out of a committed position, and many times that party will also want a way out. How can this be done? We suggest four avenues for escaping commitments.

Plan a Way Out.   One method has already been noted: When establishing a commitment, a negotiator should simultaneously plan a private way out. The negotiator may also reword a commitment to indicate that the conditions under which it applied have changed. Sometimes information provided by the other party during negotiations can permit a negotiator to say, "Given what I've learned from you during this discussion, I see I am going to have to rethink my earlier position." The same could be done for the other party. A negotiator, wanting to make it possible for the other to abandon a committed position and yet not lose credibility, might say, "Given what I've told you about the facts of the situation [or given this new information], maybe I can help you see that your earlier position no longer holds." Needless to say, the last thing a negotiator wants to do is to embarrass the other party or make judgmental statements about the shift in position; rather, the other party should be given every opportunity to retreat with dignity and without losing face.

Let It Die Silently.   A second way to abandon a commitment is to let the matter die silently. After a lapse of time, a negotiator can make a new proposal in the area of the commitment without mentioning the earlier one. A variation on this process is to make a tentative step in a direction previously excluded by the other's commitment. For example, an employee who has said that he would never accept a certain job assignment may be asked to consider the benefits to his career of a "temporary" placement in that job. If the other party, in response to either of these variations, indicates through silence or verbal comment a willingness to let things move in that direction, the negotiation should simply be allowed to progress.

Restate the Commitment.   A third route is to restate the commitment in more general terms. The party that wants to abandon a commitment will make a new proposal, changing some of the details to be more in line with his or her current needs, while ostensibly still living with the general principles of the earlier wording. For example, the purchasing agent who demanded a 10 percent volume discount may rephrase this statement later to say simply that a significant volume discount is needed. The other party can then explore what level this "significant" discount could be.

Minimize the Damage.   Finally, if the other party backs off from a committed position, it is important to minimize any possible damage to his or her self-esteem or to constituent relationships. One strategy to use in this instance is to make a public attribution about the other party's move to some noble or higher outside cause. Diplomats can withdraw from a committed position because of their deep concern for peace and humankind. A buyer or seller can back off from a point during a real estate transaction to support the economic well-being of the community. Managers can leave a committed position for the good of the company.

A committed position is a powerful tool in negotiation; it is also a rigid tool and must therefore be used with care. As with any other tool, we must be as alert to ways of denying it to the other party as we are to ways we can use it for ourselves. Unfortunately, far more commitments are made as a result of anger and the desire to stop making concessions than as a result of clearly thought-out tactical planning. In either case, the essential property of a committed position is to arrange the consequences of an action so that at some point it is no longer an item of discussion or can only be negotiated at grave risk to one or both parties. The events or consequences become inevitable unless stopped at serious risk to one or both sides. The committed position has to be believable, and what has to be believed is that nothing can be done to change the conditions—if X happens, Y is inevitable. Convincing the other party that fate is sealed on the matter at hand is a demanding task and requires preparation, time, and skill. Consequently, getting out of a committed position is not easy, but the process is made simpler by planning a secret means of escape at the time the commitment is being established. Many of the steps a negotiator can use to get out of a commitment can also be used to help the other party get out of a committed position or, even better, to keep him or her from establishing one in the first place.

CLOSING THE DEAL

After negotiating for a period of time, learning about the other party's needs, positions, and perhaps resistance point, the next challenge for a negotiator is to close the agreement. There are several tactics available to negotiators for closing a deal; choosing the best tactic for a given negotiation is as much a matter of art as science.[33]

Provide Alternatives.   Rather than making a single final offer, negotiators can provide two or three alternative packages for the other party that are more or less equivalent in value. People like to have choices, and providing a counterpart with alternative packages can be a very effective technique for closing a negotiation. This technique can also be used when a task force cannot decide on which recommendation to make to upper management. If in fact there are two distinct, defensible possible solutions, then the task force can forward both with a description of the costs and benefits of each.

Assume the Close.   Salespeople use an assume-the-close technique frequently. After having a general discussion about the needs and positions of the buyer, often the seller will take out a large order form and start to complete it. The seller usually begins by asking for the buyer's name and address before moving on to any potentially contentious issues (e.g., price, model). When using this technique, negotiators do not ask the other party if he or she would like to make a purchase. Rather, they act as if the decision to purchase something has already been made so they might as well start to get the paperwork out of the way.[34]

Split the Difference.   Splitting the difference is perhaps the most popular closing tactic. The negotiator using this tactic will typically give a brief summary of the negotiation ("We've both spent a lot of time, made many concessions, etc.") and then suggest that, because things are so close, "why don't we just split the difference?" While this can be an effective closing tactic, it does presume that the parties started with fair opening offers. A negotiator who uses an exaggerated opening offer and then suggests a split-the-difference close is using a hardball tactic (see below).

Exploding Offers.   An exploding offer contains an extremely tight deadline in order to pressure the other party to agree quickly. For example, a person who has interviewed for a job may be offered a very attractive salary and benefits package, but also be told that the offer will expire in 24 hours. The purpose of the exploding offer is to convince the other party to accept the settlement and to stop considering alternatives. This is particularly effective in situations where the party receiving the exploding offer is still in the process of developing alternatives that may or may not turn out to be viable (such as the job candidate who is still interviewing with other firms). People can feel quite uncomfortable about receiving exploding offers, however, because they feel as if they're under unfair pressure. Exploding offers appear to work best for organizations that have the resources to make an exceptionally attractive offer early in a negotiation in order to prevent the other party from continuing to search for a potentially superior offer.

Sweeteners.   Another closing tactic is to save a special concession for the close. The other negotiator is told, "I'll give you X if you agree to the deal." For instance, when selling a house the owner could agree to include the previously excluded curtains, appliances, or light fixtures to close the deal. To use this tactic effectively, however, negotiators need to include the sweetener in their negotiation plans or they may concede too much during the close.

HARDBALL TACTICS

Many popular books of negotiation discuss using hardball negotiation tactics to beat the other party.[35] Such tactics are designed to pressure targeted parties to do things they would not otherwise do, and their presence usually disguises the user's adherence to a decidedly distributive bargaining approach. It is not clear exactly how often or how well these tactics work, but they work best against poorly prepared negotiators. They also can backfire. Many people find hardball tactics offensive and are motivated for revenge when such tactics are used against them. Many negotiators consider these tactics out-of-bounds for any negotiation situation (see Chapter 7 for a discussion of negotiation ethics). We do not recommend the use of any of the following techniques. In fact, it has been our experience that these tactics do more harm than good in negotiations. They are much more difficult to enact than they are to read about, and each tactic involves risk for the person using it, including harm to reputation, lost deals, negative publicity, and the other party's revenge. But it is important that negotiators understand hardball tactics and how they work so that they can recognize and understand them if they are the targeted recipients.

Dealing with Typical Hardball Tactics

The negotiator dealing with a party who uses hardball tactics has many choices about how to respond. A good strategic response to these tactics requires that the negotiator identify the tactic quickly and understand what it is and how it works. Most of the tactics are designed either to enhance the appearance of the bargaining position of the person using the tactic or to detract from the appearance of the options available to the other party. How best to respond to a tactic depends on your goals and the broader context of the negotiation (who are you negotiating with; what are your alternatives?). No one response will work in all situations. We now discuss four main options that negotiators have for responding to typical hardball tactics.[36]

Ignore Them.   Although ignoring a hardball tactic may appear to be a weak response, it can in fact be very powerful. It takes a lot of energy to use some of the hardball tactics described below, and while the other side is using energy to play these games, you can be using your energy to work on satisfying your needs. Not responding to a threat is often the best way of dealing with it. Pretend you didn't hear it. Change the subject and get the other party involved in a new topic. Call a break and, upon returning, switch topics. All these options can deflate the effects of a threat and allow you to press on with your agenda while the other party is trying to decide what trick to use next.

Discuss Them.   A good way to deal with hardball tactics is to discuss them—that is, indicate to the other party that you know what they are doing and that you even know what the tactic is (e.g., good cop/bad cop, which we discuss below).[37] Then offer to negotiate the negotiation process (how you are to conduct the negotiations) before continuing on to the substance of the talks. Propose a shift to less aggressive methods of negotiating. Explicitly acknowledge that the other party is a tough negotiator and that you can be tough too. Then suggest that you both change to more productive methods that can allow you both to gain.

Respond in Kind.   It is always possible to respond to a hardball tactic with one of your own in turn. Although this response can frequently result in chaos and hard feelings, it is not an option that should be dismissed out of hand. Once the smoke clears, both parties will realize that they are skilled in the use of hardball tactics and may recognize that it is time to try something different. Responding in kind may be most useful when dealing with another party who is testing your resolve or as a response to exaggerated positions taken in negotiations. A participant in a negotiation seminar told one of the authors the following story about bargaining for a carpet in a northern African country:

> I knew that the value of the carpet was about $2,000 because I had been looking at carpets throughout my trip. I found the carpet that I wanted and made sure not to appear too interested. I discussed some other carpets with the vendor before moving on to the carpet that I really wanted. When I asked him the price of this carpet, he replied $9,000. I replied that I would give him *negative* $5,000. We bargained for a while and I bought the carpet for $2,000.

The purchaser in this negotiation clearly responded to a hardball tactic with one of his own. When asked if he felt comfortable with his opening bid, he responded:

> Sure. Why not? The seller knew the value of the carpet was about $2,000. If anything, he seemed to respect me when I bargained this way. If I had opened with a positive number I would have ended up having to pay more than the carpet was worth. And I really wanted the carpet.

Co-Opt the Other Party.   Another way to deal with negotiators known to use aggressive hardball tactics is to try to befriend them before they use the tactics on you. This approach is built on the theory that it is much more difficult to attack a friend than an enemy. If you can stress what you have in common with the other party and find another element upon which to place the blame (the system, foreign competition), you may then be able to sidetrack the other party and thereby prevent the use of any hardball tactics.

Typical Hardball Tactics

We will now discuss some of the more frequently described hardball tactics and their weaknesses.

Good Cop/Bad Cop.   The good cop/bad cop tactic is named after a police interrogation technique in which two officers (one kind, the other tough) take turns questioning a suspect; it can frequently be seen in episodes of popular television series such as *Law and Order* and *NYPD Blue*. The use of this tactic in negotiations typically goes as follows: The first interrogator (bad cop) presents a tough opening position, punctuated with threats, obnoxious behavior, and intransigence. The interrogator then leaves the room to make an important telephone call or to cool off—frequently at the partner's suggestion. While out of the room, the other interrogator (good cop) tries to reach a quick agreement before the bad cop returns and makes life difficult for everyone. A more subtle form of this tactic is to assign the bad cop the role of speaking only when the negotiations are headed in a direction that the team does not want; as long as things are going well, the good cop does the talking. Although the good cop/bad cop tactic can be somewhat transparent, it often leads to concessions and negotiated agreements.[38]

GOOD COP, GREAT COP

There are many weaknesses to this tactic. As mentioned above, it is relatively transparent, especially with repeated use. It can be countered by openly describing what the negotiators are doing. A humorously delivered statement like "You two aren't playing the old good cop/bad cop game with me, are you?" will go a long way to deflating this tactic even if both of the other parties deny it self-righteously. The good cop/bad cop tactic is also much harder to use than it is to read about; it typically alienates the targeted party and frequently requires negotiators to direct much more energy toward making the tactic work smoothly than toward accomplishing the negotiation goals. Negotiators using this tactic can become so involved with their gaming and acting that they fail to concentrate on obtaining their negotiation goals.

Lowball/Highball. Negotiators using the lowball (highball) tactic start with a ridiculously low (or high) opening offer that they know they will never achieve. The theory is that the extreme offer will cause the other party to reevaluate his or her own opening offer and move closer to the resistance point. The risk of using this tactic is that the other party will think negotiating is a waste of time and will therefore halt the process. Even if the other party continues to negotiate after receiving a lowball (highball) offer, however, it takes a very skilled negotiator to be able to justify the extreme opening offer and to finesse the negotiation back to a point where the other side will be willing to make a major concession toward the outrageous bid.

The best way to deal with a lowball (highball) tactic is not to make a counteroffer. The reason is that this tactic works in the split second between hearing the other party's opening offer and the delivery of your first offer. If you give in to the natural tendency to change your opening offer because it would be embarrassing to start negotiations so far apart, or because the other party's extreme opening makes you rethink where the bargaining zone may lie, then you have fallen victim to this tactic. When that happens, you have been "anchored" by the other party's extreme first offer. Good preparation for the negotiation is a critical defense against this tactic. Proper planning will help you know the general range for the value of the item under discussion and allow you to respond verbally with one of several different strategies: (1) insisting that the other party start with a reasonable opening offer and refusing to negotiate further until he or she does; (2) stating your understanding of the general market value of the item being discussed, supporting it with facts and figures, and by doing so, demonstrating to the other party that you won't be tricked; (3) threatening to leave the negotiation, either briefly or for good, to demonstrate dissatisfaction with the other party for using this tactic; and (4) responding with an extreme counteroffer to send a clear message you won't be anchored by an extreme offer from the other party.

Bogey.   Negotiators using the bogey tactic pretend that an issue of little or no importance to them is quite important. Later in the negotiation this issue can then be traded for major concessions on issues that are actually important to them. This tactic is most effective when negotiators identify an issue that is quite important to the other side but of little value to themselves. For example, a seller may have a product in the warehouse ready for delivery. When negotiating with a purchasing agent, however, the seller may ask for large concessions to process a rush order for the client. The seller can reduce the size of the concession demanded for the rush order in exchange for concessions on other issues, such as the price or the size of the order. Another example of a bogey is to argue as if you wanted a particular work assignment or project (when in fact you don't prefer it) and then, in exchange for large concessions from the other party, accept the assignment you actually preferred (but had pretended not to).

This tactic is fundamentally deceptive, and as such can be a difficult tactic to enact. Typically, the other party will negotiate in good faith and take you seriously when you are trying to make a case for the issue that you want to bogey. This can lead to a very unusual situation, one in which both negotiators may be arguing against their true wishes (the other party is asking for large concessions on other issues to give you the bogey issue that you really don't want, and you are spending time evaluating offers and making arguments for an issue that you know you do not want). It can also be very difficult to change gracefully and accept an offer in completely the opposite direction. If this maneuver cannot be done, however, then you may end up accepting a suboptimal deal—the bogey may be something you do not really want, and perhaps the other party doesn't either.

Although the bogey is a difficult tactic to defend against, being well prepared for the negotiation will make you less susceptible to it. When the other party takes a position completely counter to what you expected, you may suspect that a bogey tactic is being used. Probing with questions about why the other party wants a particular outcome may help you reduce the effectiveness of a bogey. Finally, you should be very cautious about sudden reversals in positions taken by the other party, especially late in a negotiation. This may be a sign that the bogey tactic has been in use. Again, questioning the other party carefully about why the reverse position is suddenly acceptable and not conceding too much after the other party completely reverses a position may significantly reduce the effectiveness of the bogey.

The Nibble. Negotiators using the nibble tactic ask for a proportionally small concession (for instance, 1 to 2 percent of the total profit of the deal) on an item that hasn't been discussed previously in order to close the deal. Herb Cohen describes the nibble as follows: After trying many different suits in a clothing store, tell the clerk that you will take a given suit if a tie is included for free.[39] The tie is the nibble. Cohen claims that he usually gets the tie. In a business context, the tactic occurs like this: After a considerable amount of time has been spent in negotiation, when an agreement is close, one party asks to include a clause that hasn't been discussed previously and that will cost the other party a proportionally small amount. This amount is too small to lose the deal over, but large enough to upset the other party. This is the major weakness with the nibble tactic—many people feel that the party using the nibble did not bargain in good faith (as part of a fair negotiation process, all items to be discussed during the negotiation should be placed on the agenda early). Even if the party claims to be very embarrassed about forgetting this item until now, the party who has been nibbled will not feel good about the process and will often seek revenge in future negotiations.

There are two good ways to combat the nibble. First, respond to each nibble with the question "What else do you want?" This should continue until the other party indicates that all issues are in the open; then both parties can discuss all of the issues simultaneously. Second, have your own nibbles prepared to offer in exchange. When the other party suggests a nibble on one issue, you can respond with your own nibble on another.[40]

Chicken. The chicken tactic is named after the 1950s challenge, portrayed in the James Dean movie *Rebel Without a Cause,* of two people driving cars at each other or toward a cliff until one person swerves to avoid disaster. The person who swerves is labeled a chicken, and the other person is treated like a hero. Negotiators who use this tactic combine a large bluff with a threatened action to force the other party to chicken out and give them what they want. In labor–management negotiations, management may tell the union representatives that if they do not agree to the current contract offer the company will close the factory and go out of business (or move to another state or country). Clearly this is a high-stakes gamble. On the one hand, management must be willing to follow through on the threat—if the union calls their bluff and they do not follow through, they will not be believed in the future. On the other hand, how can the union take the risk and call the bluff? If management is telling the truth, the company may actually close the factory and move elsewhere.

The weakness of the chicken tactic is that negotiation is turned into a serious game in which one or both parties find it difficult to distinguish reality from postured negotiation positions. Will the other party really follow through on his or her threats? We frequently cannot know for sure, because the circumstances must be grave in order for this tactic to be believable; but it is precisely when circumstances are grave that a negotiator may be most tempted to use this tactic. For example, President William Clinton of the United States and President Saddam Hussein of Iraq played chicken over the United Nations inspection program, designed to inspect Iraq for suspected biological and chemical warfare factories. Occasionally, this high-stakes game resulted in actual missile attacks on Iraq.

The chicken tactic is very difficult for a negotiator to defend against. To the extent that the commitment can be downplayed, reworded, or ignored, however, it could lose its power. Perhaps the riskiest response is to introduce one's own chicken tactic. At that point neither party may be willing to back down in order not to lose face. Preparation and a thorough understanding of the situations of both parties are absolutely essential for trying to identify where reality ends and the chicken tactic begins. Use of external experts to verify information or to help to reframe the situation is another option.

Intimidation.   Many tactics can be gathered under the general label of intimidation. What they have in common is that they all attempt to force the other party to agree by means of an emotional ploy, usually anger or fear. For example, the other party may deliberately *use anger* to indicate the seriousness of a position. One of the authors of this book had the following experience:

> Once while I was negotiating with a car salesman he lost his temper, destroyed his written notes, told me to sit down and listen to him, and went on to explain in a loud voice that this was the best deal in the city and if I did not accept it that evening I should not bother returning to that dealership and wasting his time. I didn't buy the car and I haven't been back, nor I suspect have any of the students in my negotiation classes, to whom I relate this story every year! I suspect that the salesman was trying to intimidate me into agreeing to the deal and realized that if I went elsewhere his deal would not look as good. What he didn't realize was that I had asked the accountant at the dealership for further information about the deal and had found that he had lied about the value of a trade-in; he really lost his cool when I exposed the lie!

Another form of intimidation includes increasing the *appearance of legitimacy.* When there is a high degree of legitimacy, there are set policies or procedures for resolving disputes. Negotiators who do not have such policies or procedures available may try to invent them and then impose them on the other negotiator while making the process appear legitimate. For example, policies that are written in manuals or preprinted official forms and agreements are less likely to be questioned than those that are delivered verbally.[41] Long and detailed loan contracts used by banks for consumer loans are seldom read completely.[42] The greater the appearance of legitimacy, the less likely the other party will be to question the process being followed or the contract terms being proposed.

Finally, *guilt* can also be used as a form of intimidation. Negotiators can question the other party's integrity or the other's lack of trust in them. The purpose of this tactic is to place the other party on the defensive so that they are dealing with the issues of guilt or trust rather than discussing the substance of the negotiation.

To deal with intimidation tactics, negotiators have several options. Intimidation tactics are designed to make the intimidator feel more powerful than the other party and to lead people to make concessions for emotional rather than objective reasons (e.g., a new fact). When making any concession, it is important for negotiators to understand why they are doing so. If one starts to feel threatened, assumes that the other party is more powerful (when objectively he or she is not), or simply accepts the legitimacy of the other negotiator's "company policy," then it is likely that intimidation is having an effect on the negotiations.

If the other negotiator is acting aggressively, then discussing the negotiation process with him or her is a good option. You can explain that your policy is to bargain in a fair and respectful manner, and that you expect to be treated the same way in return. Another good option is to ignore the other party's attempts to intimidate you, because intimidation can only have an effect on you if you let it. While this may sound too simple to be realistic, you can think about why some people you know are intimidated by authority figures and others are not—the reason often lies in the perceiver, not the authority figure.

Another effective strategy for dealing with intimidation is to use a team to negotiate with the other party. Teams have at least two advantages over individuals in acting against intimidation. First, people are not always intimidated by the same things; while you may be intimidated by one particular negotiator, it is quite possible that other members on your team won't be. In an ongoing negotiation in China when he was younger, one of the authors of this book found that his Chinese counterparts were frequently changing their team members so that older and older members appeared in each subsequent negotiation session. He decided to bring a senior colleague of his own to subsequent meetings in order not to be intimidated by the age and experience of the counterparts on the other negotiating team. The second advantage of using a team is that the team members can discuss the tactics of the other negotiators and provide mutual support if the intimidation starts to become increasingly uncomfortable.

Aggressive Behavior.   A group of tactics similar to those described under intimidation include various ways of being aggressive in pushing your position or attacking the other person's position. Aggressive tactics include a relentless push for further concessions ("You can do better than that"), asking for the best offer early in negotiations ("Let's not waste any time. What is the most that you will pay?"), and asking the other party to explain and justify his or her proposals item by item or line by line ("What is your cost breakdown for each item?"). The negotiator using these techniques is signaling a hard-nosed, intransigent position and trying to force the other side to make many concessions to reach an agreement.

When faced with another party's aggressive behavior tactics an excellent response is to halt the negotiations in order to discuss the negotiation process itself. Negotiators can explain that they will reach a decision based on needs and interests, not aggressive behavior. Again, having a team to counter aggressive tactics from the other party can be helpful for the same reasons discussed above under intimidation tactics. Good preparation and understanding both one's own and the other party's needs and interests together make responding to aggressive tactics easier because the merits to both parties of reaching an agreement can be highlighted.

Snow Job.   The snow job tactic occurs when negotiators overwhelm the other party with so much information that he or she has trouble determining which facts are real or important, and which are included merely as distractions. Governments use this tactic frequently when releasing information publicly. Rather than answering a question briefly, they release thousands of pages of documents from hearings and transcripts that may or may not contain the information that the other party is seeking. Another example of the snow job is the use of highly technical language to hide a simple answer to a question asked by a nonexpert. Any group of professionals—such as engineers, lawyers, or computer network administrators—can use this tactic to overwhelm ("snow") the other party with so much information that they cannot make sense of the answer. Frequently, in order not to be embarrassed by asking "obvious" questions, the recipient of the snow job will simply nod his or her head and passively agree with the other party's analysis or statements.

Negotiators trying to counter a snow job tactic can choose one of several alternative responses. First, they should not be afraid to ask questions until they receive an answer they understand. Second, if the matter under discussion is in fact highly technical, then negotiators may suggest that technical experts get together to discuss the technical issues. Finally, negotiators should listen carefully to the other party and identify consistent and inconsistent information. Probing for further information after identifying a piece of inconsistent information can work to undermine the effectiveness of the snow job. For example, if one piece of incorrect or inconsistent information is discovered in the complete snow job package, the negotiator can question the accuracy of the whole presentation (e.g., "Since point X was incorrect, how can I be sure that the rest is accurate?"). Again, strong preparation is very important for defending effectively against the snow job tactic.

CHAPTER SUMMARY

In this chapter we examined the basic structure of competitive or distributive bargaining situations and some of the strategies and tactics used in distributive bargaining. Distributive bargaining begins with setting your own opening, target, and resistance points. You soon learn the other party's starting points and find out his or her target points directly or through inference. Usually you won't know the resistance points, the points beyond which a party will not go, until late in negotiation because the other party often carefully conceals them. All points are important, but the resistance points are the most critical. The spread between the parties' resistance points defines the bargaining range. If positive, it defines the area of negotiation within which a settlement is likely to occur, with each party working to obtain as much of the bargaining range as possible. If negative, successful negotiation may be impossible.

It is rare that a negotiation includes only one item; more typically, there is a set of items, referred to as a bargaining mix. Each item in a bargaining mix can have opening, target, and resistance points. The bargaining mix may provide opportunities for bundling issues together, trading off across issues, or displaying mutually concessionary behavior.

Examining the structure of distributive bargaining reveals many options for a negotiator to achieve a successful resolution, most of which fall within two broad efforts: to influence the other party's belief about what is possible and to learn as much as possible about the other party's position, particularly about the resistance points. The negotiator's basic goal is to reach a final settlement as close to the other party's resistance point as possible. To achieve this goal, negotiators work to gather information about the opposition and its positions; to convince members of the other party to change their minds about their ability to achieve their own goals; and to promote their own objectives as desirable, necessary, or even inevitable.

Distributive bargaining is basically a conflict situation, wherein parties seek their own advantage—in part through concealing information, attempting to mislead, or using manipulative actions. All these tactics can easily escalate interaction from calm discussion to bitter hostility. Yet negotiation is the attempt to resolve a conflict without force, without fighting. Further, to be successful, both parties to the negotiation must feel at the end that the outcome was the best that they could achieve and that it is worth accepting and supporting. Hence, effective distributive bargaining is a process that requires careful planning, strong execution, and constant monitoring of the other party's reactions.

ENDNOTES

1. Walton and McKersie, 1965.
2. Thompson and Hrebec, 1996.
3. Raiffa, 1982.
4. Fisher and Ertel, 1995.
5. Stein, 1996.
6. For a more extensive treatment of this subject see Walton and McKersie, 1965, pp. 59–82.
7. Team negotiations are discussed in the chapter "Coalitions, Multiple Parties, and Teams," posted on the McGraw-Hill website at www.mhhe.com/lewickinegotiation.
8. Karrass, 1974.
9. See Lim and Murnighan, 1994; Roth, Murnighan, and Schoumaker, 1988; and Walton and McKersie, 1965.
10. Jacobs, 1951.
11. Cohen, 1980.
12. See Camerer and Loewenstein, 1993; and Stuhlmacher, Gillespie, and Champagne, 1998.
13. Tutzauer, 1992.
14. See Brodt, 1994; Chertkoff and Conley, 1967; Donohue, 1981; Hinton, Hamner, and Pohlan, 1974; Komorita and Brenner, 1968; Liebert, Smith, and Hill, 1968; Pruitt and Syna, 1985; Ritov, 1996; and Weingart, Thompson, Bazerman, and Carroll, 1990.
15. For further discussion of these points see Pruitt, 1981; and Tutzauer, 1991.
16. See Putnam and Jones, 1982; and Yukl, 1974.
17. Eyuboglu and Buja, 1993.
18. See Ghosh, 1996.
19. Olekalns, Smith, and Walsh, 1996.
20. See Rapoport, Erev, and Zwick, 1995.
21. Northrup, 1964; and Selekman, Selekman, and Fuller, 1958.
22. For example, Baranowski and Summers, 1972; Crumbaugh and Evans, 1967; Deutsch, 1958; and Gruder and Duslak, 1973.
23. Rubin and Brown, 1975, pp. 277–78.
24. See Pruitt, 1981.

25. Froman and Cohen, 1970; Neale and Bazerman, 1991; and Pruitt, 1981.
26. See Yukl, 1974.
27. Walton and McKersie, 1965.
28. Ibid., p. 82.
29. Pruitt, 1981.
30. Walton and McKersie, 1965.
31. See de Dreu, 1995; and Shapiro and Bies, 1994.
32. Shapiro and Bies, 1994.
33. See Cellich, 1997; and Girard, 1989.
34. See Girard, 1989.
35. See Aaronson, 1989; Brooks and Odiorne, 1984; Cohen, 1980; Levinson, Smith, and Wilson, 1999; and Schatzski, 1981.
36. See Fisher, Ury, and Patton, 1991 and Ury, 1991 for an extended discussion of these points; more generally see Adler, Rosen, and Silverstein, 1996.
37. Fisher, Ury, and Patton, 1991; also see Ury, 1991.
38. Hilty and Carnevale, 1993.
39. Cohen, 1980.
40. Landon, 1997.
41. Cohen, 1980.
42. Hendon and Hendon, 1990.

CHAPTER 4

Strategy and Tactics
of Integrative Negotiation

INTRODUCTION

Even well-intentioned negotiators often make one or more of three mistakes: failing to negotiate when they should, negotiating when they should not, or negotiating when they should but picking an inappropriate strategy. As suggested by the dual concerns model described in Chapter 1, being committed to the other party's interests as well as to one's own makes problem solving the strategy of choice. In many negotiations, there need not be winners and losers; all parties can gain. Rather than assume that all conflicts are win-lose events, negotiators can look for win-win solutions—and usually they will find them. Integrative negotiation—variously known as cooperative, collaborative, win-win, mutual gains, or problem solving—is the focus of this chapter.

In distributive bargaining, the goals of the parties are initially at odds—or at least appear that way to some or all of the parties. In contrast, in integrative negotiation the goals of the parties are not mutually exclusive. If one side achieves its goals, the other is not necessarily precluded from achieving its goals. One party's gain is not necessarily at the other party's expense. The fundamental structure of an integrative negotiation situation is such that it allows both sides to achieve their objectives. Although the conflict may appear initially to be win-lose to the parties, discussion and mutual exploration will usually suggest win-win alternatives. A description of the efforts and tactics by which negotiators discover these alternatives accounts for the major part of this chapter.[1]

What Makes Integrative Negotiation Different?

In Chapter 1, we listed elements common to all negotiations. For a negotiation to be characterized as integrative, negotiators must also:

- Focus on commonalties rather than differences.
- Attempt to address needs and interests, not positions.
- Commit to meeting the needs of all involved parties.
- Exchange information and ideas.
- Invent options for mutual gain.
- Use objective criteria for standards of performance.

These requisite behaviors and perspectives are the main components of the integrative process (see Box 4.1).

BOX 4.1
Characteristics of the Interest-Based Negotiator

A successful interest-based negotiator models the following traits:

Honesty and integrity. Interest-based negotiating requires a certain level of trust between the parties. Actions that demonstrate interest in all players' concerns will help establish a trusting environment.

Abundance mentality. Those with an abundance mentality do not perceive a concession of monies, prestige, control, and so on, as something that makes their slice of the pie smaller, but merely as a way to enlarge the pie. A scarcity or zero-sum mentality says, "anything I give to you takes away from me." A negotiator with an abundance mentality knows that making concessions helps build stronger long-term relationships.

Maturity. In his book *Seven Habits of Highly Effective Leaders*, Stephen Covey refers to maturity as having the courage to stand up for your issues and values while being able to recognize that others' issues and values are just as valid.

Systems orientation. Systems thinkers will look at ways in which the entire system can be optimized, rather than focusing on suboptimizing components of the system.

Superior listening skills. Ninety percent of communication is not in one's words but in the whole context of the communication, including mode of expression, body language, and many other cues. Effective listening also requires that one avoid listening only from his or her frame of reference.

SOURCE: Chris Laubach, "Negotiating a Gain-Gain Agreement," *Healthcare Executive* (Jan/Feb 1997), p. 14.

AN OVERVIEW OF THE INTEGRATIVE NEGOTIATION PROCESS

Past experience, biased perceptions, and the truly distributive aspects of bargaining often make it remarkable that integrative agreements occur at all. But they do, largely because negotiators work hard to overcome inhibiting factors and assertively search for common ground. Our presentation of the integrative process is analogous to much of the managerial advice on motivating others. Those wishing to achieve integrative results find that they must manage both the context and the process of the negotiation in order to gain the willing cooperation and commitment of all parties.[2] The following processes tend to be central to achieving almost all integrative agreements.

Creating a Free Flow of Information

Ample research evidence indicates that effective information exchange promotes the development of good integrative solutions.[3] For the necessary exchange to occur, negotiators must be willing to reveal their true objectives and to listen to each other carefully. In short, negotiators must create the conditions for a free and open discussion of all related issues and concerns. Willingness to share information is not a characteristic of distributive bargaining situations, in which the parties distrust one another, conceal and manipulate information, and attempt to learn about the other for their own competitive advantage.

Attempting to Understand the Other Negotiator's Real Needs and Objectives

As we noted earlier, negotiators differ in their values and preferences. What one side needs and wants may or may not be what the other side needs and wants. If you are to help satisfy another's needs, you must first understand them. Simply being aware of the possibility that the other's priorities are not the same as his or her own is sufficient to stimulate the parties to exchange more information, understand the nature of the negotiation better, and achieve higher joint profits.[4] Similarly, integrative agreements are facilitated when the parties exchanged information about their priorities for particular issues, but not necessarily about their positions on those issues.[5] Hence, throughout the process of sharing information about preferences and priorities, the parties must make a true effort to understand what the other side really wants to achieve. Again, this is in contrast to distributive bargaining, where the negotiator either makes no effort to understand the other side's needs and objectives or does so only to challenge, undermine, or even deny the other party the opportunity to have those needs and objectives met.

Emphasizing the Commonalities between the Parties and Minimizing the Differences

To sustain a free flow of information and an effort to understand the other's needs and objectives, negotiators may require a different outlook or frame of reference (see Chapter 2 for a discussion of framing). Individual goals may need to be redefined as best achievable through collaborative efforts directed toward a collective goal. Sometimes the collective goal is clear and obvious. For example, politicians in the same party may recognize that their petty squabbles must be put aside to ensure the party's victory at the polls. The saying "politics makes strange bedfellows" suggests that the quest for victory can unite political enemies. Similarly, managers who are quarreling over cutbacks in their individual department budgets may need to recognize that unless all departments sustain appropriate budget cuts, they will be unable to change an unprofitable firm into a profitable one. At other times, the collective goal is not so clear, nor so easy to keep in sight. For example, one of the authors worked as a consultant to a company that was closing down a major manufacturing plant while at the same time, opening several other plants in different parts of the country. The company was perfectly willing to transfer employees to new plants and let them take their seniority with them up to the time of the announced move; the union agreed to this arrangement. However, conflict developed over the transfer issue. Some employees were able to transfer immediately, whereas others—those who were needed to close and dismantle the old plant—could not. Because workers acquired seniority in the new plants based on the date they arrived, those who stayed to close the old plant would have comparatively less seniority once they arrived at the new plants. The union wanted everyone to go at the same time to avoid this inequity. Management adamantly maintained that this was unworkable. In the argument that resulted, both parties lost sight of the larger goal—to transfer all willing employees to the new plants with their seniority intact. Only by constantly stressing this larger goal were the parties able to maintain a focus on commonalities that eventually led to a solution; management allowed the workers to select their new jobs in advance and transferred their seniority to those jobs when the choice was made, not when the physical move actually occurred.

Searching for Solutions That Meet the Goals and Objectives of Both Sides

The success of integrative negotiation depends on a search for solutions that meet the objectives and needs of both (or all) sides. In this process, negotiators must be firm but flexible—firm about their primary interests and needs, but flexible about the manner in which these interests and needs are met.[6] When the parties are used to taking a combative, competitive orientation toward each other, they are prone to be concerned only with their own objectives. In such a competitive interaction, a low level of concern for the other's objectives may drive one of two forms of behavior. The first is making sure that what the other obtains does not take away from one's own accomplishments. The second is attempting to block the other from obtaining his or her objectives because of a strong desire to win or to "defeat the opponent." In contrast, successful integrative negotiation requires each negotiator not only to define and pursue his or her own goals but also to be mindful of the other's goals and to search for solutions that satisfy both sides. Outcomes are measured by the degree to which they meet both negotiators' goals. They are not measured by determining whether one party is doing better than the other. If the objective of one party is simply to get more than the other, integrative negotiation is difficult at best; if both strive to get more than the other, integrative negotiation may be impossible.

In summary, integrative negotiation requires a process fundamentally different from that of distributive bargaining. Negotiators must attempt to probe below the surface of the other party's position to discover his or her underlying needs. They must create a free and open flow of information, and they must use their desire to satisfy both sides as the perspective from which to structure their dialogue. If negotiators do not have this perspective—if they approach the problem and their "opponent" in win-lose terms—integrative negotiation cannot occur.

KEY STEPS IN THE INTEGRATIVE NEGOTIATION PROCESS

There are four major steps in the integrative negotiation process: identify and define the problem, understand the problem and bring interests and needs to the surface, generate alternative solutions to the problem, and evaluate those alternatives and select among them.

Identify and Define the Problem

The problem identification step is often the most difficult one; this is even more challenging when several parties are involved. Consider the following example: In a large electronics plant, considerable difficulty with one of the subassemblies occurred in the final assembly department. Various pins and fittings that held the subassembly in place were getting bent and distorted. When this happened, the unit would be laid aside as a reject. At the end of the month, the rejects would be returned to be reworked, often arriving at the subassembly department just when workers there were under pressure to meet end-of-the-month schedules and were also low on parts. As a result, the reworking effort had to be done in a rush and on overtime. The extra cost of overtime did not fit into the standard cost allocation system. The manager of the subassembly department did not want the costs allocated to his overhead charge. The manager of the final assembly department insisted that he should not pay the additional cost; he argued that the subassembly department should bear the cost because its poor work originally caused the problem. The subassembly department manager countered that the parts were in good condition when they left his area and that it was the poor workmanship in the final assembly area that created the damage. The immediate costs were relatively small. What really concerned both parties was setting a long-term precedent for handling rejects and for paying the costs.

Eventually an integrative solution was reached. During any given month, the subassembly department had a number of short slack-time periods. Arrangements were made for the final assembly department to return damaged subassemblies in small batches during those slack periods. It also became clear that many people in the final assembly department did not fully understand the parts they were handling, which may have contributed to some of the damage. These people were then temporarily transferred to the subassembly department during assembly department slack periods to learn more about subassembly and to process some of the rush orders in that department. This example helps us identify a number of key aspects of the problem definition process.[7]

Define the Problem in a Way That Is Mutually Acceptable to Both Sides. Ideally, parties should enter the integrative negotiation process with few if any preconceptions about the solution and with open minds about each other's needs. As a problem is defined jointly, it should accurately reflect both parties' needs and priorities. Regrettably, this is not what we usually encounter. An understandable and widely held fear about integrative negotiation is that during the problem definition process, the other party is manipulating information to state the problem to his or her own advantage. For positive problem solving to occur, both parties must be committed to stating the problem in neutral terms. The problem statement must be mutually acceptable to both sides and not worded so that it lays blame or favors the preferences or priorities of one side over the other. The parties may be required to work the problem statement over several times until they agree on its wording. It is critical to note that problem definition is, and should be, separate from any leap to judgment that might be expected from parties impatient with careful integrative negotiation. It is critical, though, to define problems clearly at this stage, if only to accomplish an initial structure within which parties "agree to disagree," albeit on a common, distinct issue.

State the Problem with an Eye toward Practicality and Comprehensiveness.
The major focus of an integrative agreement is to solve the core problem(s). Anything
which distracts from this focus should be removed or streamlined in order to ensure that
this objective is achieved. This approach is in stark contrast to the distributive bargaining process (see Chapter 3), in which the parties are encouraged to beef up their positions by bringing in a large number of secondary issues and concerns so they can trade
these items off during the hard-bargaining phase. If there are several issues on the table
in an integrative negotiation, the parties may want to clearly identify the link among
them and decide whether they will be approached as separate problems (which may be
packaged together later) or as one larger problem.

State the Problem as a Goal and Identify the Obstacles to Attaining This Goal.
The parties should define the problem as a specific goal to be attained (what we want
to achieve) rather than as a solution process (how we are going to achieve it). They
should then proceed to specify what obstacles must be overcome for the goal to be
attained. For example, in the previous example, the goal might have been "to minimize
the number of rejects." A clearer and more explicit definition would be "to cut the number of rejects in half." After specifying the goal, the parties would then specify what
they need to know about how the product is made, how defects occur, what must be
done to repair the defects, and so on.

One key issue is whether the obstacles specified are amenable to corrective efforts
on the parts of the negotiating parties. If the parties cannot address the obstacles effectively, given limited time or other resources, the obstacles then become boundary
markers for the negotiation playing field. A clear understanding of which obstacles are
addressable and which are not can be just as critical to realistic integrative negotiation
as an explicit awareness of what is negotiable and what is not.

Depersonalize the Problem.   As we pointed out earlier, when parties are engaged
in conflict, they tend to become evaluative and judgmental. They view their own actions,
strategies, and preferences in a positive light and the other party's actions, strategies, and
preferences in a negative light. Such evaluative judgments can get in the way of clear and
dispassionate thinking. Saying "Your point of view is wrong and mine is right" inhibits
the integrative negotiation process because you cannot attack the problem without
attacking the person who owns the problem. In contrast, depersonalizing the definition
of the problem—stating, for example, "We have different viewpoints on this problem"—
allows both sides to approach the issue as a problem "out there" rather than as a problem that belongs to one side only.

Separate the Problem Definition from the Search for Solutions.   Finally, we
will repeat the advice included in almost every discussion of problem solving: Don't
jump to solutions until the problem is fully defined. In distributive bargaining, negotiators are encouraged to state the problem in terms of their preferred solution and to
make concessions based on this statement. In contrast, parties attempting integrative
negotiation should avoid stating solutions that favor one side or the other until they have
fully defined the problem and examined as many alternative solutions as possible.

Instead of premature solutions, negotiators should develop standards by which potential solutions will be judged for goodness of fit. These standards can be assembled by asking interested parties questions such as the following:

- How will we know the problem has been solved?
- How would we know that our goal has been attained?
- How would a neutral third party know that our dispute has been settled?
- Is there any legitimate interest or position that remains unaddressed (or disenfranchised) by our outcome?

Understand the Problem Fully—Identify Interests and Needs

Many writers on negotiation—most particularly, Roger Fisher, William Ury, and Bruce Patton in their popular book, *Getting to Yes*—have stressed that a key to achieving an integrative agreement is the ability of the parties to understand and satisfy each other's *interests*. Thus, we consider identifying interests an important second step in the integrative negotiation process. Interests are different from positions in that interests are the underlying concerns, needs, desires, or fears that motivate a negotiator to take a particular position. Fisher, Ury, and Patton argue that although negotiators may have difficulty satisfying each other's specific positions, an understanding of underlying interests may permit them to invent solutions that meet those interests. In this section, we will first define interests more fully and then discuss how understanding them may be critical to effective integrative negotiation.[8]

An example reveals the essence of the difference between interests and positions:

> Consider the story of two men quarreling in a library. One wants the window open and the other wants it closed. They bicker back and forth about how much to leave it open: a crack, halfway, three-quarters of the way. No solution satisfied them both. Enter the librarian. She asks one why he wants the window open. "To get some fresh air." She asks the other why he wants it closed. "To avoid the draft." After thinking a minute, she opens wide a window in the next room, bringing in fresh air without a draft.[9]

This is a classic example of negotiating over positions and failing to understand underlying interests. The positions are "window open" and "window closed." If they continue to pursue positional bargaining, the set of possible outcomes can include only a victory for the one who wants the window open, a victory for the one who wants it shut, or some compromise in which neither gets what he wants. Note that a compromise here is more a form of lose-lose than win-win for these bargainers because one party believes that he won't get enough fresh air with the window partially open and the other believes that any opening is unsatisfactory. The librarian's questions transform the dispute by focusing on *why* each man wants the window open or closed: to get fresh air, to avoid a draft. Understanding these interests enables the librarian to invent a solution that meets the interests of both sides—a solution that was not at all apparent when the two men were arguing over their positions.

In this description, the key word is *why*—why they want what they want. When two parties begin negotiation, they usually expose their position or demands; and as we have pointed out, this position or these demands have emerged from a planning process in which the parties decided *what* they wanted and then specified opening bids, targets, and resistance points. In distributive bargaining, negotiators trade these points and positions back and forth, attempting to achieve a settlement as close to their targets as possible. However, in integrative negotiation, each negotiator needs to pursue the other party's thinking and logic to determine the factors that motivated him or her to arrive at those points. The presumption is that if both parties understand the motivating factors for the other, they may recognize possible compatibilities in interests that permit them to invent new options that both will endorse. Consider the following dialogue between a company recruiter and a job applicant over starting salary:

Recruiter:

What were you thinking about as a starting salary?

Applicant:

I would like $40,000.

Recruiter:

We can only offer $35,000.

Applicant:

That's not acceptable.

Thus far, the parties have only exposed their positions. They are $5,000 apart. Moreover, the applicant may be afraid to bargain positionally with the recruiter, whereas the recruiter may be afraid that the applicant—whom she very much wants to hire—will walk out. Now let us extend their dialogue to help them focus on interests.

Recruiter:

$40,000 is a problem for our company. Can you tell me why you decided you wanted $40,000?

Applicant:

Well, I have lots of education loans to pay off, and I will need to pay for a few more courses to finish my degree. I can't really afford to pay these bills and live comfortably for less than $40,000.

Recruiter:

Our company has a program to help new employees refinance their education loans. In addition, we also have a program to provide tuition assistance for new courses if the courses you need to take are related to your job. Would these programs help you with your problem?

Applicant:

Yes!

Types of Interests. David Lax and Jim Sebenius have suggested that several types of interests may be at stake in a negotiation and that each type may be intrinsic (the parties value it in and of itself) or instrumental (the parties value it because it helps them derive other outcomes in the future).[10]

Substantive interests are the types of interests we have just been discussing; they are like the tangible issues we mentioned in Chapter 1. Substantive interests relate to the focal issues under negotiation—economic and financial issues such as price or rate, or the substance of a negotiation such as the division of resources. These interests may be intrinsic or instrumental or both; we may want something because it is intrinsically satisfying to us and/or we may want something because it helps us achieve a long-range goal.

Process interests are related to the way a dispute is settled. One party may pursue distributive bargaining because he enjoys the competitive game of wits that comes from nose-to-nose, hard-line bargaining. Another party may enjoy negotiating because she believes she has not been consulted in the past and wants to have some say in how a key problem is resolved. In the latter case, the negotiator may find the issues under discussion less important than the opportunity they allow for her to voice her opinions at the negotiating table.[11] Process interests can also be both intrinsic and instrumental. Thus in the voice example, having a say may be intrinsically important to a group—it allows them to affirm their legitimacy and worth, and highlights the key role they play in the organization; it can also be instrumentally important, in that if they are successful in gaining voice in this negotiation, they may be able to demonstrate that they should be invited back into the negotiation on other, related issues in the future.

Relationship interests indicate that one or both parties value their relationship with each other and do not want to take actions that will damage it. Intrinsic relationship interests exist when the parties value the relationship both for its existence and for the pleasure or fulfillment that sustaining it creates. Instrumental relationship interests exist when the parties derive positive benefits from the relationship and do not wish to endanger future benefits by souring it.

Finally, Lax and Sebenius point out that the parties may have *interests in principle.*[12] Certain principles—concerning what is fair, what is right, what is acceptable, what is ethical, or what has been done in the past and should be done in the future—may be deeply held by the parties and serve as the dominant guides to their action. (These principles often involve the intangibles we described in Chapter 1.) Interests in principles can also be intrinsic (valued because of their inherent worth) or instrumental (valued because they can be applied to a variety of future situations and scenarios). Bringing their interests in principles to the surface will lead the parties to discuss explicitly the principles at stake and to invent solutions consistent with them.

Some Observations on Interests.   Based on the preceding discussion, we may make several observations about interests and types of interests:

1. There is almost always more than one type of interest in a dispute. Parties can have more than substantive interests about the issues. They can also care deeply about process, the relationship, or the principles at stake. Note that interests in principles effectively cut across substantive, procedural, and relationship interests as well, so that the categories are not necessarily exclusive.

2. Parties can have different types of interests at stake. One party may care deeply about the specific issues under discussion while the other cares about how the issues are resolved—questions of principle or process. Bringing these different interests to the surface may enable the parties to see that in fact they care about very different things, and thus to invent a solution that addresses the interests of both sides.

3. Interests often stem from deeply rooted human needs or values. Several authors have suggested that frameworks for understanding basic human needs and values are helpful for understanding interests. According to these frameworks, needs are hierarchical and satisfaction of the basic or lower order needs will be more important in negotiation than that of higher order needs.[13]

4. Interests can change. Like positions on issues, interests can change over time. What was important to the parties last week—or even 20 minutes ago—may not be important now. Interaction between the parties can put some interests to rest, but it may raise others. Thus, the parties must continually be attentive to changes in their own interests and the interests of the other side. When one party begins to talk about things in a different way—when the language or emphasis changes—the other party may look for a change in interests.

5. Getting at interests. There are numerous ways to get at interests. Sometimes people are not even sure of their own interests. Negotiators should not only ask themselves "What do I want from this negotiation?" but also "Why do I want that?" "Why is that important to me?" "What will achieving that help me do?" and "What will happen if I don't achieve my objective?" Listening to your own inner voices—fears, aspirations, hopes, desires—is important in order to bring your own interests to the surface.

6. Getting at interests is not always easy or to one's best advantage. Critics of the "interests approach" to negotiation have often identified the difficulty of defining interests and taking them into consideration. It is often not easy to define interests and that trying to focus on interests alone often oversimplifies or conceals the real dynamics of a conflict. In some cases parties do not pursue their own best objective interests but instead focus on one or more subjective interests, which may mislead the other party. Thus, a car buyer may prefer a fast, flashy car (his subjective interest) even though his objective interest is to buy a safe, conservative one.[14]

7. Finally, focusing on interests can be harmful to a group of negotiators whose consensus on a particular issue is built around a unified position rather than a more generalized set of interests. If a coalition is held together by a commitment to pursue a specific objective in negotiation, then encouraging the chief negotiator to discuss interests rather than to drive for the specific objective is clearly encouraging him or her to deviate from the coalition's purpose.

Generate Alternative Solutions

The search for alternatives is the creative phase of integrative negotiations. Once the parties have agreed on a common definition of the problem and understood each other's interests, they generate a variety of alternative solutions. The objective is to create a list of options or possible solutions to the problem; evaluating and selecting from among those options will be their task in the final phase.

A number of techniques have been suggested to help negotiators generate alternative solutions. These techniques fall into two general categories. The first requires the negotiators to redefine, recast, or reframe the problem (or problem set) so as to create win-win alternatives out of what earlier appeared to be a win-lose problem. The second takes the problem as given and creates a long list of options from which the parties can choose. In integrative negotiation over a complex problem, both types of techniques may be used and even intertwined.

Inventing Options: Generating Alternative Solutions by Redefining the Problem or Problem Set.

The techniques in this category call for the parties to define their underlying needs specifically and to develop alternatives to meet them. At least five different methods for achieving integrative agreements have been proposed.[15] Each of these methods not only refocuses the issues under dispute, but also requires progressively more information about the other side's true needs; thus, solutions move from simpler, distributive to more complex (and comprehensive), integrative ones. Accordingly, they are presented in order of increasing "cost" and difficulty. We suggest that parties begin with the easiest and least costly ("expand the pie") and progress to the more costly approaches only in the event that the simpler remedies fail. Each approach will be illustrated by the example of a husband and wife attempting to decide where to spend their two-week vacation. The husband wants to go to the mountains for the entire two weeks, and the wife wants to go to the coast for the entire two weeks. A compromise solution—to spend a week at each place—is possible, but the husband and wife want to determine whether other solutions are possible as well.

Expand the Pie.   Many negotiations begin with a shortage of resources in which it is not possible for both sides to satisfy their interests or obtain their objectives under the current allocation. A simple solution is to add resources—expand the pie—in such a way that both sides can achieve their objectives. If the married couple could persuade their employers to give them four weeks for their vacation, they could go to the mountains and the beach for two weeks each. In expanding the pie, one party requires no information about the other party except her interests; it is a simple way to solve resource shortage problems. In addition, the approach assumes that simply enlarging the resources will solve the problem. Thus, having four weeks of vacation would be a very satisfactory solution if the husband and wife both liked the mountains and the beach but each simply wanted one or the other this particular year. However, expanding the pie would not be a satisfactory solution if their conflict were based on other grounds—if, for example, the husband couldn't stand the beach or the wife wouldn't go to the mountains under any conditions. In addition, to the extent that the negotiation increases the costs of a person or organization not directly involved in the negotiation (e.g., the employers in this example), the solution may be integrative for the negotiators but parasitic to other stakeholders.[16]

Logroll.   Successful logrolling requires the parties to establish (or find) more than one issue in conflict; the parties then agree to trade off among these issues so that one party achieves a highly preferred outcome on the first issue and the other person achieves a highly preferred outcome on the second issue. If the parties do in fact have different preferences on different issues and each party gets his or her most preferred outcome on a high-priority issue, then each should be happy with the overall agreement. Thus, suppose that the husband and wife disagree not only about where to take their vacation but also about the kind of accommodations. The husband prefers informal housekeeping cabins whereas the wife prefers a luxury hotel. If the wife decides that the formality of the accommodations is more important to her than the location, the couple may be able to agree on a luxury hotel in the mountains as a way to meet both their needs.

Logrolling may be effective when the parties can combine two issues, but not when the parties take turns in successive negotiations—that is, when one party gets what he wants this time, while the other gets what she wants next time. Research shows that when parties do not expect to negotiate with the other person in the future, they are less likely to employ logrolling over time and hence may reach a suboptimal agreement in the current negotiation.[17]

Use Nonspecific Compensation.   A third way to generate alternatives is to allow one person to obtain his objectives and pay off the other person for accommodating his interests. The payoff may be unrelated to the substantive negotiation, but the party who receives it nevertheless views it as adequate for acceding to the other party's preferences. Such compensation is "nonspecific" in that it is not directly related to the substantive issues being discussed. In the vacation example, the wife could tell the husband that if he agrees to go to the coast, she will buy him a new camera or set of golf clubs. For nonspecific compensation to work, the person doing the compensating needs to know what is valuable to the other person and how seriously he is inconvenienced (i.e., how much compensation is needed to make him feel satisfied). The wife might need to test several different offers (types and amounts of compensation) to find out how much it will take to satisfy her husband. This discovery process can turn into a distributive bargaining situation itself, as the husband may choose to set very high demands as the price for going along to the beach while the wife tries to minimize the compensation she will pay.

Cut the Costs for Compliance.   Through cost cutting, one party achieves her objectives and the other's costs are minimized if he agrees to go along. In the vacation example, suppose that the husband really likes a quiet and peaceful vacation and dislikes the beach because of the crowds, whereas the wife really likes the beach because of all the activity. If peace and quiet is what the husband really wants, then he may be willing to go to the beach if the wife assures him that they will stay in a secluded place far away from the other resorts. Unlike nonspecific compensation, where the compensated party simply receives something for going along, cost cutting is specifically designed to minimize the other party's costs and suffering. The technique is thus more sophisticated than logrolling or nonspecific compensation because it requires a more intimate knowledge of the other party's real needs and preferences (the party's interests, what really matters to him, how his needs can be specifically met).

Find a Bridge Solution.   Finally, by "bridging," the parties are able to invent new options that meet their respective needs. Thus, if the husband reveals that he really wants to hunt and fish on his vacation, whereas the wife wants to swim, go shopping, and enjoy the nightlife, they may be able to discover a resort area that will allow both to have what they want. Successful bridging requires a fundamental reformulation of the problem such that the parties are no longer squabbling over their positions; instead, they are disclosing sufficient information to discover their interests and needs and then inventing options that will satisfy those needs.[18] Bridging solutions do not always remedy all concerns; the wife may not get the salt sea air at the resort, and the husband may spend more money than he wanted to, but both have agreed that taking their vacation together is more desirable than taking it separately (i.e., they have committed themselves to interdependence) and have worked to invent a solution that meets their most important needs. If negotiators fundamentally commit themselves to a win-win negotiation, bridging solutions are likely to be highly satisfactory to both sides.

As we stated earlier, the successful pursuit of these five strategies requires a meaningful exchange of information between the parties. The parties must either volunteer information or ask each other questions that will generate sufficient information to reveal win-win options. Table 4.1 presents a series of refocusing questions that may reveal these possibilities.[19]

Generating Alternative Solutions to the Problem as Given.   In addition to the techniques mentioned above, there are a number of other approaches to generating alternative solutions. These approaches can be used by the negotiators themselves or by a number of other parties (constituencies, audiences, bystanders, etc.). Several of these approaches are commonly used in small groups. Groups of people are frequently better problem solvers than single individuals, particularly because groups provide a wider number of perspectives and hence can invent a greater variety of ways to solve a given problem. However, groups also should adopt procedures for defining the problem, defining interests, and generating options lest the group process degenerate into a win-lose competition or a debating event.

Brainstorming.   In brainstorming, small groups of people work to generate as many possible solutions to the problem as they can. Someone records the solutions, without comment, as they are identified. Participants are urged to be spontaneous, even impractical, and not to censor anyone's ideas (including their own). Moreover, participants are required not to discuss or evaluate any solution as it is proposed, so they do not stop the free flow of new ideas. The success of brainstorming depends on the amount of intellectual stimulation that occurs as different ideas are tossed around. Therefore, the following rules should be observed:

1. *Avoid judging or evaluating solutions.* Criticism inhibits creative thinking. Creative solutions often come from ideas that initially seem wild and impractical. No idea should be evaluated or eliminated until the group is finished generating options.

2. *Separate the people from the problem.* Group discussion and brainstorming processes are often constrained because the parties take ownership of preferred solutions and alternatives.[20] Since competitive negotiators assume an offensive posture toward the other party, they are unlikely to see the merits of a suggested alternative that comes from that party or appears to favor that party's position. Therefore, for effective problem solving to occur, negotiators must concentrate on depersonalizing the problem and treating all possible solutions as equally viable, regardless of who initiated them.

3. *Be exhaustive in the brainstorming process.* Many times the best ideas come after a meeting is over or after a problem is solved. Sometimes this happens because the parties were not persistent enough. Research has shown that when

TABLE 4.1   Refocusing Questions to Reveal Win-Win Options

Expanding the Pie

1. How can both parties get what they want?
2. Is there a resource shortage?
3. How can resources be expanded to meet the demands of both sides?

Logrolling

1. What issues are of higher and lower priority to me?
2. What issues are of higher and lower priority to the other?
3. Are there any issues of high priority to me that are of low priority for the other, and vice versa?
4. Can I "unbundle" an issue—that is, make one larger issue into two or more smaller ones that can then be logrolled?
5. What are things that would be inexpensive for me to give and valuable for the other to get that might be used in logrolling?

Nonspecific Compensation

1. What are the other party's goals and values?
2. What could I do that would make the other side happy and simultaneously allow me to get my way on the key issue?
3. What are things that would be inexpensive for me to give and valuable for the other to get that might be used as nonspecific compensation?

Cost Cutting

1. What risks and costs does my proposal create for the other?
2. What can I do to minimize the other's risks and costs so that he or she would be more willing to agree?

Bridging

1. What are the other's real underlying interests and needs?
2. What are my own real underlying interests and needs?
3. What are the higher and lower priorities for each of us in our underlying interests and needs?
4. Can we invent a solution that meets the relative priorities, underlying interests, and needs of both parties?

---

brainstormers work at the process for a long time, the best ideas are most likely to surface during the latter part of the activity.

4. *Ask outsiders.* Often people who know nothing about the history of the negotiation, or even about the issues, can suggest options and possibilities that have not been considered. Outsiders can provide additional input to the list of alternatives, or they can help orchestrate the process and keep the parties on track.

Nominal Groups.   In the nominal group technique, negotiators must start with the problem as defined, then individually prepare a written list of possible solutions.[21] Participants are encouraged to list as many solutions as they can. Then they meet in small groups and read their solutions aloud while a recorder writes them on flip charts or a blackboard. Particularly in a large group, this approach can generate a great number of options in a short time. All those working on the problem can then examine these solutions.

Surveys.   The disadvantage of nominal groups is that they do not solicit the ideas of those who are not present at the negotiation. In addition, the nominal group technique can be time-consuming. A different approach is to distribute a written questionnaire to a large number of people, stating the problem and asking them to list all the possible solutions they can imagine. This process can be conducted in a short time. The liability, however, is that the parties cannot benefit from seeing and hearing the other people's ideas, a key advantage of the nominal group technique.

Summary.   Our discussion of the two basic approaches to generating alternative solutions—generating options to the problem as given and generating options by redefining the problem—may give the impression that if bargainers simply invent enough different options, they will find a solution to solve their problem rather easily. Although identifying options sometimes leads to a solution, solutions are usually attained through hard work and pursuit of several related processes: information exchange, focusing on interests rather than positions, and firm flexibility.[22] Information exchange will allow the parties to maximize the amount of information available. Focusing on interests will allow the parties to move beyond opening positions and demands to determine what the parties really want—what needs truly must be satisfied. Finally, firm flexibility will allow the parties to be firm with regard to what they want to achieve (i.e., interests) while remaining flexible on the means by which they achieve it. Firm flexibility recognizes that negotiators have one or two fundamental interests or principles, although a wide variety of positions, possible solutions, or secondary issues may get drawn into the negotiations. Thus, among the many viable alternatives that will satisfy a negotiator, the important ones directly address the bottom line or the top priorities. Negotiators need to be able to signal to the other side the positions on which they are firm and the positions on which they are willing to be flexible. Here are several tactics to communicate firm flexibility to the other negotiator:

1. Use contentious (competitive) tactics to establish and defend basic interests rather than to demand a particular position or solution to the dispute. State what you want clearly.

2. Send signals of flexibility and concern about your willingness to address the other party's interests. Openly express concern for the other's welfare and "acknowledge their interests as part of the problem."[23] In doing so, you communicate that you have your own interests at stake but are willing to try to address the other's as well.

3. Indicate a willingness to change your proposals if a way can be found to bridge the two parties' interests.

4. Demonstrate problem-solving capacity. For example, use experts on a negotiating team or bring them in as consultants based on their expertise at generating new ideas.

5. Maintain open communication channels. Do not eliminate opportunities to communicate and work together, if only to demonstrate continually that you are willing to work with the other party.

6. Reaffirm what is most important to you through the use of clear statements—for example, "I need to attain this; this is a must; this cannot be touched or changed." These statements communicate to the other party that a particular interest is fundamental to your position, but it does not necessarily mean that the other's interests can't be satisfied as well.

7. Reexamine any aspect of your interests that are clearly unacceptable to the other party and determine if they are still essential to your fundamental position. It is rare that negotiators will find that they truly disagree on basic interests.

8. Separate and isolate contentious tactics from problem-solving behavior to better manage the contentious behavior. This may be accomplished by clearly specifying a change in the negotiation process, by separating the two processes with a break or recess, or, in team negotiations, by having one party act contentiously and then having a second negotiator offer to engage in problem solving. This last approach, called "good cop/bad cop" or "black hat/white hat," is also frequently used as a purely distributive bargaining tactic, as we discussed in Chapter 3. In this situation, however, separate the competitive from the collaborative elements of the process by changing the individuals who represent those positions.[24]

Evaluation and Selection of Alternatives

The fourth stage in the integrative negotiation process is to evaluate the alternatives generated during the previous phase and to select the best ones to implement. When the problem is a reasonably simple one, the evaluation and selection steps may be effectively combined into a single step. For those new to or uncomfortable with the integrative process, though, we suggest a close adherence to a series of distinct steps: definitions and standards, alternatives, evaluation, and selection. Following these distinct steps is also a good idea for those confronted with complex problems or a large number of alternative options. Negotiators will need to weigh or rank-order each option against the criteria. If no option or set of options appears suitable and acceptable, this is a strong indication that the problem was not clearly defined (return to definitions), or that the standards developed earlier are not reasonable, relevant, and/or realistic (return to standards). Finally, the parties will be required to engage in some form of decision-making process, in which they debate the relative merits of each side's preferred options and come to agreement on the best options. The following guidelines should be used in evaluating options and reaching a consensus.[25]

Narrow the Range of Solution Options. Examine the list of options generated and focus on those that are strongly supported by one or more negotiators. This approach is more positive than allowing people to focus on negative, unacceptable criteria and options. Solutions not strongly advocated by at least one negotiator should be eliminated.

Evaluate Solutions on the Basis of Quality, Acceptability, and Standards. Solutions should be judged on two major criteria: how good they are, and how acceptable they will be to those who have to implement them. These are the same two dimensions that research has revealed to be critical in effective participative decision making in organizations. Negotiators will evaluate the quality dimension by determining what is best, what is most rational, what is most logical. To the degree that parties can support their arguments with statements of hard fact, logical deduction, and appeals to rational criteria, their arguments will be more compelling in obtaining the support of others. This suggests that the parties are more likely to accept a solution they perceive as fair and equitable to all concerned than one that seems biased. Thus, the parties should search for precedents, arbitration decisions, or other objectively fair outcomes and processes that can be used as benchmarks for legitimizing the fairness of the current settlement. These criteria may be different from what the negotiators judge to be most rational or the best solution. Those evaluating the solution options may also have to be prepared to make trade-offs to ensure that the criteria of both quality and acceptability (fairness) are met.[26]

Agree to the Criteria in Advance of Evaluating Options.   Ideally, negotiators should agree to the criteria for evaluating potential integrative solutions early in the process.[27] Negotiators can use these criteria when they have to narrow the choice of options down to a single alternative—for example, one candidate for a new job—or to select the option most likely to succeed. If the parties first debate their criteria and determine which ones are most important, they will be able to decide on criteria independent of the consideration of any particular candidate or option. Then, when they consider the individual candidates or options, they will pick the best one based on these criteria, not on the individual preferences of one side or the other. If the parties agree, they may revise their criteria later to improve their choice, but this should be done only by the agreement of all negotiators. In fact, it is not a bad idea to check criteria periodically and determine whether each negotiator places the same priority on them as before. Discussion of alternatives frequently leads negotiators to revise their preferences, as well as their estimates of the probability of success and the cost of particular options.

Be Willing to Justify Personal Preferences.   People often find it hard to publicly explain why they like what they like, or dislike what they dislike. "Why do you like that?" "I don't know, I just do," is usually the reply. Moreover, negotiators gain little by pressing opponents to justify themselves—doing so usually just makes them angry and defensive; they may feel that a simple statement of preference is not viewed as sufficient. For example, if the topic under negotiation is what to have for dinner, and one party states that she hates clam chowder, no amount of persuasive effort is likely to induce her to eat clam chowder. Instead, the parties would be more productive if they accepted this information and attempted to explore other options for dinner. Yet what people prefer often has a deep-seated rationale—recall our discussion of how interests, values, and needs often underlie positions. Thus, inquiries from one party about the other party's preferences may be an effort to probe behind a position and identify underlying interests and needs. If the other party elicits a little defensiveness in response to a why question, the negotiator should explain that the intent is to probe for possible underlying interests that might facilitate a collaborative settlement rather than to produce defensiveness.

Be Alert to the Influence of Intangibles in Selecting Options.   One side may favor an option because it helps satisfy some intangible—gaining recognition, looking strong or tough to a constituency, feeling like a winner, and so on. Intangibles or principles can serve as strong interests for a negotiator. Intangibles can lead the negotiator to fight harder to attain a particular solution if that option satisfies both tangibles and intangibles. Some parties may be uncomfortable with discussing intangibles, or even unaware of their nature and power in negotiation process.

Use Subgroups to Evaluate Complex Options.   Small groups may be particularly helpful when many complex options must be considered or when many people will be affected by the solution. Groups of six to eight people, composed of representatives from each faction, side, or subgroup, will be able to work more effectively than a large group.[28]

Take Time Out to Cool Off.   Even though the parties may have completed the hardest part of the process—generating a list of viable options—they may become upset if communication breaks down, they feel their preferences are not being acknowledged, or the other side pushes too hard for a particular option. If the parties become angry, they should take a break. They should make their dissatisfaction known and openly discuss the reasons for it. The parties should feel that they are back on an even emotional keel before continuing to evaluate options.

Explore Different Ways to Logroll.   Earlier we discussed a variety of ways to invent options. The strategy of logrolling is effective not only in inventing options but also as a mechanism to combine options into negotiated packages. Neale and Bazerman identify a variety of approaches in addition to simply combining several issues into a package. Three of these, in particular, relate to the matters of outcome, probabilities, and timing—in other words, *what* is to happen, the *likelihood* of it happening, and *when* it happens.[29]

Exploit Differences in Risk Preference.   Suppose two partners are discussing a future business venture. One has little to risk at the moment and everything to gain from the future; the other has a lot on the line now that he does not want to risk losing if the future is bad. If the partners simply agree to split profits in the future, the one with a large amount of current risk may feel vulnerable. Logrolling around these interests can create a solution that protects one partner's current investment first while providing long-term profits for the other partner as well.

Exploit Differences in Expectations.   In the same example, the person with a lot to lose may also have pessimistic expectations about the future of the joint venture, whereas the person with little to lose may be more optimistic about it. The optimist may thus be willing to gamble more on the future profitability and payout, whereas the pessimist may be willing to settle for a smaller but more assured payment. As with differences in risk, simple differences in expectations about what will happen can permit the parties to invent a solution that addresses the needs of both parties.

Exploit Differences in Time Preferences.   Negotiators may have different time preferences—one may be concerned about meeting short-term needs while the other may be interested in the long-term rewards of their relationship. Parties with short-term interests will need immediate gratification, whereas parties who look for long-term rewards may be willing to make immediate sacrifices to ensure a future payoff. Parties with different time preferences can invent solutions that address both their interests.

Keep Decisions Tentative and Conditional Until All Aspects of the Final Proposal Are Complete.   Even though a clear consensus may emerge about the solution option(s) that will be selected, the parties should talk about the solution in conditional terms—a sort of "soft bundling." Maintaining a tentative tone allows any side to change or revise the final package at any time. Points agreed upon in earlier discussions are not firm until the entire package is determined. Parties do not have to feel that because they gave up an earlier option they have burned their bridges behind them; rather, nothing should be considered final until everything is final.

Minimize Formality and Record Keeping Until Final Agreements Are Closed.
Parties usually do not want to lock themselves into any specific language or written agreement until they are close to a consensus. They want to make sure that they will not be held to any comments recorded in notes or transcripts. In general, the fewer the written records during the solution generating phase, the better. In contrast, when the parties are close to consensus, one side should write down the terms of the agreement. This document may then be used as a "single text" to be passed around from party to party as often as necessary until all sides agree to the phrasing and wording of their agreement.[30]

We *strongly* urge groups to avoid the apparent expediency of "voting" on final agreements or packages, if at all possible. This accomplishes only the relative disenfranchisement of the losing party and makes it more likely that "losers" will be less committed than desirable for the implementation and attainment of the negotiated outcome.

FACTORS THAT FACILITATE SUCCESSFUL INTEGRATIVE NEGOTIATION

We have stressed that successful integrative negotiation can occur if the parties are predisposed to finding a mutually acceptable joint solution. Many other factors contribute to a predisposition toward problem solving and a willingness to work together to find the best solution. In this section, we will review in greater detail these factors: the presence of a common goal, faith in one's own problem-solving ability, a belief in the validity of the other party's position, the motivation and commitment to work together, trust, clear and accurate communication, and an understanding of the dynamics of integrative negotiation.[31]

Some Common Objective or Goal

When the parties believe that they are likely to benefit more from working together than from competing or working separately, the situation offers greater potential for successful integrative negotiation. Three types of goals—common, shared, and joint—may facilitate the development of integrative agreements (see Table 4.2).

TABLE 4.2   Goal Typology

Type of Goal	Goal Characteristics
Common	Same goal, same (equal) benefit
Shared	Same goal, different benefits
Joint	Different goals (combined), different benefits

A *common goal* is one that all parties share equally, each one benefiting in a way that would not be possible if they did not work together. A town government and an industrial manufacturing plant may debate the amount of taxes owed by the plant, but they are more likely to work together if the common goal is to keep the plant open and employ half the town's workforce.

A *shared goal* is one that both parties work toward but that benefits each party differently. For example, partners can work together in a business but not divide the profits equally. One may get a larger share of the profit because she contributed more experience or capital investment. Inherent in the idea of a shared goal is that parties will work together to achieve some output that will be divided among them. The same result can also come from cost cutting, by which the parties can earn the same outcome as before by working together, but with less effort, expense, or risk. This is often described as an "expandable pie" in contrast to a "fixed pie" (see Chapter 5).

A *joint goal* is one that involves individuals with different personal goals agreeing to combine them in a collective effort. For example, people joining a political campaign can have different goals: One wants to satisfy personal ambition to hold public office, another wants to serve the community, and yet another wants to benefit from policies that will be implemented under the new administration. All will unite around the joint goal of helping the new administration get elected.

The key element of an integrative negotiation situation is the belief that all sides can benefit. Whether the sides attain the same outcome or different outcomes, all sides must believe that they will be better off by working in cooperation than by working independently or competing.

Faith in One's Problem-Solving Ability

Parties who believe they can work together usually are able to do so. Those who do not share this belief in themselves (and others) are less willing to invest the time and energy in the potential payoffs of a collaborative relationship and more likely to assume a contending or accommodating approach to conflict. Expertise in the focal problem area strengthens the negotiator's understanding of the problem's complexity, nuances, and possible solutions. Expertise increases both the negotiator's knowledge base and his or her self-confidence, both of which are necessary to approach the problem at hand with an open mind. Similarly, direct experience in negotiation increases the negotiator's sophistication in understanding the bargaining process and approaching it more creatively. Finally, there is also evidence that knowledge of integrative tactics leads to an increase in integrative behavior. Taken together, these results suggest that a faith in one's ability to negotiate integratively is positively related to successful integrative negotiations.[32]

A Belief in the Validity of One's Own Position and the Other's Perspective

In distributive bargaining, negotiators invest time and energy in inflating and justifying the value of their own point of view and debunking the value and importance of the other's perspective. In contrast, integrative negotiation requires negotiators to accept both their own and the other's attitudes, information, and desires as valid. First, you must believe in the validity of your own perspective—that what you believe is worth fighting for and should not be compromised. Research by Kemp and Smith showed that negotiators who were firmer about insisting that their own point of view become incorporated into the group solution achieved more integrative agreements than those who were less firm.[33] But one must also accept the validity of the other party's perspective. If you challenge the other party's views, he or she may become angry, defensive, and hence unproductive in the problem-solving process. The purpose of integrative negotiation is not to question or challenge the other's viewpoint, but to incorporate it into the definition of the problem and to attend to it as the parties search for mutually acceptable alternatives.

The Motivation and Commitment to Work Together

For integrative negotiation to succeed, the parties must be motivated to collaborate rather than to compete. They need to be committed to reaching a goal that benefits both of them rather than to pursuing only their own ends. They must adopt interpersonal styles that are more congenial than combative, more open and trusting than evasive and defensive, more flexible (but firm) than stubborn (but yielding). Specifically, they must be willing to make their own needs explicit, to identify similarities, and to recognize and accept differences. They must also tolerate uncertainties and unravel inconsistencies.

Motivation and commitment to problem solving can be enhanced in several ways:

1. The parties can come to believe that they share a common fate; to quote Ben Franklin, "If we do not hang together, we will surely hang separately."

2. The parties can demonstrate to each other that there is more to be gained by working together (to increase the payoffs or reduce the costs) than by working separately. The parties can emphasize that they may have to work together after the negotiations are over and will continue to benefit from the relationship they have created. In spite of these efforts, competitive and contentious behavior may persist.

3. The parties can engage in commitments to each other before the negotiations begin; such commitments have been called *presettlement settlements* and are distinguished by three major characteristics:

   a. The settlement results in a firm, legally binding written agreement between the parties (it is more than a "gentlemen's agreement").

BOX 4.2
Presettlement Settlements: An Example

In their description of the advantage of presettlement settlements (PreSS), authors James Gillespie and Max Bazerman offer the following example:

> In the international arena, perhaps the most prominent recent example of a presettlement settlement is the 1993 Oslo accords between Israel and the Palestinians. The Oslo accords sought to establish an incremental process of negotiation and reciprocation that would lead to what both parties termed "final status talks." The parties agreed to reserve the most difficult issues (e.g., borders, settlements, Jerusalem) until the final status talks. In the meantime, the Israelis and Palestinians sought to resolve less difficult issues, thereby establishing a political dialogue and working toward normalized relations. The Israelis agreed to release female prisoners, transfer disputed money, and withdraw from Hebron. The Palestinians agreed to revise their national charter, transfer suspected terrorists, and limit the size of the Palestinian police force. . . .
>
> The Oslo accords contained all three elements of a PreSS. Israel and the Palestinians signed a formal agreement containing very specific terms. Since sovereign parties were involved, the agreement was not strictly binding, but it did create obligations on both sides that would be politically costly to reduce unilaterally. The Oslo accords were intended as an initial step in a political and negotiating process leading to a comprehensive resolution of the Israeli–Palestinian dispute. Finally, this PreSS was partial because the parties deferred extremely difficult issues such as Jerusalem until the final-status talks. (p. 151)

The researchers go on to note that by 1998, the framework set out in the Oslo accords had subsequently floundered because of heated rhetoric and escalating violence, and a PreSS no longer exists between Israel and the Palestinians.

SOURCE: James Gillespie and Max Bazerman, "Pre-settlement Settlement (PreSS): A Simple Technique for Initiating Complex Negotiations," *Negotiation Journal* (April 1998), pp. 149–59.

---

b. The settlement occurs in advance of the parties undertaking full-scale negotiations, but the parties intend that the agreement will be replaced by a more clearly delineated long-term agreement which is to be negotiated.

c. The settlement resolves only a subset of the issues on which the parties disagree and may simply establish a framework within which the more comprehensive agreement can be defined and delineated.[34]

See Box 4.2 for an example of a presettlement settlement.

Trust

Although there is no guarantee that trust will lead to collaboration, there is plenty of evidence to suggest that mistrust inhibits collaboration. People who are interdependent but do not trust each other will act tentatively or defensively. Defensiveness usually means that they will not accept information at face value but instead will look for hidden, deceptive meanings. When people are defensive, they withdraw and withhold information. Defensive people also attack their opponent's statements and position, seeking to defeat their position rather than to work together. Either of these responses is likely to make the negotiator hesitant, cautious, and distrustful of the other, undermining the negotiation process.[35]

Generating trust is a complex, uncertain process; it depends in part on how the parties behave and in part on the parties' personal characteristics. When people trust each other, they are more likely to share information, communicate accurately their needs, positions, and the facts of the situation. In contrast, when people do not trust each other, they are more likely to engage in positional bargaining, use threats, and commit themselves to tough positions. As with defensiveness, mistrust is likely to be reciprocated and to lead to unproductive negotiations. To develop trust effectively, each negotiator must believe that both she and the other party choose to behave in a cooperative manner; moreover, each must believe that this behavior is a signal of the other's honesty, openness, and a similar mutual commitment to a joint solution.[36]

A number of key factors contribute to the development of trust between negotiators. First, people are more likely to trust someone they perceive as similar to them or as holding a positive attitude toward them. Second, people often trust those who depend on them; being in a position to help or hurt someone (who can do the same in return) fosters mutual trust. Third, people are more likely to trust those who initiate cooperative, trusting behavior. Acting in a cooperative, trusting manner serves as an invitation to others, especially if the invitation is repeated despite initially contentious behavior from the opponent. Fourth, there is some evidence that giving a gift to the other negotiator may lead to increased trust. Finally, people are more likely to trust those who make concessions. The more other people's behavior communicates that they are holding firm in their fundamental commitment to their own needs at the same time as they are working toward a joint solution, the more negotiators are likely to find their conduct trustworthy, in the spirit of the best joint agreement.[37]

Given that trust has to be built during the negotiation, tone-setting and other opening moves are crucial. The more cooperative, open, and nonthreatening the opening statements and actions of a party are, the more trust and cooperation are engendered in the other party. Once a cooperative position is established, it is more likely to persist. If cooperative behavior can be established at the very beginning, there is a tendency for parties to lock in to this cycle and make it continue. Finally, opening moves not only help set the tone for the negotiation but also begin the momentum. The longer the cycle of trust and cooperation continues, the easier it would be to reestablish it should the cycle break down.[38]

Clear and Accurate Communication

Another precondition for high-quality integrative negotiation is clear and accurate communication. First, negotiators must be willing to share information about themselves.[39] They must be willing to tell what they want and, more important, must be willing to state why they want it in specific, concrete terms, avoiding generalities and ambiguities. Second, the other negotiators must understand the communication. At a minimum, they must understand the meaning they each attach to their statements; hopefully, the parties each interpret the facts in the same way. Others at the negotiating table can frequently identify ambiguities and breakdowns in communication. If someone on a bargaining team makes a confusing statement, others can address it and try to clarify it. When one person on the other side does not grasp a difficult point, someone else from the same side will often be able to find the words or illustrations to bring out the meaning. Still, mutual understanding is the responsibility of both sides. The communicator must be willing to test whether the other side has received the message that was intended. Similarly, the listener must engage in active listening, testing to make sure that what he or she received and understood is the message that the sender intended.

Using multiple communication channels (i.e., opportunities for the two sides to communicate in ways other than formally across the negotiation table) will help negotiators clarify the formal communication or get information through if the formal channels break down. Conversations over coffee breaks, separate meetings between chief negotiators outside the formal sessions, and off-the-record contacts between key subordinates are all alternatives to the formal channel. The negotiators must exercise care, though, to make sure that the multiple messages and media are consistent. Sending conflicting messages in integrative negotiations can confuse the other party at best, and threaten or anger at worst.

When there are strong negative feelings or when one or more parties are inclined to dominate, negotiators may create formal, structured procedures for communication. Under these circumstances, negotiators should follow a procedure that gives everyone a chance to speak. For example, the rules of most debates limit statements to five minutes, and similar rules are often adopted in contentious open meetings or public hearings. In addition, the parties may agree to follow a previously agreed-on agenda so that everyone can be heard and their contributions noted.[40]

An Understanding of the Dynamics of Integrative Negotiation

It is possible for negotiators to have "traditional" views of negotiation that lead them to assume that the distributive bargaining process is the only way to approach negotiations. Yet several studies indicate that training in integrative negotiation enhances the ability of the parties to successfully pursue the process. Training negotiators in integrative tactics—particularly in how to exchange information about priorities across issues and preferences within issues, and how to set high goals—significantly enhanced the frequency of integrative behaviors and led the parties to achieve higher joint outcomes. This study also found that using distributive tactics, such as strongly trying to persuade the other of the validity of one's own views, was negatively related to joint outcome.[41]

Summary

We identified six fundamental preconditions for successful integrative negotiation: some form of shared or common goals, faith in one's ability to solve problems, a belief in the validity and importance of the other's position, the motivation and commitment to work together, trust in the opposing negotiator, and the ability to accurately exchange information in spite of conflict conditions. If the parties are not able to successfully meet these preconditions, they will need to resolve problems in these areas as the integrative negotiation evolves.

CHAPTER SUMMARY

In this chapter, we have reviewed the strategy and tactics of integrative negotiation. The fundamental structure of integrative negotiation is one within which the parties are able to define goals that allow both sides to achieve their objectives. Integrative negotiation is the process of defining these goals and engaging in a set of procedures that permit both sides to maximize their objectives.

The chapter began with an overview of the integrative negotiation process. A high level of concern for both sides achieving their own objectives propels a collaborative, problem-solving approach. Negotiators frequently fail at integrative negotiation because they fail to perceive the integrative potential of the negotiating problem. However, breakdowns also occur due to distributive assumptions about the negotiating problem, the mixed-motive nature of the issues, or the negotiators' previous relationship with each other. Successful integrative negotiation requires several processes. First, the parties must understand each other's true needs and objectives. Second, they must create a free flow of information and an open exchange of ideas. Third, they must focus on their similarities, emphasizing their commonalities rather than their differences. Finally, they must engage in a search for solutions that meet the goals of both sides. This is a very different set of processes from those in distributive bargaining, described in Chapter 3.

The four key steps in the integrative negotiation process are identifying and defining the problem, identifying interests and needs, generating alternative solutions, and evaluating and selecting alternatives. For each of these steps, we proposed techniques and tactics to make the process successful.

We then discussed various factors that facilitate successful integrative negotiation. First, the process will be greatly facilitated by some form of common goal or objective. This goal may be one that the parties both want to achieve, one they want to share, or one they could not possibly attain unless they worked together. Second, they must share a motivation and commitment to work together, to make their relationship a productive one. Third, the parties must be willing to believe that the other's needs are valid. Fourth, they must be able to trust each other and to work hard to establish and maintain that trust. Finally, there must be clear and accurate communication about what each one wants and an effort to understand the other's needs.

ENDNOTES

1. Carnevale and Pruitt, 1992; Filley, 1975; Fisher, Ury, and Patton, 1991; Pruitt, 1981, 1983; Pruitt and Carnevale, 1993; and Walton and McKersie, 1965.
2. Ury, 1991.
3. Butler, 1999; Pruitt, 1981; and Thompson, 1991.
4. Kemp and Smith, 1994.
5. Olekalns, Smith, and Walsh, 1996.
6. Fisher, Ury, and Patton, 1991; and Pruitt and Rubin, 1986.
7. See Filley, 1975 and Shea, 1983 for more complete treatment of these points.
8. Fisher, Ury, and Patton, *Getting to Yes*. New York: Penguin, 1991.
9. Fisher, Ury, and Patton, 1991, p. 40; originally from Follett, 1940.
10. Lax and Sebenius, 1986.
11. See Sheppard, Lewicki, and Minton, 1992, Chapter 5, for a more complete discussion of the role of "voice" in organizations.

12. Lax and Sebenius, 1986.
13. Nierenberg, 1976; Burton, 1984.
14. Provis, 1996.
15. See Neale and Bazerman, 1991; Pruitt, 1981, 1983; Pruitt and Carnevale, 1993; and Pruitt and Lewis, 1975.
16. Gillespie and Bazerman, 1997.
17. See Lax and Sebenius, 1986; Pruitt, 1981; Mannix, Tinsley, and Bazerman, 1995.
18. Butler, 1996.
19. See Pruitt and Carnevale, 1993; and Pruitt and Rubin, 1986.
20. Filley, 1975; Fisher, Ury, and Patton, 1991; and Walton and McKersie, 1965.
21. Delbecq and Van de Ven, 1971.
22. Fisher, Ury, and Patton, 1991; and Pruitt, 1983.
23. Fisher, Ury, and Patton, 1991, p. 55.
24. See Filley, 1975; Pruitt and Carnevale, 1993; Shea, 1983; and Walton and McKersie, 1965.
25. Vroom and Yetton, 1973.
26. Fisher, Ury, and Patton, 1991.
27. Ibid.
28. More information about group processes and negotiation can be found in the chapter "Coalitions, Multiple Parties, and Teams" posted on the McGraw-Hill website at www.mhhe.com/lewickinegotiation.
29. Neale and Bazerman, 1991.
30. Fisher, Ury, and Patton, 1991.
31. Filley, 1975; and Pruitt, 1981, 1983.
32. Neale and Northcraft, 1986; Thompson, 1990a; Weingart, Prietula, Hyder, and Genovese, 1999.
33. Fisher, Ury, and Patton, 1991; Kemp and Smith, 1994.
34. Gillespie and Bazerman, 1998.
35. Gibb, 1961.
36. Butler, 1999; Tenbrunsel, 1999; Kimmel, Pruitt, Magenau, Konar-Goldband, and Carnevale, 1980.
37. Solomon, 1960; Bonoma, Horai, Lindskold, Gahagan, and Tedeschi, 1969; Gahagan, Long, and Horai, 1969; Gruder and Duslak, 1973; Heller, 1967; Kleinke and Pohlan, 1971; Large, 1999; Rubin and Brown, 1975.
38. Crumbaugh and Evans, 1967; Michelini, 1971; Oskamp, 1970; Sermat and Gregovich, 1966; also see Chen, Chen, and Meindl, 1998; Pilisuk and Skolnick, 1978; Komorita and Mechling, 1967; Sermat, 1967; Swinth, 1967.
39. Neale and Bazerman, 1991.
40. For information on how third parties can help facilitate disabled communication processes, see the chapter "Managing Difficult Negotiations: Third-Party Approaches" on the McGraw-Hill website at www.mhhe.com/lewickinegotiation.
41. Weingart, Hyder, and Prietula, 1996.

CHAPTER 5

Perception, Cognition, and Communication

Perception, cognition, and communication are fundamental processes that govern how individuals construct and interpret the interaction that takes place in a negotiation. Reduced to its essence, negotiation is a form of interpersonal communication, which itself is a subset of the broader category of human perception and communication. Perception and cognition are the basic building blocks of all social encounters, including negotiation, in the sense that our social actions are guided by the way we perceive and analyze the other party, the situation, and our own interests and positions. A sound understanding of how humans perceive and communicate in general will help negotiators understand why people behave the way they do during negotiations.

We begin the chapter by examining how psychological perception is related to the process of negotiation, with particular attention to forms of perceptual distortion that can cause problems of understanding and meaning making for negotiators. We then look at how negotiators use information to make decisions about tactics and strategy—the process of cognition. Our focus here is on the various kinds of systematic errors, or "cognitive biases," in information processing that negotiators are prone to make and that may compromise negotiator performance. Following these sections on perception and cognition, we turn to the process by which negotiators communicate their own interests, positions, and goals—and in turn make sense of those of the other party and of the negotiation as a whole. We will consider *what* is communicated in a negotiation, and *how* people communicate in negotiation. The chapter ends with discussions of how to improve communication in negotiation, the effect of moods and emotions on communication, and special communication considerations at the close of negotiations.

PERCEPTION AND NEGOTIATION

The Role of Perception

Negotiators approach each negotiation guided by their perceptions of past situations and current attitudes and behaviors. Perception is the process by which individuals connect to their environment. The process of ascribing meaning to messages received is strongly influenced by the receiver's current state of mind, role, and understanding or comprehension of earlier communications.[1] Other parties' perceptions, the environment, and the receiver's own dispositions all affect how meanings are ascribed, and whether the receiver can determine exactly what the other party is saying, and what is meant. We will now examine in more detail how perceptions are created and how they affect the success of communication.

FIGURE 5.1 The Perceptual Process

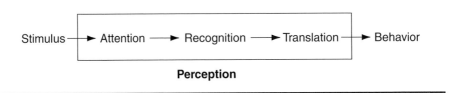

Perception is a "sense-making" process; people interpret their environment so that they can respond appropriately (see Figure 5.1). Most environments are extremely complex—they present a large number and variety of stimuli, each having different properties such as magnitude, color, shape, texture, and relative novelty. The sheer complexity of such environments makes it impossible to process all of the available information, so perception becomes selective, focusing on some stimuli while tuning out others. As a result, people have several shortcuts in their perceptual systems that allow them to process information more readily. Unfortunately, these shortcuts come with a cost—perceptual errors, which typically occur without people being aware that they are happening.

Perceptual Distortion in Negotiation

In any given negotiation, the perceiver's own needs, desires, motivations, and personal experiences may create a predisposition about the other party. Such predispositions are most problematic when they lead to biases and errors in perception and subsequent communication. We will discuss four major perceptual errors: stereotyping, halo effects, selective perception, and projection. Stereotyping and halo effects are examples of perceptual distortion by *generalization:* small amounts of perceptual information are used to draw large conclusions about individuals. Selective perception and projection are, in contrast, examples of perceptual distortion by the *anticipation* of encountering certain attributes and qualities in another person. In each case, the perceiver filters and distorts information to arrive at a consistent view.

Stereotyping is a very common distortion of the perceptual process. Stereotyping occurs when one individual assigns attributes to another solely on the basis of the other's membership in a particular social or demographic group. Stereotypes are formed about a wide variety of different groups, for example, the younger generation; males or females; Italians or Germans; or people of different races, religions, or sexual orientations. In each case, stereotypes tend to be formed in the same way. People assign an individual to a group based on one piece of perceptual information (e.g., the individual is young or old); then they assign a broad range of other characteristics of the group to this individual (e.g., "Old people are conservative; this person is old and therefore is conservative" or "Young people are disrespectful; this person is young and therefore is disrespectful"). There may be no factual basis for the conclusion that this particular older individual is conservative; the conclusion is based on the generalization of qualities that have been ascribed to the larger group. Applying other traits associated with the category to this particular individual further compounds the error. Moreover, stereotypes, once formed, are often highly resistant to change. In organizations, problems of age, race, and gender stereotyping have received much attention, yet they persist. The simple process of using a single criterion—even an arbitrary one—to divide people into groups encourages group members to begin to define themselves as "we" and the other group as "they," and then to make evaluative comparisons between them. Direct competition for resources among groups, or a conflict of values and ideologies, significantly enhances the stereotyping process.[2]

Halo effects in perception are similar to stereotypes. Rather than using a person's group membership as a basis for classification, halo effects occur when people generalize about a variety of attributes based on the knowledge of one attribute of an individual.[3] A smiling person is judged to be more honest than a frowning or scowling person, even though there is no consistent relationship between smiling and honesty. Halo effects may be positive or negative. A good attribute may be generalized so that people are seen in a very positive light, whereas a negative attribute has the reverse effect. The more prominent the attribute is in influencing the overall judgment about an individual, the more likely that it will be used to cast further information into a perspective consistent with the initial judgment. Halo effects are most likely to occur in perception (1) when there is very little experience with a person along some dimension (and hence generalization occurs about that person from knowledge of him or her in other contexts), (2) when the person is well known, and (3) when the qualities have strong moral implications.[4]

Halo effects are as common as stereotypes in negotiation. Negotiators are likely to form rapid impressions of each other based on very limited initial information, such as appearance, group membership, or initial statements. Negotiators tend to maintain these judgments as they get to know each other better, fitting each piece of new information into some consistent pattern. Finally, the mere suggestion that the other party can be viewed in moral terms—for example, honest or dishonest, ethical or unethical—is likely to affect the perception of a wide variety of their other attributes.[5]

Selective perception occurs when the perceiver singles out certain information that supports or reinforces a prior belief, and filters out information that does not confirm that belief. Selective perception has the effect of perpetuating stereotypes or halo effects—negotiators not only form quick judgments about individuals on the basis of limited information but also filter out further evidence that might disconfirm the judgment. An initial smile from the other party, which leads the negotiator to believe that he or she is honest, might also lead the negotiator to downplay any of that party's statements that demonstrate an intention to be competitive and aggressive. If the negotiator perceives the same initial smile as a smirk, then the negotiator may downplay the other party's offers to establish an honest and cooperative relationship. In both cases, the negotiator's own biases—the predisposition to view the smile as honest or dishonest—are likely to affect how the other party's behavior is perceived and interpreted.

Projection occurs when people ascribe to others the characteristics or feelings that they possess themselves. Projection usually arises out of a need to protect one's own self-concept. People have a need to see themselves as consistent and good. Negotiators tend to assume that the other party would respond in the same manner they would if they were in the same situation. For instance, if a negotiator feels that he would be frustrated if he were in the other party's position, then he is likely to perceive that the other party is frustrated. People respond differently to similar situations, however, and projecting one's own feelings and beliefs onto the other negotiator may be incorrect. For instance, if a negotiator is really bothered by delays in negotiations but needs to tell the other party that there will be an unavoidable delay, the negotiator may expect the other party to exhibit frustration at the announcement. While it is possible that the other party will be frustrated, it is also possible that he or she will welcome the delay as an opportunity to complete work on a different project, and that any frustration was only a projection from the negotiator's mind.

Framing

Another key issue in perception and negotiation is *framing*. A frame is the subjective mechanism through which people evaluate and make sense out of situations, leading them to pursue or avoid subsequent actions.[6] Framing helps explain "how bargainers conceive of ongoing sets of events in light of past experiences"; framing and reframing, along with reevaluation of information and positions, "are tied to information processing, message patterns, linguistic cues, and socially constructed meanings."[7] As we explained in Chapter 2, framing is about focusing, shaping, and organizing the world around us—making sense of complex realities and defining it in ways that are meaningful to us.

An important aspect of framing for our discussion in this chapter is the *cognitive heuristics* approach, which examines the ways in which negotiators make systematic errors in judgment when they process information.[8] Decision heuristics (or shortcuts) are important because such heuristics often lead parties to make decisions that are less than optimal or even irrational. For example, when faced with a situation where they can make decisions based only on easily available information, negotiators often fail to search for additional information that may be hard to access or understand, and thus they may frame the decision in a manner that gives the other party an advantage.

The cognitive heuristic approach to framing focuses on how a party perceives and shapes the outcome (particularly with regard to risk), and how the party's frame tends to persist regardless of the events and information that follow it. We treat this type of frame as a *cognitive bias* that may shape the negotiator's decision-making process in evaluating outcomes and alternatives; we will explore cognitive biases in depth in the next section.

COGNITIVE BIASES IN NEGOTIATION

In the last section, we examined how information is perceived and potentially distorted in the perception process. In this section, we look at how negotiators use that information to make decisions during the negotiation. Rather than being perfect processors of information, it is quite clear that negotiators have a tendency to make systematic errors when they process information.[9] These errors, collectively labeled *cognitive biases,* tend to impede negotiator performance; they include (1) the irrational escalation of commitment, (2) the mythical belief that the issues under negotiation are all fixed-pie, (3) the process of anchoring and adjustment in decision making, (4) issue and problem framing, (5) the availability of information, (6) the winner's curse, (7) negotiator overconfidence,

(8) the law of small numbers, (9) self-serving biases, (10) the endowment effect, (11) the tendency to ignore others' cognitions, and (12) the process of reactive devaluation. We will discuss each of these in more detail below.

1. Irrational Escalation of Commitment

Negotiators sometimes maintain commitment to a course of action even when that commitment constitutes irrational behavior on their part. This is an example of a broader psychological phenomenon known as "escalation of commitment," which is the tendency for an individual to make decisions that stick with a failing course of action.[10] Classic examples include a country that continues to pour military resources into an unwinnable armed conflict, or an investor who continues to put more money into a declining stock in hopes its fortunes will turn. Escalation of commitment is due in part to biases in individual perception and judgment. Once a course of action is decided, negotiators often seek supportive (confirming) evidence for that choice, while ignoring or failing to seek disconfirming evidence. Initial commitments become set in stone (see the section on anchoring and adjustment, below), and a desire for consistency prevents negotiators from changing them. This desire for consistency is often exacerbated by a desire to save face and to maintain an impression of expertise or control in front of others. No one likes to admit error or failure, especially when the other party may perceive doing so as a weakness. One way to combat these tendencies is to have an advisor serve as a reality checkpoint—someone who is not consumed by the "heat of the moment" and who can warn negotiators when they inadvertently begin to behave irrationally.

2. Mythical Fixed-Pie Beliefs

Many negotiators assume that all negotiations (not just some) involve a fixed pie.[11] Negotiators often approach integrative negotiation opportunities as zero-sum games or win-lose exchanges. Those who believe in the mythical fixed pie assume that the possibility for integrative settlements and mutually beneficial trade-offs doesn't exist, and they suppress efforts to search for such settlements or trade-offs.[12] In a salary negotiation, the job applicant who assumes that salary is the only issue may insist on $35,000 when the company is offering $32,000. Only when the two parties discuss the possibilities further do they discover that moving expenses and starting date can also be negotiated, which may make the resolution of the salary issue far easier.

The tendency to see negotiation in fixed-pie terms seems to vary depending on how people view the nature of a given conflict situation.[13] Negotiators focusing on personal interests are most likely to come under the influence of fixed-pie beliefs and approach the situation competitively. Negotiators focusing on values are less likely to see the problem in fixed-pie terms, and more inclined to approach the situation cooperatively.

3. Anchoring and Adjustment

Cognitive biases in anchoring and adjustment are related to the effect of the standard (or anchor) against which subsequent adjustments (gains or losses) are measured during negotiation. The choice of an anchor (e.g., an initial offer or an intended goal) might well be based on faulty or incomplete information and thus be misleading in and of itself. However, once the anchor is defined, parties tend to treat it as a real, valid benchmark by which to adjust other judgments, such as the size of one side's opening offer.[14] For example, research shows that real estate agents' house appraisals are strongly affected by the asking price.[15] The asking price serves as a convenient anchor to use in appraising the value of the house. Goals in negotiation—whether set realistically or carelessly—can also serve as anchors. These anchors may be visible or invisible to the other party (a published market price versus an uncommunicated expectation), and, similarly, the person who holds them may do so consciously or unconsciously (a specific expectation versus an unexamined, unquestioned expectation or norm). Thorough preparation, along with the use of a devil's advocate or reality check, can help prevent errors of anchoring and adjustment.

4. Framing

In decision theory terms, a frame is a perspective or point of view that people use when they gather information and solve problems. Frames can lead people to seek, avoid, or be neutral about risk in decision making and negotiation.[16] It is in evaluating risk that framing has a strong influence on negotiators. The way that a negotiation is framed can make negotiators more or less risk averse (or risk seeking). For instance, people respond quite differently when they are negotiating to "gain" something rather than to "not lose" something.[17] As a result, negotiators should not necessarily trust their intuitions regarding risk. Negotiators may overreact to a perceived loss when they might react more positively to the same situation if it is framed as a perceived gain. Hence, as a negotiator you must "avoid the pitfalls of being framed while, simultaneously, understanding positively and negatively framing your opponent."[18] When negotiators are risk averse, they are likely to accept any viable offer put on the table simply because they are afraid of losing. In contrast, when negotiators are risk seeking, they are likely to pass up an offer, choosing instead to wait for a better offer or for possible future concessions.

This positive/negative framing process is not inconsequential. Negotiations in which the outcomes are negatively framed tend to produce fewer concessions, reach fewer agreements, and perceive outcomes as less fair than negotiations in which the outcomes are positively framed. Remedies for framing effects are similar to those mentioned above (e.g., sufficient information, thorough analysis, and reality checks) but are more difficult to achieve because frames are often tied to deeply held values and beliefs or to other anchors that are hard to detect.

5. Availability of Information

Negotiators must also be concerned with the potential bias caused by the availability of information or how easy information is to retrieve—that is, how easily it can be recalled and used to inform or evaluate a process or a decision. In negotiation, the availability bias operates when information that is presented in vivid, colorful, or attention-getting ways becomes easy to recall, and thus also becomes central and critical in evaluating events and options. Information presented through a particularly clear chart, diagram, or formula (even one that is oversimplified) might be used or believed more readily than information presented in a confusing or detailed format—regardless of the accuracy of each. The availability of information also affects negotiation through the use of established search patterns. If negotiators have a favorite way of collecting information, or looking for key signals, they will use these patterns repeatedly and hence overvalue the information that comes from them.

6. The Winner's Curse

The winner's curse refers to the tendency of negotiators, particularly in an auction setting, to settle quickly on an item and then subsequently feel discomfort about a negotiation win that comes too easily.[19] If the other party capitulates too quickly, the negotiator is often left wondering, "Could I have gotten this for less?" or asking "What's wrong with the item/product/option?" The negotiator may suspect that the other party knows too much or has insight into an unseen advantage; thus, either "I could have done better" or "This must be a bad deal."

For example, in an antique store several years ago one of the authors of this book saw a clock that he and his wife fell in love with. After spending the afternoon deciding on a negotiation strategy (opening offer, bottom line, timing, feigned disinterest, the good guy/bad guy tactic), the author and his wife returned to the store to enact their strategy. The storeowner accepted their first offer. Upon arriving home, suffering from the winner's curse, they left the clock in the garage, where it remains collecting dust.

The best remedy for the winner's curse is to prevent it from occurring. Thorough investigation and preparation can provide negotiators with independent verification of the proper settlement point. Negotiators can also try to secure performance or quality guarantees from the other party to make sure the outcome is not faulty or defective.

7. Overconfidence

Overconfidence is the tendency of negotiators to believe that their ability to be correct or accurate is greater than is actually true. Overconfidence has a double-edged effect: (1) it can solidify the degree to which negotiators support positions or options that are incorrect or inappropriate, and (2) it can lead negotiators to discount the worth or validity of the judgments of others, in effect shutting down other parties as sources of information, interests, and options necessary for a successful integrative negotiation. One study found that negotiators who were not trained to be aware of the overconfidence heuristic tended to overestimate their probability of being successful, and they were significantly less likely to compromise or reach agreements than trained negotiators.[20] In another study, overconfident individuals were more persistent and were more concerned about their own outcomes than were the realistically confident negotiators.[21] This does not mean, however, that negotiators should always seek to suppress confidence or optimism. Research on distributive bargaining found that negotiators biased toward optimism achieved more profitable settlements compared to negotiators with accurate perceptions or a bias toward pessimism.[22]

8. The Law of Small Numbers

The law of small numbers refers to the tendency of people to draw conclusions from small sample sizes. In negotiation, the law of small numbers applies to the way negotiators learn and extrapolate from their own experience. If that experience is limited in time or in scope (e.g., if all of one's prior negotiations have been hard-fought and distributive), the tendency is to extrapolate prior experience onto future negotiations (e.g., all negotiations are distributive). This tendency will often lead to a self-fulfilling prophecy, as follows: People who expect to be treated in a distributive manner will (1) be more likely to perceive the other party's behavior as distributive, and (2) treat the other party in a more distributive manner. The other party will then be likely to interpret the negotiator's behavior as evidence of a distributive tendency, and will therefore respond in kind. The smaller the prior sample (i.e., the more limited the negotiation experience), the greater the possibility that past lessons will be erroneously used to infer what will happen in the future. Styles and strategies that worked in the past may not work in the future, and certainly will not work if future negotiations differ significantly from past experiences.

9. Self-Serving Biases

People often explain another person's behavior by making attributions, either to the person (i.e., the behaviors were caused by internal factors such as ability, mood, or effort) or to the situation (i.e., the behaviors were caused by external factors such as the task, other people, or fate).[23] In "explaining" another person's behavior, the tendency is to overestimate the causal role of personal or internal factors and underestimate the causal role of situational or external factors. As an example, consider the student who arrives late for a morning class. Perhaps she is lazy (an internal, dispositional explanation), or perhaps she had a flat tire driving to campus (an external, situational explanation). Absent other information, the professor tends to be biased toward the internal explanation (she's lazy). Perceptual biases are often exacerbated by the *actor-observer effect*, in which people tend to attribute their own behavior to situational factors, but attribute others' behaviors to personal factors, saying in effect, "If I mess up, it's bad luck (the situation, someone else's fault, etc.); if you mess up, it's your fault!"[24]

Recent research has documented the effects of self-serving biases on the negotiation process. For instance, one study found that negotiators in different school districts chose comparison school districts in a self-serving way; that is, the districts they chose as comparison standards for their own district's activities were those that made their districts look most favorable.[25] Another study found that negotiators believed that they used more constructive tactics than their counterparts and that the strength of this self-serving bias increased with the strength of the conflict between the parties.[26]

Perceptual error may also be expressed in the form of biases or distortions in the evaluation of data. For instance, the false-consensus effect is a tendency to overestimate the degree of support and consensus that exists for one's own position, opinions, or behaviors.[27] This can seriously damage a negotiation effort—negotiators subject to it would make faulty judgments regarding tactics or outcome probabilities.

10. Endowment Effect

The endowment effect is the tendency to overvalue something you own or believe you possess. The existence of the endowment effect was shown rather dramatically in a series of experiments involving coffee mugs.[28] In one experiment, some participants were asked whether they would prefer a sum of money or the mug at various possible dollar levels. Based on their responses, it could be determined that they assigned an average value of just over $3.00 to the mug. Other participants were asked to value the mug as a potential buyer; the average value they assigned to the mug was just under $3.00. Members of a third group were actually given the mug, and then asked if they would sell the mug for various amounts. Their answers indicated that they placed a value of more than $7.00 on the mug!

In negotiation, the endowment effect can lead to inflated estimations of value that interfere with reaching a good deal. Discussing endowment effects in the context of negotiations over environmental issues, Max Bazerman and his colleagues argued that the status quo serves as a "potentially dysfunctional anchor point, making mutually beneficial trades more difficult."[29]

11. Ignoring Others' Cognitions

Negotiators often just don't bother to ask about the other party's perceptions and thoughts, which leaves them to work with incomplete information, and thus produces faulty results. Failure to consider others' cognitions allows negotiators to simplify their thinking about otherwise complex processes; this usually leads to a more distributive strategy and causes a failure to recognize the contingent nature of both sides' behaviors and responses. Although this "failure to consider" might be attributed to some basic, underlying bias against the other party, research suggests that it is more often a way "to make decision making under uncertainty more manageable."[30] Research also suggests that training and awareness of this trap reduces its effects only modestly.[31] The emotional drives at work here can be very deep-seated, and they can be avoided only if negotiators explicitly focus on accurately understanding the other party's interests, goals, and perspectives.

12. Reactive Devaluation

Reactive devaluation is the process of devaluing the other party's concessions simply because the other party made them.[32] Such devaluation may be based in emotionality ("I just don't like that so-and-so") or on distrust fostered by past experience. Reactive devaluation leads negotiators to minimize the magnitude of a concession made by a disliked other, to reduce their willingness to respond with a concession of equal size, or to seek even more from the other party once a concession has been made.[33] Reactive devaluation may be minimized by maintaining an objective view of the process, or assigning a colleague to do this task; by clarifying each side's preferences on options and concessions before any are made,[34] or by using a third party to mediate or filter concession-making processes.

"Careful—it might be a trap!"

MANAGING MISPERCEPTIONS AND COGNITIVE BIASES IN NEGOTIATION

Misperceptions and cognitive biases arise automatically and out of conscious awareness as negotiators gather and process information. The question of how best to manage the negative consequences of misperception is difficult to answer. Certainly the first level of managing such distortions is to be aware that they can occur. However, awareness by itself may not be enough; research evidence shows that simply telling people about misconceptions and cognitive biases does little to counteract their effects.[35] Other research indicates that problem definition and problem evaluation are important components of reducing cognitive bias. Careful discussion of the issues and preferences by both negotiators may limit the effects of perceptual biases.[36] More research needs to be conducted to provide negotiators with advice about how to manage the negative effects of misperception and cognitive biases in negotiation. Until then, the best advice that negotiators can follow is simply to be aware of the negative aspects of these effects, and to discuss them in a structured manner within their team and with their counterparts.

Reframing

Negotiators may apply several different frames to the same negotiation. When different negotiators apply different, or mismatched, frames, they will find the bargaining process ambiguous and frustrating. In such situations, it may become necessary to reframe the negotiation systematically, to assist the other party in reframing the negotiation, or to establish a common frame or set of frames within which the negotiation may be conducted more productively. Reframing might involve any of a number of approaches. For instance, rather than perceiving a particular outcome as a loss, the negotiator might reframe it as an opportunity to gain, that is, as a bright-side alternative to approaching a given situation.[37]

Negotiators can also reframe by trying to perceive or understand the situation in a different way or from a different perspective. For instance, they can constructively reframe a problem by defining it in terms that are broader or narrower, bigger or smaller, riskier or less risky, or subject to a longer or shorter time constraint. We discussed how this could be done in Chapter 4, in our review of ways in which the parties could creatively invent options to ensure mutual gain. Because reframing requires negotiators to be flexible during the negotiation itself, during the planning phase, they should plan for multiple contingencies to occur during negotiations. Negotiators cannot completely plan the sequence of a negotiation at the outset but rather need to be prepared for shifts in the discussion.

WHAT IS COMMUNICATED DURING NEGOTIATION?

One of the fundamental questions that researchers in communication and negotiation have examined is, What is communicated during negotiation? This work has taken several different forms but generally involves audio taping or videotaping negotiation role-plays and analyzing the patterns of communication that occur in them. In one study, researchers videotaped executives who participated in a 60-minute, three-person negotiation involving two oil companies.[38] The videotapes were classified into 6,432 verbal units, which were then coded into 24 different response categories. The researchers found that over 70 percent of the verbal tactics that buyers and sellers used during the negotiation were integrative. In addition, buyers and sellers tended to behave reciprocally—when one party used an integrative tactic, the other tended to respond with an integrative tactic.

Most of the communication during negotiation is not about negotiator preferences.[39] The blend of integrative versus distributive content varies as a function of the issues being discussed, but it is also clear that the content of communication is only partly responsible for negotiation outcomes.[40] For example, one party may choose not to communicate certain things (e.g., the reason she chose a different supplier), so her counterpart (e.g., the supplier not chosen) may be unaware why some outcomes occur. We highlight five categories of communication that take place during negotiations.

1. Offers and Counteroffers

According to Tutzauer, "Perhaps the most important communications in a bargaining session are those that convey the disputants' offers and counteroffers."[41] Bargainers have definite preferences and exhibit rational behavior by acting in accordance with those preferences. A communicative framework for negotiation is based on assumptions that (1) the communication of offers is a dynamic process (the offers change or shift over time); (2) the offer process is interactive (bargainers influence each other); and (3) various internal and external factors (e.g., time limitations, reciprocity norms, alternatives, constituency pressures) drive the interaction and "motivate a bargainer to change his or her offer."[42] In other words, the offer-counteroffer process is dynamic and interactive, and subject to situational and environmental constraints. This process constantly revises the parameters of the negotiation, eventually narrowing the bargaining range and guiding the discussion toward a settlement point.

2. Information about Alternatives

Communication in negotiation is not limited to the exchange of offers and counteroffers; another important aspect is how sharing information with the other party influences the negotiation process. For instance, is simply having a best alternative to a negotiated agreement (BATNA) sufficient to give a negotiator an advantage over the other party? Should one's BATNA be communicated to the other person? Robin Pinkley and her colleagues found that the existence of a BATNA changed several things in a negotiation: (1) compared to negotiators without attractive BATNAs, negotiators with attractive BATNAs set higher reservation prices for themselves than their counterparts did; (2) negotiators whose counterparts had attractive BATNAs set lower reservation points for themselves; and (3) when both parties were aware of the attractive BATNA that one of the negotiators had, that negotiator received a more positive negotiation outcome.[43] The results of this research suggest that negotiators with an attractive BATNA should tell the other party about it if they expect to receive its full benefits.

3. Information about Outcomes

Researcher Leigh Thompson and her colleagues examined the effects of sharing different types of information in the negotiation on evaluations of success.[44] The study focused on how winners and losers evaluated their negotiation outcomes (*winners* were defined as negotiators who received more points in the negotiation simulation). Thompson and her colleagues found that winners and losers evaluated their own outcomes equally when they did not know how well the other party had done, but if they found out that the other negotiator had done better, or was simply pleased with his or her outcome, then negotiators felt less positive about their own outcome. This suggests that negotiators should be careful not to share their outcomes or even their positive reactions to the outcomes with the other party, especially if they are going to negotiate with that party again in the future.

4. Social Accounts

Communication in negotiation may also involve "social accounts" that negotiators use to explain things to the other party, especially when negotiators need to justify bad news.[45] Three types of explanations are important: (1) *explanations of mitigating circumstances,* where negotiators suggest that they had no choice in taking the positions they did; (2) *explanations of exonerating circumstances,* where negotiators explain their positions from a broader perspective, suggesting that while their current position may appear negative, it derives from positive motives (e.g., an honest mistake); and (3) *reframing explanations,* where outcomes can be explained by changing the context (e.g., short-term pain for long-term gain).[46] Sitkin and Bies suggest that negotiators who use multiple explanations are more likely to have better outcomes and that the negative effects of poor outcomes can be alleviated by communicating explanations for them.

5. Communication about Process

Lastly, some communication is about the negotiation process itself—how well it is going, or what procedures might be adopted to improve the situation. For example, some communication strategies in negotiation are used to halt conflict spirals that might otherwise lead to impasse or less-than-ideal outcomes.[47] One such strategy involves calling attention to the other party's contentious actions and explicitly labeling the process as counterproductive. Research examining conflict spirals suggests that negotiators seeking to break out of a spiral should resist the natural urge to reciprocate contentious communication from the other party.[48]

HOW PEOPLE COMMUNICATE IN NEGOTIATION

While it may seem obvious that how negotiators communicate is as important as what they have to say, research has examined different aspects of *how* people communicate in negotiation. We address two aspects related to the "how" of communication: the characteristics of language that communicators use, and the selection of a communication channel for sending and receiving messages.

Use of Language

In negotiation, language operates at two levels: the *logical* level (for proposals or offers) and the *pragmatic* level (semantics, syntax, and style). The meaning conveyed by a proposition or statement is a combination of one logical, surface message and several pragmatic (i.e., hinted or inferred) messages. In other words, it is not only what is said and how it is said that matters but also what additional, veiled, or subsurface information is intended, conveyed, or perceived in reception. By way of illustration, consider threats. We often react not only to the substance of a threatening statement but also (and frequently more strongly) to its unspoken messages. Threats can be made more or less credible or compelling by varying the intensity or immediacy of the language used to convey the threat.[49]

Whether the intent is to command and compel, sell, persuade, or gain commitment, how parties communicate in negotiation would seem to depend on the ability of the speaker to encode thoughts properly, as well as on the ability of the listener to understand and decode the intended message(s) (see again Figure 5.1). In addition, negotiators' use of idioms or colloquialisms is often problematic, especially in cross-cultural negotiations (see Chapter 8). The meaning conveyed might be clear to the speaker but confusing to the listener (e.g., "I'm willing to stay until the last dog is hung"—a statement of positive commitment on the part of some regional Americans, but confusing at best to those with different cultural backgrounds, even within the United States). Even if the meaning is clear, the choice of a word or metaphor may convey a lack of sensitivity or create a sense of exclusion, as is often done when men relate strategic business concerns by using sports metaphors ("Well, it's fourth down and goal to go; this is no time to drop the ball").

Finally, a negotiator's choice of words may not only signal a position but also shape and predict it. Tony Simons examined the linguistic patterns of communication in negotiations and found that parties whose statements communicated interests in both the substance of the negotiation (i.e., things) and the relationship with the other party (i.e., people) achieved better, more integrative solutions than parties whose statements were concerned solely with either substance or relationship.[50]

Selection of a Communication Channel

Communication is experienced differently when it occurs through different channels. We may think of negotiation as typically occurring face-to-face, but the reality is that people negotiate through a variety of communication media: over the telephone, in writing, and increasingly through electronic channels such as e-mail and teleconferencing systems (sometimes referred to as "virtual negotiations"). The use of a particular channel shapes both perceptions of the communication task at hand and norms regarding appropriate behavior; accordingly, channel variations are potentially important drivers of negotiation processes and outcomes.[51]

The key variation that distinguishes one communication channel from another is *social presence*—the ability of a channel to carry and convey subtle social cues from sender to receiver that go beyond the literal "text" of the message itself.[52] For example, as an alternative to face-to-face interaction, the telephone preserves one's ability to transmit social cues through inflection or tone of voice, but forfeits the ability to communicate through facial expressions or physical gestures. In written communication, there are only the words and symbols on paper, although one's choice of words and the way they are arranged can certainly convey tone, (in)formality, and emotion.

E-mail is an increasingly ubiquitous mode of personal and organizational communication. Treating e-mail as just another vehicle for written communication is analytically simplistic because e-mail interactions frequently substitute for communication that would otherwise occur via telephone, face-to-face, or perhaps not at all. Accordingly, it is not enough to ask how e-mail communication differs from conventional writing; we need also to understand how interaction (such as negotiation) is affected when people choose to use e-mail rather than communicate through higher social presence channels.

Researchers have been examining the effects of channels in general, and e-mail in particular, on negotiation processes and outcomes during much of the past decade. Unfortunately, there are few consistent findings that point to clear effects. We do know that interacting parties can more easily develop personal rapport in face-to-face communication compared to other channels,[53] and that face-to-face negotiators are more inclined to disclose information truthfully, increasing their ability to attain mutual gain.[54] There is evidence that negotiation through written channels is more likely to end in impasse than negotiation that occurs face-to-face or by phone.[55] There is also evidence that e-mail negotiators reach agreements that are more equal (a balanced division of resources) than face-to-face negotiators.[56] By giving the individual a chance to ponder

BOX 5.1
Top Ten Rules for Virtual Negotiation

1. Take steps to create a face-to-face relationship before negotiation, or early on, so that there is a face or voice behind the e-mail.

2. Be explicit about the normative process to be followed during the negotiation.

3. If others are present in a virtual negotiation (on either your side or theirs) make sure everyone knows who is there and why.

4. Pick the channel (face-to-face, videophone, voice, fax or e-mail, etc.) that is most effective at getting all the information and detail on the table so that it can be fully considered by both sides.

5. Avoid "flaming"; when you must express emotion, label the emotion explicitly so the other knows what it is and what's behind it.

6. Formal turn-taking is not strictly necessary, but try to synchronize offers and counter-offers. Speak up if it is not clear "whose turn it is."

7. Check out assumptions you are making about the other's interests, offers, proposals, or conduct. Less face-to-face contact means less information about the other party, and a greater chance that inferences will get you in trouble, so ask questions.

8. In many virtual negotiations (e.g., e-mail) everything is communicated in writing, so be careful not to make unwise commitments that can be used against you. Neither should you take undue advantage of the other party in this way; discuss and clarify until there is agreement by all.

9. It may be easier to use unethical tactics in virtual negotiation because facts are harder to verify. But resist the temptation: the consequences are just as severe, and perhaps more so, given the incriminating evidence available when virtual negotiations are automatically archived.

10. Not all styles work equally well in all settings. Work to develop a personal negotiation style (collaboration, competition, etc.) that is a good fit with the communication channel you are using. One of the most difficult aspects of negotiation is the actual give-and-take that occurs at the table. Should I stick with this point, or is it time to fold? Should I open the bidding or wait for the other side to take the lead? It requires good judgment to make these.

SOURCE: Adapted from R. J. Lewicki and B. R. Dineen, "Negotiation in Virtual Organizations," in R. Heneman, ed., *Human Resource Management in the Virtual Organization* (2002).

at length the other party's message, and to review and revise one's own communication, e-mail may help less interpersonally skilled parties improve their performance, especially when the alternative is negotiating spontaneously (face-to-face or by phone) with a more accomplished other party. However, negotiators using e-mail may need to work harder at building personal rapport with the other party if they are to overcome limitations of the channel. (See Box 5.1 for a list of ways to maximize effectiveness when negotiations occur in virtual environments.)

HOW TO IMPROVE COMMUNICATION IN NEGOTIATION

Given the many ways that communication can be disrupted and distorted, we can only marvel at the extent to which negotiators can actually understand each other. Failures and distortions in perception, cognition, and communication are the most dominant contributors to breakdowns and failures in negotiation. Research consistently demonstrates that even those parties whose actual goals are compatible or integrative may either fail to reach agreement or reach suboptimal agreements because of the misperceptions of the other party or because of breakdowns in the communication process. We highlight three techniques for improving communication in negotiation: the use of questions, listening, and role reversal.

The Use of Questions

Questions are essential elements in negotiations for securing information; asking good questions enables negotiators to secure a great deal of information about the other party's position, supporting arguments, and needs.

Questions can be divided into two basic categories: those that are manageable, and those that are unmanageable and cause difficulty.[57] Manageable questions cause attention or prepare the other person's thinking for further questions ("May I ask you a question?"), get information ("How much will this cost?"), and generate thoughts ("Do you have any suggestions for improving this?"). Unmanageable questions cause difficulty, give information ("Didn't you know that we couldn't afford this?"), and bring the discussion to a false conclusion ("Don't you think we've talked about this enough?"). Unmanageable questions may produce defensiveness and anger in the other party. Although these questions may yield information, they are likely to make the other party feel uncomfortable and less willing to provide information in the future.

Negotiators can also use questions to manage difficult or stalled negotiations, for example, to pry or lever a negotiation out of a breakdown or an apparent dead end. Table 5.2 identifies a number of such situations and suggests specific questions for dealing with them.[58] The value of such questions seems to be in their power to assist or force the other party to face up to the effects or consequences of his or her behavior, intended and anticipated or not.

Listening

Active listening and *reflecting* are terms that are commonly used in the helping professions such as counseling and therapy.[59] Counselors recognize that communications are frequently loaded with multiple meanings and that the counselor must try to identify these different meanings without making the communicator angry or defensive. There are three major forms of listening:

1. *Passive listening* involves receiving the message while providing no feedback to the sender about the accuracy or completeness of reception. Sometimes

TABLE 5.1   Questions in Negotiation

Manageable Questions	Examples
Open-ended questions—ones that cannot be answered with a simple yes or no. *Who, what, when, where,* and *why* questions.	"Why do you take that position in these deliberations?"
Open questions—invite the other's thinking.	"What do you think of our proposal?"
Leading questions—point toward an answer.	"Don't you think our proposal is a fair and reasonable offer?"
Cool questions—low emotionality.	"What is the additional rate that we will have to pay if you make the improvements on the property?"
Planned questions—part of an overall logical sequence of questions developed in advance.	"After you make the improvements to the property, when can we expect to take occupancy?"
Treat questions—flatter the opponent at the same time as you ask for information.	"Can you provide us with some of your excellent insight on this problem?"
Window questions—aid in looking into the other person's mind.	"Can you tell us how you came to that conclusion?"
Directive questions—focus on a specific point.	"How much is the rental rate per square foot with these improvements?"
Gauging questions—ascertain how the other person feels.	"How do you feel about our proposal?"

Unmanageable Questions	Examples
Close-out questions—force the other party into seeing things your way.	"You wouldn't try to take advantage of us here, would you?"
Loaded questions—put the other party on the spot regardless of the answer.	"Do you mean to tell me that these are the only terms that you will accept?"
Heated questions—high emotionality, trigger emotional responses.	"Don't you think we've spent enough time discussing this ridiculous proposal of yours?"
Impulse questions—occur "on the spur of the moment," without planning, and tend to get conversation off the track.	"As long as we're discussing this, what do you think we ought to tell other groups who have made similar demands on us?"
Trick questions—appear to require a frank answer, but really are "loaded" in their meaning.	"What are you going to do—give in to our demands, or take this to arbitration?"
Reflective trick questions—reflects the other into agreeing with your point of view.	"Here's how I see the situation—don't you agree?"

SOURCE: From Gerard Nierenberg, *Fundamentals of Negotiating* (New York: Hawthorn Books, 1973), pp. 125–26. Used with permission of the author.

TABLE 5.2   Questions for Tough Situations

The Situation	Possible Questions
"Take it or leave it" ultimatums	"If we can come up with a more attractive alternative than that, would you still want me to 'take or leave' your offer?" "Do I have to decide now, or do I have some time to think about it?" "Are you feeling pressure to bring the negotiation to a close?"
Pressure to respond to an unreasonable deadline	"Why can't we negotiate about this deadline?" "If you're under pressure to meet this deadline, what can I do to help remove some of that pressure?" "What's magical about this afternoon? What about first thing in the morning?"
Highball or lowball tactics	"What's your reasoning behind this position?" "What would *you* think I see as a fair offer?" "What standards do you think the final resolution should meet?"
An impasse	"What else can either of us do to close the gap between our positions?" "Specifically what concession do you need from me to bring this to a close right now?" "If it were already six weeks from now and we were looking back at this negotiation, what might we wish we had brought to the table?"
Indecision between accepting and rejecting a proposal	"What's your best alternative to accepting my offer right now?" "If you reject this offer, what will take its place that's better than what you know you'll receive from me?" "How can you be sure that you will get a better deal elsewhere?"
A question about whether the offer you just made is the same as that offered to others	"What do you see as a fair offer, and given that, what do you think of my current offer to you?" "Do you believe that I think it's in my best interest to be unfair to you?" "Do you believe that people can be treated differently, but still all be treated fairly?"
Attempts to pressure, control, or manipulate	"Shouldn't we both walk away from this negotiation feeling satisfied?" "How would you feel if our roles were reversed, and you were feeling the pressure I'm feeling right now?" "Are you experiencing outside pressures to conclude these negotiations?"

SOURCE: Adapted from the book *What to Ask When You Don't Know What to Say* by Sam Deep and Lyle Sussman ©1993. Used by permission of the publisher, Prentice Hall/A Division of Simon & Schuster, Englewood Cliffs, NJ.

passive listening is itself enough to keep a communicator sending information. Negotiators whose counterpart is talkative may find that their best strategy is to sit and listen while the other party eventually works into, or out of, a position on his or her own.

2. *Acknowledgment* is the second form of listening, slightly more active than passive listening. When acknowledging, receivers occasionally nod their heads, maintain eye contact, or interject responses like "I see," "Mm-hmm," "Interesting," "Really," "Sure," "Go on," and the like. These responses are sufficient to keep communicators sending messages, but a sender may misinterpret them as the receiver's agreement with his or her position, rather than as simple acknowledgments of receipt of the message.

3. *Active listening* is the third form of listening. When receivers are actively listening, they restate or paraphrase the sender's message in their own language.

Active listening has generally been recommended for counseling communications, such as employee counseling and performance improvement. In negotiation, it may appear initially that active listening is unsuitable because, unlike a counselor, the receiver normally has a set position and may feel strongly about the issues. By recommending active listening we are not suggesting that receivers should automatically agree with the other party's position and abandon their own. Rather, we are suggesting that active listening is a skill that encourages people to speak more fully about their feelings, priorities, frames of reference, and, by extension, the positions they are taking. When the other party does so, negotiators will better understand his or her positions, the factors and information that support it, and the ways that the position can be compromised, reconciled, or negotiated in accordance with their own preferences and priorities.

Role Reversal

Continually arguing for one particular position in debate leads to a "blindness of involvement," or a self-reinforcing cycle of argumentation that prohibits negotiators from recognizing the possible compatibility between their own position and that of the other party.[60] Through active listening one seeks an understanding of the other party's perspective or frame of reference. Active listening is, however, a somewhat passive process. Role-reversal techniques allow negotiators to understand more completely the other party's positions by actively arguing these positions until the other party is convinced that he or she is understood. For example, someone can ask you how you would respond to the situation that he or she is in. In doing so, you can come to understand that person's position, perhaps can come to accept its validity, and can discover how to modify both of your positions to make them more compatible.

Research suggests that role reversal can be a useful tool for improving communication and the accurate understanding and appreciation of the other party's position in negotiation.[61] However, such understanding does not necessarily lead to easy resolution of the conflict, particularly when accurate communication reveals a fundamental incompatibility in the positions of the two sides.

MOOD, EMOTION, AND NEGOTIATION

Research on negotiation has been dominated by views that have favored rational, cognitive, economic analyses of the negotiation process. These approaches have tended to analyze the rationality of negotiation, examine how negotiators make judgment errors that deviate from rationality, or assess how negotiators can optimize their outcomes. But this overlooks the role played by emotions in the negotiation process.

The role of mood and emotion in negotiation has been the subject of an increasing body of recent theory and research during the last decade.[62] The distinction between mood and emotion is based on three characteristics: specificity, intensity, and duration. Mood states are more diffuse, less intense, and more enduring than emotion states, which tend to be more intense and directed at more specific targets.[63] There are many new and exciting developments in the study of mood, emotion, and negotiation, and we can present only a limited overview here. The following are some selected findings.

Negotiations Create Both Positive and Negative Emotions. Positive emotions can result from being attracted to the other party, feeling good about the development of the negotiation process and the progress that the parties are making, or liking the results that the negotiations have produced.[64] Conversely, negative emotions can result from being turned off by the other party, feeling bad about the development of the negotiation process and the progress being made, or disliking the results. Positive emotions tend to be classified under the single term *happiness,* but we tend to discriminate more precisely among negative emotions.[65] Some negative emotions may tend to be based in dejection while others are based in agitation. Dejection-related emotions (e.g., disappointment, frustration) may lead negotiators to act aggressively, while agitation-related emotions (e.g., fear, anxiety) may lead negotiators to try to retaliate or to get out of the situation.[66]

Positive Emotions Generally Have Positive Consequences for Negotiations. Positive emotions can lead to the following consequences:

- *Positive feelings are more likely to lead the parties toward integrative processes.* Researchers have shown that negotiators who feel positive emotions are more likely to strive for integrative agreements,[67] and are more likely to be flexible in how they arrive at a solution to a problem.[68]

- *Positive feelings promote persistence.* If negotiators feel positively attracted, they are more likely to feel confident and, as a result, to persist in trying to get their concerns and issues addressed in the negotiation, and to achieve better outcomes.[69]

- *Positive feelings result from fair procedures during negotiation.* Researchers have explored how emotional responses are related to the experience of fairness during the negotiation process. Findings indicated that negotiators who see the process as fair experience more positive feelings and are less inclined to express negative emotions following the encounter.[70]

We note, however, that positive feelings may create negative consequences as well. First, negotiators in a positive mood may be less likely to examine closely the arguments put forward by the other party. As a result, they may be more susceptible to deceptive tactics used by a competitive opponent.[71] In addition, because negotiators with positive feelings are less focused on the arguments being made by the other party, they may end up with less-than-optimal outcomes.[72] Finally, if positive feelings create strong positive expectations, parties who are not able to find an integrative agreement are likely to experience the defeat more strongly and perhaps treat the other party more harshly.[73]

Negative Emotions Generally Have Negative Consequences for Negotiations. As we noted above, negative feelings may be based either in dejection or in agitation, and one or both parties may feel the emotions, or the behavior of one may prompt the emotional reaction in the other. Some more specific results from studies are as follows:

- *Negative emotions may lead parties to define the situation as competitive or distributive.* A negative mood increases the likelihood that the actor will increase belligerent behavior toward the other.[74] In a negotiation situation, this negative behavior is most likely to take the shape of a more distributive posture on the issues.

- *Negative emotions may lead parties to escalate the conflict.* When the mood is negative—more specifically, when both parties are dejected, are frustrated, and blame the other—conflict is likely to become personal, the number of issues in the conflict may expand, and other parties may become drawn into the dispute.[75]

- *Negative emotions may lead parties to use retaliatory behavior and obtain poorer outcomes.* When the parties are angry with each other, and when their previous interaction has already led one party to seek to punish the other, the other may choose to retaliate.[76] Negative emotions may also actually lead to less effective outcomes. The more that a negotiator holds the other responsible for destructive behavior in a previous interaction, the more anger and less compassion he or she feels for the other party; this reduces the likelihood of discovering mutually beneficial negotiated solutions.[77]

- *Negative emotions may result from impasse.* When a negotiation ends in impasse, negotiators are more likely to experience negative emotions such as anger and frustration compared to negotiators who successfully reach agreement. However, research suggests that people with more confidence in their negotiating ability are less likely to experience negative emotion in the wake of impasse.[78] This is important because impasse is not always a bad thing—the goal is outcome, not merely reaching an agreement.

Just as positive emotions can create negative outcomes, it is clear that negative emotions can create positive consequences for negotiation. First, negative emotion has information value. It alerts the parties that the situation is problematic and needs attention, which may motivate them to either leave the situation or resolve the problem.[79] An expression of anger may alert the other party that there is a problem in the relationship and lead both parties to work on fixing the problem. Anger can thus serve as a danger signal that motivates both parties to confront the problem directly and search for a resolution.[80]

Emotions Can Be Used Strategically as Negotiation Tactics.   Finally, we have been discussing emotions here as though they were genuine. Given the power that emotions may have in swaying the other side toward one's own point of view, emotions may also be used strategically and manipulatively as influence tactics within negotiation. For example, negotiators may intentionally manipulate emotion in order to get the other side to adopt certain beliefs or take certain actions.[81] In addition to the strategic expression of one's own (genuine or fabricated) emotions, negotiators may also engage in the regulation or management of the emotions of the other party. Effective negotiators are able to adjust their messages to adapt to the emotional state that they perceive is held by the other party.[82] Some psychologists regard the ability to perceive and regulate emotions as a stable individual difference that has come to be known as *emotional intelligence.*[83]

SPECIAL COMMUNICATION CONSIDERATIONS AT THE CLOSE OF NEGOTIATIONS

As negotiations come to a close, negotiators must attend to two key aspects of communication and negotiation simultaneously: the avoidance of fatal mistakes, and the achievement of satisfactory closure in a constructive manner.

Avoiding Fatal Mistakes

Achieving closure in negotiation generally concerns making decisions to accept offers, to compromise priorities, to trade off across issues with the other party, or some combination of these elements. Such decision-making processes can be broken down into four key elements: framing, gathering intelligence, coming to conclusions, and learning from feedback.[84] The first three of these elements we have discussed elsewhere; the fourth element, that of learning (or failing to learn) from feedback, is largely a communication issue, which involves "keeping track of what you expected would happen, systematically guarding against self-serving expectations, and making sure you review the lessons your feedback has provided the next time a similar decision comes along."[85] Russo and Schoemaker warn of 10 decision traps that can ensnare decision makers, resulting in suboptimal decisions (see Box 5.2). Although some of these traps occur in earlier stages of the negotiation, we suspect that a number of them occur at the end of a negotiation, when parties are in a hurry to wrap up loose ends and cement a deal.

Achieving Closure

Gary Karrass, focusing on sales negotiations in particular, has specific advice about communication near the end of a negotiation.[86] Karrass enjoins negotiators to "know when to shut up," to avoid surrendering important information needlessly, and to refrain from making "dumb remarks" that push a wavering counterpart away from the agreement he or she is almost ready to endorse. The other side of this is to "beware of garbage and the garbage truck" by recognizing the other party's faux pas and dumb remarks for what they are, and refusing to respond or be distracted by them. Karrass also reminds of the need to watch out for last-minute hitches, such as nit-picking or second-guessing by parties who didn't participate in the bargaining process but who have

BOX 5.2

Decision Traps and Learning from Negotiation Feedback

1. *Plunging in* involves reaching a conclusion to a problem before fully identifying the essence or crux of the problem (e.g., forcing negotiations into the end stage prematurely by pushing for a quantitative or substantive resolution to a problem that has been incompletely defined or is basically relational).

2. *Overconfidence in one's own judgment* involves blocking, ignoring, or failing to seek factual information that might contradict one's own assumptions and opinions (e.g., strictly adhering to a unilateral strategy, regardless of other information that emerges during the course of the negotiation).

3. *Frame blindness* involves perceiving, then solving, the wrong problem, accompanied by overlooking options and losing sight of objectives because they do not fit the frame being used (e.g., forcing resolution of a complex, mixed-motive dispute into some simplistic, concrete measure of performance such as money).

4. *Lack of frame control* involves failing to test different frames to determine if they fit the issues being discussed, or being unduly influenced by the other party's frame (e.g., agreeing to a suboptimal outcome, because the other party has taken advantage of our aversion to not reaching an agreement—see Neale and Bazerman, 1992).

5. *Shortsighted shortcuts* involves misusing heuristics or rules of thumb, such as convenient (but misleading) referent points (e.g., accepting the other party's commitment to turning over a new leaf when past experience suggests that he or she is really unlikely to do so).

6. *Shooting from the hip* involves managing too much information in one's head rather than adopting and using a systematic process of evaluation and choice (e.g., proceeding on gut feelings or eye contact alone in deciding to accept a resolution, trusting that problems will not occur or that they will be easily worked out if they do).

7. *Group failure* involves not managing the group process effectively and instead assuming that smart and well-intentioned individuals can invariably produce a durable, high-quality group decision (see Janis's 1982 work on "groupthink"; e.g., in order to move stalled decisions, a group might take a vote on accepting a resolution, thereby disenfranchising the minority who do not vote for the resolution and stopping the deliberative process short of achieving its integrative possibilities).

8. *Fooling yourself about feedback* involves failing to use feedback correctly, either to protect one's ego or through the bias of hindsight (e.g., dealing with the embarrassment of being outmaneuvered by the other party because of a lack of good information or a failure to prepare rigorously).

9. *Not keeping track* involves assuming that learning occurs automatically and thus not keeping systematic records of decisions and related outcomes (e.g., losing sight of the gains and deals purchased with concessions and trade-offs made during the negotiation, or not applying the lessons of one negotiation episode to future negotiations).

10. *Failure to audit one's own decision processes* involves failing to establish and use a plan to avoid the traps mentioned here or the inability or unwillingness to fully understand one's own style, warts and all (thus, doggedly adhering to a flawed or inappropriate approach to negotiation, even in the face of frequent failures and suboptimal outcomes).

SOURCE: Adapted from Russo and Schoemaker, 1989.

the right or responsibility to review it. Karrass says to expect such hitches and to be prepared to manage them with aplomb. Finally, Karrass notes the importance of reducing the agreement to written form, recognizing that the party who writes the contract is in a position to achieve clarity of purpose and conduct for the deal.

CHAPTER SUMMARY

In this chapter we have taken a multifaceted look at the role of perception and communication in negotiation. We examined how negotiators make sense of negotiation and the role that communication processes play in negotiation processes and outcomes.

The first portion of the chapter discussed perception and negotiation, beginning with a brief overview of the perceptual process. We discussed how framing influences perceptions in negotiation, and how reframing and issue development both change negotiator perceptions during negotiations. The chapter then reviewed the research findings on important cognitive biases in negotiation, and considered ways to manage misperception and cognitive biases in negotiation.

Our discussion then shifted to a discussion of *what* is communicated during negotiation. Rather than simply being an exchange of preferences about solutions, negotiations can cover a wide-ranging number of topics in an environment where each party is trying to influence the other. This was followed by an exploration of two issues related to *how* people communicate in negotiation: the use of language, and the selection of a communication channel.

In the final three sections of the chapter we considered how to improve communication in negotiation, mood and emotion in negotiation, and special communication considerations at the close of negotiation.

ENDNOTES

1. Babcock, Wang, and Loewenstein, 1996; de Dreu and van Lange, 1995; Thompson, 1995; Thompson and Hastie, 1990a.
2. Sherif, Harvey, White, Hood, and Sherif, 1988.
3. Cooper, 1981.
4. Bruner and Tagiuri, 1954.
5. Ibid.
6. Bateson, 1972; Goffman, 1974.
7. Putnam and Holmer, 1992, p. 129.
8. The foundations of this approach are in behavioral decision theory and the prospect theory of human judgment and decision making (e.g., Bazerman, 1998; Neale and Bazerman 1991; Tversky and Kahnemann, 1981).
9. For reviews, see Bazerman and Carroll, 1987; Neale and Bazerman, 1992b; Thompson and Hastie, 1990b. Whether negotiators misperceive information or misprocess information remains a technical debate in the communication and negotiation literature that is beyond the scope of this book.
10. Brockner, 1992; Staw, 1981.
11. Bazerman, Magliozzi, and Neale, 1985; Bazerman and Neale, 1983; Thompson, 1990b.
12. Pinkley, Griffith, and Northcraft, 1995; Thompson and Hastie, 1990a, 1990b.

13. Harinck, de Dreu, and Van Vianen, 2000.
14. Diekmann, Tenbrunsel, Shah, Schroth, and Bazerman, 1996; Kristensen and Garling, 1997; Ritov, 1996.
15. Northcraft and Neale, 1987.
16. Tversky and Kahneman, 1981.
17. Bazerman, Magliozzi, and Neale, 1985; de Dreu, Carnevale, Emans, and van de Vliert, 1994; Neale, Huber, and Northcraft, 1987; Schurr, 1987. However, Bottom (1998) provides evidence that the influence of framing and risk propensity on negotiation outcomes varies with nature of the negotiation task.
18. Neale and Bazerman, 1992a, p. 50.
19. Ball, Bazerman, and Carroll, 1991; Bazerman and Samuelson, 1983; Foreman and Murnighan, 1996.
20. Neale and Bazerman, 1983.
21. Lim, 1997.
22. Bottom and Paese, 1999.
23. Heider, 1958.
24. Jones and Nisbett, 1976.
25. Babcock, Wang, and Loewenstein, 1996.
26. de Dreu, Nauta, and van de Vliert, 1995.
27. Ross, Greene, and House, 1977.
28. Kahneman, Knetsch, and Thaler, 1990.
29. Bazerman, Moore, and Gillespie, 1999, p. 1288.
30. Carroll, Bazerman, and Maury, 1988.
31. Carroll, Delquie, Halpern, and Bazerman, 1990.
32. Stillenger, Epelbaum, Keltner, and Ross, 1990.
33. Neale and Bazerman, 1992b.
34. Stillenger et al., 1990.
35. Babcock and Loewenstein, 1997; Foreman and Murnighan, 1996; Thompson and Hastie, 1990a.
36. Arunachalam and Dilla, 1995.
37. Kahneman and Tversky, 1979.
38. Alexander, Schul, and Babakus, 1991.
39. Carnevale, Pruitt, and Seilheimer, 1981.
40. Weingart, Hyder, and Prietula, 1996; Olekalns, Smith, and Walsh, 1996.
41. Tutzauer, 1992, p. 67.
42. Ibid., p. 73.
43. Pinkley, 1995; Pinkley, Neale, and Bennett, 1994.
44. Thompson, Valley, and Kramer, 1995.
45. Bies and Shapiro, 1987; Shapiro, 1991.
46. Sitkin and Bies, 1993.
47. Brett, Shapiro, and Lytle, 1998.
48. Ibid.
49. Gibbons, Bradac, and Busch, 1992.
50. Simons, 1993.
51. Bazerman, Curhan, Moore, and Valley, 2000; Lewicki and Dineen, 2002.
52. Short, Williams, and Christie, 1976.
53. Drolet and Morris, 2000.
54. Valley, Moag, and Bazerman, 1998.
55. Ibid.

56. Croson, 1999.
57. Nierenberg, 1976.
58. Deep and Sussman, 1993.
59. Rogers, 1957, 1961.
60. Rapoport, 1964.
61. Johnson, 1971; Walcott, Hopmann, and King, 1977.
62. For reviews of research literature on emotion in negotiation, see Allred, Mallozzi, Matsui, and Raia, 1997; Barry, Fulmer, and Van Kleef, 2002; Barry and Oliver, 1996; Kumar, 1997.
63. Forgas, 1992; Parrott, 2001.
64. Carver and Scheir, 1990.
65. Kumar, 1997.
66. Higgins, 1987; Berkowitz, 1989.
67. Carnevale and Isen, 1986.
68. Isen and Baron, 1991.
69. Kramer, Pommerenke, and Newton, 1993.
70. Hegtvedt and Killian, 1999.
71. Bless, Bohner, Schwartz, and Strack, 1988.
72. Kumar, 1997.
73. Parrott, 1994.
74. Veitch and Griffith, 1976.
75. Kumar, 1997.
76. Allred, 1998; Bies and Tripp, 1998.
77. Allred, Mallozzi, Matsui, and Raia, 1997.
78. O'Connor and Arnold, 2001.
79. van de Vliert, 1985.
80. Daly, 1991.
81. Barry, 1999.
82. Thompson, Nadler, and Kim, 1999.
83. Mayer, Salovey, and Caruso, 2000.
84. Russo and Schoemaker, 1989.
85. Ibid., p. 3.
86. Karrass, 1985.

CHAPTER 6

Finding and Using Negotiation Leverage

In this chapter, we focus on leverage in negotiation. By *leverage,* we mean the tools negotiators can use to give themselves an advantage or increase the probability of achieving their objectives. All negotiators want leverage; they want to know what they can do to put pressure on the other party, persuade the other to see it their way, get the other to give them what they want, get one up on the other, or change the other's mind. We have already talked about many leverage tactics in Chapters 3 and 4; the tactics of distributive bargaining and integrative negotiation are leverage tactics, used in the service of achieving the best deal for one or both parties.

In this chapter, we dissect the concept of leverage in relation to the use of *power* and *influence*. It is important to be clear about the distinction between the two. We treat power as the potential to alter the attitudes and behaviors of others that an individual brings to a given situation. Influence, on the other hand, can be thought of as power in action—the actual messages and tactics an individual undertakes in order to change the attitudes and/or behaviors of others. To put it concisely, power is potential influence, while influence is kinetic power.[1]

We begin by defining the nature of power and discussing some of the dynamics of its use in negotiation. We will focus on the power sources that give negotiators the capacity for leverage. We will consider three major ones: information and expertise, control over resources, and one's position in an organization or network. We then move to discussing the process for managing this power—influence—which we will view as attempts to change the other's perspective, position, or behavior.

LEVERAGE AS ADVANTAGE: WHY IS POWER IMPORTANT TO NEGOTIATORS?

Leverage is often used synonymously with *power*. Most negotiators believe that power is important in negotiation, because it gives one negotiator an advantage over the other party. Negotiators who have this advantage usually want to use it to secure a greater share of the outcomes or achieve their preferred solution. Seeking leverage in negotiation usually arises from one of two perceptions:

1. The negotiator believes he or she currently has *less* leverage than the other party. In this situation, a negotiator believes the other party already has some advantage that can and will be used, so he or she seeks power to offset or counterbalance that advantage.

2. The negotiator believes he or she needs *more* leverage than the other party to increase the probability of securing a desired outcome. In this context, the negotiator believes that added power is necessary to gain or sustain an advantage in the upcoming negotiation.

Embedded in these two beliefs are significant questions of tactics and motives. The tactics may be designed to enhance the negotiator's own power or to diminish the other's power, and to create a state of either power equalization (both parties have relatively equal or countervailing power) or power difference (one's power is greater than the other's). The motive questions relate to why the negotiator is using the tactics. Most commonly, negotiators employ tactics designed to equalize power as a way to level the playing field. Such tactics minimize the capacity for either side to dominate the relationship and often serve as the groundwork for moving discussions toward a compromising or collaborative, integrative agreement. In contrast, negotiators may employ tactics designed to create power difference as a way to gain advantage or to block the other party's power moves. Such tactics enhance the capacity for one side to dominate the relationship, and often serve as the groundwork for a competing or dominating strategy and a distributive agreement. Box 6.1 presents a framework on the merits of using power as a negotiating tactic.

In general, negotiators who don't care about their power or who have matched power—equally high or low—will find that their deliberations proceed with greater ease and simplicity toward a mutually satisfying and acceptable outcome. In contrast, negotiators who do care about their power and seek to match or exceed the other's power are probably seeking a solution in which they either do not lose the negotiation (a defensive posture) or win the negotiation (an offensive posture).

Power is implicated in the use of many negotiation tactics, such as hinting to the other party that you have good alternatives (a strong BATNA) in order to increase your leverage. Nevertheless, relatively few research studies have focused specifically on power and influence tactics in negotiation. Many of the findings discussed in this chapter are drawn from broader studies of how managers influence one another in organizations, and how to use persuasion effectively in communication and marketing. We will apply those findings to negotiation situations as appropriate.

A DEFINITION OF POWER

In a broad sense, people have power when they have "the ability to bring about outcomes they desire" or "the ability to get things done the way [they want] them to be done."[2] But there is a problem here: This definition seems to focus on power as absolute and coercive, which is too restrictive for understanding how power is used in negotiation. We prefer what may be called a *relational* definition of power:

> an actor . . . has power in a given situation (situational power) to the degree that he can *satisfy the purposes (goals, desires, or wants) that he is attempting to fulfill in that situation.* Power is a relational concept; it does not reside in the individual but rather in the relationship of the person to his environment. Thus, the power of an actor in a given situation is determined by the characteristics of the situation as well as by his own characteristics.[3]

Before moving forward, we want to draw attention to the weakness of any discussion of power. It would be nice to be able to write this chapter and delineate a comprehensive

---

BOX 6.1
Interests, Rights, and Power in Negotiation

One way of thinking about the role of power in negotiation is in relation to other, alternative strategic options. In Chapter 2 we introduced a framework developed by Ury, Brett, and Goldberg[4] that compares three different strategic approaches to negotiation: interests, rights, and power.

- Negotiators focus on *interests* when they strive to learn about each other's interests and priorities as a way to work toward a mutually satisfying agreement that creates value.

- Negotiators focus on *rights* when they seek to resolve a dispute by drawing upon decision rules or standards grounded in principles of law, fairness, or perhaps an existing contract.

- Negotiators focus on *power* when they use threats or other means to try to coerce the other party into making concessions.

This framework assumes that all three approaches can potentially exist in a single situation; negotiators make choices about where to place their focus. But do negotiators really use all three? Should they? A study by Anne Lytle, Jeanne Brett, and Debra Shapiro of a simulated contract dispute between two companies found that most negotiators cycled through all three strategies—interests, rights, and power—during the same encounter. They also found that negotiators tended to reciprocate these strategies. A coercive power strategy, for example, may be met with a power strategy in return, which can lead to a negative conflict spiral and a poor (or no) agreement.

Their findings suggest that power tactics (and rights tactics) may be most useful when the other party refuses to negotiate or when negotiations have broken down and need to be restarted. In these situations, not much is risked by making threats based on rights or power, but the threat itself may help the other party appreciate the severity of the situation.

The success of power tactics (and rights tactics) depends to a great extent on *how* they are implemented. To be effective, threats must be specific and credible, targeting the other party's high-priority interests. Otherwise, the other party has little incentive to comply. Make sure that you leave an avenue for the other party to "turn off" the threat, save face, and reopen the negotiations around interests.

SOURCE: Adapted from A. L. Lytle, J. M. Brett, and D. L. Shapiro, "The Strategic Use of Interests, Rights, and Power to Resolve Disputes," *Negotiation Journal* 15(1) (1999), pp. 31–51.

---

review of the power sources available to negotiators, the major configurations of power bases assembled as influence strategies, and the conditions under which each should be used. Unfortunately, such a task is not just daunting but impossible, for two principal reasons. First, the effective use of power requires a sensitive and deft touch, and its consequences may vary greatly from one person to the next. In the hands of one user, the tools of power can craft a benevolent realm of prosperity and achievement, whereas in the hands of another, they may create a nightmare of tyranny and disorder. Second, not only do the key actors and targets change from situation to situation, but the context in which the tools of power operate changes as well. As a result, the best we can do is to identify a few key sources of power and the major influence strategies that accompany them.

TABLE 6.1 Sources of Power

Sources of Power	Description
Information and expertise	The accumulation and presentation of data intended to change the other person's point of view or position on an issue; and (for expertise) an acknowledged accumulation of information, or mastery of a body of information, on a particular problem or issue.
Control over resources	The accumulation of money, raw material, labor, time, and equipment that can be used as incentives to encourage compliance or as punishments for noncompliance.
Position	Power derived from being located in a particular position in an organizational or communication structure; leads to two different kinds of leverage: • Formal authority, derived from occupying a key position in a hierarchical organization. • Access to or control over information or supply flows, derived from location within a network.

SOURCES OF POWER—HOW PEOPLE ACQUIRE POWER

Understanding the different ways in which power can be exercised is best accomplished by looking first at the various sources of power. In their seminal work on power, French and Raven identified five major types: expert power, reward power, coercive power, legitimate power, and referent power.[5] Although many contemporary discussions of power are still grounded in this typology, we will focus our attention on three specific variations: information and expertise, control over resources, and position power (see Table 6.1).

Power Based on Information and Expertise

Within the context of negotiation, information is perhaps the most common source of power. Information power is derived from the negotiator's ability to assemble and organize data to support his or her position, arguments, or desired outcomes. Negotiators may also use information as a tool to challenge the other party's position or desired outcomes, or to undermine the effectiveness of the other's negotiating arguments. Even in the simplest negotiation, the parties take a position and then present arguments and facts to support that position. I want to sell a used motorcycle for $1,500; you say it is worth only $1,000. I proceed to tell you how much I paid for it, point out what good condition it is in and what attractive features it has, and explain why it is worth $1,500. You point out that it is five years old, emphasize the paint chips and rust spots, and comment that the tires are worn and need to be replaced. You also tell me that you can't afford to spend $1,500. After 20 minutes of discussion about the motorcycle, we have exchanged extensive information about its original cost, age, depreciation, and current condition, as well as your financial situation and my need to raise cash. We then settle

---

BOX 6.2
Planning for a Car-Buying Negotiation

Before the age of electronic information, many consumers approached buying a car with the same enthusiasm as visiting the dentist. Customers knew their role was to scoff at the asking price, threaten to walk away from the vehicle, and generally engage in tough negotiation postures in order to get the best deal. Still, after they drove the car off the lot, nagging doubts remained about whether or not they paid too much for their new car.

Savvy customers have always known that they should determine their real requirements for an automobile, find several cars that meet their objectives, determine the book value of each car, contact current owners to determine their satisfaction, and keep from becoming emotionally attached to a particular automobile. These strategies certainly have helped people prepare for negotiations with their local dealer. However, customers still had to rely largely on guesswork to determine what price offers would be acceptable to the dealership.

Today, however, price information on new and used cars is readily available through the Internet and other sources. Customers can enter negotiations with car dealers armed with accurate facts and figures about the car's cost to the dealership, the actual price for various options, prices in neighboring states, and the customer and dealer incentives in place at a given time. Car buyers who take the time to gather information about "real" prices report saving hundreds or even thousands of dollars on automobiles. This wealth of information gives consumers more power in negotiations with dealers. Ultimately, that power leads to lower prices on new automobiles (Blumstein, R., "Haggling in cyberspace transforms car sales." *The Wall Street Journal,* December 30, 1977, pp. B1, B6. McGraw, D., "Will he own the road?" *U.S. News & World Report.,* October 20, 1977, pp. 45–54.).

---

on a price of $1,300, including a "loan" of $300 I have given you. (See Box 6.2 on the power of information in buying a new car.)

The exchange of information in negotiation is also at the heart of the concession-making process. As each side presents information, a common definition of the situation emerges. The amount and kind of information shared, and the way the negotiators share it, allow both parties to derive a common (and hopefully realistic) picture of the current condition of the motorcycle, its market worth, and the preferences of each side. Moreover, this information need not be 100 percent accurate to be effective; bluffs, exaggerations, omissions, and outright lies may work just as well. I may tell you I paid $2,200 for the bike when I paid only $2,000; I may not tell you that the clutch needs to be replaced. You may not tell me that you actually can pay $1,500 but simply don't want to spend that much, or that you plan to buy this bike regardless of what you have to pay for it. (We return to these issues of bluffing and misrepresentation in Chapter 7, when we discuss the ethics of lying and deception.)

Power derived from expertise is a special form of information power. The power that comes from information is available to anyone who assembles facts and figures to support arguments, but expert power is accorded to those who are seen as having achieved some level of command and mastery of a body of information. Experts are accorded respect, deference, and credibility based on their experience, study, or accomplishments.

One or both parties in a negotiation will give experts' arguments more credibility than those of nonexperts—but only to the extent that the expertise is seen as functionally relevant to the persuasion situation.[6] For example, someone knowledgeable about cars may not be an expert on motorcycles.

Power Based on Control over Resources

People who control resources have the capacity to give them to someone who will do what they want, and withhold them (or take them away) from someone who doesn't do what they want. *Resources* can be many things. Particular resources are more useful as instruments of power to the extent that they are highly valued by participants in the negotiation. In an organizational context, some of the most important resources are the following:

1. Money, in its various forms: cash, salary, budget allocations, grants, bonus money, expense accounts, and discretionary funds.
2. Supplies: raw materials, components, pieces, and parts.
3. Human capital: available labor supply, staff that can be allocated to a problem or task, temporary help.
4. Time: free time, the ability to meet deadlines, the ability to control a deadline. If time pressure is operating on one or both parties, the ability to help someone meet or move a deadline can be extremely powerful.
5. Equipment: machines, tools, technology, computer hardware and software, vehicles.
6. Critical services: repair, maintenance, upkeep, installation and delivery, technical support, transportation.
7. Interpersonal support: verbal praise and encouragement for good performance or criticism for bad performance. This is an interesting resource, because it is available to almost anyone, does not require significant effort to acquire, and is quite powerful on its own.

The ability to control and dispense resources is a major power source in organizations.[7] Power also comes from creating a resource stockpile in an environment where resources appear to be scarce. Jeffrey Pfeffer in his book *Managing with Power* illustrated how powerful political and corporate figures build empires founded on resource control.[8] During his early years in Congress, Lyndon Johnson took over the "Little Congress" (a speaker's bureau for clerical personnel and aides to members of Congress) and leveraged it into a major power base that led him to become Speaker of the House and eventually president. Similarly, Robert Moses, beginning as the parks commissioner of New York City, built a power empire that resulted in the successful construction of 12 bridges, 35 highways, 751 playgrounds, 13 golf courses, 18 swimming pools, and more than 2 million acres of park land in the New York metropolitan area—a base he used to become a dominant power broker in the city.

To use resources as a basis for power, negotiators must develop or maintain control over some scarce commodity that the other party wants, such as physical space, jobs, budget authorizations, or raw materials. Successful control over resources also requires that the other party must deal directly with the power holder. Finally, the power holder must be willing to allocate resources depending on the other's compliance or cooperation with the power holder's requests. The increasing scarcity of resources of all kinds has led to the new golden rule of organizations: "Whoever has the gold makes the rules."

Power Based on One's Position

We discuss two kinds of power in this section: legitimate power, and power derived from location in an organizational structure. Legitimate power is derived from occupying a particular job, office, or position in an organizational hierarchy. In this case, the power resides in the title, duties, and responsibilities of the job itself. Thus, a newly promoted vice president acquires some legitimate power merely from being a vice president. The second type of power also comes from location in an organizational structure, but not necessarily a hierarchical structure. In this case, power is derived from whatever flows through that particular location in the structure (usually information and resources, such as money). The person occupying a certain position may not have a formal title or office; his or her leverage comes from the ability to control and manage what "flows" through that position. We will now describe each kind of power in more detail.

Legitimate Power. There are times when people respond to directions from another, even directions they do not like, because they feel it is proper (legitimate) for the other to direct them and proper (obligatory) for them to obey. This is the effect of legitimate power.

Legitimate power is at the foundation of our social structure. When individuals and groups organize into any social system—a small business, a combat unit, a union, a political action organization, a sports team, a task force—they almost immediately create some form of structure and hierarchy. They elect or appoint a leader and may introduce formal rules about decision making, work division, allocation of responsibilities, and conflict management. Without this social order, either the group can take little coordinated action (chaos prevails), or everyone is required to participate in every decision and thus group coordination takes forever. Social structures are efficient and effective, and this fact creates the basis for legitimate power. People are willing to give up their right to participate in every decision by vesting authority in someone who can act on their behalf (a president, leader, or spokesperson). By creating a group structure that gives one person a power base, group members also create an obligation in themselves to obey that person's directives.

People can acquire legitimate power in several ways. First, it may be acquired at birth. Elizabeth II has the title of Queen of England and all of the stature the title commands (although she has little actual power in terms of her ability to run the day-to-day affairs of Britain). Second, legitimate power may be acquired by election to a designated office: the president of the United States has substantial legitimate power derived from the constitutional structure of the American government. Third, legitimate power is derived simply by appointment or promotion to some organizational position. Thus, holding the title of director or general manager entitles a person to all the rights, responsibilities, and privileges that go with that position. Finally, some legitimate authority comes to an individual who occupies a position for which other people simply show respect. Usually, such respect is derived from the intrinsic social good or important social values of that person's position or organization. In many societies, the young listen to and obey the old. People also listen to college presidents or the members of the clergy. They follow their advice because they believe it is proper to do so. Clergy members, college presidents, and many others may have precious little they can actually give to individuals as rewards or use against them as coercive punishments, yet they have considerable legitimate power.[9]

The effectiveness of formal authority is derived from the willingness of followers to acknowledge the legitimacy of the organizational structure and the system of rules and regulations that empowers its leaders.[10] In short, legitimate power cannot function without obedience, or the consent of the governed. If enough British citizens question the legitimacy of the queen and her authority—even given the hundreds of years of tradition and law on which the monarchy is founded—her continued rule will be in serious jeopardy. If the president's cabinet and key advisers are unwilling to act on and dispatch presidential orders, then the president's effectiveness is nullified. When enough people begin to distrust the authority or discredit its legitimacy, they will begin to defy it and thereby undermine its potential as a power source. Because legitimate power can be undermined if followers choose to no longer recognize the power holder's authority, it is not uncommon for power holders to accumulate other power sources (such as resource control or information) to fortify their power base.

Location in an Organizational Structure.   Even without a lofty position or title, individuals can become powerful because of the way that their actions and responsibilities are embedded in a larger organization. For example, individuals who have access to a large amount of information, who are responsible for collecting vital data and resources, or who are in jobs the organization deems central to its mission may become very powerful.[11] The job may not have a fancy title, a big budget, or a large corner office, but it can confer a significant amount of power by virtue of the amount of information and resource control associated with it.

Understanding power in this way entails thinking about an organization not as a hierarchy, but as a network of interrelationships. Network schematics represent key individuals as circles or nodes, and relationships between individuals as lines of transaction. See Figure 6.1 for an example of a network, as compared to an organizational hierarchy. These lines connect individuals who interact or need to interact with each other in the organization. Through information and resources as the primary focus of transactions, personal relationships and authority may also be negotiated across network lines. In formal hierarchy terms, authority is directly related to how high the position is on the vertical organization chart and how many people report to that individual from lower levels. In network terms, in contrast, power is determined by location within the set of relationships. Key location concepts include centrality, criticality, flexibility, and visibility.

Centrality.   The more central a node is in a network of exchanges and transactions, the more power that node's occupant will have. Centrality may be determined by the amount of information that passes through a node, the number of transactions that

FIGURE 6.1   Comparing Organization Hierarchies and Networks

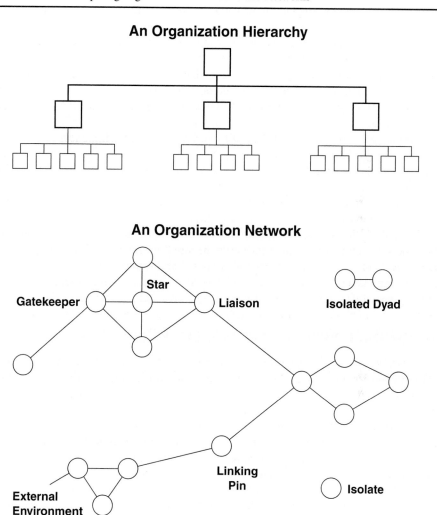

occur through the node, or the degree to which the node is central to managing information flow. In the network depicted in Figure 6.1, the "star" has greater centrality, and therefore more power.

Criticality and Relevance.   A second source of network power is the criticality of the node. Although a node may not have a large amount of information or resources flowing through it, what does flow through it may be essential to the organization's mission, major task, or key product. People who depend highly on others may become critical to the degree that they are charged with assembling information from many locations. In Figure 6.1, "liaisons" and "linking pins" perform this role.

Flexibility. A third source of network power lies in the position's flexibility, or the degree to which the key individual can exercise discretion in how certain decisions are made or who gains access. Flexibility is often related to criticality (see preceding discussion). A classic example of flexibility is the role of "gatekeeper" (Figure 6.1), the person in a network who controls the access to a key figure or group.

Visibility. Finally, nodes differ in their degree of visibility—that is, how visible the task performance is to others in the organization. If a negotiator gains significant concessions from the other party while being watched, the team will give that negotiator a great deal of affirmation. A node with high centrality and criticality may not be visible, but if it is not, it is much less likely to be recognized and rewarded.

Summary

In this section, we considered three major sources of leverage: information and expertise, control over resources, and structural position. Imbalances in these power sources across the table are inevitable, but effective negotiators can take steps to alter the power dynamics before and during the negotiation. Box 6.3 offers some insights into how negotiators recognize and remedy power imbalances.

We turn next to a detailed examination of how negotiators implement these power sources through the strategies and tactics of interpersonal influence.

MANAGING POWER: INFLUENCE AND PERSUASION

During negotiations, actors frequently need to convince the other party they have offered something of value, that their offer is reasonable, and that they cannot offer more. Negotiators may also want to alter the other party's beliefs about the importance of his own objectives and convince him that his concessions are not as valuable as he first believed. Negotiators may portray themselves as likable people who should be treated decently. All these efforts are designed to use information, as well as the qualities of the sender and receiver of that information, to adjust the other party's positions, perceptions, and opinions; we call this group of tactics *influence*.

People differ widely in their ability to use influence effectively. Some observers think that the ability to persuade is something with which people are born—something they either have or don't have. Although the natural persuasive abilities of people do differ, persuasion is as much a science as a native ability; improving persuasive skills is an opportunity open to everyone.

Our discussion of influence is based on an approach developed by Richard Petty and John Cacioppo that suggests that there are two general paths by which people are persuaded.[12] The first path occurs consciously and involves integration of the message into the individual's previously existing cognitive structures (thoughts, intellectual frameworks, etc.). Petty and Cacioppo have labeled this path to persuasion the *central route*, which "occurs when motivation and ability to scrutinize issue-relevant arguments are relatively high."[13] The other route to persuasion, the *peripheral route*, is characterized by subtle cues and context, with less cognitive processing of the message. Persua-

---

BOX 6.3
The Shadow Negotiation

How do negotiators manage unequal power at the bargaining table? Researchers Deborah Kolb and Judith Williams interviewed hundreds of executives about their negotiation experiences. From their interviews, Kolb and Williams came to see the existence of what they call the "shadow negotiation"—the subtle yet complex interaction lurking beneath the formal negotiation itself where issues of power imbalance, conversational tone, and influence over process are settled. Kolb and Williams identify three strategic levers available to help people navigate the shadow negotiation:

- *Power moves* are designed to bring reluctant bargainers back to the table. They can take the form of incentives offered to help the other side recognize that they will benefit from negotiation, pressure tactics that lead the other to realize that the status quo is unacceptable, and the enlistment of allies to help the other party see the advantage of negotiating.

- *Process moves* are designed to alter the negotiation process itself through adjustments to the agenda, sequencing, decision rules, and the like. For example, a competitive mindset may favor those who talk loudest or longest, or who like bluffing and gamesmanship. A negotiator who is uncomfortable with this dynamic can try to reframe the process, for example, by redefining what was a competition of resources into a collaborative group process.

- *Appreciative moves* are designed to break cycles of contentiousness that may have led to deteriorating communication, acrimony, or even silence. Examples of appreciative moves are tactics that help the other party save face in an argument, maintain dialogue and information exchange in the face of pressures to disengage, or invite new perspectives into the discussion to try to break a logjam or reverse a skid toward stalemate.

SOURCE: Adapted from D. M. Kolb and J. Williams, "Breakthrough Bargaining," *Harvard Business Review* 79(2) (2001), pp. 89–97.

---

sion via the peripheral route is thought to occur automatically (i.e., out of conscious awareness), leading to "attitude change without argument scrutiny."[14] Because the information is not integrated into existing cognitive structures, persuasion occurring via this route is likely to last a shorter time than persuasion occurring via the central route. A simple example of peripheral-route persuasion is the listener who is convinced by the impressive credentials of the speaker rather than by the arguments the speaker is actually presenting.

For clarity of presentation, we will represent elements from both paths in a single diagram (Figure 6.2). Many of the common elements used to increase leverage are part of the central route: the structure and content of the message, or the relationship between sender and receiver. However, several influence strategies are designed to persuade

FIGURE 6.2   Leverage: Two Routes to Influence

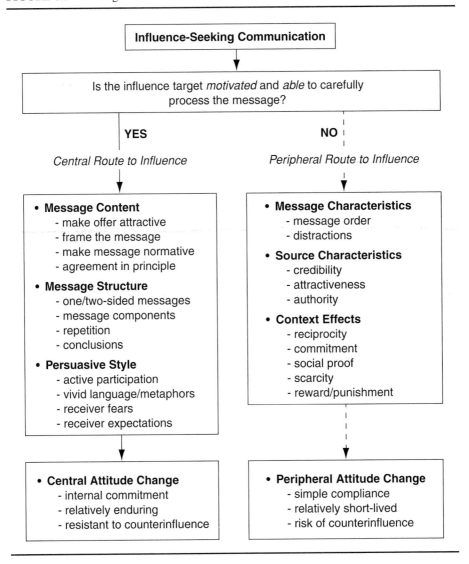

through the indirect or peripheral route, such as enhancing the attractiveness and cred-ibility of the source, invoking the principle of reciprocity (you should do something for me because I did something for you), or drawing on appeals to popularity (you should think this way because many others do). The remainder of this chapter will address the leverage factors presented in Figure 6.2. We organize this discussion according to the distinction between central and peripheral routes to influence.

THE CENTRAL ROUTE TO INFLUENCE:
THE MESSAGE AND ITS DELIVERY

Facts and ideas are clearly important in changing another person's opinions and perceptions, but the effectiveness of a persuasion effort depends on how the facts and ideas are selected, organized, and presented. There are three major issues to consider when constructing a message: the *content* of the message (the facts and topics that should be covered), *structure* of the message (how the topics and facts should be arranged and organized), and the *delivery style* (how the message should be presented).

Message Content

When constructing arguments to persuade the other party, negotiators need to decide what topics and facts they should include. In this section, we discuss four questions negotiators need to consider when constructing persuasive arguments: (1) how to make the offer attractive to the other party, (2) how to frame the message so the other party will say yes, (3) how to make messages normative, and (4) how to obtain agreements in principle.

1. Make the Offer Attractive to the Other Party.   In structuring the message, negotiators should emphasize the advantage the other party gains from accepting the proposal.[15] Although this may seem obvious, it is surprising how many negotiators spend more time on explaining what aspects of their offer are attractive to themselves than on identifying what aspects are likely to be attractive to the other party. Experienced negotiators ensure that the other party understands what he or she will gain by accepting an offer. To do this well, negotiators need to understand the other party's needs.

When negotiators are on the *receiving* end of a proposal, they frequently choose not to talk about the attractive features of an offer but rather to highlight why certain features are undesirable. The negotiator making the offer stresses its attractive features, hoping to minimize further concessions. The receiver of the offer stresses its unattractive features, hoping to receive more concessions. The better a negotiator understands the other's real needs and concerns, the more that he or she can anticipate the other's objections and structure the presentation to counteract them.

2. Frame the Message So the Other Party Will Say "Yes."   Advertisers discovered long ago that people who agree with one statement or proposal, even though it may be minor, are likely to agree with a second, more significant statement or proposal from the same person or on the same topic.[16] Hence, if you can get the other party to agree to something—almost anything—then you have laid the foundation for subsequent agreement. The task is to find something that the other party can agree with that puts him or her in the mind-set of saying yes. A real estate salesperson who gets potential buyers to agree that the house they are visiting is in a nice neighborhood or has a nice yard for their children has made the first step toward getting them to say yes to buying the house (even if it is not the ideal size, layout, or price).

3. Make the Message Normative.   It is easy to assume that people are driven only by self-interest. There is plenty of evidence, however, to indicate that people are motivated to behave consistently with their values, that is, their religious, social, or ethical standards. These standards become part of people's self-image, a concept in their mind of what they are really like. People will go to considerable lengths to act or say things consistent with their self-image. At times, people act politely when in fact they are feeling quite hostile. People can act generously when they are actually financially strained and feel like being greedy.[17]

A powerful argument in negotiation is to show the other person that by following a course of action (your proposal), she will be acting in accordance both with her values, and with some higher (more noble, moral, or ethical) code of conduct. At times, the simple statement "This is the right (or proper) thing to do" may carry considerable weight. People work hard to take responsibility for actions that lead to positive outcomes.[18]

4. Suggest an "Agreement in Principle."   There are times when getting the other party to accept an "agreement in principle" may be a valuable step in a negotiation. For example, when there is bitter conflict between two parties who cannot seem to agree on anything, getting agreement on a general principle, such as a cease-fire, may be the first "yes" statement to which both parties can ascribe. In the negotiations between Israel and Egypt over the Sinai, no details were settled about the fate of the Palestinians, but an agreement on the principle of Palestinian self-rule was reached. Although an agreement in principle is desirable when other options are blocked, it still takes a great deal of work to turn such an agreement into one that contains specific details and action proposals. Principles sound good, and most people may agree with what they advocate, but there is usually great uncertainty about how a principle applies to a specific situation.

Message Structure

People are influenced not only by what negotiators say but also by how they arrange the words. Any writer or speaker faces the question of how to present material in the most logical or persuasive manner. There has been a considerable amount of research on the persuasive power of different message structures. Here we discuss four aspects of messages: (1) one- and two-sided messages, (2) message components, (3) repetition, and (4) conclusions.

1. One- and Two-Sided Messages.   When negotiators try to persuade the other party it is because they believe that the other holds an opinion different from theirs. Many people deal with this problem by completely ignoring arguments and opinions that might support the other party's position—a *one-sided* approach. Many politicians, for example, not only do not mention their opponent's point of view but may never even mention their opponent's name. An alternate approach to ignoring the competition is to mention and describe the opposing point of view, and then show how and why it is less desirable than the presenter's point of view—a *two-sided* approach.

In general, *two-sided messages are considered to be more effective than one-sided messages.*[19] More specifically, two-sided messages appear to be most effective (1) when the other party is well educated, (2) when the other party initially disagrees with the position, (3) when the other party will be exposed to people who will argue points of view different from the position advocated, and (4) when the issue discussed is already familiar. When dealing with reasonably intelligent receivers, it is a mistake to ignore the impact of counterarguments.

2. Message Components.   Big ideas or large propositions are hard to grasp and accept, especially when they are significantly different from your own. Negotiators can help the other party understand and accept their arguments by breaking them into smaller, more understandable pieces.[20] It is even better if they can show that the component parts contain statements that the other party has already accepted or agreed with. For example, a company that is having trouble getting the union to accept a whole package of rule changes could break its presentation down into separate discussions of specific rules: transfers between departments within a plant, transfers between plants, temporary changes in work classifications, and so on. Breaking down complex arguments into smaller parts also helps the parties to see possibilities to logroll, bundle, and trade off across issues (see Chapter 4) because the issues appear in sharper focus.

3. Repetition.   We only have to think of the regular blitz of typical television or radio advertisements to realize the power of repetition in getting a message across. Repetition also encourages central-route processing and thus enhances the likelihood that the message will be understood.[21] However, repeating a point is effective only for the first few times. After that, additional repetition does not significantly change attitudes[22] and may lead people to react against the message.

4. Conclusions.   Some writers or speakers will make an argument and then state the conclusion; others will let the listeners draw their own conclusions. Research suggests that when negotiating with people who are very intelligent, or have not yet made up their minds, leaving the conclusion open is a good approach. In contrast, for people whose ideas are already well-formulated and strong, to leave the conclusion unstated is to leave the most important part of the persuasive effort undone. In general, do not assume that given a set of facts or arguments, the other party will reach the same conclusion you would reach; rather, draw explicit conclusions for listeners to ensure that they have understood the argument completely.[23]

Persuasive Style: How to Pitch the Message

When negotiators select a delivery style for the message they have constructed, they are setting the emotional tone of their presentation. Some people are belligerent; others are accommodating. Some people make speeches; others start a dialogue. Some present detailed facts; others use metaphors and paint beautiful pictures with words. We will consider four major elements of persuasive style: (1) active participation versus passive responding, (2) use of vivid language and metaphors, (3) use of threats to incite fears, and (4) violation of the receiver's expectations.

1. Encourage Active Participation.   People are more likely to change their attitudes and beliefs for the long term when they are actively involved in the process of learning new material.[24] Good teachers know this—rather than lecture, they ask questions and start discussions. Teachers are even more effective when they can get students both intellectually and emotionally involved. Role-plays and cases can help negotiators make use of the power of active participation. Negotiators who can use active approaches are generally more persuasive than those who don't, since an active approach requires the receiver to exert effort, which leads to involvement, which leads to attitude change.

2. Use Vivid Language and Metaphors.   The vividness and intensity of the language negotiators use have a major effect on their persuasiveness. Saying "This is certainly the best price you will get" is more intense than saying "This is quite a good price." Similarly, the statement "I don't feel like going out tonight" is not as intense as "You could not drag me out tonight with a team of horses." The intensity of language can also be increased through the use of colorful metaphors, profanity, or a change in intonation—from quiet to loud or loud to quiet.

You might think that the most intense language would also be the most persuasive, but to the contrary, language of relatively low intensity can be more effective.[25] Evidence indicates that people react negatively to persuasive attempts using language they perceive as too intense.[26] People under stress seem to be particularly receptive to messages using low-intensity language and more inclined to reject those using high-intensity language.[27] However, the effect of intense language depends in part on who uses it. Sources with high credibility can use more intense language than those who are not seen as credible.[28]

Metaphors and analogies are a particularly useful way to elevate the vividness of a message in the service of persuasion.[29] An auto salesperson can give the potential customer details about a car's carburetor, the miles per gallon of gasoline used at different speeds, and rates of acceleration, but can make these points just as well by saying, "This car flies like the wind and doesn't guzzle gas." The same salesperson could show a car's fine finish, point out the body undercoating, and draw attention to the immaculate condition of the engine, or he could say, "This car is as sleek as a cat." Using metaphors to excess may lead the other party to believe that you're filled with hot air (itself a metaphor for not having the facts to support arguments), but using them to summarize some facts or to establish clear visual impressions can be valuable in persuasion.

3. Incite Fears.   Messages that contain threats—threats of strikes by unions or lockouts by management, threats to harm the other party's reputation, or threats to break off negotiations—can be useful when a negotiator needs to underscore the absolute importance of a point being made. In essence, threats are if–then statements with serious negative consequences attached: "If you do X, then I will be forced to do Y." Negotiators must be prepared to follow through with the consequences threatened, however, or they will be perceived as making empty threats and thereby lose credibility.

Because of their dramatic nature and the emotional response they evoke, threats may be tempting to use. In fact, threats are probably used less frequently than one might expect. One reason is that the other person's reaction to a threat is hard to predict. A second reason is that it is hard to know how menacing the threat appears to the other party.

Often threats appear more powerful to the people who make them than they do to the receivers. Third, threats put other parties in a position where they can call the bluff, forcing the negotiator to carry out the threat. Finally, threats may produce compliance, but they do not usually produce commitment. People can find many ways to avoid or undermine arrangements they were forced to comply with but to which they are not committed.

4. Violate the Receiver's Expectations. People who argue positions that are thought to be counter to their self-interest are generally more persuasive because they violate the receiver's expectation about what the sender should be advocating.[30] For instance, an automobile mechanic recently suggested that one of the authors of this book should use mid- or high-octane gas in his car to reduce fuel-injector maintenance and save money. This message was persuasive because the mechanic was arguing against his own self-interest (future car repairs) when he suggested the change in gas (his business does not sell gasoline).

Another way that receivers' expectations can be violated occurs when they expect one style of delivery from the speaker and then experience a totally different style. For example, when one expects to be subjected to intense language (loud, volatile, provocative, etc.), one prepares defenses and counterarguments. If one instead encounters moderate, casual, reasonable language, one can relax one's defenses, listen to the message less critically, and be more likely to be persuaded.[31] Great orators such as Winston Churchill and Martin Luther King, Jr. have used this style, frequently changing the intensity of their voices to hold the audience's attention. Although this is not a stylistic tactic that everyone can use, strong orators have a valuable tool at their disposal. Clearly, the process may also work in reverse—an emotionally intense speaker may equally persuade audiences who expect quiet, controlled, highly rational discourse.

PERIPHERAL ROUTES TO INFLUENCE

Thus far, we have focused on organizing the structure and content of the message in order to create leverage through the "central" route to influence. In this section, we will consider ways that a person can influence others through the "peripheral" route. In such cases, the receiver attends less to the substance of persuasive arguments and is instead susceptible to more "automatic" influence through subtle cues. This usually occurs when the target of influence is either unmotivated or unable to attend carefully to the substance contained within a persuasive message. As we suggested earlier, persuasion that occurs through the peripheral route is less likely to bring about real attitude change, is more likely to last a shorter time, and is more vulnerable to counterinfluence.

In our discussion of peripheral routes to influence we draw in part on the work of psychologist Robert Cialdini, who spent many years investigating why people comply with requests that, upon further reflection, they would rather not have agreed to.[32] His research represents a skillful blend of laboratory research and observation of "compliance experts" such as salespeople, fund-raisers, and marketing and advertising experts.

Our discussion of peripheral routes to influence will consider three sets of strategies (refer again to Figure 6.2): message aspects, attributes of the persuader, and elements of the influence context.

Aspects of Messages That Foster Peripheral Influence

When targets of influence are unmotivated or unable to pay close attention to the influence seeker's message, they are susceptible to being influenced by message elements that exist apart from the actual arguments involved. We discuss two such elements here: the way in which the influence seeker chooses to order those arguments, and the use of distraction to interfere with the target's ability to think about the arguments.

Message Order.   In preparing a persuasive argument, negotiators usually have one major point, piece of information, or illustration that is particularly important or compelling. Where should it be placed in the message? Research tells us one thing clearly—do not place the important point in the middle of the message.[33] Should it be at the beginning or at the end? When the topics are familiar, interesting, or controversial to the receiver, the important points should be made early, exposing the receiver to the *primacy effect:* The first item in a long list of items is the one most likely to be remembered. In contrast, when the topic is uninteresting, unfamiliar, or not very important to the receiver, the most critical point should be placed at the end of the message to take advantage of the *recency effect:* the tendency for the last item presented to be the best remembered.[34]

Distractions.   Persuasion is complex because people start to defend themselves against being persuaded as soon as they suspect that someone is trying to persuade them. As they listen, part of their attention is devoted to what is being said, but a large portion is also devoted to developing counterarguments.[35] Persuasion efforts are more effective if they can reduce the other party's efforts to develop defensive counterarguments. One way to do this is to have a *distraction* occur at the same time the message is sent. When receivers are distracted, they are less able to engage in issue-relevant thinking and hence may be more susceptible to processing peripheral cues that may push them toward a particular choice. For example, during an oral presentation of the economic advantages of an offer, negotiators could lay out papers with charts and graphs, hand them to the other party, and help that person turn from one chart to another as the oral presentation continues. Presumably, the charts and graphs absorb that part of the other party's attention that might normally go into formulating counterarguments. Distractions seem to inhibit the receiver's subvocalization (what people say to themselves as they hear a message).

Source Characteristics That Foster Peripheral Influence

When the recipients of a persuasive message are unmotivated or unable to attend closely to the substance of the persuasive appeal, they become vulnerable to source effects. In other words, someone who is not paying close attention to the message may be unduly influenced by the characteristics of the person or organization delivering the message. A wide variety of source effects can potentially have an effect on the recipient of a persuasive message. We group them here into three broad categories: credibility, attractiveness, and authority.

Source Credibility. During a negotiation, both parties exchange information, opinions, and interpretations. What, and how much, should be believed? As a negotiator, you cannot check every fact and statement. The more information one is willing to accept from the other party without independent verification, the easier that person's job will be. The reverse is also true—the more credible you are to the other party, the more persuasive you will be.

Source credibility depends mostly on three things: the qualifications of the source, the perceived trustworthiness of the source, and source likability.

First, qualifications: When people are determining how much to believe another person, they often ask, "Is this person in a position to possess the information he or she claims to have? That is, is he or she competent and qualified?" The stronger the person's perceived qualifications and expertise, the higher the credibility.[36] Second, trustworthiness: "Is this person reporting accurately what he or she knows? That is, is he or she personally believable or trustworthy?" Third, likeability: People appear more or less credible because of their *presence*—the way they present themselves to others. Three components of behavior are instrumental in creating a favorable presence: composure, sociability, and extroversion.[37] A person who seems hesitant, confused, or uncertain when giving information is not as convincing as a person who appears calm, confident, and comfortable. A friendly, open person is easier to talk to (and therefore to believe) than someone who is distant, abrasive, or haughty. A person with a dynamic vocal style and a strong delivery is often more persuasive than one without these attributes. Trustworthiness and qualifications are more powerful characteristics in determining your perception of another's credibility than his or her self-presentation is, but all three play a critical role.

Many other factors contribute to source credibility. Below we discuss several that negotiators can control.

Personal Reputation for Integrity. Integrity is character—the personal values and ethics that ground your behavior in high moral principles. Integrity is the quality that assures people you can be trusted, you will be honest, and you will do as you say. If people trust you with confidential information, you will not disclose that information to others. Finally, if you make an agreement, you will abide by its terms and conditions, and follow through on it.[38] Conversely, people with a reputation for being dishonest or insincere have an extremely difficult time in negotiations—they tend not to be believed, even when they tell the truth.

Intention to Persuade. Does a negotiator initially come across as a huckster or as cool, poised, and polished? While people may give the benefit of the doubt in their initial judgment, the more they detect that a negotiator's mission is to change their minds, the more suspicious and resistant they may become. For instance, when the phone rings unexpectedly, it is often easy to identify the telemarketer who mispronounces your name and tries to involve you in friendly chit-chat ("How are you this evening?") while she eases into her prepared sales pitch ("I'm glad you're well. Do you ever have problems with . . ."). By the time she has gotten to the sales pitch, your defenses are most likely already well fortified. In contrast, communicating with natural enthusiasm, sincerity, and spontaneity may take the edge off persuasive communication and reduce defensive reactions.

Use or Minimize Status Differences.   Status is signaled by a variety of criteria: occupation, age, education level, the neighborhood where a person lives, dress, type of automobile, and the like. A president of a major corporation, for example, has more status than a university professor, but less than a justice of the Supreme Court. High-status people generally have more influence than low-status people, in several ways. First, status gives people visibility, which allows them to get attention and be heard. It also confers prestige, lending the image that certain people are worth listening to.[39] However, a status difference may also increase resistance, because receivers expect to be persuaded and therefore increase their defenses against the effort.

Appearance and Self-Presentation.   It is not an earth-shaking revelation to note that how you dress, speak, and behave will influence how credible you appear to others. What may not be as obvious is how you should adjust your appearance to increase your credibility. Often appearance and dress are tied to the status difference and intent-to-persuade issues. In general, researchers have found that it is best to be "normal," meaning to act appropriately, naturally, and unaffectedly.[40]

Associates.   Whom you associate with also can influence how you are perceived, in terms of both status and expertise. Judicious name dropping (i.e., mentioning well-known people who are also credible and prestigious) and even arranging for introductions or endorsements by people who can add to your reputation can be useful steps.

Perceived Expertise.   Sometimes your occupation, education, or past experiences will establish your expertise and therefore the perception of your competence.[41] At other times, there are no obvious ways to make your expertise known. In situations where you are unknown or likely to be viewed stereotypically, you need to make an extra effort to establish your expertise. There are numerous things you can do to establish your expertise:

- Find ways to introduce your education or experience into the conversation: "When I went to law school, we were taught that . . ."
- Cite other credible sources of information: "According to this morning's *New York Times . . .*"
- Ask questions or draw quick conclusions that could only be derived from in-depth, firsthand knowledge or experience.

Persistence and Tenacity.   Persistence and tenacity are valuable personal qualities in a negotiator. Children are often considered great negotiators because they are so wonderfully persistent in pursuing what they want. Part of persistence is doggedly pursuing the objective, but another part is finding new, unique, and creative ways to pursue the same request.

Personal Attractiveness.   People will treat others better when they like them than when they don't. They are less likely to feel that attractive negotiators will be dishonest or attempt to coerce them, and more likely to accept their influence, to believe them, and to trust them.[42] Being nice and pleasant is a logical step to being more persuasive. It is not clear why personal attractiveness increases persuasiveness. People may have a tendency to let their guard down and trust attractive people more readily. The following tactics are some of the many ways that an individual can enhance his or her personal attractiveness to a target of influence or a negotiating opponent.

Friendliness.   A critically important attribute that a negotiator can have is the ability to be friendly and outgoing and to establish personal relationships with others—particularly the other parties in the negotiation. Warmth, empathy, and simple direct, personal interest in others all help to soften the harder edges of some of the other power sources. Friendliness also involves a strong emotional component, and therefore it appeals to the other party's moods and feelings as well as to his or her intellect. Rather than immediately getting down to business, successful negotiators use friendliness to make the other party feel comfortable and at ease, to get to know the other negotiator, and to discover things that they may have in common.

Ingratiation.   Ingratiation involves flattering or enhancing the other's self-image or reputation through statements or actions, and thus enhancing one's own image in the same way.[43] Flattering another person by giving compliments is perhaps the most obvious form of ingratiation. Because it is obvious, it is used often and sometimes abused. Compliments can be a potent means of ingratiation, not only because people like to receive them, but also because the norm of reciprocity leaves the other party with the obligation to return something for the compliment.[44] But when people are complimented for attributes they do not have or actions they know they did not perform well, or when the praise seems excessive, they are likely to become wary, wondering what the flatterer is after.

Likability.   The liking principle is quite straightforward: People you like have more influence over you. If you like the sender, you are more likely to be persuaded by him or her, although research has shown that likability is less important than other credibility factors, such as expertise.[45]

The effects of the liking principle are insidious. Liking can occur through many different approaches, and defending against them all would be impossible. Cialdini points out that it would be useless to try to prevent yourself from liking others.[46] Rather, you should let the liking occur and then explore *why* you like the other person. If you find that you like the person more than you would typically like another person under similar circumstances, then it is time to be wary. Separating liking the other party from an evaluation of the deal should be enough to moderate the influence of the liking principle in your negotiations.

Perceived Similarity.   When meeting for the first time, people often try to find something they have in common. The more similarities they find, the more bonds they establish, the better both parties feel, and more important, the more receptive they will be to each other's messages and efforts at persuasion.[47] A useful negotiating tactic, therefore, is to identify and discuss experiences, characteristics, and opinions you hold in common with the other party. But if it is to your advantage to find and explore commonalities in experience, attitude, and background with the other party, it is also to your disadvantage to highlight those areas where you differ. There is no point to starting a conversation on a politically controversial topic when you know or suspect that the other holds a completely different view from yours.

Emotion.   We discussed emotion earlier in this chapter in connection with the use of language to construct a message, but emotion can also be a source factor. Emotion combined with persistence leads to assertiveness and determination. Used effectively, emotion may enhance a message source's attractiveness by instilling in listeners the

Pepper . . . and Salt

THE WALL STREET JOURNAL

**"Remember, no sobbing.
It makes them jittery."**

From *The Wall Street Journal*. Used with permission of Cartoon Features Syndicate.

belief that the speaker holds appealing deep-seated values (this may also enhance the speaker's credibility).

Authority. The principle of authority is quite simple: People with authority have more influence than those without authority. Researchers have long been interested in the effects of authority figures on human behavior. Stanley Milgram's classic studies of obedience to authority suggest that people will go to great lengths when their behavior is legitimized by an authority figure.[48] Most people will obey the orders of a person wearing a uniform, even if there is no war or apparent emergency. This, too, is an effect of the principle of authority.

In negotiation, the principle of authority can be used in many ways. First, written rules may carry more weight than those given verbally.[49] Thus, a procedure is more likely to be followed if it is in the policy manual or fine print of the contract than if it is merely expressed orally. The use of a title, such as *doctor* or *professor,* gives the user more authority and thus more influence.[50] A friend of one of the authors uses the title *doctor* whenever ordering airline tickets. He found out early in his career that airlines would telephone doctors when there was a flight delay but would ignore the other passengers. This simple illustration shows the esteem with which some titles (or positions) are held in society.

Cialdini offers the following advice about dealing with authority figures who may have influence over you. Ask two questions: "Is this authority truly an expert?" and "How truthful can you expect this expert to be?"[51] The first question forces you to verify that the person really does have expertise in the situation and not just the appearance (title, attire) of expertise. The second question suggests that you examine the motive of the expert who is offering advice.

Aspects of Context That Foster Peripheral Influence

Finally, we explore aspects of the situation beyond the message itself and the sender of the message that create opportunities to pursue the peripheral route to influence. Five strategies are discussed: reciprocity, commitment, social proof, scarcity, and reward and punishment.

Reciprocity. The norm of reciprocity has been studied for years by philosophers, anthropologists, sociologists, and other social scientists. This norm suggests that when you receive something from another person, you should respond in the future with a favor in return. This norm is thought to be pan-cultural in that groups around the world appear to respect it.[52]

The norm of reciprocity plays an important role in negotiations. Negotiators give concessions and expect concessions in return. For instance, negotiator A does a small favor for negotiator B and later asks for a larger favor from B in return. The net advantage goes to A. Although one may think that the norm of reciprocity should apply only to favors of the same size, this does not appear to be the case. In fact, many sales pitches rely on giving the consumer a small gift early in an exchange and then asking for a large concession from the consumer later.

Similar opportunities exist in other negotiation situations. A compliment, such as a reference to the other party's positive behavior in a prior discussion, will make that person feel good and set the scene for him or her to act positively. Giving a quick concession on an issue that the other party wants will both please that party and create the implicit obligation for him or her to do the same.

Given the apparent powerfulness of the norm of reciprocity, how can the negotiator counter its effects? One possibility is to refuse all favors in a negotiation setting, but this would probably cause more problems than it resolves. For instance, refusing a cup of coffee from your host may remove the effects of the norm of reciprocity but at the same time may insult the host, especially if five minutes later you go out to get a cup of coffee yourself. Perhaps the other person was simply being polite. Perhaps he or she was setting a positive tone for the meeting. Or perhaps he or she was trying to use the norm of reciprocity to create a small sense of indebtedness.[53] Cialdini suggests that you should respond politely to a favor and accept what is offered if it is something you want. If it becomes apparent that the favor was an attempt at manipulation, however, then you should redefine the event as a trick rather than a favor. This will remove the obligation of the rule of reciprocity because the "rule says that favors are to be met with favors; it does not require that tricks be met with favors."[54]

Commitment.   Researchers have long recognized that once people have decided something, they can be remarkably persistent in their beliefs. This process has been labeled *commitment to a position,* and it relies heavily on the common need that people have to appear consistent, both to themselves and to others. Most people are familiar with the bait-and-switch sales technique. Unscrupulous organizations advertise merchandise for sale at an incredibly low price but "run out" of stock by the time you arrive at the store. They then try to sell you alternate merchandise at a higher price. Why does this technique work? One reason is that once you have made the decision to purchase a product (a commitment), you almost automatically follow through with the commitment (even at a higher price).

Commitment strategies are very powerful devices for making people comply. One way to increase commitment is to write things down. Some encyclopedia companies that have customers complete their own order forms have a far lower cancellation rate than those companies that have salespeople write out the form. Many consumer-product companies have people write testimonials about their products in order to enter a drawing for a prize. Why? Apparently, writing testimonials increases the commitment to buy the product.[55] Research has shown that even signing a petition can increase your compliance with a request to do something more intrusive several days later.[56]

How can commitment work in a negotiation? Usually, it is incremental. Agreement to innocuous statements early in the negotiation may be used as a foundation for further and further concessions. Such strategies are very difficult to combat. Frequently, one will have already been influenced and agreed to something before even realizing that the manipulation has taken place. To some extent, being forewarned about these techniques is being forearmed. Cialdini suggests that your body will send two types of warning signals when these techniques are in use.[57] Either you will feel uncomfortable when subtle commitments are being made, or something in the deal will just not seem quite right. If you encounter these thoughts or feelings when negotiating, look out for use of a commitment strategy by the other party. At the very least, be aware of all the agreements you strike during a negotiation, even those small, innocuous ones. They may be the setup for the next move.

Social Proof.   The principle of social proof suggests that people look to others to determine the correct response in many situations. This principle suggests that people often behave in certain ways because everyone else is doing so. This is the principle that makes laugh tracks so effective on television comedies.[58] It also explains why some influence agents like to mention the names of previously satisfied customers; if other people used the product and liked it, then it must be good. Celebrities are hired to endorse products for similar reasons.

In negotiation situations, the principle of social proof can act as a powerful influence strategy. Salespeople will show lists of satisfied customers, knowing that few people will take the time to verify the list. ("If it wasn't true, why would the salesperson show me the list?") Sweepstakes advertisements highlight previous winners and feature celebrities. Negotiators will talk about how popular their new product is and how sales have really increased this year. Real estate agents will be sure that you are aware that many other people are interested in the house that you are considering buying.

The principle of social proof works because false information ("Everyone thinks this product is good") is given weight in decisions. One way to reduce this influence is to identify the false information and give it the weight it deserves.[59] In negotiations, this means careful preparation and being aware of "facts" about the others' advocated views that do not seem to match your preparation. When the other party offers "evidence" about the popularity of an item, do not automatically trust that the other party is being completely honest; rather, ask the other to substantiate the claims.

Scarcity. The principle of scarcity suggests that when things are less available, they will have more influence. Frequently, salespeople will tell customers that they are not sure if the product the customers would like to purchase is currently in stock.[60] Before making the trip to the stockroom they ask if they should grab one before another sales-person gets it. Typically shoppers will say yes and will feel relieved (or lucky) when the salesperson returns with the "last one" in the store. This is the scarcity principle at work; people are easier to influence when they feel that they are obtaining a scarce resource.

In negotiation situations, the scarcity influence strategy may be operating when-ever there appears to be a great demand for a product. Some organizations deliberately keep their products in short supply to give the appearance that they are very popular (e.g., popular Christmas toys). Anytime negotiators talk about "exclusive opportunities" and "time-limited offers," they are using the scarcity principle. Auctions also rely on the principle of scarcity, by selling off unique (one-of-a-kind) pieces to the highest bidder—the more scarce the item, the higher the bids.

The scarcity principle is very difficult to combat when used effectively. It creates in the victim an activity trap focused on obtaining the item and effectively suspends cognitive evaluation of the broader situation. Cialdini suggests that people need to be aware of the emotional trappings that this principle arouses; when confronted with a strong emotional response to obtain a scarce good, they should carefully evaluate their reasons for wanting the item in the first place.[61]

Use of Reward and Punishment. Earlier in this chapter, we indicated that con-trol over resources was a strong source of power. These resources can be used in at least two major ways. First, negotiators can offer resources, or favors (promises and assis-tance), to secure the other's compliance and cooperation. Exchange relies on resources that can be translated into rewards for the other—favors, benefits, incentives, treats, perks, and the like. Thus, exchange frequently invokes the use of promises and com-mitments as persuasive tools—obligations that you are willing to make in exchange for the other's cooperation, compliance, or commitment to give you what you want.

A second way that negotiators attempt to use this power is through pressure—that is, by the threat of punishment. An agent can make demands, suggest consequences about what will happen if the demands are not met, engage in frequent surveillance to determine whether the demands are carried out, remind the other person frequently about what is expected, and eventually follow through with the actual punishment if the demand is not met on time. A sales manager may cut a salesperson's pay for repeatedly failing to achieve sales target projections. A supplier may put a late charge on an over-due bill to a customer. Like reward power and the use of praise, coercive or punishment power can be as effective in the verbal form as in the withdrawal or denial of tangible resources. If the sales manager berates a salesperson for failing to make target sales quotas (rather than firing him or her), the impact may be just as great.

David Kipnis proposed a number of reasons why a power holder may decide to use pressure.[62] First, pressure may be used as a way to express anger, gain retribution, or get even for something the target person has done. Second, pressure may be used as an expression of role behavior—the job (or role) requires it. For example, a banker forecloses on a loan "because bank rules mandate it," or a dean terminates a poorly performing student because university policy must be upheld. Negotiators are most likely to use pressure when they expect that the other party has little or no desire to meet their expectations, does not share the same deadline, or will not comply unless directly threatened with severe negative consequences.

Pressure tactics produce, at best, short-term compliance with requests, but they also are likely to elicit resistance from the other party. Frequent use of pressure tactics alienates the other party and leads to very high resistance, in which case the agent must consistently escalate the severity of consequences for noncompliance and the willingness to invoke them. Pressure tactics should be used selectively and sparingly because their use is likely to corrode the relationship between the parties, and frequent use is likely to destroy it.

THE ROLE OF RECEIVERS—TARGETS OF INFLUENCE

We conclude this chapter with a discussion of factors related to the person who is the target of influence. At first glance, one might think that there is not much that receivers can do to exert leverage. Not true! Just as negotiators-as-message-senders can work to increase their credibility and attractiveness, receivers can signal the sender about the general acceptability and favorableness of the message being sent, and senders can monitor the receiver's receptiveness and adapt the message accordingly. Receivers need to be conscious about the signals they send; senders need to monitor the other's receptiveness, avoid taking the "defensive/combative" stance that lets people turn off persuasive communication, and help receivers hear and understand better. Let us review a few key factors.

Attending to the Other

Much of what people communicate to one another is transmitted not only with words and sentences, but also with body language: the way they position their body, their tone of voice, their head movements. Many nonverbal acts are very important in connecting with another person; they let the other know that you are listening and prepare the other party to receive your message. We will mention three important behaviors: eye contact, body position, and encouraging.

Make Eye Contact.   Dishonest people and cowards are not supposed to be able to look people in the eye. Poets claim that the eye is the lens that permits us to look into a person's soul. These and other bits of conventional wisdom illustrate how important people believe eye contact to be. In general, making eye contact is one way to show others you are paying attention and listening, and that you consider them important. In making eye contact, however, people should not keep their eyes continually fixed on the other person. Otherwise they might be accused of staring, which usually leads to suspicion rather than trust.

When persuading someone, it is important to make eye contact when delivering the most important part of the message.[63] This is the equivalent of staring inside the other person, talking directly to his heart and soul. Having the verbal and nonverbal systems in parallel at this point emphasizes the importance of the message that is being sent. Also, one should maintain eye contact not only when speaking but when receiving communication as well.[64]

It is important to recognize, however, that the patterns described above are characteristic of Western society. In other parts of the world, different patterns prevail. In parts of the Far East, for example, to keep one's eyes down while the other is speaking is a sign of respect.[65]

Adjust Body Position.   Parents frequently advise their children about how to stand and sit, particularly when they are in formal settings such as school, church, or dinner parties. The command "Sit up!" is often accompanied by "And pay attention!" Here the parent is teaching the child another widely held belief—one's body position indicates whether or not one is paying attention to the other party. To ensure that others know you are attentive to them, hold your body erect, lean slightly forward, and face the other person directly.[66] If you accept and endorse the others' message, care needs to be taken not to show *dis*respect with body position by slouching, turning away, or placing feet on the table.[67]

Nonverbally Encourage or Discourage What the Other Says.   One can indicate attention and interest in what another is saying through a variety of simple behaviors. A head nod, a simple hand gesture to go on, or a murmured "Unh hunh" to indicate understanding all tell the other person to continue, that you are listening. In fact, one can encourage someone to continue to speak about many subjects by simply nodding your head as he or she is speaking. Brief eye contact or a smile and a nod of the head will both provide encouraging cues. Similarly, a frown, a scowl, a shake of the head, or a grab of one's chest in mock pain will signal disapproval of the other's message.

Exploring or Ignoring the Other's Position

Negotiators frequently give little attention to the other party's opinions and point of view. This is unfortunate, because it is very much to your advantage to understand what the other party really wants, how things look to him, and how he developed his position. One can explore the other party's perspective with questions designed to reveal his or her needs and interests (see Chapter 5). Exploring the other person's outlook not only provides more information, which can lead you to design solutions to meet both sides' needs, but further increases the other party's feeling of being listened to and makes him or her more receptive to meeting your needs. However, questions are often used as a weapon of attack. Questions such as "How in the world can you say that?" or "What possible justi-fication can you have for that position?" are likely to make the other party feel tense and combative and may make the tone of the negotiations quite negative.

Selectively Paraphrase.   Paraphrasing ensures that both parties have under-stood each other accurately. It is important to restate your understanding after being corrected, to make sure you have understood. Repeat in your own words what was said. In addition, vocalizing the other person's ideas helps you remember them better than simply hearing them. Do not literally repeat the other person's words; repeat the mes-sage in your own words, starting with "Let me see if I understand the point you just made." When people have an important message to get across, they will talk vigorously and at length, often emphasizing the same point over and over. Once your paraphras-ing indicates that the other person has been understood, he or she will usually stop repeating the same point and move on; hence, paraphrasing can be very helpful in mov-ing a discussion forward.

You can also ask the other party to restate or paraphrase what you have said. You might say, "What I have said is very important to me, and I would appreciate it if you could restate what you understood to be my main points." This asks the other party to listen closely, gives you the opportunity to check out the accuracy of his or her under-standing, and emphasizes the most important points of your presentation.

Reinforce Points You Like in the Other Party's Proposals.   Negotiators are frequently ineffective because they respond only to what they dislike in the other party's statement or proposal and ignore the things they like. Responding in this way ignores a powerful means of shaping and guiding what the other party is saying.

The simplest way to reward people for what they say during a negotiation is to acknowledge and support a point that they have made: "That is an interesting point." "I had not heard that before." Give a simple "Mm-hmm" or a nod of the head. State-ments and actions like these separate a key statement from other points the speaker has made. Second, compliment speakers when they make points you want emphasized, and express appreciation to them for considering your interests and needs. A third approach is to separate particular parts of a statement that you like from those parts you don't like and to encourage the other party to develop the favorable points. A fourth approach is to return favors. If the other party makes a concession and offers you something you want, you can reward this behavior by making a concession or offering a favor in return.

Resisting the Other's Influence

In addition to the variety of things a negotiator can do to encourage, support, or direct the other's communication, there are at least three major things that listeners can do to resist the other's influence efforts: have a best alternative to a negotiated agree-ment (BATNA), make a public commitment (or get the other party to make one), and inoculate yourself against the other's persuasive message.

Have a BATNA, and Know How to Use It.   Several authors identify a BATNA as a source of power.[68] There is no question that having a BATNA enables negotiators to walk away from a given negotiation, since it means that they can get their needs met and interests addressed somewhere else. Of course, having a BATNA is a source of leverage at the negotiation table only if the other party is aware of it. To use a BATNA effectively, a negotiator must assess the other party's awareness that it exists and, if necessary, share that fact. This often must be done deftly—conveying the existence of a BATNA could be interpreted by the other party as an imminent threat to walk away. Keep in mind also that a BATNA can always be improved. Good negotiators will work to improve their BATNA before and even during an ongoing negotiation as a way to improve their leverage.

Make a Public Commitment.   One of the most effective ways of getting people to stand firm on a position is to have them make a public commitment to that position. Union leaders have said things to their rank and file like, "I will resign before I settle for a penny less than . . ." After making that statement, the union leader faces several pressures. One is the potential loss of face with union members that would come with backing away from that position—the leader may be unceremoniously thrown out of office if he or she does not actually resign. A second pressure is that the leader's credibility with management will be sharply reduced in the future if he or she does not follow through on the commitment. Finally, the leader may have his or her own cognitive inconsistency to deal with because failing to resign will be inconsistent with his or her earlier commitment.

Negotiators can also get the other party to make a public commitment. If you can get the other party to make a public statement that supports something you want, that party will be hard-pressed not to stand by the statement, even though he or she may have a desire to abandon it later on. Sometimes negotiators make a statement such as "I'm committed to finding an agreement that we can both benefit from," and then invite the other party to make a similar statement. Even better than eliciting statements of commitment is enticing the other party to make a behavioral commitment. For example, retail merchants use down payments and layaway plans to get a behavioral commitment from customers when it is not possible to complete the total sale at that time.

Sometimes, however, negotiators want to prevent the other party from making public commitments to positions that counter their interests. They can do so by downplaying statements of commitment, not responding to them, or looking for a rationale to explain why the commitment does not apply at that time.

Inoculate Yourself against the Other Party's Arguments.   One of the likely outcomes of listening carefully to the other party and exploring and understanding his or her point of view is that negotiators may change some of their own positions. At times they may not want to change their position, and therefore they may want to "inoculate" themselves against the other party's arguments.[69] For instance, managers who must support organizational policies with which they disagree may want to inoculate themselves against subordinates' arguments by preparing and rehearsing counterarguments that can be used to refute the key points the other is likely to make.

There are three approaches for inoculating against the arguments of other parties:

1. prepare supporting arguments *for your position only*.

2. develop arguments *against your position only* and then develop counterarguments, that is, find ways to refute them in the points you make.

3. develop arguments *both for your original position and against your position*, and then develop counterarguments to refute both (this is a combination approach).

Research reveals that the best way to inoculate against being influenced is to use the combination approach (point 3 above)—developing arguments both for and against your position, and counterarguments to refute them.[70] Developing arguments against your position only plus counterarguments (point 2 above) is also effective, but to a lesser extent. The least effective, by a large margin, is the first approach—developing arguments in support of your position only.

CHAPTER SUMMARY

In this chapter, we discussed the nature of leverage in negotiation. By leverage, we mean the process of gaining or using various sources of power in order to obtain and use temporary advantage over the other negotiating party. We began by exploring three sources of power: information and expertise, control over resources, and the location within an organizational structure (which leads to either formal authority or informal power based on where one is located relative to flows of information or resources).

We then turned to examine a very large number of influence (leverage) tools that one could use in negotiation. These tools were considered in two broad categories: influence that occurs through the *central* route to persuasion, and influence that occurs through the *peripheral* route to persuasion.

In the last major section of the chapter, we considered how the receiver—the target of influence—either can shape and direct what the sender is communicating, or can intellectually resist the persuasive effects of the message. Effective negotiators are skilled not only at crafting persuasive messages, but also at playing the role of skilled "consumers" of the messages that others direct their way.

ENDNOTES

1. French and Raven, 1959.
2. Salancik and Pfeffer, 1977.
3. Deutsch, 1973, pp. 84–85.
4. Ury, Brett, and Goldberg, 1993.
5. French and Raven, 1959.
6. Cronkhite and Liska, 1976, 1980.
7. Pfeffer and Salancik, 1974.
8. Pfeffer, 1992.
9. Cialdini, 2001, discusses illusions of authority that may accrue to occupants of certain social positions.
10. Barnard, 1938.

11. See Charan, 1991; Kaplan, 1984; Krackhart and Hanson, 1993.
12. See Chaiken, 1987; Petty and Cacioppo, 1986a, 1986b.
13. Petty & Cacioppo, 1986b, p. 131.
14. Ibid., p. 132.
15. Michener and Suchner, 1971.
16. Fern, Monroe, and Avila, 1986; Freedman and Fraser, 1966; Seligman, Bush, and Kirsch, 1976.
17. Reardon, 1981.
18. Schlenker and Riess, 1979.
19. Jackson and Allen, 1987.
20. Fisher, 1964; Ikle, 1964.
21. Cacioppo and Petty, 1985.
22. McGuire, 1973.
23. Feingold and Knapp, 1977; Hovland and Mandell, 1952; McGuire, 1964.
24. Bettinghaus, 1966; Johnson and Eagly, 1989, 1990; Petty and Cacioppo, 1990.
25. Bowers, 1964.
26. Burgoon and King, 1974.
27. Jones and Burgoon, 1975.
28. Burgoon and Stewart, 1975.
29. Bowers and Osborn, 1966; Burgoon and King, 1974; Conger, 1998.
30. O'Keefe, 1990.
31. Miller and Burgoon, 1979.
32. Cialdini, 2001.
33. Bettinghaus, 1966.
34. Clark, 1984; Rosnow and Robinson, 1967.
35. Brock, 1963; Festinger and Maccoby, 1964; Petty and Brock, 1981.
36. See Ostermeier, 1967; Swenson, Nash, and Roos, 1984.
37. McCroskey, Jensen, and Valencia, 1973.
38. Shapiro, Sheppard, and Cheraskin, 1992.
39. Bettinghaus, 1980.
40. Ibid.
41. Swenson, Nash, and Roos, 1984.
42. Chaiken, 1986; Eagly and Chaiken, 1975; Tedeschi, Schlenker, and Bonoma, 1973.
43. Jones, 1964.
44. Cialdini, 2001; Jones, 1964.
45. Eagly and Chaiken, 1975.
46. Cialdini, 2001.
47. O'Keefe, 1990.
48. Milgram, 1974.
49. Cohen, 1980.
50. Cialdini, 2001.
51. Ibid., p. 197.
52. Gouldner, 1960.
53. Note that many public-sector bargaining laws prohibit negotiators from even buying a cup of coffee for each other. Negotiators need to be aware of the laws and norms that may have implications for compliance strategies. In addition, there are cross-cultural differences in refusing a gift, and negotiators need to prepare carefully for such instances when they negotiate across borders.
54. Cialdini, 2001, p. 47.
55. Cialdini, 2001.

56. Freedman and Fraser, 1966.
57. Cialdini, 2001.
58. See Fuller and Sheehy-Skeffington, 1974.
59. Cialdini, 2001.
60. Ibid.
61. Ibid.
62. Kipnis, 1976.
63. Beebe, 1980; Burgoon, Coker, and Coker, 1986; Kleinke, 1986.
64. Kellerman, Lewis, and Laird, 1989.
65. Ivey and Simek-Downing, 1980.
66. Ibid.
67. Stacks and Burgoon, 1981.
68. Pinkley, Neale, and Bennett, 1994.
69. McGuire, 1964.
70. Ibid.; Tannenbaum and Norris, 1966.

CHAPTER 7

Ethics in Negotiation

In this chapter, we explore the question of whether there are, or should be, accepted ethical standards for behavior in negotiations. This topic has received increased attention from researchers in recent years. It is our view that fundamental questions of ethical conduct arise in every negotiation. The effective negotiator must recognize when the questions are relevant and what factors must be considered to answer them.

WHY DO NEGOTIATORS NEED TO KNOW ABOUT ETHICS?

Consider the following situations:

1. You are a manager badly in need of additional clerical assistance for your office. Although work is getting done, a large and often unpredictable volume is creating periodic delays. Some of your staff members are complaining that the work flow could be managed much more effectively if another clerk were added. However, you also know that your boss is not sympathetic; she thinks that the problem could be solved if all the current clerks simply agreed to work a bit harder or volunteer a few hours of overtime. Moreover, your department's budget is very tight, and to get a new clerical position approved, you will have to demonstrate clearly to senior management (particularly your boss) that you need additional personnel. You see the following options open to you:

- Document the amount of work that each of your clerks is doing and the amount of work that is being delayed or not done properly, and make a complete report to your boss.

- Give each of your clerks a lot of extra jobs to do now, particularly ones that could really be deferred for a few months (such as cleaning out and completely reorganizing the files). Thus, you will create an artificial backlog of incomplete work that can be used to argue for more help.

- Talk to your clerks and stress that the most important standard by which they should do their jobs is to follow procedures exactly and to focus on quality rather than on getting everything done. This will probably create a slowdown and a backlog that you can then use to argue for more help.

- You've been watching the operation of the payroll office down the hall. Many of those clerks are standing around drinking coffee half the time. Talk to your boss about your observation and ask to have one of these clerks transferred to your department.

Question: Are some of these approaches more ethical than others? Which ones? Which ones would you try?

2. You are an entrepreneur interested in acquiring a business that is currently owned by a competitor. The competitor, however, has not shown any interest in either selling his business or merging with your company. To gain inside knowledge of his firm, you hired a consultant you know to call contacts in your competitor's business and ask if the company is having any serious problems that might threaten its viability. If there are such problems, you might be able to use the information to either hire away the company's employees or get the competitor to sell.

Question: Is this ethical? Would you be likely to do it if you were the entrepreneur?

3. You are a vice president of human resources, negotiating with a union representative for a new labor contract. The union has insisted that it will not sign a new contract until the company agrees to raise the number of paid holidays from six to seven. Management has calculated that it will cost approximately $150,000 for each paid holiday, and has argued to the union that the company cannot afford to meet the demand. However, you know that, in reality, money is not the issue—the company simply doesn't think the union's demand is justified. To convince the union leaders that they should withdraw their demand, you have been considering the following alternatives:

- Tell the union representatives that their request is simply unacceptable to you because they haven't justified why they need seven paid holidays.
- Tell the union that the company simply can't afford it (without explanation).
- Prepare some erroneous financial statements that show that it will cost about $300,000 per paid holiday, which you simply can't afford.
- Offer the union leaders an all-expenses-paid "working" trip to a Florida resort if they will simply drop the demand entirely.

Question: Do any of the strategies raise ethical concerns? Which ones? Why?

4. You are about to graduate from the MBA program of a leading university. You specialized in management information systems (MIS) and will be taking a job with a company that commercially develops Web pages. While you did a lot of your work on machines at the university, you owned a very powerful personal computer of your own. You have decided to sell all of your personal hardware now, and then buy some new equipment after you see what kinds of projects your employer has you working on. So you post a note on several campus bulletin boards about the equipment for sale. You have decided not to tell prospective buyers that your hard drive acts like it is about to fail and that the computer occasionally crashes without warning.

Question: Is this ethical? Would you be likely to do this if you were this particular student?

5. You buy a new pair of shoes on sale. The printed receipt states very clearly that the shoes are not returnable. After you get them home, you wear the shoes around the house for a day and decide that they just don't fit you correctly. So you take the shoes back to the store. The clerk points to the message on the receipt; but you don't let that deter you. You start to yell angrily about the store's poor quality service, so that people in the store start to stare. The clerk calls the store manager; after some discussion, the manager agrees to give you your money back.

Question: Is this ethical? Would you be likely to do this if you were this customer?

These situations are hypothetical; however, the problems they present are real ones for negotiators. Managers are frequently confronted with important decisions about the strategies they will use to achieve important objectives, particularly when a variety of influence tactics are open to them. In this chapter, we will turn our attention to the major ethical questions that arise in negotiation. We will consider several questions:

1. What are ethics and how do they apply to negotiation?
2. What major types of ethical and unethical conduct are likely to occur in negotiation?
3. How can negotiators deal with the other party's use of deception?

WHAT ARE ETHICS AND
WHY DO THEY APPLY TO NEGOTIATION?

In this chapter, we are going to discuss the ethics of negotiation. *Ethics* are broadly applied social standards for what is right or wrong in a particular situation, or a process for setting those standards. They differ from *morals,* which are individual and personal beliefs about what is right and wrong. Ethics proceed from particular philosophies, which purport to (*a*) define the nature of the world in which we live, and (*b*) prescribe rules for living together.

We want to be clear that it is not our intention to advocate a specific ethical position for all negotiators or for the conduct of all negotiations. Many treatises on business ethics take a strongly prescriptive or normative position, advocating what a person should do. Instead, in this chapter we will simply describe the ethical issues that arise in negotiations. We will briefly identify the major ethical dimensions raised in negotiations, describe how people tend to think about these ethical choices, and provide a framework for making informed ethical decisions. Finally, we will summarize the research that has already been done in this area.

We also wish to distinguish among different criteria for judging and evaluating a negotiator's actions, particularly when questions of ethics might be involved. Many writers on business ethics have suggested several standards. Hitt suggests that there are at least four standards for evaluating strategies and tactics in business and negotiation:

- Make the decision on the basis of expected results, or what would give us the greatest return on investment.
- Make the decision on the basis of what the law says, on the legality of the matter.

- Make the decision on the basis of the strategy and values of my organization.
- Make the decision on the basis of my own personal convictions and what my conscience told me to do.[1]

Each of these approaches reflects a fundamentally different approach to ethical reasoning. The first may be called *end-result ethics,* in that the rightness of an action is determined by evaluating the pros and cons of its consequences. The second may be called *rule ethics,* in that the rightness of an action is determined by existing laws and contemporary social standards that define what is right and wrong and where the line is. The third may be called *social contract ethics,* in that the rightness of an action is based on the customs and norms of a particular society or community. Finally, the fourth may be called *personalistic ethics,* in that the rightness of the action is based on one's own conscience and moral standards. (See an overview of these four approaches in Table 7.1.)

Each of these approaches could be used to resolve the concerns we raised in the five situations at the beginning of the chapter. Going back to the clerk problem (Situation 1), if you as the manager believed in end-result ethics, then you would do whatever was necessary (lie, create an artificial overload) in order to get the boss to agree that another clerk should be hired. If you believed in rule ethics, you might believe that it is never appropriate to lie and might therefore use any tactic that does not require outright lying. If you believed in social contract ethics, you would make your decision on tactics based on what you thought was appropriate conduct for the way people behaved in your society and in your specific organization's culture; if they lie, you lie. Finally, if you believed in personalistic ethics, you would consult your conscience and decide whether the problem of getting more clerks justified using deceptive or dishonest tactics.

Discussions of business ethics frequently confuse ethical versus prudent versus practical versus legal criteria for judging appropriate conduct; that is, debate over these issues often confuses what is ethical (appropriate as determined by some standard of moral conduct) versus what is prudent (wise, based on trying to understand the efficacy of the tactic and the consequences it might have on the relationship with the other) versus what is practical (what a negotiator can actually make happen in a given situation) versus what is legal (what the law defines as acceptable practice).[2] In earlier chapters, we evaluated negotiation strategies and tactics by the prudence and practicality criteria; in this chapter, we turn to ways by which we can judge negotiation strategies and tactics by ethical criteria.

HOW DO NEGOTIATORS CHOOSE TO USE ETHICAL OR UNETHICAL TACTICS?

Why do some negotiators choose to use tactics that may be unethical? The first answer that occurs to many people is that such negotiators are corrupt, degenerate, or immoral. However, that answer is much too simplistic. In addition, it reflects a systematic bias in the way negotiators tend to perceive the other party and explain the reasons for his or her behavior. Simply put, this bias encourages people to attribute the causes of other people's behavior to their personalities, while attributing the causes of their own behavior to factors in the social environment.[3] Thus, in attempting to explain

TABLE 7.1 Four Approaches to Ethical Reasoning

Ethical System	Definition	Major Proponent	Central Tenets	Major Concerns
End-result ethics	Rightness of an action is determined by considering consequences.	Jeremy Bentham (1748–1832) John Stuart Mill (1806–1873)	• One must consider all likely consequences. • Actions are more right if they promote more happiness, more wrong as they produce unhappiness. • Happiness is defined as presence of pleasure and absence of pain. • Promotion of happiness is generally the ultimate aim. • Collective happiness of all concerned is the goal.	• How does one define happiness, pleasure, or utility? • How does one measure happiness, pleasure, or utility? • How does one trade off between short-term vs. long-term happiness? • If actions create happiness for 90% of the world and misery for the other 10%, is it still ethical?
Rule ethics	Rightness of an action is determined by laws and standards.	Immanuel Kant (1724–1804)	• Human conduct should be guided by primary moral principles, or "oughts." • Individuals should stand on their principles and restrain themselves by rules. • The ultimate good is a life of virtue (acting on principles) rather than pleasure. • We should not adjust moral law to fit our actions, but adjust our actions to fit moral law.	• By what authority do we accept particular rules or the "goodness" of those rules? • What rule do we follow when rules conflict? • How do we adapt general rules to fit specific situations? • How do rules change as circumstances change? • What happens when good rules produce bad consequences? • Are there rules without any exceptions?

(Continued)

TABLE 7.1 *(Concluded)*

Ethical System	Definition	Major Proponent	Central Tenets	Major Concerns
Social contract ethics	Rightness of an action is determined by the customs and norms of a community.	Jean-Jacques Rousseau (1712–1778)	• People must function in a social, community context to survive. • Communities become "moral bodies" for determining ground rules. • Duty and obligation bind the community and the individual to each other. • What is best for the common good determines the ultimate standard. • Laws are important, but morality determines the laws and standards for right and wrong.	• How do we determine the general will? • What is meant by the "common good"? • What do we do with independent thinkers who challenge the morality of the existing social order (e.g., Jefferson, Gandhi, Martin Luther King)? • Can a state be corrupt and its people still be "moral" (e.g., Nazi Germany)?
Personalistic ethics	Rightness of an action is determined by one's conscience.	Martin Buber (1878–1965)	• Locus of truth is found in human existence. • Conscience within each person calls them to fulfill their humanness and to decide between right and wrong. • Personal decision rules are the ultimate standards. • Pursuing a noble goal by ignoble means leads to an ignoble end. • There are no absolute formulas for living. • One should follow one's group but also stick up for what one individually believes.	• How could we justify ethics other than by saying, "it felt like the right thing to do"? • How could we achieve a collective definition of what is ethical if individuals disagreed? • How could we achieve cohesiveness and consensus in a team that only fosters personal perspectives? • How could an organization assure some uniformity in ethics?

SOURCE: Derived from W. Hitt, *Ethics and Leadership: Putting Theory into Practice* (Columbus, OH: Battelle Press, 1990).

why the other party used an ethically questionable negotiating tactic, a negotiator might say that this individual was unprincipled, profit-driven, or willing to use any tactic to get what he or she wanted. In contrast, when attempting to explain why you as the negotiator might use the same tactic, you would tend to say that you are highly principled but had very good reasons for deviating from those principles just this one time. Another way to describe this is in terms of the "absolutist–relativist" disparity: In general, people tend to perceive others in absolutist terms and attribute the causes of their behavior to a violation of some absolutist principles (e.g., "It is wrong to lie"), whereas they tend to perceive their own behavior in more relativistic terms and permit themselves an occasional minor transgression because they had good reasons (e.g., "The lie I told was perfectly justifiable under the circumstances").

Building in part on the material already covered in this chapter, we propose a relatively simple model to help explain how a negotiator decides whether to employ one or more deceptive tactics (see Figure 7.1). Negotiators begin by being in a situation where they must influence the other party and need to decide which tactics they will use. They then identify a range of possible influence tactics that may be effective in a given situation, but ones that they might judge as deceptive, inappropriate, or marginally ethical. Once these tactics are identified, they may decide to actually use one or more of these tactics. The selection and use of this tactic are likely to be influenced by the negotiators' own motivations and their perception/judgment of the tactic's appropriateness. Once the tactic is employed, negotiators will evaluate the consequences on three standards: (1) whether the tactic worked (produced the desired result), (2) how they feel about themselves after using the tactic, and (3) how they may be judged by the other party or by neutral observers. Negative or positive conclusions on any of these three standards may lead the negotiators to try to explain or justify their use of the tactic, but will also eventually affect their decision to employ similar tactics in the future. We will now explore the components of this model in greater detail, referring to some recent research that has improved our understanding of how these components work together.

Ethical Tactics in Negotiation Are Mostly about Truth Telling

Most of the ethics issues in negotiation are concerned with standards of truth telling—how honest, candid, and disclosing a negotiator should be. The attention here is more on what negotiators say they will do than on what they do . Some negotiators may cheat (violate formal and informal rules—e.g., claiming that rules about deadlines or procedures don't apply to them) or steal (e.g., break into the other party's or competitor's database or headquarters to secure confidential documents or briefing memoranda), but most of the attention in negotiator ethics has been on lying behavior.

Most negotiators would probably place a high value on a reputation for being truthful. Yet what does *being truthful* mean? The questions about what constitutes truth telling are quite straightforward, but once again the answers are not so clear. First, how does one define *truth?* Do you follow a clear set of rules, determine what the social contract is for truth in your group or organization, or follow your conscience? Second, how does one define and classify deviations from the truth? Are all deviations *lies,* no matter

FIGURE 7.1 A Simple Model of Ethical Decision Making

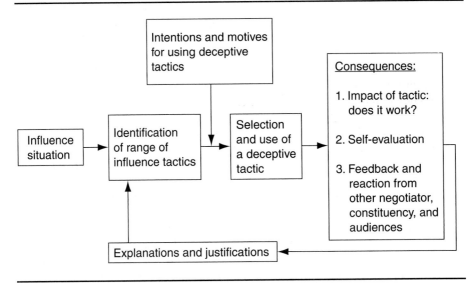

how small and minor they are? Finally, one can add a relativistic dimension to these questions: Should a person tell the truth all the time, or are there times when not telling the truth is an acceptable (or even necessary) form of conduct? These are questions of major concern to negotiators who are trying to decide what they can and cannot say and still remain ethical.

A number of articles in business journals have addressed the ethical issues surrounding truth telling. For example, Carr argued in a controversial *Harvard Business Review* article that strategy in business is analogous to strategy in a game of poker.[4] He advocated that, short of outright cheating (the equivalent of marking cards or hiding an ace up your sleeve), businesspeople ought to play the game as poker players do. Just as good poker playing often involves concealing information and bluffing (convincing others that you have the cards when you really don't), so do many business transactions. From time to time, most executives find themselves compelled, for their own interests or the interests of their companies, to practice some form of deception in their dealings with customers, suppliers, labor unions, government officials, or even other key executives. Through conscious misstatements, concealment of pertinent facts, or exaggeration—in short, bluffing—they seek to persuade others to agree with them. Carr argues that if an executive refuses to bluff periodically—if he or she feels obligated to tell the truth, the whole truth, and nothing but the truth all the time—he or she is probably ignoring opportunities permitted under the rules of business and is probably at a heavy disadvantage in business dealings.[5]

Bluffing, exaggeration, and concealment or manipulation of information, Carr maintained, are legitimate ways for both individuals and corporations to maximize their self-interest. Such strategies may be either advantageous or disadvantageous. An executive might plead poverty in a contract negotiation with a key employee and thereby save a significant amount of money for the company. However, a similar cost-cutting focus might lead the same executive to fail to make safety or quality improvements on one of the company's products, which could have severe long-term business consequences. As you can well imagine, Carr's position sparked lively debate among *Harvard Business Review* readers. A number of critics argued that individual businesspeople and corporations should be held to higher standards of ethical conduct, and they took Carr to task for his position.

Questions and debate regarding the ethical standards for truth telling in negotiation are ongoing. As we pointed out when we discussed interdependence (Chapter 1), negotiation is based on the exchange of information regarding the true preferences and priorities of the other negotiator.[6] Arriving at a clear, precise, effective negotiated agreement depends on the willingness of the parties to share accurate information about their own preferences, priorities, and interests. At the same time, because negotiators may also be interested in maximizing their self-interest, they may want to disclose as little as possible about their positions—particularly if they think they can do better by manipulating the information they disclose to the other party (see Chapter 3). This results in two fundamental negotiation dilemmas: the dilemma of trust and the dilemma of honesty (see Chapter 1). For our purposes here, the implication of the *dilemma of trust* is that negotiators believe everything the other says and can be manipulated by his or her dishonesty. The implication of the *dilemma of honesty* is that negotiators tell the other party all about their exact requirements and limits and will therefore never do better than this minimum level.[7] "To sustain the bargaining relationship, each party must select a middle course between the extremes of complete openness toward, and deception of, the other. Each must be able to convince the other of his integrity while not at the same time endangering his bargaining position."[8]

Typologies of Deceptive Tactics

Deception and disguise may take several forms in negotiation. Researchers have been working to identify the nature of these tactics, and their underlying structure, for almost 20 years.[9] The general approach has been to ask students and executives to rate a list of tactics on several dimensions: the appropriateness of the tactic, the rater's likelihood of using the tactic, and/or the perceived efficacy of using the tactic. Analyzing these questionnaire results, six clear categories of tactics emerged and have been confirmed by additional data collection and analysis.[10] These categories are listed in Table 7.2. It is interesting to note that of the six categories, two—emotional manipulation, and the use of "traditional competitive bargaining" tactics—are those which are viewed as generally appropriate and likely to be used. These tactics, therefore, while mildly inappropriate, are nevertheless seen as appropriate and effective in successful distributive bargaining. The other four categories—misrepresentation, bluffing, misrepresentation to opponent's network, and inappropriate information collection—generally include those tactics seen as inappropriate and unethical in negotiation.

TABLE 7.2   Categories of Marginally Ethical Negotiating Tactics

Category	Example
Traditional competitive bargaining	Not disclosing your walkaway; making an inflated opening offer
Emotional manipulation	Faking anger, fear, disappointment; faking elation, satisfaction
Misrepresentation	Distorting information or negotiation events in describing them to others
Misrepresentation to opponent's networks	Corrupting your opponent's reputation with his peers
Inappropriate information gathering	Bribery, infiltration, spying, etc.
Bluffing	Insincere threats or promises

SOURCE: Adapted from R. Robinson, R. J. Lewicki, and E. Donahue, "Extending and Testing a Five Factor Model of Ethical and Unethical Bargaining Tactics: The SINS Scale," *Journal of Organizational Behavior,* 2000, 21, 649–664; and B. Barry, I. S. Fulmer, and A. Long, *Ethically Marginal Bargaining Tactics: Sanction, Efficacy, and Performance.* Presented at the annual meeting of the Academy of Management, Toronto, August, 2000.

INTENTIONS AND MOTIVES TO USE DECEPTIVE TACTICS

The purpose of using marginally ethical negotiating tactics is to increase the negotiator's power in the bargaining environment. As we discussed in Chapter 6, information is one of the major sources of leverage in negotiation. Information has power because negotiation is intended to be a rational activity involving the exchange of information and the persuasive use of that information. One view of negotiation is that it is primarily an exchange of facts, arguments, and logic between two wholly rational information-processing entities. Often, whoever has better information, or uses it more persuasively, stands to "win" the negotiation.

In such a view, we assume that the information is accurate and truthful. To assume otherwise—that it is not truthful—is to question the very assumptions on which daily social communication is based, and to question the honesty and integrity of the presenter of that information. We seldom have reason to raise these questions and are naturally concerned that if we did raise them, we might insult the other and reduce the implied trust we placed in them. Moreover, investigating the others' truthfulness and honesty is time and energy consuming. So any inaccurate and untruthful statements (i.e., lies) introduced into this social exchange manipulate information in favor of the introducer. A lie changes the balance of information power in the negotiating relationship, creating the image that the liar either has better information than the other party or is using it in a more persuasive and convincing manner. Through the tactics we described earlier—bluffing, falsification, misrepresentation, deception, and selective disclosure—the liar gains advantage. The receiver either accepts the information at face value or has to decide whether there is a basis for challenging the other person's accuracy, credibility, and intentions (and/or must attempt to independently verify that information). Thus, a

---

BOX 7.1
Why Do Racers Cheat?

The *Boston Globe* investigated incidents of cheating in the Boston Marathon and other similar competitions around the country. The report listed the following explanations:

1. Some cheaters were angry or disturbed, often demonstrating a pattern of erratic, unethical, or illegal behaviors.

2. More typically, cheaters were described as middle-aged males who were often successful in many parts of their lives and found it difficult not to be equally successful in racing.

3. Some people were categorized as "unintentional cheaters"; these were people who simply were caught up in the racing moment and did not fully realize what they were doing at the time.

4. Cheaters typically sought recognition rather than prize money or other material gain. Ironically, many reported that the negative publicity surrounding their cheating caused friends, neighbors, and even family members to view them negatively, even if they had never misbehaved before.

SOURCE: Larry Tye, "They're Not in It for the Long Haul," *The Columbus (Ohio) Dispatch,* April 19, 1998, p. 10E.

---

negotiator uses inaccurate or misleading information to change the other party's preferences or priorities.

Different types of deception can serve different purposes in negotiation. For example, one study examined factors that affected the tendency of negotiators to lie about material facts.[11] Students took part in a role-play in which they had to sell a car with a defective transmission. Students could lie by omission—by simply failing to mention the defective transmission—or by commission—by denying that the transmission was defective even when asked by the other party. Far more students were willing to lie by omission (not revealing the whole truth) than by commission (falsely answering a question when asked). This finding clearly reinforces the norm of caveat emptor (let the buyer beware), suggesting that it is up to the buyer to ask the right questions and be appropriately skeptical when accepting the other's sales pitch.

The Motivation to Behave Unethically

The motivation of a negotiator can clearly affect his or her tendency to use deceptive tactics. (For example, see Box 7.1 for a discussion of the motives of cheaters in running.) In an early study on tactics, Lewicki and Spencer asked negotiators about their predisposition to use marginally ethical tactics. One part of the questionnaire explicitly instructed the respondents to assume either a competitive or a cooperative motivational orientation toward the other party, and to assume that the other party would be taking either a competitive or a cooperative motivational orientation. The authors predicted that (1) when motivated to be competitive, and when expecting the other to be competitive, the negotiator would see the marginally ethical tactics as appropriate, and (2) when both parties were competitively motivated, they would exhibit the greatest tendency to employ marginally ethical tactics. The results revealed that differences in the negotiators' own motivational orientation—cooperative versus competitive—did *not* cause differences in their view of the appropriateness of using the tactics, but the negotiators' perception of the other's expected motivation did! In other words, negotiators were significantly more likely to see the marginally ethical tactics as appropriate if they anticipated that the other would be competitive versus cooperative. Although these findings are preliminary, they do suggest that motives and intentions may be integrally tied together. Negotiators may rationalize the use of marginally ethical tactics in anticipated defense of the other's expected conduct, rather than take personal responsibility for using these tactics in the service of their own competitive orientation.[12]

The Consequences of Unethical Conduct

A negotiator who employs an unethical tactic will experience positive or negative consequences. The consequences are based on whether the tactic is effective; how the other person, constituencies, and audiences evaluate the tactic; and how the negotiator evaluates the tactic. First, consequences will occur depending on whether the tactic worked or not—that is, whether the negotiator got what he or she wanted as a result of using the tactic. A second set of consequences may result depending on how the negotiator evaluates his or her own use of the tactic—whether using the tactic creates any discomfort, personal stress, or even guilt—or, in contrast, whether the actor sees no problem in using the tactic again and even begins to consider how to use it more effectively. As we note elsewhere in this chapter, negotiators often fail to understand how the use of these tactics can seriously affect their reputation in the marketplace as a fair and ethical person. Finally, a third set of consequences may come from the judgments and evaluations of that negotiator—from the opponent, from constituencies, or from audiences that can observe the tactic. Depending on whether these parties recognize the tactic and whether they evaluate it as proper or improper to use, the negotiator may receive a great deal of feedback.

Let us first consider the consequences that occur based on whether the tactic is successful or not. It should be fairly clear that the tactic's effectiveness should have some impact on whether it is more or less likely to be used in the future (essentially, a simple learning and reinforcement process). If using the tactic allows negotiators to attain rewarding outcomes that would be unavailable to them if they behaved ethically, and if the unethical conduct is not punished by others, the frequency of unethical conduct is likely to increase because the negotiator believes he or she can get away with it. Thus, real consequences—rewards and punishments that arise from using a tactic or not using it—should not only motivate a negotiator's present behavior but also affect his or her predisposition to use similar strategies in similar circumstances in the future. (For the moment, we will ignore the consequences of these tactics on the negotiator's reputation and trustworthiness, an impact that most deceptive negotiators ignore in the short term.) These propositions have not been tested in negotiating situations, but they have been tested extensively in other research studies on ethical decision making. For example, research by Hegarty and Sims appears to support both of these assertions. In that study, when research participants expected to be rewarded for making an unethical decision by participating in a laboratory-simulated kickback scheme, they not only participated but also were willing to participate again when a second opportunity arose. Moreover, when there were also strong pressures on the research subjects to compete with others—for example, announcing how well each person had done on the task and giving a prize to the one with the highest score—the frequency of unethical conduct increased even further.[13]

To our knowledge, no research has been performed on the second set of consequences: the negotiator's own reactions to the use of unethical tactics. But a final set of consequences occurs when the negotiator experiences the reaction of the target person. If the target person is unaware that a deceptive tactic has been used, he or she shows no reaction other than disappointment at having lost the negotiation. However, if the target discovers that deception has occurred, he or she is likely to react strongly. People who discover that they have been deceived or exploited are typically angry. In addition to having lost the negotiation, they feel foolish for having allowed themselves to be manipulated or deceived by a clever ploy. As a result of both the actual loss they may have suffered in negotiations and the embarrassment they feel at having been deceived, most victims are likely to seek retaliation and revenge. Thus, although the use of unethical tactics may lead to short-term success for the negotiator, it may also create an adversary who is bent on revenge and retribution.[14] For example, one study showed that victims had strong emotional reactions to deception when they had an intimate relationship with the subject, when the information at stake was very important, and when they saw lying as an unacceptable type of behavior for that relationship (i.e., when strong expectations of truth telling were clearly violated). In almost two-thirds of the cases reported, the discovery of the lie was instrumental in an eventual termination of the relationship with the other person, and in most cases the termination was initiated by the victim. Finally, the importance of the information that was lied about was the most significant predictor of whether the relationship would eventually terminate. If the information was about something that was serious, personal, and highly consequential for whether the parties could fundamentally trust each other or not, then the discovered deception was highly destructive to the relationship.[15]

NON SEQUITUR   **by WILEY**

NON SEQUITUR © Wiley Miller. Dist. by UNIVERSAL PRESS SYNDICATE. Reprinted with permission. All rights reserved.

Explanations and Justifications

From the negotiator's perspective, as we stated earlier, the primary motivation to use a deceptive tactic is to gain a temporary power advantage. The negotiator may have made the decision to use such a tactic casually and quickly in order to seize a tactical advantage or after long and careful evaluation of the various options and their likely consequences. When a negotiator has used a tactic that may produce a reaction—as we described above—the negotiator must prepare to defend the tactic's use to himself (e.g., "I see myself as a person of integrity, and yet I have decided to do something that might be viewed as unethical"), to the victim, or to constituencies and audiences who may express their concerns. The primary purpose of these explanations and justifications is to rationalize, explain, or excuse the behavior—to verbalize some good, legitimate reason why this tactic was necessary. Some examples include:[16]

- *The tactic was unavoidable.* Negotiators frequently justify their actions by claiming that the situation made it necessary for them to act the way they did. The negotiator may feel that she was not in full control of her actions or had no other option, and hence should not be held responsible. Perhaps the negotiator had no intent to hurt anyone but was pressured to use the tactic by someone else.

- *The tactic was harmless.* The negotiator may say that what he did was really trivial and not very significant. People tell white lies all the time. For example, you may greet your neighbor with a cheery "Good morning, nice to see you" when, in fact, it may not be a good morning, you are in a bad mood, and you wish you hadn't run into your neighbor because you are angry about his dog barking all night. Exaggerations, bluffs, or peeking at the other party's private notes during negotiations can all be easily explained away as harmless actions. Note, however, that this particular justification interprets the harm from the actor's point of view; the victim may not agree and may have experienced significant harm or costs as a result.

- *The tactic will help to avoid negative consequences.* When using this justification, negotiators are arguing that the ends justify the means. In this case, the justification is that the tactic helped to avoid greater harm. It is okay to lie to an armed robber about where you have hidden your money in order to avoid being robbed. Similarly, negotiators may see lying (or any other means–ends tactic) as justifiable if it protects them against even more undesirable consequences should the truth be known.

- *The tactic will produce good consequences, or the tactic is altruistically motivated.* Again, the end justifies the means, but in a positive sense. As we stated earlier, a negotiator who judges a tactic on the basis of its consequences is acting in accord with the tenets of act utilitarianism—that the quality of any given action is judged by its consequences. Act utilitarians will argue that certain kinds of lies or means–ends tactics are appropriate because they may provide for the larger good— for example, Robin Hood tactics in which someone robs from the rich to make the poor better off. Another tack on this is the "I was only trying to help you . . ." explanation. In reality, most negotiators use deceptive tactics for their own advantage,

Pepper ... and Salt

THE WALL STREET JOURNAL

"I swear to tell the truth, as I see it."

From *The Wall Street Journal.* Used with permission of Cartoon Features Syndicate.

not for the general good. In this case, others are likely to view these actions as less excusable than tactics that avoid negative consequences.

- *"They had it coming,"* or *"They deserve it,"* or *"I'm just getting my due."* All these justifications are variations on the theme of using lying and deception either against an individual who may have taken advantage of you in the past or against some generalized source of authority (i.e., "the system"). The pollster Daniel Yankelovich has noted the problem of a national erosion of honesty. Increasingly, people believed that it was appropriate to take advantage of the system in various ways—through tax evasion, petty theft, shoplifting, improper declaration of bankruptcy, journalistic excesses, and distortion in advertising. A decade later, newer statistical surveys show that the problem has increased dramatically on almost every front.[17]

- *"They were going to do it anyway, so I will do it first."* Sometimes a negotiator legitimizes the use of a tactic because he or she anticipates that the other intends to use similar tactics. In an insightful study, Anne Tenbrunsel also shows how the magnitude of temptation to act unethically affects both the perceptions of the other party and one's own desire to use the tactic. Research participants were given opportunities to misrepresent the value of a fictitious firm in order to win either a small prize or a large one, and competed against each other to win the prize. Individuals whose partners were more tempted to misrepresent information expected the other to be less honest than individuals whose partners were less tempted. In addition, the reverse logic also operated: The more an individual was tempted to engage in misrepresentation, the more he or she believed that the other would also misrepresent information. Thus, one's own temptation to misrepresent creates a self-fulfilling logic in which one believes one needs to misrepresent because the other is likely to do it as well. At the same time, subjects in this study consistently rated themselves as more ethical than the other party, which suggests that people experience some combination of positive illusions about themselves and their own behavior, and negative illusions about the other and the other's likely behavior.[18]

- *The tactic is fair or appropriate to the situation.* This approach uses situational relativism as a rationale or justification. Most social situations, including negotiations, are governed by a set of generally well-understood rules of proper conduct and behavior. For example, recall the earlier arguments of Carr, that business is a game and that the game has a special ethos to it that legitimizes normally unethical actions.[19] Others have countered these arguments, both to show that deceit in business is just as immoral as it is in other areas of life, and that the game analogy of business no more legitimizes unethical conduct than other analogies (see Box 7.2).[20]

Summary.   Explanations and justifications are self-serving rationalizations for one's own conduct. First, they allow the negotiator to convince others—particularly the victim—that conduct that would ordinarily be wrong in a given situation is acceptable. The adequacy of these explanations to others has a strong effect on mitigating the impact of deceptive behavior.[21] In addition, explanations and justifications help people to rationalize the behavior to themselves as well. We propose that the more frequently negotiators engage in this self-serving justification process, the more their judgments about ethical standards and values will become biased, leading to a lessened ability to make accurate judgments about the truth. Moreover, although the tactics were initially used to gain power in a negotiation, the negotiators who use them frequently will experience a loss of power over time. These negotiators will be seen as having low credibility or integrity, and will be treated as people who will act exploitatively if the opportunity arises. Negotiators with these characteristics will probably be unsuccessful over time unless they are skillful at continually staying ahead of the negative reputation generated by their conduct.

HOW CAN NEGOTIATORS DEAL WITH THE OTHER PARTY'S USE OF DECEPTION?

A chapter such as this would not be complete without briefly noting some of the things that you as a negotiator can do when you believe the other party is using deceptive tactics. If you think the other party is using deceptive tactics (see Table 7.3), in general you can do the following:

Ask Probing Questions.   When the other party is committing acts of omission—that is, not fully disclosing a problem (recall the fourth situation at the beginning of this chapter, about selling the computer with a defective hard drive)—asking a number of

BOX 7.2
When Is It Acceptable to Lie in the Office?

Most large organizations (and many smaller ones) have adopted a formal code of ethics that calls for honesty in all interactions and full accountability for opinions and behavior. However, some researchers believe that there are instances where a lack of personal accountability—and even dishonesty—may be preferable to these codified norms. These situations include the following:

- *When evaluating your boss.* Many companies have instituted a program of "360-degree feedback," in which employees provide input into their supervisors' performance evaluation. Recent research (Antonioni, 1994) suggests that employees who are asked to provide feedback on their supervisors will respond more honestly and constructively when their appraisals are anonymous. Employees who were personally accountable for their ratings evaluated their managers more positively, while providing less valuable constructive feedback.

- *When dealing with customers.* Salespeople are often at a disadvantage when they are held to strict standards of truth telling. For example, a real estate salesperson who discloses her client's interest in a home too soon in the bargaining process may negate her client's competitive advantage in future negotiations. Hamilton and Strutton (1994) have developed the following guidelines for resolving truth-telling problems in business transactions (a yes answer to any of these questions indicates that truth or full disclosure is morally required in this situation):

Does the receiver have a right, based on legal, contractual, or human rights standards, to truth telling or full disclosure?

Would a reasonable person expect the truth/full disclosure?

Does the prospect/customer actually expect truth/full disclosure?

Does the salesperson's or organization's reputation require truth telling or full disclosure in this situation?

Should the salesperson's or organization's reputation require truth telling/full disclosure in situations such as this?

SOURCE: Adapted from D. Antonioni, "The Effects of Feedback Accountability on Upward Appraisal Ratings," *Personnel Psychology* 47 (1994), pp. 247–56; and J. B. Hamilton and D. Strutton, "Two Practical Guidelines for Resolving Truth Telling Problems in Business Transactions," *Journal of Business Ethics* 13 (1994), pp. 899–912.

probing questions about the other's position, point of view, information, and so on may help you uncover the key information that was omitted. Research (by Schweitzer) shows that most buyers fail to ask questions, and that asking questions can reveal a great deal of information, some of which may be intentionally undisclosed by the negotiator.[22] While asking questions may not always expose lies of commission—that is, those in which the actor is intentionally changing information or misrepresenting an issue—excellent and complete questioning may expose some. Police interrogators and

TABLE 7.3 Detecting Deception

Researchers have identified a number of verbal tactics that you can use to determine whether the other party is acting deceptively.

Tactic	Explanation and Examples
Intimidation	Force the other to admit he is using deception by intimidating him into telling the truth. Make a no-nonsense accusation of the other. Criticize the other. Hammer the other with challenging questions. Feign indifference to what he has to say ("I'm not interested in anything you have to say on the matter").
Futility portrayal	Emphasize the futility and impending danger associated with continued deceit: "The truth will come out someday," "Don't dig the hole deeper by trying to cover it up," "If you try to cover it up, it will only be worse in the future," "You are all alone in your deception."
Discomfort and relief	State the maxim "Confession is good for the soul." Help the other reduce the tension and stress associated with being a known deceiver.
Bluffing	Lie to the other to make her believe you have uncovered her deception: "Your sins are about to be uncovered." Indicate that you know what she knows but will not discuss it.
Gentle prods	Encourage the other to keep talking so that he gives you information that may help you separate true facts from deceptions. Ask him to elaborate on the topic being discussed. Ask questions but indicate that you are asking because "other people want to know." Play devil's advocate and ask playful questions. Praise the other so as to give him confidence and support that may lead to information sharing.
Minimization	Play down the significance of any deceptive act. Help the other find excuses for why she was deceptive; minimize the consequences of the action; indicate that others have done worse; shift the blame to someone else.
Contradiction	Get the other to tell his story fully in order to discover more information that will allow you to discover inconsistencies and contradictions in his comments or reports. Point out and ask for explanations about apparent contradictions. Ask the speaker the same question several times and look for inconsistencies in his response. Present contradictions back and ask the speaker to explain. Put pressure on the speaker and get him to slip up or say things he doesn't want to say.
Altered information	Alter information and hopefully trick the other into revealing deception. Exaggerate what you believe is the deception, hoping that the other will jump in to "correct" the statement. Ask the suspected deceiver a question containing incorrect information and hope she corrects you.

TABLE 7.3   *(Concluded)*

Tactic	Explanation and Examples
A chink in the defense	Try to get the other to admit a small or partial lie about some information, and use this to push for admission of a larger lie: "If you lied about this one little thing, how do I know you have not lied about other things?"
Self-disclosure	Reveal a number of things about yourself, including, perhaps, dishonesty on your own part, hoping the other will begin to trust you and reciprocate with disclosures of dishonesty.
Point of deception cues	Point out behaviors you detect in the other that might be an indication he is lying: sweating, nervousness, change of voice, inability to make eye contact, and so on.
Concern	Indicate your true concern for the other's welfare: "You are important to me," "I care deeply about you," "I feel your pain."
Keeping the status quo	Admonish the other to be truthful in order to maintain her good name. "What will people think?" Appeal to her pride and desire to maintain a good reputation.
Direct approach	"Simply tell me the truth." "Let's be honest here." "Surely you have no objection to telling me everything you know."
Silence	Create a "verbal vacuum" that makes the other uncomfortable and gets him to talk and disclose information. When he tells a lie, simply maintain direct eye contact but remain silent.

SOURCE: Adapted from Pamela J. Kalbfleisch, "The Language of Detecting Deceit," *Journal of Language and Social Psychology* 13, no. 4 (1994), pp. 469–96.

prosecuting attorneys have learned to master the art of questioning to discover both lies of omission and commission. Refer back to Chapter 5 for a more extensive examination of asking good questions.

Recognize the Tactic.   In Chapter 3 we extensively discuss how to respond when the other party is using distributive tactics or dirty tricks. Deceptive tactics certainly fall into the latter category. To summarize, negotiators can do the following things:

Ignore the tactic. If you are aware that the other party is bluffing or lying, simply ignore it.

• *Ask questions.* Asking questions can help a negotiator determine whether a negotiator is being deceptive. But such "cross-examination" may actually increase the seller's tendency to be deceptive in areas where questions are not being asked.[23]

• *"Call" the tactic.* Indicate to the other side that you know he is bluffing or lying. Do so tactfully but firmly, and indicate your displeasure. (Recall, though, that spotting lies is not always easy—see Box 7.3.)

BOX 7.3
Is There Such a Thing as an "Honest Face"?

Though people in general are not particularly good at spotting lies, some people continue to believe that they can tell by looking into someone's face if that person is inclined to be dishonest or truthful on a regular basis. But how accurate are such assessments?

A study asked participants to view photographs of the same people as children, adolescents, and adults and to rate their attractiveness and honesty based on an assessment of their faces. These results were compared to self-reports of honest behavior provided by the people in the photographs. The results demonstrated that structural qualities of the face, such as attractiveness, "babyfaceness," eye size, and symmetry each individually contributed to perceptions of greater honesty in observers. The self-reports revealed that men who looked more honest early in life actually were more honest as they grew older. On the other hand, women whose behavior was less honest when they were young grew to appear more honest as they aged, even though their behavior did not change significantly. Study participants were able to correctly identify the most honest men in the group as they aged, but their assessment of women was largely inaccurate. The researchers concluded that men's faces accurately reflected their tendency toward honesty, but women's faces were not particularly valid indicators of their truthfulness.

SOURCE: Adapted from L. A. Zebrowitz, L. Voinescu, and M. A. Collins, "Wide-Eyed and Crooked-Faced: Determinants of Perceived and Real Honesty across the Life Span," *Personality and Social Psychology Bulletin* 22 (1996), pp. 1258–69.

• *Respond in kind.* If the other party bluffs, you bluff more. If she misrepresents, you misrepresent. We do not recommend this course of action at all, because it simply escalates the destructive behavior and drags you into the mud with the other party, but if she recognizes that you are lying too, she may also realize that the tactic is unlikely to work.

• *Discuss what you see and offer to help the other party change to more honest behaviors.* This is a variation on calling the tactic but instead tries to assure the other party that telling the truth is, in the long term, more likely to get him what he wants than any form of bluffing or deception will.

CHAPTER SUMMARY

In this chapter, we have discussed the primary factors that negotiators consider when they decide whether particular tactics are deceptive and unethical. We have included this chapter because we believe that the negotiation process raises several critical ethical issues. Much of what has been written on negotiating behavior has been strongly normative about ethics and has prescribed "shoulds" and "should nots." We do not believe that this approach facilitates the understanding of how negotiators actually make decisions about when and where to use specific tactics. To understand this process better, we have approached the study of tactic choice from a decision-making framework, examining the ethical overtones of these choices. We also briefly discussed the ways in which negotiators can respond to another party who may be using deceptive tactics.

We began by considering several negotiation cases, showing how ethical questions can be critical to the selection of particular strategic and tactical options.

We proposed that negotiators who choose to use an unethical tactic usually decide to do so to increase their negotiating power. Power is gained by manipulating the perceived base of accurate information in the negotiation, getting better information about the other party's plan, or undermining the other party's ability to achieve his or her objectives. We then presented a simple model of ethical decision making (Figure 7.1).

Research on negotiator ethics and on various aspects of this model leads us to the following conclusions:

1. While individual negotiators may disagree as to which negotiating tactics are ethical and which are unethical, the research reported here suggests that there is much more convergence than might have been expected.

2. The decision to use a deceptive tactic can probably best be understood through a decision-making model. It is clear that many individual differences and situational variables are also likely to affect that decision.

3. In deciding to use a deceptive tactic, a negotiator is likely to be more heavily influenced by (*a*) his or her own motivations, (*b*) expectations of what the other negotiator will do, and (*c*) the expected future relationship between the negotiator and the other party.

4. Negotiators who have considered the use of deceptive tactics in the past or who are considering their use in the future should ask themselves the following questions:

    (*a*) Will they really enhance my power and help me achieve my objective?

    (*b*) How will the use of these tactics affect the quality of my relationship with the other party in the future?

    (*c*) How will the use of these tactics affect my reputation as a negotiator?

Negotiators frequently overlook the fact that, although unethical or expedient tactics may get them what they want in the short run, these same tactics typically lead to diminished effectiveness in the long run.

ENDNOTES

1. Hitt, 1990. See also Green, 1993; Nash, 1990.
2. Missner, 1980.
3. Miller and Ross, 1975.
4. Carr, 1968.
5. Ibid., p. 144.
6. Kelley and Thibaut, 1969.
7. Kelley, 1966.
8. Rubin and Brown, 1975.
9. See Lewicki, 1983; Lewicki and Spencer, 1990: Lewicki and Robinson, 1998; Robinson, Lewicki, and Donahue, 1998; Barry, Fulmer, and Long, 2001.
10. Robinson, Lewicki, and Donahue, 2000; Barry, Fulmer, and Long, 2000.

11. Schweitzer, 1997; Schweitzer and Croson, 2001.
12. Lewicki and Spencer, 1991.
13. Hegarty and Sims, 1978.
14. Bies and Moag, 1986; Miller and Vidmar, 1981; Werth and Flannery, 1986.
15. McCornack and Levine, 1990.
16. Examples drawn from Bok, 1978.
17. Yankelovich, 1982; Patterson and Kim, 1991.
18. Tenbrunsel, 1998.
19. Carr, 1968.
20. Bowie, 1993; Koehn, 1997.
21. Shapiro, 1991.
22. Schweitzer, 1997; Schweitzer and Croson, 2001.
23. Schweitzer and Croson, 2001.

CHAPTER 8

Global Negotiation

The number of global negotiations is increasing rapidly. People today travel more frequently and farther, and business is more international in scope and extent than ever before. For many people and organizations, global negotiations have become the norm rather than an exotic activity that occurs only occasionally. Numerous books and articles, from both academic and practitioner perspectives, have been written about the complexities of negotiating across borders, be it with a person from a different country, culture, or region. Although the term *culture* has many possible definitions, we will use it to refer to the shared values and beliefs of a group of people. Culture describes group-level characteristics, which may or may not be accurate descriptors of any given individual within the group.[1] Countries can have more than one culture, and cultures can span national borders. With these caveats in mind, we will use the terms *culture* and *country* loosely in this chapter to refer to negotiation across borders (legal or cultural). As we discussed in Chapter 1, negotiating is a social process that is embedded in a much larger context.[2] This context increases in complexity when more than one culture is involved, making negotiation a highly complicated process when it occurs across borders.[3]

So much has been written on this topic that we cannot summarize it all in one chapter.[4] Recent additions in this area are studies of negotiations occurring in newly developing economies[5] and intracultural comparisons of negotiators from several different countries, including Norway and Mexico;[6] China and Canada;[7] China and Hong Kong;[8] the United States and Taiwan;[9] and the United States and Mexico;[10] among others. Our goal is to highlight and discuss some of the most recent and interesting work that has been written on this topic.

It is important to recognize that this book has been written from a North American perspective, and that this cultural filter has influenced how we think about negotiation, what we consider to be important aspects of negotiation, and our advice about how to become a better negotiator. This chapter also reflects our own cultural filter, both in our choices about what we discuss, and because we use Americans as the base from which to make comparisons to other cultures. That is not to say that all Americans share the same culture. In fact, there is evidence that people from countries as similar as the United States and Canada negotiate differently.[11] Within the United States and Canada, there are systematic regional and cultural differences (e.g., among English and French Canadians, and among Hispanics, African Americans, Southerners, New Yorkers, and other groups in many areas of the United States). At some level, however, Americans do share (more or less) a common culture that is different from that of other countries. While recognizing the differences within the United States, we will use some common aspects of American culture in our discussion of international and intercultural negotiation.

This chapter is organized in the following manner. First we discuss the American negotiating style, from both non-American and American perspectives. Next we present the results of a program of research that has demonstrated that negotiators in different countries use different negotiation processes to reach similar negotiation outcomes. Then we will discuss some of the factors that make negotiations across borders difficult, including both the environmental context (macropolitical factors) and the immediate context (microstrategic factors). We then turn to a discussion of perhaps the most critical issue of cross-border negotiation: the effect of culture, be it national, regional, or organizational. The chapter concludes with a discussion of some culturally responsive strategies available to the global negotiator. There are many factors to think about when negotiating with people from other cultures.[12]

THE AMERICAN NEGOTIATING STYLE

Several authors have written about the American negotiation approach.[13] Labeling any culture's traits is risky business, however, because labels are at best a guide to an average person from the country or culture in question, and there is a great deal of variation around that average. Labels tend to constrain our thinking and expectations such that we may perceive more consistency in the other person than actually exists, and labels may lock us into perceiving the other party's behavior in a historically dated manner. For instance, it is likely that negotiators from countries undergoing economic restructuring will become increasingly influenced by the new organizational cultures that develop rather than the old national culture, perhaps making national-level trait descriptions less useful as time passes.[14] With this caution in mind, cultural or national trait labels can provide us with at least a good starting point for knowing how to negotiate across borders.

We'll start by looking at how some non-Americans describe the American style, and conclude this section with an American's own view of the American negotiating style. Tommy Koh, the former ambassador from Singapore to the United States, had the opportunity to observe American negotiators in the international political arena for several years. Koh notes the following strengths of the American negotiators: (1) good preparation; (2) clear and plain speaking; (3) a focus on pragmatism over doctrine; (4) strong ability to recognize the other party's perspective, and to recognize that negotiations do not have to be win-lose; (5) good understanding of the concession-making process that is fundamental to negotiation; and (6) candid and straightforward communication.[15] In contrast, he lists the following as major weaknesses of American political negotiators: (1) serious intergovernmental agency conflicts that cause problems in reaching consensus within the American team; (2) the separation of political power between the presidency and Congress, which complicates the negotiation process; (3) the influence of interest groups on negotiations; (4) media interference, which makes it more difficult to negotiate sensitive parts of an agreement discreetly; (5) negotiator impatience; and (6) cultural insensitivity. Koh says that the strengths of American political negotiators outweigh their weaknesses, but he also cautions to focus on the individual characteristics of each negotiator and not to be guided by trait labels alone.

A much more biting view of the American negotiating style is offered by Samfrits Le Poole in his article "Negotiating with Clint Eastwood in Brussels."[16] Le Poole writes that American business negotiators have an arrogant ignorance that handicaps them when negotiating globally. Le Poole, a European, argues that Europeans are much more adept at cross-border negotiations because the geography of Europe provides them with the opportunity to understand an international perspective from a very early age. For Le Poole, American business negotiators are always in a hurry, do not understand the role of small talk in building relationships, and are too quick to concede in negotiations. Le Poole argues that these characteristics weaken the American negotiator dealing with a European. For instance, knowing the Americans' love for efficiency and their tendency to give large concessions, many European negotiators will deliberately delay the negotiation process and reap the benefits of more concessions. Le Poole's central argument is that all negotiators need to understand the ways in which their own culture influences how they negotiate across borders.

McDonald offers an American perspective on the American negotiating style. From his 40 years of experience as a U.S. diplomat and international negotiator, McDonald's balanced view of the American negotiating style dovetails nicely with the perspectives of Koh and Le Poole. For McDonald, the weaknesses of American negotiators include (1) impatience, (2) arrogance, (3) poor listening skills, (4) insularity, (5) legalism, and (6) naïveté.[17] On the other hand, McDonald perceives the following strengths of American negotiators: (1) friendliness, (2) fairness and honesty, (3) flexibility, (4) innovativeness, (5) pragmatism, (6) preparedness, and (7) cooperativeness.

NOT EVERYONE NEGOTIATES LIKE AMERICANS!

John Graham and his colleagues have conducted a series of experiments comparing negotiators from the United States and several other countries.[18] These studies each used the same research materials—a version of the buyer/seller negotiation simulation developed by Kelley, in which negotiators have to decide on the prices of three products (televisions, typewriters, air conditioners).[19] The participants in the studies were business people who were attending either management seminars or graduate business courses. Participants in the studies negotiated with people from their own countries (thus, these were intracultural, not cross-cultural, negotiations). The major dependent measures in these studies were (1) the individual profit level made by the two negotiators in the simulation and (2) the level of satisfaction that the negotiators had with the negotiation outcomes.

The results of this research have been quite consistent across studies. Graham and his colleagues found no differences in the profit levels obtained by negotiators in the simulation from the United States and the other countries studied, which included Japan;[20] China;[21] Canada;[22] Brazil;[23] and Mexico.[24] Taken as a whole, these results suggest that negotiators from different countries were equally effective in obtaining negotiation outcomes when they negotiate with other people from their own country.

Graham and Adler did find, however, that there were significant differences in the negotiation *process* in the countries that they studied.[25] In other words, although negotiators from different countries obtained the same average outcomes, the ways in which they negotiated to obtain those outcomes were quite different. For instance, Graham concludes that "in American negotiations, higher profits are achieved by making opponents feel *un*comfortable, while in Japanese negotiations, higher profits are associated with making opponents feel comfortable."[26] In addition, Graham reports that Brazilian negotiators who used powerful and deceptive strategies were more likely to receive higher outcomes; these strategies were not related to the outcomes attained by the American negotiators.[27] Further, Adler, Graham, and Schwartz report that representational strategies (gathering information) were negatively related to profits attained by Mexican and French-Canadian negotiators, whereas these strategies were unrelated to the profits that American negotiators received.[28] Finally, although Adler, Brahm, and Graham found that Chinese and American negotiators used similar negotiation strategies when they negotiated, their communication patterns were quite different—the Chinese asked more questions, said no less frequently, and interrupted each other more frequently than did American negotiators.[29]

Adler and Graham also compared intracultural and cross-cultural negotiation outcomes and processes. They found that Japanese and English-Canadian negotiators received lower profit levels when they negotiated cross-culturally than when they negotiated intraculturally; American and French-Canadian negotiators negotiated the same average outcomes in cross-cultural and intracultural negotiations.[30] These results support Adler and Graham's hypothesis that cross-cultural negotiations will result in poorer outcomes compared to intracultural negotiations, at least some of the time. In addition, Adler and Graham found some differences in the cross-cultural negotiation process. For instance, French-Canadian negotiators used more cooperative strategies in cross-cultural negotiations than in intracultural negotiations, and American negotiators reported higher levels of satisfaction with their cross-cultural negotiations (versus intracultural negotiations).

A study by Natlandsmyr and Rognes generally supports and extends Graham's research.[31] Natlandsmyr and Rognes examined the negotiation process and outcome of Mexican and Norwegian negotiators who participated in a negotiation simulation similar to the one used by Graham and his colleagues in their research. Natlandsmyr and Rognes found that when negotiating intraculturally, Norwegian negotiators reached higher joint outcomes than Mexican negotiators. During intercultural negotiations, however, the Mexican–Norwegian dyads reached agreements closer to the intracultural Mexican dyads than to the intracultural Norwegian dyads. Natlandsmyr and Rognes report that the progression of offers that Mexican and Norwegian negotiators made was different, and they suggest that culture may have a significant effect on the negotiation process.

In summary, research suggests that negotiators from different cultures (countries) use different negotiation strategies and communication patterns when negotiating intraculturally than when negotiating cross-culturally. However, it is important to note that there were few differences in the negotiation outcomes attained by the negotiators across these studies. This suggests that there are many different ways to negotiate agreements that are, on average, worth the same value, and that negotiators should employ the process that fits the culture they are in. Further, the culture of the negotiator appears to be an important predictor of both the negotiation process that will occur and how the chosen negotiation strategies will influence negotiation outcomes. In addition, this research suggests that cross-cultural negotiations may yield poorer outcomes than intracultural negotiations, at least on some occasions.

FIGURE 8.1   The Contexts of International Negotiations

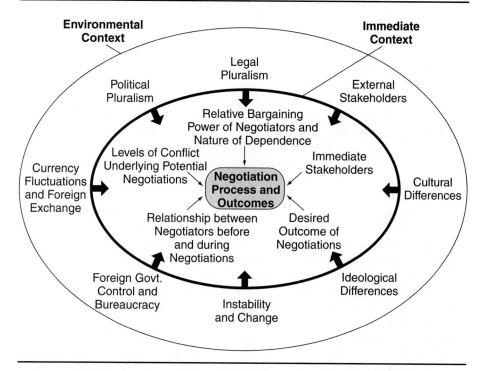

SOURCE: Adapted from A.V. Phatak and M.H. Habib, "The Dynamics of International Business Negotiations," *Business Horizons* 39 (1996), pp. 30–38; and from J.W. Salacuse, "Making Deals in Strange Places: A Beginner's Guide to International Business Negotiations," *Negotiation Journal* 4 (1988), pp. 5–13.

WHAT MAKES CROSS-BORDER NEGOTIATIONS DIFFERENT?

Phatak and Habib suggest that two overall contexts have an influence on cross-border negotiations: the environmental context and the immediate context (see Figure 8.1).[32] The *environmental context* includes "forces in the environment that are beyond the control of either party" that influence the negotiation.[33] The *immediate context* "includes factors over which the negotiators have influence and some measure of control."[34] In order to understand the complexity of cross-border negotiations, one must understand how the factors in both the environmental and the immediate contexts can influence negotiation processes and outcomes.

Environmental Context

In an important article about the environmental context, Salacuse suggested six factors that make global negotiations more challenging than domestic negotiations: political and legal pluralism, international economics, foreign governments and bureaucracies, instability, ideology, and culture.[35] Phatak and Habib have suggested an additional factor: external stakeholders.[36] These factors can act to limit or constrain organizations that operate in the international arena, and it is important that negotiators who bargain across borders understand and appreciate their effects.

Political and Legal Pluralism.   When organizations make business deals that cross a national border, they come into contact with the legal and political system of another country. There may be implications for the taxes that an organization pays, the labor codes or standards that it must meet, and the different codes of contract law and standards of enforcement (e.g., case law versus common law versus no functioning legal system). In addition, political considerations may enhance or detract from the conduct of business negotiations in various countries at different times. For instance, the open business environment in the former Soviet republics in the 1990s is quite different than the closed environment of the 1960s.

International Economics.   The value of international currencies naturally fluctuates, and this factor must be considered when making deals across borders. In which currency will the deal be made? According to Salacuse, the risk is typically greater for the party who must pay in the other country's currency.[37] The less stable the currency, the greater the risk for both parties. In addition, any change in the value of a currency (upward or downward) can significantly affect the value of the deal for both parties, changing a mutually valuable deal into a windfall profit for one and a large loss for the other. Many countries also control the currency flowing across their borders. Frequently, purchases within these countries may be made only with hard currencies that are brought into the country by foreign parties, and domestic organizations are unable to purchase foreign products or negotiate outcomes that require payment in foreign currencies.

Foreign Governments and Bureaucracies.   Countries differ in the extent to which the government regulates industries and organizations. Organizations in the United States are relatively free from government intervention, although some industries are more heavily regulated than others (e.g., power generation, defense) and some states have tougher environmental regulations than others. Generally, however, business negotiations in the United States occur without government approval, and the parties to a negotiation decide whether or not to engage in a deal based on business reasons alone. In contrast, the governments of many developing and (former) communist countries closely supervise imports and joint ventures;[38] frequently, an agency of the government has a monopoly in dealing with foreign organizations.[39] In addition, political considerations, such as the effect of the negotiations on the government treasury and the general economy of the country, may influence the negotiations more heavily than what Western business people would consider to be legitimate business reasons.

Instability.   Although the world continues to change rapidly, business people negotiating domestically in the United States are accustomed to a degree of stability that is not present in many areas of the world. Instability may take many forms, including a lack of resources that Americans commonly expect during business negotiations (paper, electricity, computers); shortages of other goods and services (food, reliable transportation, potable water); and political instability (coups, sudden shifts in government policy, major currency revaluations). The challenge for international negotiators is to predict changes accurately and with enough lead-time to adjust for their consequences if they occur. Salacuse suggests that negotiators faced with unstable circumstances should include clauses in their contracts that allow for easy cancellation or neutral arbitration, and consider purchasing insurance policies to guarantee contract provisions. This advice presumes that contracts will be honored and that specific contract clauses will be culturally acceptable to the other party.

Ideology.   Negotiators within the United States generally share a common ideology of the benefits of individualism and capitalism. According to Salacuse, Americans believe strongly in individual rights, the superiority of private investment, and the importance of making a profit in business.[40] Negotiators from other countries do not always share this ideology. For example, negotiators from some countries (e.g., China, France) may instead stress group rights as more important than individual rights and public investment as a better allocation of resources than private investment; they may also have different prescriptions for earning and sharing profit. Ideological clashes increase the communication challenges in cross-border negotiations in the broadest sense because the parties may disagree at the most fundamental levels about what is being negotiated.

Culture.   The most frequently studied construct in research examining global negotiation is culture.[41] While many international negotiation experts consider culture the critical factor in negotiations across borders, there are in fact many different meanings of the concept of culture.[42] As we suggested earlier, people from different cultures appear to negotiate differently.[43] In addition to behaving differently, people from different cultures may also interpret the fundamental processes of negotiations differently (such as what factors are negotiable and the purpose of the negotiations). According to Salacuse, people in some cultures approach negotiations deductively (they move from the general to the specific) whereas people from other cultures are more inductive (they settle on a series of specific issues that become the area of general agreement).[44] Sebenius argues that culture has an important effect on both decision making during negotiation as well as the negotiation process itself, including who participates in the negotiation, who makes decisions during the negotiation, and the informal factors that help or hinder negotiations.[45] In some cultures, the parties negotiate the substantive issues while considering the relationship between the parties to be more or less incidental. In other cultures, the relationship between the parties is the main focus of the negotiation, and the substantive issues of the deal itself are more or less incidental.[46] There is also evidence that preference for conflict resolution models varies across cultures,[47] while others suggest that culture influences the emotions displayed during negotiation as well as face-saving behavior.[48]

Clearly there is a large challenge negotiating across borders when the fundamental beliefs about what negotiation is and how it occurs are different. We will spend the latter part of this chapter exploring various aspects of this issue in more detail.

External Stakeholders.   Phatak and Habib defined external stakeholders as "the various people and organizations that have an interest or stake in the outcome of the negotiations."[49] These stakeholders include business associations, labor unions, embassies, and industry associations. For example, labor unions often oppose negotiations with foreign companies because they are afraid that domestic jobs will be lost. International negotiators can receive a great deal of promotion and guidance from their government via the trade section of their embassy, and from other business people via their chamber of commerce in the country in which they are negotiating.

Immediate Context

Throughout this book we have discussed many of the immediate context factors in reference to domestic negotiations. In this section, we will discuss the concepts in the Phatak and Habib model from a cross-border perspective; more detailed discussion of the theories and models underlying this model can be found elsewhere in this book.

Relative Bargaining Power.   One factor in cross-border negotiations that has received considerable research attention is the relative bargaining power of the two parties in the negotiation. Joint ventures have been the subject of a great deal of research on cross-border negotiations, and relative power has frequently been operationalized as the amount of equity (financial and other investment) that each side is willing to invest in the new venture.[50] The presumption is that the party that invests more equity has more power in the negotiation and therefore will have more influence on the negotiation process and outcome. Research by Yan and Gray questions this perspective, however, and suggests that relative power is not simply a function of equity, but appears to be due to management control, which was found to be heavily influenced by negotiating.[51] In addition, several factors seem to be able to influence relative power, including special access to markets (e.g., in current or former communist countries); distribution systems (e.g., in Asia, where creating a new distribution system is so expensive that it may be a barrier to entering markets); or managing government relations (e.g., where the language and culture are quite different).

Levels of Conflict.   The level of conflict and type of interdependence between the parties to a cross-border negotiation will also influence the negotiation process and outcome. High-conflict situations, or conflicts that are ethnically, identity, or geographically based, will be more difficult to resolve.[52] Ongoing conflicts in Northern Ireland, the Middle East, East Timor, and Sudan are but a few examples. There is historical evidence, however, that civil wars concluded through a comprehensive, institutionalized agreement that prohibits the use of coercive power and promotes the fair distributions of resources and political power lead to more stable settlements.[53] Also important is the extent to which negotiators frame the negotiation differently or conceptualize what the negotiation concerns (see Chapters 2 and 5 for a discussion of framing), and this appears to vary across cultures, as do the ways in which negotiators respond to conflict.[54] For example, Fisher, Ury, and Patton discuss how conflicts in the Middle East were difficult to deal with for several years because the different parties had such different ways of conceptualizing what the dispute was about (e.g., security, sovereignty, historical rights).[55]

Relationship between Negotiators.   Phatak and Habib suggest that the relationship the principal negotiating parties develop before the actual negotiations will also have an important impact on the negotiation process and outcome.[56] Negotiations are part of the larger relationship between two parties. The history of relations between the parties will influence the current negotiation (e.g., how the parties frame the negotiation), just as the current negotiation will become part of any future negotiations between the parties.[57]

Desired Outcomes.   Tangible and intangible factors will play a large role in determining the outcomes of cross-border negotiations. In the political arena, countries often use international negotiations to achieve both domestic and international political goals. For instance, one of the main goals of the North Vietnamese during the Paris Peace Talks to end the war in Vietnam was to be recognized formally by the other parties to the negotiation. Similarly, in recent ethnic conflicts around the world, numerous parties have threatened that unless they are recognized at the formal negotiation table they will disrupt the successful resolution of the conflict (e.g., Northern Ireland). Ongoing tension can exist between one party's short-term objectives for the current negotiations and their influence on the parties' long-term relations. In trade negotiations between the United States and Japan, both sides often settle for less than their desired short-term outcomes because of the importance of the long-term relationship.

Immediate Stakeholders.   The immediate stakeholders in the negotiation include the negotiators themselves as well as the people they directly represent, such as their managers, employers, or boards of directors.[58] Stakeholders can influence negotiators in many ways. The skills, abilities, and international experience of the negotiators themselves clearly can have a large impact on the process and outcome of cross-border negotiations. In addition, the personal motivations of the principal negotiators and the other immediate stakeholders can have a large influence on the negotiation process and outcomes. People may be motivated by several intangible factors in the negotiation, including how the process or outcome will make them look in the eyes of both the other party and their own superiors, as well as other intangible factors like their personal career advancement.

In summary, Phatak and Habib's model provides a good overview of how several factors in the environmental and immediate contexts can have a large influence on cross-border negotiations. The next section of this chapter provides examples of how these factors can interact to determine the processes and outcomes of negotiations.

HOW DO WE EXPLAIN GLOBAL NEGOTIATION OUTCOMES?

As we have seen in the discussion of the Phatak and Habib model, global negotiations can be much more complicated than domestic negotiations. At times it may be tempting to attribute the outcomes of negotiations to a single variable, such as cultural differences or the relative power of a country (the size of the national economy, for instance). This would be a serious mistake, however. Recent studies of negotiations in very different contexts suggest that simple, one-variable arguments cannot explain conflicting global negotiation outcomes.[59]

Schoppa examined the results of five different discussions between Japan and the United States under the 1989 Structural Impediments Initiative, which focused on changing trade relations between the two countries.[60] These negotiations were between the same countries during the same time period, so one would expect that similar explanations should be found for the outcome of each negotiation. For instance, if the United States were more powerful than Japan, or if the Japanese were better listeners than the Americans, then this should more or less equally influence the outcomes of all five negotiations. Schoppa found that the results of the five negotiations (whose subjects were public investment, distribution systems, land policy, exclusionary business practices, and Keiretsu groups) were quite different, and that no single variable could explain them. Schoppa also found that different negotiation strategies had different levels of effectiveness across the different issues. For instance, a strategy of expanding the number of participants involved in the negotiation process seemed to produce concessions in the public investment and distribution system negotiations, but had no effect in the exclusionary business practices and Keiretsu negotiations.

Derong and Faure's study of the negotiation process between Chinese companies and the various levels of government in China is also enlightening.[61] The study examined a series of negotiations between a high-technology company in Beijing and six government regulatory bureaus. Much has been written about the Chinese negotiation style (e.g., the need for harmony, the meaning of time, etc.[62]), and we would expect intra-Chinese negotiations to be more or less similar. What Derong and Faure found, however, was that a wide variety of different strategies and tactics were used in the negotiations, depending on the goals of the negotiators and the situation. While the national culture appeared to determine the overall negotiation process, the role of the organization and the organizational culture also appeared important. With respect to time, for instance, Derong and Faure found that "the [government] bureaus act according to the usual temporality of bureaucracies which requires a huge amount of time to attain any result. On the other hand, the company works on the unspoken assumption that time is a limited resource whose use has a cost in managerial terms."[63] The interplay between organizational culture and national culture, and how this changes as countries reform their economic systems, will make it even less likely that researchers can use simplistic explanations of global negotiations.

In summary, models such as Phatak and Habib's are very good devices for guiding our thinking about global negotiations. It is always important to remember, however, that negotiation processes and outcomes are influenced by many factors, and that the influence of these factors can change in magnitude over time.[64] The challenge for every global negotiator is to understand the simultaneous, multiple influences of several factors on the negotiation process and outcome, and to update this understanding regularly as circumstances change. This also means that planning for global negotiations is especially important, as is the need to adjust plans as new information is obtained through monitoring the environmental and immediate contexts.

HOFSTEDE'S DIMENSIONS OF CULTURE

Hofstede's research defines culture as the shared values and beliefs held by members of a group, and is considered the most comprehensive and extensive program of research on cultural dimensions in international business.[65] Hofstede examined data on values that had been gathered from over 100,000 IBM employees from around the world; to date, over 53 cultures and countries have been included in his study. Statistical analysis of this data suggests that four dimensions could be used to describe the important differences among the cultures in the study.[66] Table 8.1 lists the countries included in Hofstede's study and their ranking on the four dimensions described below.

TABLE 8.1   Ranking of Countries/Cultures on Cultural Dimensions
Reported by Hofstede (1991)

	Rank Order on:			
Country	*Individualism*	*Power Distance*	*Masculinity*	*Uncertainty Avoidance*
Arab countries	26/27	7	23	27
Argentina	22/23	35/36	20/21	10/15
Australia	2	41	16	37
Austria	18	53	2	24/25
Belgium	8	20	22	5/6
Brazil	26/27	14	27	21/22
Canada	4/5	39	24	41/42
Chile	38	24/25	46	10/15
Colombia	49	17	11/12	20
Costa Rica	46	42/44	48/49	10/15
Denmark	9	51	50	51
East Africa	33/35	21/23	39	36
Ecuador	52	8/9	13/14	28
Finland	17	46	47	31/32
France	10/11	15/16	35/36	10/15
Germany F.R.	15	42/44	9/10	29
Great Britain	3	42/44	9/10	47/48
Greece	30	27/28	18/19	1
Guatemala	53	2/3	43	3
Hong Kong	37	15/16	18/19	49/50
India	21	10/11	20/21	45
Indonesia	47/48	8/9	30/31	41/42
Iran	24	29/30	35/36	31/32
Ireland (Rep.)	12	49	7/8	47/48
Israel	19	52	29	19
Italy	7	34	4/5	23
Jamaica	25	37	7/8	52
Japan	22/23	33	1	7
Malaysia	36	1	25/26	46
Mexico	32	5/6	6	18
Netherlands	4/5	40	51	35
New Zealand	6	50	17	39/40
Norway	13	47/48	52	38
Pakistan	47/48	32	25/26	24/25

(Continued)

TABLE 8.1   *(Concluded)*

		Rank Order on:		
Country	*Individualism*	*Power Distance*	*Masculinity*	*Uncertainty Avoidance*
Panama	51	2/3	34	10/15
Peru	45	21/23	37/38	9
Philippines	31	4	11/12	44
Portugal	33/35	24/25	45	2
Salvador	42	18/19	40	5/6
Singapore	39/41	13	28	53
South Africa	16	35/36	13/14	39/40
South Korea	43	27/28	41	16/17
Spain	20	31	37/38	10/15
Sweden	10/11	47/48	53	49/50
Switzerland	14	45	4/5	33
Taiwan	44	29/30	32/33	26
Thailand	39/41	21/23	44	30
Turkey	28	18/19	32/33	16/17
Uruguay	29	26	42	4
U.S.	1	38	15	43
Venezuela	50	5/6	3	21/22
West Africa	39/41	10/11	30/31	34
Yugoslavia	33/35	12	48/49	8

SOURCE: Based on G. Hofstede, *Culture and Organizations: Software of the Mind* (London, England: McGraw-Hill, 1991). Reproduced with permission of the McGraw-Hill Companies.

Individualism/Collectivism

The individualism/collectivism dimension describes the extent to which the society is organized around individuals or the group. Individualistic societies encourage their young to be independent and to look after themselves. Collectivistic societies integrate individuals into cohesive groups that take responsibility for the welfare of each individual. Individualistic countries include the United States, Great Britain, and Australia, while collectivistic countries include Indonesia, Pakistan, and Costa Rica. Hofstede suggests that the focus on relationships in collectivist societies plays a critical role in negotiations—negotiations with the same party can continue for years, and changing a negotiator changes the relationship, which may take a long time to rebuild. Contrast this with individualistic societies, in which negotiators are considered interchangeable and competency, rather than relationship, is an important consideration when choosing a negotiator. The implication is that negotiators from collectivist cultures will strongly depend on cultivating and sustaining a long-term relationship, whereas negotiators from individualistic cultures may be more likely to swap negotiators, using whatever short-term criteria seem appropriate. In addition, Smith, Dugan, Peterson, and Leung found that within collectivistic countries disagreements are resolved based on rules, whereas in individualistic countries conflicts tend to be resolved through personal experience and training.[67]

The individualism/collectivism dimension of culture has received considerable attention from negotiation researchers, and it appears to influence a broad range of negotiation processes, outcomes, and preferences for conflict resolution procedures.

Negotiation Processes. Cai demonstrated how individualism/collectivism influenced negotiation planning: negotiators from a more collectivist culture (Taiwan) spent more time planning for long-term goals, while negotiators from a more individualistic culture (U.S.) spent more time planning for short-term goals.[68] Gelfand and Christakopoulou found that negotiators from a relatively individualistic culture (U.S.) were more susceptible to fixed-pie errors (see Chapter 5) than were negotiators from a more collectivist culture (Greece).[69] In addition, examination of the negotiation process revealed that negotiators from the more individualistic culture made more extreme offers during the negotiation than did negotiators from the more collectivist culture. Individualism/collectivism also appears to influence the effects of negotiator accountability on the negotiation process. Gelfand and Realo found that "high accountability enhanced competition for representatives with low levels of collectivism, yet enhanced cooperation for those with high levels of collectivism."[70]

Negotiation Outcomes. Researchers have also found that the effects of individualism/collectivism may also influence negotiation outcomes. Lituchy reported that negotiators from a more collectivist culture (Japan) reached more integrative solutions than negotiators from a more individualist culture (U.S.) or negotiation dyads where both cultures were present (Japan, U.S.).[71] Arunachalam, Wall, and Chan found that negotiators from a more collectivistic culture (Hong Kong) reached higher joint outcomes on an integrative negotiation task than did negotiators from a more individualistic culture (U.S.).[72] Brett and Okumura did not find a direct effect of individualism/collectivism on negotiation outcomes but, rather, found that same-culture negotiators (Japan-Japan or U.S.-U.S. dyads) reported higher joint gains than intercultural dyads (Japan-U.S.).[73] Brett and Okumura suggest that lack of information sharing in intercultural dyads may have caused lower integrative outcomes in these groups. More research on the effects of individualism/collectivism on negotiation outcomes needs to be conducted in order to understand better the extent of its influence on negotiation.

Conflict Resolution Styles. Kim and Kitani demonstrated how individualism/collectivism influenced preference for conflict resolution styles in romantic relationships as partners from a more collectivist culture (Asian Americans) preferred obliging, avoiding, and integrating conflict management styles, while partners from a more individualistic culture (Caucasian Americans) preferred a dominating conflict management style.[74] Similarly, Pearson and Stephan found that negotiators from a more collectivist culture (Brazil) preferred accommodation, collaboration, and withdrawal compared to negotiators from a more individualist culture (U.S.), who had a stronger preference for competition.[75] A study by Mintu-Wimsatt and Gassenheimer provided further evidence of the effects of individualism/collectivism on conflict resolution styles as they found that exporters from the Philippines (a "high context" culture that is more collectivist) preferred less confrontational problem solving than did exporters from the United States (a "low context" culture that is more individualistic).[76] Gire found that while negotiators from both a more individualistic culture (Canada) and more collectivist culture (Nigeria) preferred negotiation to arbitration as a conflict management procedure, negotiators from the more collectivist culture had a stronger preference for negotiation than did negotiators from the more individualistic culture, who much preferred arbitration compared to negotiators from the more collectivist culture.[77] In addition, Arunachalam, Wall, and Chan found that mediation had a stronger effect on negotiation outcomes with negotiators from a more individualistic culture (U.S.) than those with negotiators from a more collectivist culture (Hong Kong).[78]

In summary, the individualism/collectivism dimension of culture appears to influence a broad range of negotiation processes, outcomes, and preferences for conflict resolution procedures. More systematic research is required to further explicate the extent of these effects, however, as well as to identify what specific aspects of differences in individualism/collectivism account for these findings.

Power Distance

The power distance dimension describes "the extent to which the less powerful members of organizations and institutions (like the family) accept and expect that power is distributed unequally."[79] According to Hofstede, cultures with greater power distance will be more likely to have decision making concentrated at the top, and all of the important decisions will have to be finalized by the leader. Cultures with low power distance are more likely to spread the decision making throughout the organization, and while leaders are respected, it is also possible to question their decisions. Countries that are high in power distance include Malaysia, Guatemala, and Panama, while countries that are low in power distance include Norway, Sweden, and Great Britain. The consequences for international negotiations are that negotiators from comparatively high power distance cultures may need to seek approval from their supervisors more frequently, and for more issues, leading to a slower negotiation process. In addition, Smith, Dugan, Peterson, and Leung found that "out group" disagreements were less likely to occur in high power distance cultures than lower power distance cultures.[80]

Masculinity/Femininity

Hofstede found that cultures differed in the extent to which they held values that were traditionally perceived as masculine or feminine. Masculine cultures were characterized by "assertiveness, the acquisition of money and things, and *not* caring for others, the quality of life, or people."[81] Feminine cultures were characterized by concern for relationships, nurturing, and quality of life. Countries that are higher in masculinity include Japan, Austria, and Venezuela, while countries that are higher in femininity include Costa Rica, Chile, and Finland. According to Hofstede, this dimension influences negotiation by increasing the competitiveness when negotiators from masculine cultures meet; negotiators from feminine cultures are more likely to have empathy for the other party and to seek compromise.[82]

Uncertainty Avoidance

Uncertainty avoidance, the fourth dimension identified by Hofstede, "indicates to what extent a culture programs its members to feel either uncomfortable or comfortable in unstructured situations."[83] Unstructured situations are characterized by rapid change and novelty, whereas structured situations are stable and secure. Countries that are higher in uncertainty avoidance include Greece, Portugal, and Guatemala, while countries that are lower in uncertainty avoidance include Sweden, Hong Kong, and Ireland. Negotiators from uncertainty avoidance cultures are less comfortable with ambiguous situations and are more likely to seek stable rules and procedures when they negotiate. Negotiators from cultures more comfortable with unstructured situations are likely to adapt to quickly changing situations and will be less uncomfortable when the rules of the negotiation are ambiguous or shifting.

Summary

Hofstede's dimensions have received a great deal of attention in cross-cultural research and international business. Although the model is not without its critics,[84] it has become a dominating force in cross-cultural research in international business. Other than work on individualism/collectivism, however, little systematic research exploring the effects of Hofstede's dimensions on negotiation has been conducted, and the extent to which these dimensions influence cross-cultural and intracultural negotiations needs to be further explored.[85] In addition, there is evidence of considerable variation within more individualistic or more collectivist cultures. For instance, Miyahara, Kim, Shin, and Yoon studied preferences for conflict resolution styles in Japan and Korea, which are both collectivist cultures.[86] Miyahara et al. found significant differences between Japanese and Koreans, with Koreans reporting more concern about avoiding impositions and avoiding dislike during conflict resolution, while Japanese reported more concern about obtaining clarity than the Koreans. For these reasons, interpretations of the effects of Hofstede's dimensions on negotiations should be considered tentative.

HOW DO CULTURAL DIFFERENCES INFLUENCE NEGOTIATIONS?

Given that cultural differences exist, can be measured, and operate on different levels, the issue becomes how they influence negotiations. Drawing upon work by Weiss and Stripp, Foster, and others, we suggest that culture can influence negotiations across borders in at least eight different ways:[87]

1. *Definition of negotiation.* The fundamental definition of negotiation, what is negotiable, and what occurs when we negotiate can differ greatly across cultures.[88] For instance, "Americans tend to view negotiating as a competitive process of offers and counteroffers, while the Japanese tend to view the negotiation as an opportunity for information-sharing."[89]

2. *Selection of negotiators.* The criteria used to select who will participate in the negotiations vary across cultures. These criteria can include knowledge of the subject matter being negotiated, seniority, family connections, gender, age, experience,

and status. Different cultures weigh these criteria differently, leading to varying expectations about what is appropriate in different types of negotiations.

3. *Protocol.* Cultures differ in the degree to which protocol, or the formality of the relations between the two negotiating parties, is important. American culture is among the least formal cultures in the world. A generally familiar communication style is quite common; first names are used, for example, while titles are ignored. Contrast this with the situation in other cultures. Many European countries (e.g., France, Germany, England) are very formal, and not using the proper title when addressing someone (e.g., Mr., Dr., Professor, Lord) is considered insulting.[90] The formal calling cards or business cards used in many countries in the Pacific Rim (e.g., China, Japan) are essential for introductions there. Negotiators who forget to bring business cards or who write messages on them are frequently breaching protocol and insulting their counterpart.[91] Even the ways that business cards are presented, hands are shaken, or dress codes are observed are subject to interpretation by negotiators and can be the foundation of attributions about a person's background and personality.

4. *Communication.* Cultures influence how people communicate, both verbally and nonverbally. There are also differences in body language across cultures; a behavior that may be highly insulting in one culture may be completely innocuous in another.[92] To avoid offending the other party in negotiations across borders, the international negotiator needs to observe cultural rules of communication carefully. For example, placing feet on a desk in the United States signals power or relaxation; in Thailand, it is considered very insulting. Clearly, there is a lot of information about how to communicate that an international negotiator must remember in order not to insult, anger, or embarrass the other party during negotiations. Culture-specific books and articles can provide considerable advice to international negotiators about how to communicate in various cultures; seeking such advice is an essential aspect of planning for global negotiations.[93]

5. *Time.* Cultures largely determine what time means and how it affects negotiations.[94] In the United States, people tend to respect time by appearing for meetings at an appointed hour, being sensitive to not wasting the time of other people, and generally holding that "faster" is better than "slower" because it symbolizes high productivity. Other cultures have quite different views about time. In more traditional societies, especially in hot climates, the pace is slower than in the United States. This tends to reduce the focus on time, at least in the short term. Americans are perceived by other cultures as enslaved by their clocks, because time is watched carefully and guarded as a valuable resource. In some cultures, such as China and Latin America, time per se is not important. The focus of negotiations is on the task, regardless of the amount of time that it takes. The opportunity for misunderstandings because of different perceptions of time is great during cross-cultural negotiations. Americans may be perceived as always being in a hurry and as flitting from one task to another, while Chinese or Latin American negotiators may appear to the Americans to be doing nothing and wasting time.

6. *Risk propensity.* Cultures vary in the extent to which they are willing to take risks. Some cultures tend to produce bureaucratic, conservative decision makers

who want a great deal of information before making decisions. Other cultures produce negotiators who are more entrepreneurial and who are willing to act and take risks when they have incomplete information (e.g., "nothing ventured, nothing gained"). According to Foster, Americans fall on the risk-taking end of the continuum, as do some Asian cultures (e.g., the "Dragons"), and some European cultures are quite conservative (e.g., Greece).[95] The orientation of a culture toward risk will have a large effect on what is negotiated and the content of the negotiated outcome. Negotiators in risk-oriented cultures will be more willing to move early on a deal and will generally take more chances. Those in risk-avoiding cultures are more likely to seek further information and take a wait-and-see stance.

7. *Groups versus individuals.* Cultures differ according to whether they emphasize the individual or the group. The United States is very much an individual-oriented culture, where being independent and assertive is valued and praised. Group-oriented cultures, in contrast, favor the superiority of the group and see individual needs as second to the group's needs. Group-oriented cultures value fitting in and reward loyal team players; those who dare to be different are socially ostracized—a large price to pay in a group-oriented society. This cultural difference can have a variety of effects on negotiation. Americans are more likely to have one individual who is responsible for the final decision, whereas group-oriented cultures like the Chinese are more likely to have a group responsible for the decision. Decision making in group-oriented cultures involves consensus and may take considerably more time than American negotiators are used to. In addition, because so many people can be involved in the negotiations in group-oriented cultures, and because their participation may be sequential rather than simultaneous, American negotiators may be faced with a series of discussions over the same issues and materials with many different people. In a negotiation in China, one of the authors of this book met with more than six different people on successive days, going over the same ground with different negotiators and interpreters, until the negotiation was concluded.

8. *Nature of agreements.* Culture also has an important effect both on concluding agreements and on what form the negotiated agreement takes. In the United States, agreements are typically based on logic (e.g., the low-cost producer gets the deal), are often formalized, and are enforced through the legal system if such standards are not honored. In other cultures, however, obtaining the deal may be based on who you are (e.g., your family or political connections) rather than on what you can do. In addition, agreements do not mean the same thing in all cultures. Foster notes that the Chinese frequently use memorandums of agreement to formalize a relationship and to signal the start of negotiations (mutual favors and compromise).[96] Frequently, however, Americans will interpret the same memorandum of agreement as the completion of the negotiations that is enforceable in a court of law. Again, cultural differences in how to close an agreement and what exactly that agreement means can lead to confusion and misunderstandings when we negotiate across borders.

In summary, a great deal has been written about the importance of culture in cross-border negotiations. While academics and practitioners may use the word *culture* to mean different things, they agree that it is a critical aspect of international negotiation that can have a broad influence on many aspects of the process and outcome of negotiations across borders.

CULTURALLY RESPONSIVE NEGOTIATION STRATEGIES

Although a great deal has been written about international negotiation and the extra challenges that occur when negotiating across borders, cultures, or nationalities, far less attention has been paid to what the individual negotiator should specifically *do* when faced with negotiating with someone from another culture. The advice by many theorists in this area, either explicitly or implicitly, has been, "When in Rome, act as the Romans do."[97] In other words, negotiators are advised to be aware of the effects of cultural differences on negotiation and to take them into account when they negotiate. Much of the material discussed in this chapter reflects this tendency. Many theorists appear to assume implicitly that the best way to manage cross-border negotiations is to be sensitive to the cultural norms of the person with whom you are negotiating and to modify your strategy to be consistent with behaviors that occur in that culture. Contrast this with the less culturally sensitive view, "Business is business everywhere in the world," which suggests that the other party can adapt to your style of negotiating, that style is unimportant, or, more arrogantly, that your style should dictate what other people do. Although it is important to avoid cultural gaffes when negotiating, it is not clear that the best approach is to modify your strategy to match the other person's approach.

Several factors indicate that cross-border negotiators should not make large modifications to their approach:

1. Negotiators may not be able to modify their approach *effectively*. It takes years to understand another culture deeply, and you may not have the time necessary to gain this understanding before beginning negotiations. Although a little understanding of another culture is clearly better than total ignorance, it may not be enough to let you make effective adjustments to your negotiation strategy. Attempting to match the strategies and tactics used by negotiators in another culture is a daunting task that requires fluency in their language as only one of many preconditions. Even simple words may be translated in several different ways with different nuances, making the challenge of communicating across languages a daunting task.[98]

2. Even if negotiators can modify their approach effectively, it does not mean that this will translate automatically into a better negotiation outcome for their side. It is quite possible that those on the other side will modify their approach too. The results in this situation can be disaster, with each side trying to act like the other "should" be acting, and both sides not really understanding what the other party is doing. Consider the following example contrasting typical American and Japanese negotiation styles. Americans are more likely to start negotiations with an extreme offer in order to leave room for concessions. Japanese are more likely to start negotiations with gathering information in order to understand whom they

are dealing with and what the relationship will be. Assume that both parties understand their own and the other party's cultural tendencies (this is a large assumption that frequently is not met). Now assume that each party, acting out of respect for the other, decides to "act like the Romans do" and to adopt the approach of the other party. The possibilities for confusion are endless. When the Americans gather information about the Japanese, are they truly interested or are they playing a role? It will be clear that they are not acting like Americans, but the strategy that they are using may not be readily identified. How will the Americans interpret the Japanese behavior? The Americans have prepared well for their negotiations and understand that the Japanese do not present extreme positions early in negotiations. When the Japanese *do* present an extreme position early in negotiations (in order to adapt to the American negotiation style), how should the Americans interpret this behavior? The Americans likely will think, "That must be what they really want, because they don't open with extreme offers." Adopting the other party's approach does not guarantee success, and in fact may lead to more confusion than acting like yourself (where at least your behavior is understood within your own cultural context).

3. Research suggests that negotiators may naturally negotiate differently when they are with people from their own culture than when they are with people from other cultures.[99] The implications of this research are that a deep understanding of how people in other cultures negotiate, such as Costa Ricans negotiating with each other, may not help an American negotiating with a Costa Rican.[100]

4. Research by Francis suggests that moderate adaptation may be more effective than "acting as the Romans do."[101] In a simulation study of Americans' responses to negotiators from other countries, Francis found that negotiators from a familiar culture (Japan) who made moderate adaptations to American ways were perceived more positively than negotiators who made no changes or those who made large adaptations. Although these findings did not replicate for negotiators from a less familiar culture (Korea), more research needs to be conducted to understand why. At the very least, the results of this study suggest that large adaptations by international negotiators will not always be effective.

Stephen Weiss has advanced our understanding of the options that people have when negotiating with someone from another culture.[102] Weiss observes that a negotiator may be able to choose among up to eight different culturally responsive strategies. These strategies may be used individually or sequentially, and the strategies can be switched as the negotiation progresses. According to Weiss, when choosing a strategy, negotiators should be aware of their own and the other party's culture in general, understand the specific factors in the current relationship, and predict or try to influence the other party's approach. Weiss's culturally responsive strategies may be arranged into three groups, based on the level of familiarity (low, moderate, high) that a negotiator has with the other party's culture. Within each group there are some strategies that the negotiator may use individually (unilateral strategies) and others that involve the participation of the other party (joint strategies).

Low Familiarity

Employ Agents or Advisers (Unilateral Strategy).   One approach for negotiators who have very low familiarity with the other party's culture is to hire an agent or adviser who is familiar with the cultures of both parties. This relationship may range from having the other party conduct the negotiations under your supervision (agent) to receiving regular or occasional advice during the negotiations (adviser). Although agents or advisers may create other problems (such as tensions between that person and you), they may be quite useful for negotiators who have little awareness of the other party's culture and little time to become aware.

Bring in a Mediator (Joint Strategy).   Many types of mediators may be used in cross-cultural negotiations, ranging from someone who conducts introductions and then withdraws to someone who is present throughout the negotiation and takes responsibility for orchestrating the negotiation process.[103] Interpreters will often play this role, providing both parties with more information than the mere translation of words during negotiations. Mediators may encourage one side or the other to adopt one culture's approaches or a third cultural approach (the mediator's home culture).

Induce the Other Party to Use Your Approach (Joint Strategy).   The third option is to persuade the other party to use your approach. There are many ways to do this, ranging from making a polite request to asserting rudely that your way is best. More subtly, you can continue to respond to the other party's requests in your own language because you "cannot express yourself well enough" in the other's language. Although this strategy has many advantages for the negotiator with low familiarity, there are also some disadvantages. For instance, the other party may become irritated at or insulted by having to make the extra effort to deal with you on your own cultural terms. In addition, the other party may also have a strategic advantage because he or she may now attempt more extreme tactics and, if you object, excuse their use on the basis of his or her "cultural ignorance" (after all, you can't expect the other party to understand everything about how you conduct business).

Moderate Familiarity

Adapt to the Other Party's Approach (Unilateral Strategy).   This strategy involves making conscious changes to your approach so that it is more appealing to the other party. Rather than trying to act like the other party, negotiators using this strategy maintain a firm grasp on their own approach but make modifications to help relations with the other person. These modifications may include acting in a less extreme manner, eliminating some behaviors, and including some of the other party's behaviors. The challenge in using this strategy is to know which behaviors to modify, eliminate, or adopt. In addition, it is not clear that the other party will interpret your modifications in the way that you have intended.

Coordinate Adjustment (Joint Strategy).   This strategy involves both parties making mutual adjustments to find a common process for negotiation. Although this can be done implicitly, it is more likely to occur explicitly ("How would you like to proceed?"), and it can be thought of as a special instance of negotiating the process of negotiation. This strategy requires a moderate amount of knowledge about the other party's culture and at least some facility with his or her language (comprehension, if not the ability to speak). Coordinate adjustment occurs on a daily basis in Montreal, the most bilingual city in North America (85 percent of Montrealers understand both English and French). It is standard practice for businesspeople in Montreal to negotiate the process of negotiation before the substantive discussion begins. The outcomes of this discussion are variations on the theme of whether the negotiations will occur in English or French, with a typical outcome being that either party may speak either language. Negotiations often occur in both languages, and frequently the person with the best second-language skills will switch languages to facilitate the discussion. Another outcome that occasionally occurs has both parties speaking in their second language (i.e., the French speaker will negotiate in English while the English speaker will negotiate in French) to demonstrate respect for the other party. Another type of coordinate adjustment occurs when the two negotiating parties adopt aspects of a third culture to facilitate their negotiations. For instance, during a recent trip to Latin America, one of the authors of this book conducted discussions in French with a Latin American colleague who spoke Spanish and French, but not English. On a subsequent trip to China, negotiations were conducted in French, English, and Chinese since each of the six participants spoke two of the three languages.

High Familiarity

Embrace the Other Party's Approach (Unilateral Strategy).   This strategy involves adopting completely the approach of the other party. To be used successfully, the negotiator needs to be completely bilingual and bicultural. In essence, the negotiator using this strategy doesn't act like a Roman, he or she *is* a Roman. This strategy is costly (in preparation time and expense) and places the negotiator using it under considerable stress (it is difficult to switch back and forth rapidly between cultures). However, there is much to gain by using this strategy because the other party can be approached and understood completely on his or her own terms.

Improvise an Approach (Joint Strategy).   This strategy involves crafting an approach that is specifically tailored to the negotiation situation, other party, and circumstances. To use this approach, both parties to the negotiation need to have high familiarity with the other party's culture and a strong understanding of the individual characteristics of the other party. The negotiation that emerges with this approach can be crafted with aspects from both cultures adopted when they will be useful. This approach is the most flexible of the eight strategies, which is both its strength and weakness. Flexibility is a strength because it allows the approach to be crafted to the circumstances at hand, but it is a weakness because there are few general prescriptive statements that can be made about how to use this strategy.

Effect Symphony (Joint Strategy).   This strategy works to "transcend exclusive use of either home culture" and instead allows the negotiation parties to create a new approach that may include aspects of either home culture or adopt practices from a third culture.[104] Professional diplomats use such an approach when the customs, norms, and language that they use transcend national borders and form their own culture (diplomacy). Use of this strategy is complex and involves a great deal of time and effort. It works best when the parties are familiar with each other, familiar with both home cultures, and have a common structure (like that of professional diplomats) for the negotiation. Risks of using this strategy include costs due to confusion, lost time, and the overall effort required to make it work.

CHAPTER SUMMARY

This chapter examined various aspects of a growing field of negotiation that explores the complexities of negotiating across borders. We began the chapter with a discussion of the American negotiating style, from both American and non-American perspectives. While there is a great deal of consistency in perceptions of the American negotiating style (e.g., Americans are straightforward, impatient), it is important to remember that there is also a lot of variability within cultures (i.e., not every American negotiates in the same way).

Next, we examined the results of a research program by John Graham and his colleagues that compared American negotiators with negotiators from several countries. Graham and his colleagues found that regardless of where negotiators were from, they negotiated the same level of outcomes on a standard negotiation task. The process of negotiation differed across countries, however, suggesting that there is more than one way to attain the same negotiation outcome. Finally, this research program also suggested that negotiators seem to use different strategies when negotiating with people domestically and internationally.

We then examined some of the factors that make cross-border negotiations different. Phatak and Habib suggest that both the environmental and the immediate context have important effects on global negotiations. We then discussed Salacuse's description of the environmental factors that influence global negotiations: (1) political and legal pluralism, (2) international economics, (3) foreign governments and bureaucracies, (4) instability, (5) ideology, and (6) culture. We added one more environmental factor—external stakeholders—from Phatak and Habib. Phatak and Habib's five immediate context factors were discussed next: (1) relative bargaining power, (2) levels of conflict, (3) relationship between negotiators, (4) desired outcomes, and (5) immediate stakeholders. Each of these environmental and immediate context factors acts to make cross-border negotiations more difficult, and effective international negotiators need to understand how to manage them. We concluded this section of the chapter with a discussion of how to make sense of global negotiation outcomes in light of the multiple factors that can simultaneously influence them.

Next, we turned to a discussion of Hofstede's work on culture, the factor that has been most frequently used to explain differences in negotiations across borders. Hofstede defines culture as the shared values and beliefs held by a group of people, and is the most comprehensive study of cultural dimensions in international business. He concluded that four dimensions could summarize cultural differences: (1) individualism/collectivism, (2) power distance, (3) masculinity/femininity, and (4) uncertainty avoidance.

We then examined how cultural differences can influence negotiations. Foster, adapting work by Weiss and Stripp, suggests that culture can influence global negotiations in several ways, including (1) the definition of negotiation, (2) the selection of negotiators, (3) protocol, (4) communication, (5) time, (6) risk propensity, (7) groups versus individuals, and (8) the nature of agreements.

The chapter concluded with a discussion of how to manage cultural differences when negotiating across borders. Weiss presents eight different culturally responsive strategies that negotiators can use with a negotiator from a different culture. Some of these strategies may be used individually, whereas others are used jointly with the other negotiator. Weiss indicates that one critical aspect of choosing the correct strategy for a given negotiation is the degree of familiarity (low, moderate, or high) that a negotiator has with the other culture. However, even those with high familiarity with another culture are faced with a daunting task if they want to modify their strategy completely when they deal with the other culture.

ENDNOTES

1. Avruch, 2000.
2. Also see the chapter "Social Context," posted on the McGraw-Hill website at www.mhhe.com/lewickinegotiation.
3. Sebenius, 2002.
4. For example, see Binnendijk, 1987; Brett, 2001; Fisher, Schneider, Borgwardt, and Ganson, 1997; Foster, 1992; Habeeb, 1988; Hendon and Hendon, 1990; Kremenyuk, 1991; Lukov, 1985; Mautner-Markhof, 1989; and Weiss, 1996; for earlier work, see Fayerweather and Kapoor, 1976; Hall, 1960; and Van Zandt, 1970.
5. Arino, Abramov, Rykounina, and Villa, 1997; Brouthers and Bamossy, 1997; and Pfouts, 1994.
6. Natlandsmyr and Rognes, 1995.
7. Tse, Francis, and Walls, 1994.
8. Leung and Yeung, 1995.
9. Drake, 1995.
10. Husted, 1996.
11. Adler and Graham, 1987; and Adler, Graham, and Schwarz, 1987.
12. See Acuff, 1993; Hendon and Hendon, 1990; and Kennedy, 1985 for extensive examples.
13. See Druckman, 1996; Koh, 1996; Le Poole, 1989; and McDonald, 1996.
14. See Derong and Faure, 1995.
15. Koh, 1996.
16. Le Poole, 1989.
17. McDonald, 1996.
18. See Graham, 1993 for a review.
19. Kelley, 1966.
20. Graham, 1983, 1984.
21. Adler, Brahm, and Graham, 1992.
22. Adler and Graham, 1987; and Adler, Graham, and Schwarz, 1987.
23. Graham, 1983.
24. Adler, Graham, and Schwarz, 1987.
25. Also see Graham, Evenko, and Rajan, 1992.
26. Graham, 1983, p. 63.

27. Ibid.
28. Adler, Graham, and Schwarz, 1987.
29. Adler, Brahm, and Graham, 1992.
30. Adler and Graham, 1989.
31. Natlandsmyr and Rognes, 1995.
32. Phatak and Habib, 1996.
33. Ibid., p. 30.
34. Ibid.
35. Salacuse, 1988.
36. Phatak and Habib, 1996.
37. Salacuse, 1988.
38. See Brouthers and Bamossy, 1997; Derong and Faure, 1995; and Pfouts, 1994.
39. Salacuse, 1988.
40. Ibid.
41. For reviews see Brett, 2001; and Gelfand and Dyer, 2000.
42. See Avruch, 2000; and Janosik, 1987.
43. See Graham and Mintu-Wimsatt, 1997.
44. See Xing, 1995.
45. Sebenius, 2002.
46. See Tinsley, 1997.
47. Tinsley, 1997, 1998.
48. See George, Jones, and Gonzalez, 1998; Ogawa, 1999; and Ting-Toomey and Kurogi, 1998.
49. Phatak and Habib, 1996, p. 34.
50. See Yan and Gray, 1994 for a review.
51. Ibid.
52. See Isajiw, 2000; Ross, 2000; Stein, 1999; and Zartman, 1997.
53. Hartzell, 1999.
54. Abu-Nimer, 1996; Ohbuchi and Takahashi, 1994; Tinsley, 1998; and Weldon and Jehn, 1995.
55. Fisher, Ury, and Patton, 1991.
56. Phatak and Habib, 1996.
57. See the chapter "Social Contest," posted on the McGraw-Hill website at www.mhhe.com/lewickinegotiation, for a detailed discussion of this point.
58. Ibid.
59. Mayer, 1992.
60. Schoppa, 1993.
61. Derong and Faure, 1995.
62. See Faure, 1999; Pye, 1992; and Solomon, 1987.
63. Derong and Faure, 1995, p. 49.
64. Yan and Gray, 1994.
65. Hofstede, 1980a, 1980b, 1989, 1991.
66. Subsequent research by Hofstede and Bond (1988) suggested that a fifth dimension, labeled Confucian Dynamism, be added. Confucian Dynamism contains three elements: work ethic, time, and commitment to traditional Confucian values. The dimension has received little attention in the negotiation literature (cf., Chan, 1998).
67. Smith, Dugan, Peterson, and Leung, 1998.
68. Cai, 1998.
69. Gelfand and Christakopoulou, 1999.
70. Gelfand and Realo, 1999, p. 730.

71. Lituchy, 1997.
72. Arunachalam, Wall, and Chan, 1998.
73. Brett and Okumura, 1998.
74. Kim and Kitani, 1998.
75. Pearson and Stephan, 1998.
76. Mintu-Wimsatt and Gassenheimer, 2000.
77. Gire, 1997.
78. Arunachalam, Wall, and Chan, 1998.
79. Hofstede, 1989, p. 195.
80. Smith, Dugan, Peterson, and Leung, 1998.
81. Hofstede, 1980a, p. 46.
82. Hofstede, 1989.
83. Ibid., p. 196.
84. See Kale and Barnes, 1992; and Triandis, 1982.
85. See Foster, 1992; Kozan, 1997; and Tse, Francis, and Walls, 1994.
86. Miyahara, Kim, Shin, and Yoon, 1998.
87. Weiss and Stripp, 1985; and Foster, 1992.
88. See Ohanyan, 1999; and Yook and Albert, 1998.
89. Foster, 1992, p. 272.
90. Braganti and Devine, 1992.
91. Foster, 1992.
92. Axtell, 1990, 1991, 1993.
93. Binnendijk, 1987; Graham and Sano, 1989; Pye, 1992; and Tung, 1991.
94. Mayfield, Mayfield, Martin, and Herbig, 1997.
95. Foster, 1992.
96. Ibid.
97. See Francis, 1991; and Weiss, 1994 for reviews of the oversimplicity of this advice.
98. Adachi, 1998.
99. Adler and Graham, 1989; and Natlandsmyr and Rognes, 1995.
100. Drake, 1995; and Weldon and Jehn, 1995.
101. Francis, 1991.
102. Weiss, 1994.
103. See Kolb, 1983.
104. Weiss, 1994, p. 58.

CHAPTER 9

Managing Difficult Negotiations: Individual Approaches

INTRODUCTION

Michele is having a terrible dispute with her neighbor in the condo next door. The neighbor, who recently moved in to the apartment, brought a large German Shepherd dog with her that barks ALL the time. Michele is a writer who likes to work at home in the morning, but the dog is so distracting that she cannot get anything done. Michele has talked to the neighbor, who has apologized for the problem but has done nothing to keep the dog quiet. Michele is considering filing a nuisance complaint with the police and taking the neighbor to court.

Donna and her coworker Max are at it again. They both work as website administrators for a major marketing firm. Max just can't seem to get to work on time, and Donna always has to cover for him on the website problems that crop up during the night before. She and Max have talked about it; he promises to get to work earlier, and for a few days he is fine, but then he slips back into his old pattern. Donna doesn't want to report him to the boss, but she doesn't see any other alternative.

Simon, a manufacturer's representative for a machine tool company, finds that a client's recent expansion has resulted in Simon having to follow the client into another sales representative's territory. Simon is sure that the problem can be worked out to everyone's satisfaction and advantage, but so far the other rep seems to want it all—in fact, he seems to act like it's some sort of contest.

In this chapter, we address situations where negotiations become especially difficult, often to the point of stalemate or breakdown. As we have noted several times, negotiation is a conflict management process, and all conflict situations have the potential for becoming derailed. The parties become angry or entrenched in their positions. Perceptions become distorted, and judgments are biased. The parties cease to communicate effectively and instead accuse and blame each other. One party maintains a negotiation style that is not compatible with the other. Issues are viewed in such a way that the parties do not believe that there is any possible compatibility between them, or they cannot find a middle ground where agreement is possible. In short, destructive conflict processes override the negotiation, and the parties cannot proceed.

When negotiations become difficult to resolve, <u>problems</u> may be traced to one or more of the following causal elements:

- Characteristics of the *way parties perceive* themselves or other negotiators (the parties involved directly and indirectly—their styles, preferences, and behaviors).

- Characteristics of the *content* of their communication (i.e., the substance of the negotiation, or how the parties view the substance).

- Characteristics in the *process* used to negotiate or manage conflict (the play of the game, or the actual conduct of negotiation).

- Characteristics of the *context* of their negotiation (the negotiation setting—temporal, relational, and/or cultural).

As the title suggests, the current chapter deals with managing difficult negotiations and remedies that negotiators can use on their own, without outside assistance. The chapter is organized into three major sections. In the first section, we discuss the nature of negotiations that are "difficult to resolve." We examine the causes of stalemate, impasse, or breakdown, and explore characteristics of difficult negotiations, including characteristics of the parties, the types of issues involved, and the process in play. In the second section, we will discuss the specific actions that the parties can take *jointly* to try to move the conflict back to a level where successful negotiation and conflict resolution can ensue. Finally, in the third section, we will discuss *mismatched* situations where one party wants to negotiate to an integrative resolution, and the other party is being "difficult"—and hence, what the integrative party can do to draw the other into a more constructive process.

THE NATURE OF "DIFFICULT TO RESOLVE" NEGOTIATIONS AND WHY THEY OCCUR

It is not uncommon for negotiations, especially distributive ones, to become contentious to the point of breakdown. In extreme cases, conflict escalates and interpersonal enmity increases. What are the characteristics of these "difficult to resolve" negotiations, and what actions are most effective in making them easier to resolve? Not unsurprisingly, any number of things can go wrong.

Negotiations are "difficult to resolve" to the extent that the process of conflict resolution is characterized by the following dynamics:

1. The atmosphere is charged with anger, frustration, and resentment. Mistrust and hostility are directed at the opposing negotiator.

2. Channels of communication, previously used to exchange information and supporting arguments for each party's position, are now closed or constrained. Each party uses communication channels to criticize and blame the other, while simultaneously attempting to limit the same type of communication from the other party.

3. The original issues at stake have become blurred and ill defined, and perhaps new issues have been added. Negotiators have become identified with positions on issues, and the conflict has become personalized. Even if a negotiator could make a concession, he or she would not make it due to a strong dislike for the other party.

4. The parties tend to perceive great differences in their respective positions. Conflict heightens the magnitude of these differences and minimizes areas of perceived commonality and agreement. The parties see themselves as further apart than they may actually be, and they do not recognize areas where they may be in agreement.

5. As anger and tension increase, the parties become more locked in to their initial negotiating positions. Rather than searching for ways to make concessions and move toward agreement, the parties become firmer in stating their initial demands, and they resort to threats, lies, and distortions to force the other party to comply with those demands. The other usually meets these threats with counterthreats and retaliation.

6. If there is more than one person on a side, those on the same side tend to view each other favorably. They see the best qualities in the people on their side and minimize whatever differences exist, yet they also demand conformity from their team members and will accept a militant, autocratic form of leadership. If there is dissension in the group, it is hidden from the other party; group members always attempt to present a united front to the other side.[1]

The techniques for conflict reduction and resolution presented in this chapter are designed to respond to each of the above dynamics. Moreover, we suggest that the most productive procedure for resolving a highly polarized dispute is to use the steps for conflict management in the order presented. The first step should be some effort at reducing tension, followed by efforts to improve the accuracy of communication and to control the proliferation of issues. Finally, the parties should engage in techniques for establishing commonalities and enhancing the attractiveness of each other's preferred alternatives. This procedure is by no means firm and inflexible; many disputes have been successfully resolved by invoking the steps in a different order. However, the order in which we present these procedures is the one most frequently used by third parties in resolving disputes, and hence we believe it also will be the most effective if employed by the negotiators themselves. If the conflict cannot be controlled effectively, third-party intervention may become necessary.

STRATEGIES FOR RESOLVING IMPASSE: JOINT APPROACHES

Mayer suggests that dispute resolution involves three major components:

1. *Cognitive resolution.* The purpose of cognitive resolution is to change how the parties view the situation. For parties to achieve cognitive resolution, ". . . they must *perceive* that the key issues have been resolved, think that they have reached closure on the situation, and view the conflict as part of their past as opposed to their future . . ." Cognitive resolution is often difficult to achieve because people tenaciously hang on to beliefs and perceptions in spite of new data to the contrary. New information and reframing are often key to this process.

2. *Emotional resolution* involves the way the parties feel about the impasse and the other party, and the amount of emotional energy they put into the negotiation. When parties have emotionally resolved an impasse, they no longer experience negative feelings, relations with the other are less intense, and they have reached some kind of "emotional closure" on the conflict events. Emotional resolution often involves trust rebuilding, forgiveness, and apology.

3. _Behavioral resolution_ processes address exactly what people will do in the future, and what agreements they make about how that future will be realized. Behavioral resolution agreements usually specify ways that the parties can discontinue the problematic conflict dynamics, and mechanisms for instituting those new behaviors which prompt resolution.[2]

In this section, we will describe five major conflict-reduction strategies that can be used to resolve impasses. For the most part, and since we wish to prescribe strategies for changed behavior, all of these processes are aimed at behavioral resolution. However, it will be clear that these behaviors are also aimed at cognitive and emotional resolution as well. The strategies are:

1. Reducing tension and synchronizing the de-escalation of hostility.
2. Improving the accuracy of communication, particularly improving each party's understanding of the other's perspective.
3. Controlling the number and size of issues in the discussion.
4. Establishing a common ground on which the parties can find a basis for agreement.
5. Enhancing the desirability of the options and alternatives that each party presents to the other.

Before describing each of these approaches in detail, it is important to note that there is nothing firm or rigid about the number of different techniques for resolving impasses. Research on the nature of conflict and its resolution has suggested a wide array of different dispute resolution techniques that can be assembled and applied in several different ways.[3]

Reducing Tension and Synchronizing De-escalation

Unproductive deliberations can easily become highly emotional. Parties are frustrated, angry, and upset. They are strongly committed to their viewpoints and have argued strenuously for their preferred alternatives, seeing themselves as firm, principled, or deserving. The other side, behaving the same way, is seen as stubborn, bull-headed, inflexible, and unreasonable. The longer the parties debate, the more likely it is that emotions will overrule reason—name-calling and verbal assaults replace logic and reason. When the negotiation becomes personalized, turning into a win-lose feud between individuals, all hope of productivity is lost. Several approaches for controlling conflict are specifically directed at defusing volatile emotions.

Separating the Parties.   The most common approach to de-escalating conflict is to break off face-to-face relations. Declare a recess, call a caucus, or agree to adjourn and come back later when there has been a chance to unwind. The parties should acknowledge explicitly that the purpose of the caucus is to allow tempers to cool so the dialogue will become less emotional. Each party should also agree to return with a renewed effort to make deliberations more productive—either by simply regaining composure or by attempting a new or different way to address the issue that created the anger.

Tension Release.   Tension is a natural by-product of negotiations. Consequently, negotiators should be aware that it is bound to increase, and they should know how to act to address or diminish it. Some negotiators who are sensitive to increases in tension know how to make a witty remark or crack a joke that causes laughter and releases tension. Others know that it is sometimes appropriate to let the other party ventilate pent-up anger and frustration without having to respond in kind. Skilled negotiators also know that allowing the other party such a catharsis will clear the air and may permit negotiations to return to a calmer pace.

Acknowledging the Other's Feelings: Active Listening.   When one party states her views and the other openly disagrees, the first negotiator often hears the disagreement as more than just disagreement. She may hear a challenge, a put-down, an assertion that her statement is wrong or not acceptable, an accusation of lying or distorting of the facts, or another form of personal attack. Whether or not this is the message that was intended is beside the point; the negotiator has to deal with the way it was received. Understandably, such misinterpretations escalate conflict.

There is a difference between accurately hearing what the other party has said and agreeing with it. One can let the other party know that both the content and the emotional strength of his or her message have been heard and understood, but that does not mean that one agrees with or accepts it. This technique is called *active listening,*[4] and it is frequently used in interviews and therapy settings as a way of encouraging a person to speak more freely (see Chapter 5). Rather than challenging and confronting the other negotiator's statements by bolstering one's own statements and position, you respond with statements that probe for confirmation and elaboration. Comments may include: "You see the facts this way," "You feel very strongly about this point," and "I can see that if you saw things this way, you would feel threatened and upset by what I have said." Again, these statements do not indicate that a negotiator agrees with the other party; rather, they communicate that you have accurately heard him or her.

Synchronized De-escalation.   Charles Osgood, writing about the cold war and disarmament, suggested a unilateral strategy for conflict de-escalation called "graduated and reciprocated initiatives in tension reduction" (GRIT).[5] The party who desires to de-escalate a conflict initiates the action. He or she decides on some small concession that each side could make to signal both sides' good faith and desire to de-escalate. The concession should be large enough to be read as an unambiguous signal of a desire to change the relationship, but not so large that if only one side followed through it would be weak or vulnerable. The party should then make a public announcement stating:

1. Exactly what the concession is.
2. That the concession is part of a deliberate strategic policy to reduce tension.
3. That the other side is explicitly invited to reciprocate in some specified form.
4. That the concession will be executed on some stated time schedule.
5. That each party commits to execute the concession without knowing whether the other will reciprocate.

The party who initiated the de-escalation then executes the concession. The specific concession should be something that is obvious, unambiguous, and subject to easy verification. Making it public and symbolic also helps. If the opposing party does not respond, then the initiator goes through with the action and repeats the sequence, selecting a simple, low-risk concession in an effort to attract the other into synchronized de-escalation. If the other does respond, then the initiator proposes a second action, slightly riskier than the first, and once again initiates the sequence. As the synchronized de-escalation takes hold, the parties can both propose larger and riskier concessions that will bring them back into a productive negotiating relationship.

Improving the Accuracy of Communication

The second step in conflict reduction is to ensure that both parties accurately understand the other's position. (For a broader treatment of communication processes in negotiation, see Chapter 5.) When conflict becomes heated, communication efforts concentrate on managing emotions and directing the next assault at the other. Effective listening decreases. Each party thinks that they know what the other side is going to say and does not care to listen anymore. During impasses listening becomes so diminished that the parties are frequently unaware that their positions may have much in common. Rapoport labeled this the "blindness of involvement" because it inhibits the development of trust and the problem-solving process.[6] Several approaches can be used to rectify this situation (see also Box 9.1).

Role Reversal.   Although it is often easy to see the logic, rationale, and potential commonalities on both sides of a conflict when one is an outsider, recognizing them when you are personally involved in a conflict is another matter. Role reversal can help negotiators to put themselves in the other party's shoes and look at the issue from his or her perspective. A manager can take the position of an employee, a salesperson that of a customer, a purchasing agent that of a supplier. Negotiators can play out scenarios in their imagination, ask a friend or colleague to assume the other role and act out a dialogue, or, more effectively, include role reversal as part of a unilateral strategy-preparation process. Although role reversal will not tell you exactly how the other party thinks and feels about the issues, the process can provide useful and surprising insights (for example, see Box 9.2 on dealing with offensive comments).[7]

Imaging.   Imaging, like role reversal, is a method for gaining insight into the other party's perspective. In the imaging process, parties in conflict are asked to engage in the following activities separately:

1. Describe how they see themselves.
2. Describe how the other party appears to them.
3. State how they think the other party would describe them.
4. State how they think the other party sees themselves.

The parties then exchange this information, in order. The two sets of statements frequently reveal dissimilarities and inconsistencies. Imaging usually produces animated

BOX 9.1
Language Strategies to Facilitate Communication

Linguist Deborah Tannen argues that Americans live in an argument culture, where the language we use in talking about issues reflects a preference for adversarial relationships. The words we choose to describe our interactions shape our perceptions of the experience. Consequently, when we refer to the "opponent" in a "debate," we shape our communication as adversarial and are more likely to escalate the conflict.

Tannen proposed the following naming alternatives to help defuse the argument culture:

Instead of This . . .	*Say This . . .*
Battle of the sexes	Relations between women and men
Critique	Comment
Fight	Discussion
Both sides	All sides
Debate	Discuss
The other side	Another side
Having an argument	Making an argument
The opposite sex	The other sex
War on drugs	Solving the drug problem
Litigation	Mediation
Provocative	Thought-provoking
Most controversial	Most important
Polarize	Unify
Attack-dog journalism	Watchdog journalism
Automatic opposition	Genuine opposition
Focus on differences	Search for common ground
Win the argument	Understand another point of view
The opposition party	The other party
Prosecutorial reporting	Investigative reporting
The argument culture	The dialogue culture

SOURCE: From Deborah Tannen, "How to Turn Debate into Dialogue," *USA Weekend,* February 27–March 3, 1998, pp. 4–5.

discussion as the parties clarify and substantiate what they have said or heard. A common result is that the parties recognize that many apparent differences and areas of conflict are not real, and thus they begin to understand those that are real. One source gives an example of imaging in negotiations between top executives who met to work out an organizational structure for a new firm that resulted from a merger of two organizations. Executives from both sides were deeply concerned that they would be outmaneuvered by the other and would "lose" as a result of the merger. A consultant suggested having an imaging meeting prior to actual negotiations. This meeting sharply altered the perceptions of both parties, and successful integrative negotiations became possible.[8]

When parties complete role reversal or imaging processes, they have usually accomplished several things. First, they have clarified and corrected misconceptions and

BOX 9.2
What Did You Say?

When you are on the receiving end of offensive comments in a negotiation setting, your first response may be to offend back, or to stalk off in anger and displeasure. For important negotiations, though, this creates the risk of denying you (as well as the other parties) any mutual gains from the exchange, as well as diverting your attention from the issues that brought you to the table in the first place. Andrea Schneider suggests that your basic options when faced with offensive comments involve first trying to understand why the offense occurred and then deciding what to do about it. To understand the behavior, she suggests four steps:

Check your assumptions

- Check the data on which your assumptions are based.
- Seek and evaluate other data, even (or especially) if those data tend to disconfirm your assumptions.
- Evaluate and adjust your assumptions, as appropriate.

Once your assumptions seem correct and appropriate, then decide whether to handle the behavior by

- Ignoring it (just act like it never occurred).
- Confronting it (i.e., counterattack: "That's racist," or "How juvenile").
- Deflecting it (i.e., acknowledge it and move on—a sense of humor often helps here).
- Engaging it (talk with the other party about his or her purpose in being offensive, and about your reaction to the offense).

SOURCE: Adapted from A. K. Schneider, "Effective Responses to Offensive Comments," *Negotiation Journal* 10 (1994), pp. 107–15.

misinterpretations. In addition, they have brought to the surface both parties' interests, goals, and priorities, as well as limitations, which can then be used in the problem-solving process. One side often gains an understanding of the other side's true needs. Finally, and perhaps even more important, the process sets a positive tone for the negotiation. Parties find that they can make their needs and concerns heard and not be interrupted. This reduces defensiveness and encourages people to listen. Most people begin the negotiation process with a rather clear idea of what they need from the other party; in this phase, they learn more about what the other needs from them. Joint problem solving moves from being an unattainable ideal to an achievable process.

Controlling Issues

A third major difficulty that inhibits parties from reaching agreement is that as conflict intensifies, the size and number of the issues expand. As the impasse escalates, it snowballs; bits and pieces of other issues accumulate into a large, unmanageable mass. Although small conflicts can be managed satisfactorily one at a time, large conflicts become unwieldy and less amenable to easy resolution. The problem for negotiators in escalated impasses, therefore, is to develop strategies to contain issue proliferation and reduce the negotiation to manageable proportions.

"Fractionating" is a method of issue control that involves dividing a large conflict into smaller parts. According to Fisher, fractionating can involve several actions: reducing the number of parties on each side; controlling the number of substantive issues involved; stating issues in concrete terms rather than as principles; restricting the precedents involved, both procedural and substantive; searching for ways to narrow the big issues; and depersonalizing issues, separating them from the parties advocating them. We will examine each of these approaches in more detail below.[9]

1. *Reduce the Number of Parties on Each Side.*   When there is an impasse, both parties seek to build alliances for strength or to bring their constituencies into the negotiation; either they increase the number of parties at the negotiation or they bring more clout to the table. Additional parties, such as lawyers, experts, or parties with formal authority, are often brought into negotiations for the information or the leverage they can provide. Because the sheer number of parties at the table can considerably increase the complexity of the negotiation (more parties equal more perspectives on the issues, more time needed to hear each side, more opportunities for disagreement, etc.), negotiation ground rules should provide ways to limit how many people can be added. One way to control an impasse that has escalated is to reduce the number of actors. Having fewer actors present, or even limiting the discussion to two individuals, will increase the chances of reaching a settlement.

2. *Control the Number of Substantive Issues Involved.*   A second way to fractionate a conflict is to keep the number of issues small enough to manage. When conflict builds to impasse, the size and number of issues proliferate. Some negotiations escalate to the point where there are too many issues to manage constructively. At the same time, limiting negotiations to a very few issues also raises problems. Single-issue negotiations are frequently harder to manage because they quickly lead to win-lose polarization over the issue. In such circumstances, it is often desirable to expand the number of issues so both sides can see themselves as having gained something and achieves an integrative solution. The number of issues can be expanded by defining the issue broadly enough so that resolution can benefit both sides or by coupling the issue with another issue so that each party can receive a preferred settlement on at least one issue. (We discussed defining the bargaining mix, bundling and packaging issues, and inventing options in Chapters 2, 3, and 4.)

3. *State Issues in Concrete Terms Rather Than as (General) Principles.*   Negotiation issues become difficult to control when events or issues are treated as matters of principle. Small conflicts can rapidly become intractable disputes when their resolution is not treated as an isolated event but instead must be consistent with a broader policy or principle. Negotiators may view any deviation from policy as a threat to that policy. Because it is far more difficult to change broad policy than to make a concession on a single issue, negotiations can immediately become problematic. For example, an employee needs to take her child to the doctor during her work hours and requests an excused absence from the company. The company does not have a policy that permits employees to take time off for this reason, and the employee's supervisor tells her she

has to take sick leave or vacation time instead. "It's a matter of principle," the manager asserts. Resorting to arguments of principle and policy is often a strategic defense by high-power parties against any change from the status quo; however, the longer the discussion remains at the level of policy or principle, the less likely it is that the dispute can be successfully resolved.

There are, of course, times when a single event is properly seen as indicative of a new principle or policy. When this is the case, negotiations should be arranged specifically to address the policy or principle. Many times, people are reluctant to address principles because they know negotiations over principles are difficult and lengthy. However, attempting to negotiate a concrete issue when the negotiation really should address the broader principle may result only in frustration and a sense of futility. If this occurs, it is wise to face the issue and raise it directly. There are at least two strategies that can be used to do so:

- Question whether the issue needs to be addressed at the principle or policy level. Inquire about the link between the specific issue and the broader policy or principle. If none exists, and one party wants to look at the matter from a policy or principle level, suggest that the immediate concrete issue be handled and discussed separately from the underlying principle or policy. If need be, the parties can agree that the concrete issue can be settled in this instance, with no expectation as to how the policy will later be established.

- Point out that exceptions can be made to all policies, and that principles and policies can be maintained even if deviations are agreed to under special circumstances. The parties may be willing to agree that this specific case might be one of those times.

4. Restrict the Precedents Involved, Both Procedural and Substantive.   Another type of issue magnification occurs when the parties treat concessions on a single issue as violations of some substantive or procedural precedent. When a substantive precedent is at stake, one party will imply that to concede on this issue at this time will render him or her vulnerable to conceding on the same issue, or a similar issue, in the future. To return to our previous example, the manager is likely to argue that if she grants the employee an excused absence in this case, when no policy exists, then she will be obligated to grant every other employee the same request. Belief in the power of precedent is strong. The high-power party, who supports the precedent, believes that if she gives in to this one request, there will be no end to the number and types of requests she may get in the future. In contrast, procedural precedents are at stake when parties agree to follow a process they haven't followed before. In the same employment example, the manager may not want to give the employee the excused absence because the employee did not submit any proof that she was, in fact, taking a child to the doctor. So they agree that the employee will return with some evidence that the doctor's visit was made.

Issues of precedent are usually as thorny to control as issues of principle. Once again, a negotiator trying to move a conflict toward de-escalation and resolution should try to prevent single issues from being translated into major questions of precedent. Focusing the dialogue on the key issue and persisting in arguments that concessions on this issue at this time do not necessarily dictate any precedents—substantive or procedural—for the future.

5. Search for Ways to Fractionate the Big Issues.   Fisher calls these "salami tactics": ways to slice a large issue into smaller pieces. Issues that can be expressed in quantitative measurable units are easy to slice. For example, compensation demands can be cut up into pennies-per-hour increments, or lease rates can be reduced to dollars per square foot. When working to fractionate issues of principle or precedent, parties may use the time horizon (when the principle goes into effect or how long it will last) as a way to fractionate the issue, or vary the number of ways that the principle may be applied. For example, a company may devise a family emergency leave that allows employees the opportunity to be away from the company for a period of no longer than three hours, and no more than once a month, for illness in the employee's immediate family.

6. Depersonalize Issues: Separate Them from the Parties Advocating Them. Positional bargaining tends to create conflict over the issues and enhance tension in the relationship between negotiators. People become identified with positions on issues, and vice versa. Effective negotiation requires separating the issues from the parties, not only by working to establish a productive relationship between the parties (leaving only the issue conflict at stake), but also by trying to resolve the issues in a fair and impartial way independent of the parties who hold the conflicting views. Effective integrative negotiation is tough on the negotiating problem but soft on the people.[10]

Establishing Common Ground

As we noted earlier, parties in escalated conflict tend to magnify perceived differences and to minimize perceived similarities.[11] The parties tend to see themselves as further apart and having less in common than may actually be the case. Therefore, a fourth major action that parties can take to de-escalate conflict is to establish common ground and focus on common objectives. Several approaches are possible: establishing common (superordinate) goals, aligning against common enemies, agreeing to follow a common procedure, or establishing a common framework for approaching the negotiation problem. As we discussed in Chapter 2, these approaches might also be viewed as efforts to reframe the conflict away from a focus on differences and toward a focus on common areas. Once this reframing has occurred, it becomes possible to use fewer distributive negotiation approaches, and to move from a purely distributive approach to one that accommodates a mix of distributive and integrative strategies.

Superordinate Goals.   Superordinate goals are common goals; both parties desire them, and both parties must cooperate to achieve them. In a corporation, for example, people perform different jobs (e.g., marketing, manufacturing, distribution) that have different objectives, yet they must work together (e.g., to get the product to the customer) or the corporation will not survive. A local city council may disagree with community members about the ways to spend limited funds for community development; however, the two sides may be able to agree if it is possible for them to write a joint grant proposal that will provide enough money to meet all objectives. Two entrepreneurs may be in a heated conflict over how to resolve a design problem in a new product, but if they share the common objective of resolving the problem in time to present their case to a group of venture capitalists who could fund the design, they may improve their chances of finding a solution.

Common Enemies.   A common enemy is a negative form of superordinate goal. The parties find new motivation to resolve their differences to avoid intervention by a third party, or to pool resources to defeat a common enemy. Political leaders of all persuasions often invoke outside enemies (the other political party) to bring their own constituencies together. Managers who are in conflict learn that if they don't resolve their differences themselves, someone else (their boss) will make the decision for them. Labor and management may behave more collaboratively when threatened with binding arbitration, declining market share, foreign competition, or government intervention.

Common Expectations.   We noted earlier in this chapter that parties can manage the social context by creating common ground rules to govern their conflict. However, ground rules are often badly introduced and mismanaged, such that efforts to use and monitor them become part of the conflict rather than a process for effectively managing it. For example, ground rules are often introduced in a directive manner; they are formal, limiting, and prohibitive, trying to prevent people from doing (the wrong) things rather than encouraging people to do (the right) things; they are not consistently applied, deviations are handled arbitrarily, and there is no agreed-upon procedure for revisiting and revising the ground rules. As a result, the more effective process is to move from ground rules to "higher ground," a process that is more about creating common and shared expectations. The process of creating common or shared expectations—a process for how the parties will move forward—is called "creating a group covenant."[12]

A group covenant is a process for addressing differences, managing expectations, establishing ground rules, and so on for moving a group to "higher ground." There are six key elements to this process:

1. Establish the need for creating shared expectations.
2. Educate and inspire people to create a new covenant that all will agree to follow.
3. Begin by envisioning desired outcomes for the future, and then develop common ground rules that will enable the group to reach that future.
4. Promote full participation by giving everyone a voice in the process.
5. Be accountable by honoring the agreements contained in the new covenant.
6. Evaluate, modify, revise, and recommit to these new principles as necessary.[13]

Each of these steps needs to be enacted to create a new covenant to work in a way that will facilitate agreement rather than sidetrack it.

Manage Time Constraints and Deadlines.   Time, while a source of power and leverage in many negotiations (see Chapter 6), can also be an impediment to integrative bargaining. One author suggests that time and timing are critical aspects of effective group process. Not only should parties try to agree to a time schedule for moving discussions along, but they also should realize that under the time pressure of an approaching deadline, any substantive issues that remain unresolved may surface, changing one or both parties to a more competitive, less collaborative frame of mind.[14] The remedies for this problem are fairly straightforward:

- Conduct thorough and open problem diagnosis and issue identification steps so as to identify both parties' motives.
- To the extent possible, address and identify the clearly distributive issues, and do so early enough that they will not linger and derail the collaborative process when a deadline approaches.
- Be generous in estimating the time necessary to accomplish the negotiation, making allowances for extra time to manage difficult or linked issues.
- Recognize tentative deadlines for what they are, reserving the right (if not the obligation) of benchmarking progress against the time allotted, and be willing to let both sides sleep on tentative settlements before closing on them.
- Be willing to entertain the possibility of extending the deadline set early in the negotiation. If the deadline is not movable, pay additional attention to timing, pacing, and benchmarking.

Reframe the Parties' View of Each Other.   Earlier we discussed the power of frames in shaping the way the parties view each other, the issues, and the conflict management process. For example, Lewicki, Gray, and Elliott offer many detailed examples of the ways that frames shape (or misshape) the ways that parties view "difficult to resolve" environmental disputes and the processes available for their resolution.[15] In an examination of several of the approaches by which disputes can be "reframed," Lewicki et al. suggest that parties must be able to gain perspective on the dispute. This perspective-taking requires standing back from the negotiation, observing it, and reflecting on it in a way that allows parties to recognize that there is more than one way to view the other party, the issues, and the process of resolving it.[16] Many of the processes we describe in this chapter presume that the parties are able to engage in this perspective-taking on their own.

Build an Integrative Framework.   Though often time-consuming, diligent application of the integrative process (as described in Chapter 4) can produce lasting resolutions to thorny, complex problems. In the terms of the dual concerns model (Chapter 1), both parties are committed to pursue both their own interests *and* the other's; each party wants to ensure a substantive win-win agreement as well as to strengthen the future relationship. How do parties build an integrative framework to maximize their ability to achieve a mutually acceptable agreement?

Integrative frameworks are ways of redefining issues to create a common perspective from which initial positions appear more compatible. By defining negotiated issues in terms of positions—my position on this issue is X—parties tend to simplify complex phenomena by defining a single point and then refusing to move from it. To create movement, parties must establish ways of redefining the conflict so that they can explore compatible interests.[17] Recall the classic example from Chapter 4. Two men are quarreling in a library about whether a window should be open or shut. They bicker back and forth about how much to leave it open. Enter the librarian. She asks one why he wants the window open, and he responds that he wants some fresh air. She asks the other why he wants it closed, and he responds that he wants to avoid a draft. So she goes into the next room and opens a window, meeting the needs of both parties.[18]

There are four approaches to reorienting a "difficult" negotiation toward a more integrative process: building trust, training the parties, seeking semantic resolutions, and generating creative alternatives.

*i) **Build Trust.*** Strong, constructive bargaining relationships are typically marked by conditions of high trust (characterized by hope, faith, confidence, assurance, and initiative) and low distrust (characterized by the absence of fear, skepticism, and cynicism), and are accompanied by low vigilance and low monitoring behaviors between the parties.[19] Healthy interdependence, characterized by strong trust and either low distrust or the effective management of any distrust that exists, will likely support the pursuit of mutually beneficial opportunities. The collaborative ideal of high trust/low distrust refers to each party's expectation that the other will cooperate, will be predictable, and will be committed to solving the problem.[20]

*ii) **Train the Parties in Integrative Negotiation and Interactive Problem Solving.*** One study has shown how negotiation can be employed as a process of interactive problem solving, with the goal of transforming the relationship between the parties, through developing an agreement that addresses the fundamental needs and fears of both parties on a basis of reciprocity. Four components of negotiation—identification and analysis of the problem, joint shaping of ideas for a solution, influencing the other side, and creating a supportive political environment—can lead to specific prescriptions for each component.[21] Training in interactive problem solving (compared to distributive and integrative bargaining models) led Jewish and Arab students to be less pessimistic about their ethnic conflict and showed positive change in attitudes toward members of the other group.[22]

*iii) **Search for Semantic Resolutions.*** Negotiations where the parties are negotiating over specific words and ideas—contract language, setting policy, or establishing memoranda of agreement—can lead to an impasse over key words, phrases, and expressions. Sometimes these discussions can be reduced to irrelevant linguistic hairsplitting, yet to the parties involved the wording is significant in both meaning and intent. Discovering how parties attach different meanings to some words, or exploring language that can accommodate both sides, is another alternative for achieving an integrative framework. More specific treatment of the integrative solution-building process can be found in Chapter 4.

*iv) **Generate Creative Alternatives.*** For many negotiators, the prescriptive advice to create value (see Chapter 4) is easy to say but hard to accomplish. Perhaps part of the difficulty lies in the tendency to see all or most negotiations in competitive winlose terms; this perception leads to the unconscious assumption that winning the substantive contest is all that matters. Even when collaboration may be the appropriate strategy, it may be very difficult to convince oneself and the other party to engage in the creative processes necessary to secure a collaborative outcome. One needs to generate creative alternatives, where creativity refers to "the process by which novel outcomes are developed that are viewed as acceptable, and satisfying to a given audience."[23] The long-standing interest in creative thinking is testimony to the depth and breadth of this problem.[24]

Enhancing the Desirability of Options to the Other Party

Another method that parties can use to increase the likelihood of agreement is to make their desires and preferences appear more palatable to the other. We have noted that as conflict escalates, the parties may lock into a rigid position on an issue. If the other party does not readily comply with a negotiator's position or policy, the negotiator's tendency is to escalate demands or increase the magnitude threats for noncompliance. These actions make impasse more likely.

Roger Fisher suggests that most influence situations can be characterized by a demand (what you want) and offers and threats (the consequences of meeting or not meeting the demand).[25] The who, what, when, and why of this influence process are depicted in Table 9.1. Fisher suggests that in most negotiation situations, the parties tend to emphasize the demand and the threat. Rather, negotiators should direct their efforts to the following question: How can we get the other party to make a choice that is best for us, given that our interests diverge? This approach is largely a matter of focusing on the other's interests rather than one's own. Like role reversal, it requires negotiators to focus less on their own position, and more on clearly understanding and addressing the other party's needs. Moreover, once those needs are understood, effort should be invested in moving toward the other party, not in getting the other party to come to you. This can be done in most cases by making offers rather than demands and threats. Fisher suggests several alternative strategies:

Give the Other Party a "Yesable" Proposal. Rather than emphasizing one's own position and letting the other party suggest alternatives that can be approved or overruled, a negotiator should direct effort to understanding the other side's needs and devising a proposal that will meet those needs. Fisher terms this a "yesable" proposal, one to which the only answer can be "Yes, it is acceptable."

Ask for a Different Decision. Rather than making demands more general, to fit with their policy, negotiators should endeavor to make demands more specific. Negotiators must determine what specific elements of their demands are most palatable or offensive to the other party, then use this information to refine the demand. "Ask for a different decision," asserts Fisher. Reformulate, repackage, reorganize, or rephrase. Fractionate, split, divide, or make more specific.[26]

Sweeten the Offer Rather Than Intensifying the Threat. Negotiators can also make options more palatable by enhancing the attractiveness of accepting them. Again, this is a matter of placing the emphasis on the positive rather than the negative. In the language of traditional carrot-and-stick tactics for motivating workers, the approach should make the carrot more attractive rather than making the stick larger. Promises and offers can be made more attractive in several ways: maximizing the attractive qualities and minimizing the negative ones, showing how the offer meets the other party's needs,

TABLE 9.1 Fisher's "Demand" Dynamics

	Decision (The Decision You Desire)	Offer (The Consequences of Making the Decision)	Threat (The Consequences of Not Making the Decision)
Who?	Who is to make the decision?	Who benefits if the decision is made?	Who gets hurt if the decision is not made?
What?	Exactly what decision is desired?	If the decision is made, what benefits/costs can be expected?	If the decision is not made, what risks/ potential benefits can be expected?
When?	By what time does the decision have to be made?	What, if ever, will be the benefit of making the decision occur?	How soon will the consequences of not making the decision be felt?
Why?	What makes this a right, proper, and lawful decision?	What makes these consequences fair and legitimate?	What makes these consequences fair and legitimate?

Every feature of an influence problem can be located somewhere on this schematic map. The nature of a given problem can be discovered through estimating how the presumed adversary would answer the above questions.

SOURCE: R. Fisher, *International Conflict for Beginners* (New York: Harper & Row, 1969), p. 48. Used with permission.

reducing the disadvantages of accepting the offer, making offers more credible (i.e., you will do what you promise to do), or setting deadlines on offers so they expire if not accepted quickly.

Use Legitimacy or Objective Criteria to Evaluate Solutions. Finally, negotiators may insist that alternative solutions be evaluated by objective criteria that meet the tests of fairness and legitimacy. Negotiators on all sides should be able to demonstrate that their demands are based on sound facts, calculations, and information, and that preferred solutions are consistent with those facts and information. This procedure will frequently require disclosing and sharing those facts, rather than disguising and distorting them. "Here's how we arrived at our proposal. Here are the facts we used, the cost data we used in our estimates, the calculations we made. You can verify these by the following procedures." The more this data is open to public verification and demonstrated to be within the bounds of fairness and legitimacy, the more convincing it will be that the position is independent of the negotiator who advocates it, and the more persuasive the position will be in achieving a settlement.

Summary

In this section, we reviewed five major strategies that negotiators can use to get derailed negotiations back on track and return to a more productive flow of events: reducing tension, improving communication, controlling issues, finding common ground, and making options more attractive for joint resolution. Taken together, these strategies create a large portfolio of alternatives that negotiators can pursue to manage derailed discussions, enhance deteriorating communications, and find ways to invent acceptable solution alternatives.

MISMATCHED MODELS: INTENTIONAL AND OTHERWISE

In this section, we address methods negotiators can use when dealing with an intentionally difficult party. We then proceed to explain the skills and behaviors needed to defend against such parties and/or to convert them to use a more productive negotiation process. Quite simply, what the collaborative party is trying to do is to change the game, that is, to convince the other party to move from distributive to integrative negotiations. At least four challenges exist:

- What to do when the other side uses hard distributive tactics.
- What to do if the other side is more powerful.
- What to do if the other side is just generally difficult to deal with.
- The special problem of ultimatums.

We will now discuss the tactical responses to each of these situations.

Responding to the Other Side's Hard Distributive Tactics

By *hard tactics* we mean the distributive tactics that the other party applies in a negotiation to put pressure on negotiators to do something that is not in their best interest to do. The temptation to use hard tactics is inherent in the distributive model: get information, but don't give it; convince the other party of the value of staying in the deal, or the cost of leaving it; and so on. Distributive tactics were presented in Chapter 3, where we also discussed strategies for responding to or dealing with these tactics. To summarize briefly, as a pressured party you can respond to these tactics in any of these ways:

1. *Ignore them.* A tactic ignored is, essentially, a tactic defeated; even if it is recognized later, it has no power to bring undue pressure to bear. Unfortunately, some bargainers are slow learners; if you ignore them, they may simply not get the message that you want something different to happen.

2. *Call them on it.* Negotiators should let the other party know they are aware of what they are trying to do when they use hard tactics by identifying the tactic and raising it to the level of open discussion. This should be done tactfully, but firmly. Negotiators may indicate their distress or displeasure with the tactic and explain why it is problematic. Sometimes, the embarrassment value of such an observation is sufficient to make negotiators disavow the tactic and abandon its future use, or even convert their behavior to more win-win negotiating.

3. *Respond in kind.* The possibility of responding to a hard tactic with a hard tactic was discussed in Chapter 3. Recall, however, that responding in kind is likely to escalate the conflict, and it is not consistent with the principles we are proposing here.

4. *Offer to change to more productive methods.* Negotiators may announce that they have noted the other party's behavior and suggest a better way to negotiate. Fisher, Ury, and Patton, in advising well-intentioned bargainers not to let themselves be victimized, suggest a comprehensive strategy: "Recognize the tactic, raise the issue explicitly, and question the tactic's legitimacy and desirability—negotiate over it."[27] The logic of this advice lies in the assumption that once the trickster understands that (1) their behavior is understood and (2) continuing this behavior will entail certain costs (including the possibility that you will walk away from the negotiation), he or she will respond to a suggestion for a more integrative exchange.

Responding When the Other Side Has More Power

Relative power can be a good predictor of how a conflict will evolve. Other things being equal, when power is unequal, victory typically goes to the more powerful party. Power imbalances in negotiation can represent clear dangers to the satisfaction of personal needs and to the collaborative process. First, high-power parties tend to pay little heed to the needs of low-power parties, who either don't get their needs met or use disruptive, attention-getting tactics that make collaboration very difficult.[28] Second, low-power parties are not usually in a position to trigger and advance an integrative process. Integrative negotiation requires a tolerance of change and flexibility, which often requires negotiators to give up some control over outcomes; low-power parties "have less to give, and thus less flexibility to offer the other party."[29]

When dealing with a party with more power, negotiators have at least four alternatives. They can

1. Protect themselves.
2. Cultivate their best alternative (BATNA).
3. Formulate a "trip wire alert system."
4. Correct the power imbalance.

Negotiators can *protect themselves* by keeping in mind that they have real interests, that negotiation may be the preferred approach of achieving those interests, and that excessive accommodation to the high-power party will not serve them well over the long term. A note of caution, though: Knowing the resistance point may provide a clear measure of minimum acceptability (lowest price, maximum monthly payment, etc.), but too strict an adherence to it may deprive negotiators of creativity and flexibility, which are critical components to the design of an integrative arrangement. It may also limit the ability to use information that emerges during the exchange.[30]

Alternatively, negotiators should *cultivate their BATNA,* which represents the best they can accomplish without the negotiation. Many negotiators bargain without a clear definition of their BATNA; we pointed out in Chapters 3 and 4 that the lack of such a critical reference point gives negotiators less power and limits what they can achieve in the current negotiation.[31]

A clear, strong BATNA may also be reinforced by additional safety measures. Low-power negotiators are also advised to *formulate a trip wire alert system,* which serves as an early warning signal when bargaining enters the safety zone close to the walkaway option or the BATNA.[32] The trip wire tells the negotiator to exercise special caution and pay increased attention to the negotiation in progress. Given that negotiations often become intense and engrossing at such points, it might be appropriate to assign a co-negotiator to attend to the trip wire and to notify the involved negotiator at the critical time.

The foregoing options involve dealing with an extant power imbalance. A final option for dealing with more powerful parties is to *correct the imbalance*. Three approaches to this are possible: low-power parties taking power, high-power parties giving power, and third parties managing the transfer and balance of power. The first approach, power-taking, is typically not feasible in negotiations; as we already mentioned, using disruptive or attention-getting actions to try to take power typically contributes to a distributive exchange, generating in-kind responses from the high-power party. However, as we pointed out in Chapter 6, power in negotiation is multifaceted, and power may be gained on dimensions different from those currently held by the high-power party. The third approach—using a third party to manage power transfer—*is* feasible and is commonly used.

The middle, remaining approach is for the high-power party to give power to the other party. Such actions include sharing resources; sharing control over certain processes or outcomes (e.g., agendas or decisions); focusing on common interests rather than solely on the high-powered party's interests; or educating the low-power party about what power he or she does have and how to use it more effectively.[33] The immediate question is why high-power parties would ever choose to give power away. The answer is complex, but there are good reasons. First, sharing power may facilitate a better integrative process. Second, even if one party does have power over the other, the best the high-power party can hope for is compliance rather than enthusiastic cooperation. Finally, no power imbalance exists forever, and when the low-power party does gain a power base or a BATNA, he or she is likely to either sever the relationship or look for some form of revenge.

The Special Problem of Handling Ultimatums

One particularly troublesome hard tactic used by distributive negotiators is the use of ultimatums. An ultimatum is an attempt "to induce compliance or force concessions from a presumably recalcitrant opponent."[34] Ultimatums typically have three components: (1) a demand; (2) an attempt to create a sense of urgency, such that compliance is required; and (3) a threat of punishment if compliance does not occur.[35] For example, one particular type of ultimatum is the "exploding offer," in which one party presents the other with a classic no-win, "use-it-or-lose-it" dilemma. An exploding offer has a specific time limit or deadline attached to it, forcing the other party to decide on a less-than-attractive offer or run the risk of going without anything.[36] Such offers have several other components, including:

- A clear asymmetry of power between the parties.
- A pressure-inducing test of faith for the respondent.
- A restricted set of options.

- A lack of consideration and respect for the offerer by the respondent.
- An apparent lack of good faith on the offerer's part.[37]

While one analysis of ultimatums might suggest that such a take-it-or-leave-it tactic should be successful, given that something (anything) must be preferable to nothing (a failed negotiation), empirical studies have not found this to be so.[38] Conflicts involving ultimatums often fall prey to escalation problems, as noted elsewhere in this chapter, through severe "action–reaction" spirals.

Robinson has developed one possible response to ultimatums, which he calls the "farpoint gambit" (after the name of a maneuver on a *Star Trek* episode). The success of the response hangs on the ability to say "Yes, but . . ." to an ultimatum. (Robinson cautions—and we agree—that this approach is a last resort; other remedies should be exhausted first.) When first presented with an ultimatum, negotiators should probably try a reasonable approach: be forthright in addressing the ultimatum; make sensible, reasonable counteroffers; or attempt to engage the offerer in joint problem solving. If that fails, Robinson suggests "an exploding offer can be defused by *embracing it*"—that is, agree to the ultimatum provisionally, subject to some qualifying event or condition.

Responding When the Other Side Is Being Difficult

Responding to Difficult People. Sometimes problems in negotiation can be traced to difficulties in the other's behavioral style. The subject of how to deal with difficult people in the workplace has received increasing attention in recent years from several authors,[39] who make several important points. First, everyone can exhibit difficult behaviors or be difficult to deal with at times; some people, however, are *invariably* difficult, and their behavior conforms to predictable and identifiable patterns. Second, what is difficult behavior to one person may not be difficult for another. Labeling an action "difficult" may say as much about the receiver as it does about the sender. Person A may have a great deal of difficulty contending with a very aggressive negotiator, whereas Person B has no difficulty with that person. Third, difficult people do what they do because it works for them. Their behavior gives them control, feels comfortable, and lets them get their way. By giving in to it, negotiators reinforce the behavior, providing the difficult person ample reasons to continue behaving in ways that were useful in the past. Difficult people also may continue their difficult ways because they honestly are not aware of the long-term costs to people and organizations that must contend with them. Finally, it is possible to cope with invariably difficult people—contending with their behavior on equal behavioral terms—as opposed to giving in to them, accepting their behavior, or getting them to change their values, beliefs, or attitudes. In short, negotiators must effectively counterbalance the potential power these behaviors give to those who use them. Box 9.3 offers a general framework for coping with a difficult other.[40]

CHAPTER SUMMARY

Through any number of different avenues—breakdowns in communication, escalation of anger and mistrust, polarization of positions and refusal to compromise, the

BOX 9.3
Why, You No Good, Uncooperative, Double-Dealing, . . . Etc.

Emotionality is frequently an aspect of difficult, high-stakes negotiation. All the same, emotion run wild can be detrimental to the process, distorting perceptions and diverting attention from the real issues. Adler, Rosen, and Silverstein looked at the problem and effects of fear and anger in negotiations, and suggest some tactics for managing such emotions.

Regarding your *own* emotions, you can

- Determine which situations tend to trigger inappropriate anger.
- Decide, when angry, whether or not to display your anger.
- Use behavioral techniques (e.g., taking a break, counting to 10) to reduce your anger.
- Express your anger and disappointment effectively (e.g., openly and in a nonaccusatory fashion).
- Avoid the negotiator's bias ("I'm fair and reasonable, you're not . . .").
- Try to promote trust.

Regarding the *other party's* emotions, you can

- Defuse emotional buildups by direct confrontation ("You seem angry; are you?").
- Assess the real significance of emotional displays (Is it an act? A distributive dirty trick?).
- Address the other's anger directly, perhaps apologizing for a comment or pointing out the effects of a bad situation.
- Respond to the other's anger strategically (call a break, use silence to "wit him out," make a modest concession, etc.).
- Help the other party save face (especially when losing face contributed to his anger).
- Consider calling in a mediator when you anticipate anger rising.

SOURCE: R. S. Adler, B. Rosen, and E. M. Silverstein, "Emotions in Negotiation: How to Manage Fear and Anger," *Negotiation Journal* 14, No. 2 (1998), pp. 161–79.

issuance of ultimatums, or even the avoidance of conflict—negotiations often hit an impasse. Productive dialogue stops. The parties may continue talking, but the communication is usually characterized by trying to sell or force one's own position, talking about the other's unreasonable position and uncooperative behavior, or both. When these breakdowns occur, the parties may simply agree to recess, cool off, and come back tomorrow. More commonly, however, the parties break off negotiation and walk away angry and upset. Although they may privately wish there was some way to get back together, they usually don't know how to arrange a reconciliation.

This chapter explored five major strategies that the parties could use to attempt to resolve a dispute on their own:

- Reduce tension by separating themselves from one another through cooling-off periods, talking about emotions and feelings, or attempting to synchronize de-escalation of the conflict.

- Improve the accuracy of communication by role reversal or mirroring the other's statements.

- Keep the number of issues under control so that issues are managed effectively, new issues are not carelessly added, and large issues are divided into smaller ones.

- Search for common ground through exploring superordinate goals, common enemies, creating common ground rules and effective time management, developing common expectations through a "covenant," and reframing.

- Enhancing the desirability of the options and alternatives for both parties by providing "yesable" proposals, asking for different decisions, sweetening offers, and using objective criteria to evaluate solutions.

The tools that we discussed are broad in function and in application, and they represent self-help for negotiators in dealing with stalled or problematic exchanges. None of these methods and remedies is a panacea, and each should be chosen and applied with sensitivity to the needs and limitations of the situations and of the negotiators involved. A truly confrontational breakdown, especially one that involves agreements of great impact or importance, sometimes justifies the introduction of individuals or agencies who themselves are not party to the dispute.

ENDNOTES

1. Adler, Rosen, and Silverstein, 1998; Blake and Mouton, 1961a, 1961b, 1961c; Corwin, 1969; Harvey, 1953; Keltner and Robinson, 1993.
2. Mayer, 2000.
3. Deutsch, 1973; Deutsch and Coleman, 2000; Pruitt and Rubin, 1986; Susskind, McKearnan, and Larmer, 1999; Walton, 1987.
4. Rogers, 1961.
5. Osgood, 1962.
6. Rapoport, 1964.
7. Johnson and Dustin, 1970.
8. Alderfer, 1977.
9. Fisher, 1964.
10. Fisher, Ury, and Patton, 1991.
11. Pruitt and Rubin, 1986.
12. Dukes, Piscolish, and Stephens, 2000.
13. Ibid., p. 83.
14. Gersick, 1988, 1989.
15. Lewicki, Gray, and Elliott, 2003.
16. Schon and Rein, 1994.
17. Eisenman, 1978; Fisher, Ury, and Patton, 1991.
18. Follett, 1940.
19. Lewicki, McAllister, and Bies, 1998; Lewicki and Stevenson, 1998.
20. Ross and LaCroix, 1996.
21. Cross and Rosenthal, 1999.
22. Coleman and Lim, 2001.
23. Spector, 1995.
24. DeBono, 1990; Sternberg, 1988; Whiting, 1958.
25. Fisher, 1969.

26. Fisher, Ury, and Patton, 1991.
27. Ibid., p. 130.
28. Donohue and Kolt, 1992.
29. Ibid., p. 107.
30. Fisher, Ury, and Patton, 1991.
31. Ibid.
32. Ibid.
33. Donohue and Kolt, 1992.
34. Kramer, Shah, and Woerner, 1995, p. 285.
35. George, 1993.
36. Robinson, 1995.
37. Ibid., pp. 278–79.
38. Guth, Schmittberger, and Schwarze, 1982; Guth and Tietz, 1990.
39. Bernstein and Rosen, 1989; Bramson, 1981, 1992; Solomon, 1990.
40. Bramson, 1981; Solomon, 1990; Ury, 1991.

Bibliography

Aaronson, K. (1989). *Selling on the fast track.* New York: Putnam.

Abu-Nimer, M. (1996). Conflict resolution approaches: Western and Middle Eastern lessons and possibilities. *American Journal of Economics and Sociology, 55,* 35–52.

Acuff, F. L. (1993). *How to negotiate anything with anyone anywhere around the world.* New York: AMA-COM.

Adachi, Y. (1998). The effects of semantic difference on cross-cultural business negotiation: A Japanese and American case study. *The Journal of Language for International Business, 9,* 43–52.

Adler, N. J., Brahm, R., & Graham, J. L. (1992). Strategy implementation: A comparison of face-to-face negotiations in the People's Republic of China and the United States. *Strategic Management Journal, 13,* 449–466.

Adler, N. J., & Graham, J. L. (1987). Business negotiations: Canadians are not just like Americans. *Canadian Journal of Administrative Sciences, 4,* 211–238.

Adler, N. J., & Graham, J. L. (1989). Cross-cultural interaction: The international comparison fallacy? *Journal of International Business Studies, 20,* 515–537.

Adler, N. J., Graham, J. L., & Schwarz, T. (1987). Business negotiations in Canada, Mexico, and the United States. *Journal of Business Research, 15,* 411–429.

Adler, R., Rosen, B., & Silverstein, E. (1996). Thrust and parry: The art of tough negotiating. *Training and Development, 50,* 42–48.

Adler, R. S., Rosen, B., & Silverstein, E. M. (1998). Emotions in negotiation: How to manage fear and anger. *Negotiation Journal, 14,* 161–179.

Albin, C. (1993). The role of fairness in negotiation. *Negotiation Journal, 9,* 223–243.

Alderfer, C. P. (1977). Group and intergroup relations. In J. R. Hackman & J. L. Suttle (Eds.), *Improving life at work: Behavioral science approaches to organizational change* (pp. 227–296). Santa Monica, CA: Goodyear.

Alexander, J. F., Schul, P. L., & Babakus, E. (1991). Analyzing interpersonal communications in industrial marketing negotiations. *Journal of the Academy of Marketing Science, 19,* 129–139.

Allred, K. G. (1998). Anger-driven retaliation: Toward an understanding of impassioned conflict in organizations. In R. Bies, R. J. Lewicki, & B. H. Sheppard (Eds.), *Research on negotiation in organizations* (Vol. 7), in press.

Allred, K. G., Mallozzi, J. S., Matsui, F., & Raia, C. P. (1997). The influence of anger and compassion on negotiation performance. *Organizational Behavior and Human Decision Processes, 70,* 175–187.

Arino, A., Abramov, M., Rykounina, I., & Vila, J. (1997). Partner selection and trust building in west European–Russian joint ventures. *International Studies of Management and Organization, 27,* 19–37.

Arunachalam, V., & Dilla, W. N. (1995). Judgment accuracy and outcomes in negotiation: A causal modeling analysis of decision-aiding effects. *Organizational Behavior and Human Decision Processes, 61,* 289–304.

Arunachalam, V., Wall, J. A., Jr., & Chan, C. (1998). Hong Kong versus U.S. negotiations: Effects of culture, alternatives, outcome scales, and mediation. *Journal of Applied Social Psychology, 28,* 1219–1244.

Asherman, I. G., & Asherman, S. V. (1990). *The negotiation sourcebook.* Amherst, MA: Human Resource Development Press.

Avruch, K. (2000). Culture and negotiation pedagogy. *Negotiation Journal, 16,* 339–346.

Axtell, R. E. (1990). *Do's and taboos of hosting international visitors.* New York: John Wiley and Sons.

Axtell, R. E. (1991). *Gestures: The do's and taboos of body language around the world.* New York: John Wiley and Sons.

Axtell, R. E. (1993). *Do's and taboos around the world* (3rd ed.). New York: John Wiley and Sons.

Babcock, L., Wang, X., & Loewenstein, G. (1996). Choosing the wrong pond: Social comparisons in negotiations that reflect a self-serving bias. *The Quarterly Journal of Economics, 111,* 1–19.

Ball, S. B., Bazerman, M. H., & Carroll, J. S. (1991). An evaluation of learning in the bilateral winner's curse. *Organizational Behavior and Human Decision Processes, 48,* 1–22.

Baranowski, T. A., & Summers, D. A. (1972). Perceptions of response alternatives in a prisoner's dilemma game. *Journal of Personality and Social Psychology, 21,* 35–40.

Barnard, C. (1938). *The functions of the executive.* Cambridge, MA: Harvard University Press.

Barry, B. (1999). The tactical use of emotion in negotiation. In R. Bies, R. J. Lewicki, & B. H. Sheppard (Eds.), *Research on negotiation in organizations* (Vol. 7, pp. 93–121), Stamford, CT: JAI Press.

Barry, B., Fulmer, I. S., & Long, A. (2000). Ethically marginal bargaining tactics: Sanction, efficacy, and performance. Presented at the annual meeting of the Academy of Management, Toronto.

Barry, B., Fulmer, I. S., & Van Kleef, G. A. (2002). I laughed, I cried, I settled: The role of emotion in negotiation. In M. Gelfand and J. Brett (Eds.), *Culture and negotiation: Integrative approaches to theory and research,* in press.

Barry, B., & Oliver, R. L. (1996). Affect in dyadic negotiation: A model and propositions. *Organizational Behavior and Human Decision Processes, 67,* 127–143.

Bateson, B. (1972). *Steps to an ecology of mind.* New York: Ballantine Books.

Bazerman, M. (1998). *Judgment in managerial decision making* (4th ed.). New York: John Wiley and Sons.

Bazerman, M. H., & Carroll, J. S. (1987). Negotiator cognition. In B. Staw & L. L. Cummings. *Research in organizational behavior* (Vol. 9, pp. 247–288), Greenwich, CT: JAI Press.

Bazerman, M. H., Curhan, J. R., Moore, D. A., & Valley, K. L. (2000). Negotiation. *Annual Review of Psychology, 51,* 279–314.

Bazerman, M. H., Magliozzi, T., & Neale, M. A. (1985). Integrative bargaining in a competitive market. *Organizational Behavior and Human Decision Processes, 35,* 294–313.

Bazerman, M. H., Moore, D. A., & Gillespie, J. J. (1999). The human mind as a barrier to wiser environmental agreements. *The American Behavioral Scientist, 42,* 1277–1300.

Bazerman, M. H., & Neale, M. A. (1983). Heuristics in negotiation: Limitations to effective dispute resolution. In M. Bazerman & R. J. Lewicki. *Negotiating in organizations.* Beverly Hills, CA: Sage.

Bazerman, M. H., & Neale, M. A. (1992). *Negotiating rationally.* New York: Free Press.

Bazerman, M. H., & Samuelson, W. F. (1983). I won the auction but don't want the prize. *Journal of Conflict Resolution, 27,* 618–634.

Beebe, S. A. (1980). Effects of eye contact, posture, and vocal inflection upon credibility and comprehension. *Australian SCAN: Journal of Human Communication, 7–8,* 57–70.

Beisecker, T., Walker, G., & Bart, J. (1989). Knowledge versus ignorance in bargaining strategies: The impact of knowledge about other's information level. *The Social Science Journal, 26,* 161–172.

Berkowitz, L. (1989). The frustration-aggression hypothesis: An examination and reformulation. *Psychological Bulletin, 106,* 59–73.

Bernstein, J., & Rosen, S. (1989). *Dinosaur brains: Dealing with all those impossible people at work.* New York: John Wiley and Sons.

Bettinghaus, E. P. (1966). *Message preparation: The nature of proof.* Indianapolis: Bobbs-Merrill.

Bettinghaus, E. P. (1980). *Persuasive communication* (2nd ed.). New York: Holt, Rinehart & Winston.

Bies, R., & Moag, J. (1986). Interactional justice: Communication criteria of fairness. In R. J. Lewicki, B. H. Sheppard, and M. H. Bazerman (Eds.), *Research on negotiation in organizations* (Vol. 1, pp. 43–55). Greenwich, CT: JAI Press.

Bies, R., & Shapiro, D. (1987). Interactional fairness judgments: The influence of causal accounts. *Social Justice Research, 1,* 199–218.

Bies, R., & Tripp, T. (1998). Revenge in organizations: The good, the bad and the ugly. In R. W. Griffin, A. O'Leary-Kelly, & J. Collins (Eds.), *Dysfunctional behavior in organizations, Volume 1: Violent behavior in organizations* (pp. 49–68). Greenwich, CT: JAI Press.

Binnendijk, H. (1987). *National negotiating styles.* Washington, DC: Foreign Service Institute, Department of State.

Blake, R. R., & Mouton, J. S. (1961a). *Group dynamics: Key to decision making.* Houston, TX: Gulf Publications.

Blake, R. R., & Mouton, J. S. (1961b). Comprehension of own and outgroup positions under intergroup competition. *Journal of Conflict Resolution, 5,* 304–310.

Blake, R. R., & Mouton, J. S. (1961c). Loyalty of representatives to ingroup positions during intergroup competition. *Sociometry, 24,* 177–183.

Bless, H., Bohner, G., Schwarz, N., & Strack, F. (1988). Happy and mindless: Moods and the processing of persuasive communication. Unpublished manuscript, Mannheim, GR.

Bok, S. (1978). *Lying: Moral choice in public and private life.* New York: Pantheon.

Bonoma, T., Horai, J., Lindskold, S., Gahagan, J. P., & Tedeschi, J. T. (1969). Compliance to contingent threats. *Proceedings of the 77th Annual Convention of the American Psychological Association, 4,* 395–396.

Bottom, W. P. (1998). Negotiator risk: Sources of uncertainty and the impact of reference points on negotiated agreements. *Organizational Behavior and Human Decision Processes, 76,* 89–112.

Bottom, W. P., & Paese, P. W. (1999). Judgment accuracy and the asymmetric cost of errors in distributive bargaining. *Group Decision & Negotiation, 8,* 349–364.

Bowers, J. W. (1964). Some correlates of language intensity. *Quarterly Journal of Speech, 50,* 415–420.

Bowers, J. W., & Osborn, M. M. (1966). Attitudinal effects of selected types of concluding metaphors in persuasive speeches. *Speech Monographs, 33,* 147–155.

Bowie, N. (1993). Does it pay to bluff in business? In T. L. Beauchamp & N. E. Bowie (Eds.), *Ethical theory and business* (pp. 449–454). Englewood Cliffs, NJ: Prentice Hall.

Braganti, N. L., & Devine, E. (1992). *European customs and manners: How to make friends and do business in Europe* (rev. ed.). New York: Meadowbrook Press.

Bramson, R. (1981). *Coping with difficult people.* New York: Anchor Books.

Bramson, R. (1992). *Coping with difficult bosses.* New York: Carol Publishing Group.

Brett, J. M. (2001). *Negotiating globally.* San Francisco: Jossey-Bass.

Brett, J. M., & Okumura, T. (1998). Inter- and intracultural negotiation: U. S. and Japanese negotiators. *Academy of Management Journal, 41,* 495–510.

Brett, J. M., Shapiro, D. L., & Lytle, A. L. (1998). Breaking the bonds of reciprocity in negotiation. *Academy of Management Journal, 41,* 410–424.

Brock, T. C. (1963). Effects of prior dishonesty on post-decision dissonance. *Journal of Abnormal and Social Psychology, 66,* 325–331.

Brockner, J. (1992). The escalation of commitment to a failing course of action: Toward theoretical progress. *Academy of Management Review, 17,* 39–61.

Brodt, S. E. (1994). "Inside information" and negotiator decision behavior. *Organizational Behavior and Human Decision Processes, 58,* 172–202.

Brooks, E., & Odiorne, G. S. (1984). *Managing by negotiations.* New York: Van Nostrand.

Brouthers, K. D., & Bamossy, G. J. (1997). The role of key stakeholders in international joint venture negotiations: Case studies from Eastern Europe. *Journal of International Business Studies, 28,* 285–308.

Bruner, J. S., & Tagiuri, R. (1954). The perception of people. In G. Lindzey (Ed.), *The handbook of social psychology* (Vol. 2, pp. 634–654). Reading, MA: Addison-Wesley.

Buechler, S. M. (2000). *Social movements in advanced capitalism.* New York, Oxford University Press.

Burgess, G., & Burgess, H. (1995). Constructive confrontation: A transformative approach to intractable conflicts. *Mediation Quarterly, 13,* 305–322.

Burgoon, J. K., Coker, D. A., & Coker, R. A. (1986). Communication of gaze behavior: A test of two contrasting explanations. *Human Communication Research, 12,* 495–524.

Burgoon, M., & King, L. B. (1974). The mediation of resistance to persuasion strategies by language variables and active-passive participation. *Human Communication Research, 1,* 30–41.

Burgoon, M., & Stewart, D. (1975). Empirical investigations of language: The effects of sex of source, receiver, and language intensity on attitude change. *Human Communication Research, 1,* 244–248.

Burnstein, D. (1995). *Negotiator pro.* Beacon Expert Systems, 35 Gardner Road, Brookline, MA.

Burton, J. (1984). *Global conflict.* Center for International Development, University of Maryland, College Park, MD.

Butler, J. K. Jr. (1996). Two integrative win-win negotiating strategies. *Simulation and Gaming, 27,* 387–392.

Butler, J. K. Jr. (1999). Trust expectations, information sharing, climate of trust, and negotiation effectiveness and efficiency. *Group and Organization Management, 24,* 217–238.

Cacioppo, J. T., & Petty, R. E. (1985). Central and peripheral routes to persuasion: The role of message repetition. In L. F. Alwitt & A. A. Mitchell (Eds.), *Psychological processes and advertising effects: Theory, research, and application* (pp. 91–111). Hillsdale, NJ: Lawrence Erlbaum.

Cai, D. A. (1998). Culture, plans, and the pursuit of negotiation goals. *Journal of Asian Pacific Communication, 8,* 103–123.

Camerer, C. F., & Loewenstein, G. (1993). Information, fairness, and efficiency in bargaining. In *Psychological perspectives on justice. Theory and applications* (pp. 155–179). Cambridge: Cambridge University Press.

Carnevale, P. J., & Isen, A. M. (1986). The influence of positive affect and visual access on the discovery of integrative solutions in bilateral negotiation. *Organizational Behavior and Human Decision Processes, 37,* 1–13.

Carnevale, P. J. D., & Pruitt, D. G. (1992). Negotiation and mediation. In M. Rosenberg & L. Porter (Eds.), *Annual Review of Psychology* (Vol. 43, pp. 531–582). Palo Alto, CA: Annual Reviews, Inc.

Carnevale, P. J. D., Pruitt, D. G., & Seilheimer, S. D. (1981). Looking and competing: Accountability and visual access in integrative bargaining. *Journal of Personality and Social Psychology, 40,* 111–120.

Carr, A. Z. (1968, January–February). Is business bluffing ethical? *Harvard Business Review, 46,* 143–153.

Carroll, J., Bazerman, M., & Maury, R. (1988). Negotiator cognitions: A descriptive approach to negotiators' understanding of their opponents. *Organizational Behavior and Human Decision Processes, 41,* 352–370.

Carroll, J., Delquie, P., Halpern, J., & Bazerman, M. (1990). *Improving negotiators' cognitive processes.* Working paper, Massachusetts Institute of Technology, Cambridge, MA.

Carver, C. S., & Scheir, M. E. (1990). Origins and foundations of positive and negative affect: A control process view. *Psychological Review, 97,* 19–35.

Cellich, C. (1997). Closing your business negotiations. *International Trade Forum, 1,* 14–17.

Chaiken, S. (1986). Physical appearance and social influence. In C. P. Herman, M. P. Zanna, & E. T. Higgins (Eds.), *Physical appearance, stigma, and social behavior: The Ontario symposium* (Vol. 3, pp. 143–177). Hillsdale, NJ: Lawrence Erlbaum.

Chaiken, S. (1987). The heuristic model of persuasion. In M. Zanna, J. Olson, & C. Herman (Eds.), *Social influence: The Ontario symposium* (Vol. 5, pp. 3–39). Hillsdale, NJ: Lawrence Erlbaum.

Chan, C. W. (1998). Transfer pricing negotiation outcomes and the impact of negotiator mixed-motives and culture: empirical evidence from the U.S. and Australia. *Management Accounting Research, 9*, 139–161.

Charan, R. (1991). How networks reshape organizations—for results. *Harvard Business Review, 69*(5), Sept./Oct., pp. 104–115.

Chen, C. C., Chen, X., & Meindl, J. R. (1998). How can cooperation be fostered? The cultural effects of individualism-collectivism. *Academy of Management Review, 23*, 285–304.

Chertkoff, J. M., & Conley, M. (1967). Opening offer and frequency of concessions as bargaining strategies. *Journal of Personality and Social Psychology, 7*, 181–185.

Cialdini, R. B. (2001). *Influence: Science and practice* (4th ed.). Boston: Allyn and Bacon.

Clark, R. A. (1984). *Persuasive messages.* New York: Harper & Row.

Cohen, H. (1980). *You can negotiate anything.* Secaucus, NJ: Lyle Stuart.

Cohen, S. P., Kelman, H. C., Miller, F. D., & Smith, B. L. (1977). Evolving intergroup techniques for conflict resolution: An Israeli–Palestinian pilot workshop. *Journal of Social Issues, 33*, 165–189.

Coleman, P., & Lim, Y. Y. J. (2001). A systematic approach to evaluating the effects of collaborative negotiation training on individuals and groups. *Negotiation Journal*, October, 364–392.

Conger, J. A. (1998). The necessary art of persuasion. *Harvard Business Review, 76*(3), 84–95.

Cooper, W. (1981). Ubiquitous halo. *Psychological Bulletin, 90*, 218–244.

Corley, R. N., Black, R. L., & Reed, O. L. (1977). *The legal environment of business* (4th ed.). New York: McGraw-Hill.

Corwin, R. G. (1969). Patterns of organizational conflict. *Administrative Science Quarterly, 14*, 504–520.

Coser, L. (1956). *The functions of social conflict.* New York: Free Press.

Cronkhite, G., & Liska, J. (1980). The judgment of communicant acceptability. In M. E. Roloff & G. R. Miller (Eds.), *Persuasion: New directions in theory and research* (pp. 101–139). Beverly Hills, CA: Sage.

Croson, R. T. A. (1999). Look at me when you say that: An electronic negotiation simulation. *Simulation & Gaming, 30*, 23–37.

Cross, S., & Rosenthal, R. (1999). Three models of conflict resolution: Effects on intergroup experiences and attitudes. *Journal of Social Issues, 55*(3), 561–580.

Crumbaugh, C. M., & Evans, G. W. (1967). Presentation format, other persons' strategies and cooperative behavior in the prisoner's dilemma. *Psychological Reports, 20*, 895–902.

Daly, J. (1991). The effects of anger on negotiations over mergers and acquisitions. *Negotiation Journal, 7*, 31–39.

De Bono, E. (1990). *Lateral thinking: Creativity step-by-step* (Reissue ed.). New York: Harper Collins.

de Dreu, C. K. W. (1995). Coercive power and concession making in bilateral negotiation. *Journal of Conflict Resolution, 39*, 646–670.

de Dreu, C. K. W., Carnevale, P. J. D., Emans, B. J. M., & van de Vliert, E. (1994). Effects of gain-loss frames in negotiation: Loss aversion, mismatching, and frame adoption. *Organizational Behavior and Human Decision Processes, 60*, 90–107.

de Dreu, C. K. W., Nauta, A., & van de Vliert, E. (1995). Self-serving evaluations of conflict behavior and escalation of the dispute. *Journal of Applied Social Psychology, 25*, 2049–2066.

de Dreu, C. K. W., & van Lange, P. A. M. (1995). The impact of social value orientation on negotiator cognition and behavior. *Personality and Social Psychology Bulletin, 21*, 1178–1188.

Deep, S., & Sussman, L. (1993). *What to ask when you don't know what to say: 555 powerful questions to use for getting your way at work.* Englewood Cliffs, NJ: Prentice Hall.

Delbecq, A. L., & Van de Ven, A. H. (1971). A group process model for problem identification and program planning. *Journal of Applied Behavioral Science, 7*, 466–492.

Derong, C., & Faure, G. O. (1995). When Chinese companies negotiate with their government. *Organization Studies, 16*, 27–54.

Deutsch, M. (1958). Trust and suspicion. *Journal of Conflict Resolution, 2,* 265–279.

Deutsch, M. (1962). Cooperation and trust: Some theoretical notes. In M. R. Jones (Ed.), *Nebraska symposium on motivation* (pp. 275–318). Lincoln, NE: University of Nebraska Press.

Deutsch, M. (1973). *The resolution of conflict.* New Haven, CT: Yale University Press.

Deutsch, M., & Coleman, P. (2000). *The handbook of conflict resolution.* San Francisco: Jossey-Bass.

Diekmann, K. A., Tenbrunsel, A. E., Shah, P. P., Schroth, H. A., & Bazerman, M. H. (1996). The descriptive and prescriptive use of previous purchase price in negotiations. *Organizational Behavior and Human Decision Processes, 66,* 179–191.

Donohue, W. A. (1991). *Communication, marital dispute and divorce mediation.* Hillsdale, NJ: Lawrence Erlbaum.

Donohue, W. A., & Kolt, R. (1992). *Managing interpersonal conflict.* Newbury Park, CA: Sage.

Donohue, W. A., & Roberto, A. J. (1996). An empirical examination of three models of integrative and distributive bargaining. *The International Journal of Conflict Management, 7,* 209–299.

Douglas, A. (1962). *Industrial peacemaking.* New York: Columbia University Press.

Drake, L. E. (1995). Negotiation styles in intercultural communication. *The International Journal of Conflict Management, 6,* 72–90.

Drolet, A. L., & Morris, M. W. (2000). Rapport in conflict resolution: Accounting for how face-to-face contact fosters mutual cooperation in mixed-motive conflicts. *Journal of Experimental Social Psychology, 36,* 26–50.

Druckman, D. (1996). Is there a U.S. negotiating style? *International Negotiation, 1,* 327–334.

Dudley, B. S., Johnson, D. W., & Johnson, R. T. (1996). Conflict-resolution training and middle school students' integrative negotiation behavior. *Journal of Applied Social Psychology, 26,* 2038–2052.

Dukes, E. F., Piscolish, M. A., & Stephens, J. B. (2000). *Reaching for higher ground in conflict resolution.* San Francisco: Jossey-Bass.

Eagly, A. H., & Chaiken, S. (1975). An attribution analysis of the effect of communicator characteristics on opinion change: The case of communicator attractiveness. *Journal of Personality and Social Psychology, 32,* 136–144.

Eiseman, J. W. (1978). Reconciling incompatible positions. *Journal of Applied Behavioral Science, 14,* 133–150.

Eyuboglu, N., & Buja, A. (1993). Dynamics of channel negotiations: Contention and reciprocity. *Psychology & Marketing, 10,* 47–65.

Faure, G. O. (1999). The cultural dimension of negotiation: The Chinese case. *Group Decision and Negotiation, 8,* 187–215.

Fayerweather, J., & Kapoor, A. (1976). *Strategy and negotiation for the international cooperation.* Cambridge, MA: Ballinger.

Feingold, P. C., & Knapp, M. L. (1977). Anti-drug abuse commercials. *Journal of Communication, 27,* 20–28.

Felstiner, W. L. F., Abel, R. L., & Sarat, A. (1980–81). The emergence and transformation of disputes: Naming, blaming, and claiming. *Law and Society Review, 15,* 631–654.

Fern, E. F., Monroe, K. B., & Avila, R. A. (1986). Effectiveness of multiple request strategies: A synthesis of research results. *Journal of Marketing Research, 23,* 144–152.

Festinger, L. A., & Maccoby, N. (1964). On resistance to persuasive communication. *Journal of Abnormal and Social Psychology, 68,* 359–366.

Filley, A. C. (1975). *Interpersonal conflict resolution.* Glenview, IL: Scott Foresman.

Fisher, R. (1964). Fractionating conflict. In R. Fisher (Ed.), *International conflict and behavioral science: The Craigville papers.* New York: Basic Books.

Fisher, R. (1969). *International conflict for beginners.* New York: Harper & Row.

Fisher, R., & Ertel, D. (1995). *Getting ready to negotiate: The getting to yes workbook.* New York: Penguin.

Fisher, R., Schneider, A. K., Borgwardt, E., & Ganson, B. (1997). *Coping with international conflict.* Upper Saddle River, NJ: Prentice Hall.

Fisher, R., Ury, W., & Patton, B. (1991). *Getting to yes: Negotiating agreement without giving in* (2nd ed.). New York: Penguin.

Folger, J. P., Poole, M. S., & Stutman, R. K. (1993). *Working through conflict: Strategies for relationships, groups and organizations* (2nd ed.). New York: HarperCollins.

Follett, M. P. (1940). *Dynamic administration: The collected papers of Mary Parker Follett.* H. C. Metcalf & L. Urwick (Eds.). New York: Harper & Brothers.

Follett, M. P. (1942). Constructive conflict. In H. C. Metcalf & L. Urwick (Eds.), *Dynamic administration: The collected papers of Mary Parker Follett* (pp. 30–49). New York: Harper & Brothers.

Foreman, P., & Murnighan, J. K. (1996). Learning to avoid the winner's curse. *Organizational Behavior and Human Decision Processes, 67,* 170–180.

Forgas, J. P. (1992). Affect in social judgments and decisions: A multiprocess model. *Advances in Experimental Social Psychology, 25,* 227–275.

Foster, D. A. (1992). *Bargaining across borders: How to negotiate business successfully anywhere in the world.* New York: McGraw-Hill.

Francis, J. N. P. (1991). When in Rome? The effects of cultural adaptation on intercultural business negotiations. *Journal of International Business Studies, 22,* 403–428.

Freedman, J. L., & Fraser, S. C. (1966). Compliance without pressure: The foot in the door technique. *Journal of Personality and Social Psychology, 4,* 195–202.

French, J. R. P., & Raven, B. (1959). The bases of social power. In D. Cartwright (Ed.), *Studies in social power.* Ann Arbor, MI: Institute for Social Research.

Froman, L. A., & Cohen, M. D. (1970). Compromise and logrolling: Comparing the efficiency of two bargaining processes. *Behavioral Sciences, 15,* 180–183.

Fuller, R. G. C., & Sheehy-Skeffington, A. (1974). Effects of group laughter on responses to humorous materials: A replication and extension. *Psychological Reports, 35,* 531–534.

Gahagan, J. P., Long, H., & Horai, J. (1969). Race of experimenter and reactions to black preadolescents. *Proceedings of the 77th Annual Meeting of the American Psychological Association, 4,* 397–398.

Gelfand, M. J., & Christakopoulou, S. (1999). Culture and negotiator cognition: Judgment accuracy and negotiation processes in individualistic and collectivistic cultures. *Organizational Behavior and Human Decision Processes, 79,* 248–269.

Gelfand, M. J., & Dyer, N. (2000). A cultural perspective on negotiation: Progress, pitfalls, and prospects. *Applied Psychology: An International Review, 49,* 62–99.

Gelfand, M. J., & Realo, A. (1999). Individualism-collectivism and accountability in intergroup negotiations. *Journal of Applied Psychology, 84,* 721–736.

George, A. L. (1993). *Bridging the gap: Coercive diplomacy as an alternative to war.* Washington, DC: U.S. Institute of Peace Press.

George, J. M., Jones, G. R., & Gonzalez, J. A. (1998). The role of affect in cross-cultural negotiations. *Journal of International Business Studies, 29,* 749–772.

Gersick, C. J. G. (1988). Time and transition in work teams: Toward a new model of group development. *Academy of Management Journal, 31,* 9–41.

Gersick, C. J. G. (1989). Making time: Predictable transitions in task groups. *Academy of Management Journal, 32,* 274–309.

Geyelin, M. (1997). Mississippi becomes first state to settle suit against big tobacco companies. *Wall Street Journal,* July 7, p. B1.

Ghosh, D. (1996). Nonstrategic delay in bargaining: An experimental investigation. *Organizational Behavior and Human Decision Processes, 67,* 312–325.

Gibb, J. (1961). Defensive communication. *Journal of Communication, 3,* 141–148.

Gibbons, P., Bradac, J. J., & Busch, J. D. (1992). The role of language in negotiations: Threats and promises. In L. Putnam & M. Roloff (Eds.), *Communication and negotiation* (pp. 156–175). Newbury Park, CA: Sage.

Gillespie, J. J., & Bazerman, M. H. (1998, April). Pre-settlement settlement (PreSS): A simple technique for initiating complex negotiations. *Negotiation Journal, 14,* 149–159.

Gillespie, J. J., & Bazerman, M. H. (1997). Parasitic integration: Win-win agreements containing losers. *Negotiation Journal, 13,* 271–282.

Girard, J. (1989). *How to close every sale.* New York: Warner Books.

Gire, J. T. (1997). The varying effect of individualism-collectivism on preference for methods of conflict resolution. *Canadian Journal of Behavioural Science, 29,* 38–43.

Goffman, E. (1969). *Strategic interaction.* Philadelphia, PA: University of Philadelphia Press.

Goffman, E. (1974). *Frame analysis.* New York: Harper & Row.

Gouldner, A. W. (1960). The norm of reciprocity: A preliminary statement. *American Sociological Review, 25,* 161–178.

Graham, J. L. (1983). Brazilian, Japanese, and American business negotiations. *Journal of International Business Studies, 14,* 47–61.

Graham, J. L. (1984). A comparison of Japanese and American business negotiations. *International Journal of Research in Marketing, 1,* 50–68.

Graham, J. L. (1993). The Japanese negotiation style: Characteristics of a distinct approach. *Negotiation Journal, 9,* 123–140.

Graham, J. L., Evenko, L. L., & Rajan, M. N. (1992). An empirical comparison of Soviet and American business negotiations. *Journal of International Business Studies, 23,* 387–418.

Graham, J. L., & Mintu-Wimsatt, A. (1997). Culture's influence on business negotiations in four countries. *Group Decision and Negotiation, 6,* 483–502.

Graham, J. L., & Sano, Y. (1989). *Smart bargaining.* New York: Harper Business.

Gray, B. (1991). *The framing of disputes: Partners, processes and outcomes in different contexts.* Paper presented at the annual conference of the International Association of Conflict Management, Den Dolder, The Netherlands.

Gray, B. (1994). The gender-based foundation of negotiation theory. In B. H. Sheppard, R. J. Lewicki, & R. Bies (Eds.), *Research on negotiation in organizations* (Vol. 4, pp. 3–36). Greenwich, CT: JAI Press.

Gray, B. (1997). Framing and reframing of intractable environmental disputes. In *Research on negotiation in organizations.* R. J. Lewicki, R. Bies, & B. Sheppard (Eds). 6: 163–188.

Gray, B., & Donnellon, A. (1989). *An interactive theory of reframing in negotiation.* Unpublished manuscript.

Green, R. M. (1993). *The ethical manager.* New York: Macmillan.

Greenhalgh, L. (2001). *Managing strategic relationships.* New York: Free Press.

Gruder, C. L., & Duslak, R. J. (1973). Elicitation of cooperation by retaliatory and nonretaliatory strategies in a mixed motive game. *Journal of Conflict Resolution, 17,* 162–174.

Guth, W., Schmittberger, R., & Schwarze, B. (1982). An experimental analysis of ultimatum bargaining. *Journal of Economic Behavior and Organization, 3,* 367–388.

Guth, W., & Tietz, R. (1990). Ultimatum bargaining behavior: A survey and comparison of experimental results. *Journal of Economic Psychology, 11,* 417–449.

Habeeb, W. M. (1988). *Power and tactics in international negotiation.* Baltimore, MD: Johns Hopkins University Press.

Hall, E. T. (1960, May–June). The silent language of overseas business. *Harvard Business Review, 38,* 87–96.

Hall, J. (1969). *Conflict management survey: A survey of one's characteristic reaction to and handling conflict between himself and others.* Conroe, TX: Teleometrics International.

Harinck, F., de Dreu, C. K. W., & Van Vienen, A. E. M. (2000). The impact of conflict issues on fixed-pie perceptions, problem solving, and integrative outcomes in negotiation. *Organizational Behavior and Human Decision Processes, 81,* 329–358.

Hartzell, C. A. (1999). Explaining the stability of negotiated settlements to intrastate wars. *Journal of Conflict Resolution, 43,* 3–22.

Harvey, O. J. (1953). An experimental approach to the study status relations in informal groups. *Sociometry, 18,* 357–367.

Hegarty, W., & Sims, H. P. (1978). Some determinants of unethical decision behavior: An experiment. *Journal of Applied Psychology, 63,* 451–457.

Hegtved, K. A., & Killian, C. (1999). Fairness and emotions: Reactions to the process and outcomes of negotiations. *Social Forces, 78,* 269–303.

Heider, F. (1958). *The psychology of interpersonal relations.* New York: John Wiley and Sons.

Heller, J. R. (1967). The effects of racial prejudice, feedback, strategy, and race on cooperative– competitive behavior. *Dissertation Abstracts International, 27,* 2507–2508b.

Hendon, D. W., & Hendon, R. A. (1990). *World-class negotiating: Dealmaking in the global marketplace.* New York: John Wiley and Sons.

Higgins, E. T. (1987). Self discrepancy theory: A theory relating self and affect. *Psychological Review, 94,* 319–340.

Hilty, J. A., & Carnevale, P. J. (1993). Black-hat/white-hat strategy in bilateral negotiation. *Organizational Behavior and Human Decision Processes, 55,* 444–469.

Hinton, B. L., Hamner, W. C., & Pohlan, N. F. (1974). Influence and award of magnitude, opening bid and concession rate on profit earned in a managerial negotiating game. *Behavioral Science, 19,* 197–203.

Hitt, W. (1990). *Ethics and leadership: Putting theory into practice.* Columbus, OH: Battelle Press.

Hochberg, A. M., & Kressel, K. (1996). Determinations of successul and unsuccessful divorce negotiations. *Journal of Divorce & Remarriage, 25,* 1–21.

Hocker, J. L., & Wilmot, W. W. (1985). *Interpersonal conflict* (2nd ed.). Dubuque, IA: Wm. C. Brown.

Hofstede, G. (1980a). Motivation, leadership, and organization: Do American theories apply abroad? *Organizational Dynamics, 9,* 42–63.

Hofstede, G. (1980b). *Culture's consequences: International differences in work related values.* Beverly Hills, CA: Sage.

Hofstede, G. (1989). Cultural predictors of national negotiation styles. In. F. Mautner-Markhof (Ed.), *Processes of international negotiations* (pp. 193–201). Boulder, CO: Westview Press.

Hofstede, G. (1991). *Culture and organizations: Software of the mind.* London: McGraw-Hill.

Hofstede, G., & Bond, M. H. (1988). Confucius and economic growth: New trends in culture's consequences. *Organizational Dynamics, 16,* 4–21.

Hovland, C. I., & Mandell, W. (1952). An experimental comparison of conclusion drawing by the communicator and by the audience. *Journal of Abnormal and Social Psychology, 47,* 581–588.

Husted, B. W. (1996). Mexican small business negotiations with U. S. companies: Challenges and opportunities. *International Small Business Journal, 14,* 45–54.

Ikle, F. C. (1964). *How nations negotiate.* New York: Harper & Row.

Isajiw, W. W. (2000). Approaches to ethnic conflict resolution: paradigms and principles. *International Journal of Intercultural Relations, 24,* 105–124.

Isen, A. M., & Baron, R. A. (1991). Positive affect as a factor in organizational behavior. In B. M. Staw & L. L. Cummings (Eds.), *Research in organizational behavior* (Vol. 13, pp. 1–53). Greenwich, CT: JAI Press.

Ivey, A. E., & Simek-Downing, L. (1980). *Counseling and psychotherapy.* Englewood Cliffs, NJ: Prentice Hall.

Jackson, S., & Allen, M. (1987). *Meta-analysis of the effectiveness of one-sided and two-sided argumentation.* Paper presented at the annual meeting of the International Communication Association, Montreal, Quebec.

Jacobs, A. T. (1951). *Some significant factors influencing the range of indeterminateness in collective bargaining negotiations.* Unpublished doctoral dissertation, University of Michigan, Ann Arbor, MI.

Janosik, R. J. (1987). Rethinking the culture-negotiation link. *Negotiation Journal, 3,* 385–395.

Johnson, B. T., & Eagly, A. H. (1989). Effects of involvement on persuasion: A meta-analysis. *Psychological Bulletin, 106,* 290–314.

Johnson, B. T., & Eagly, A. H. (1990). Involvement and persuasion: Types, traditions, and the evidence. *Psychological Bulletin, 107,* 375–384.

Johnson, D. W. (1971). Role reversal: A summary and review of the research. *International Journal of Group Tensions, 1,* 318–334.

Johnson, D. W., & Dustin, R. (1970). The initiation of cooperation through role reversal. *Journal of Social Psychology, 82,* 193–203.

Johnston, R. W. (1982, March–April). Negotiation strategies: Different strokes for different folks. *Personnel, 59,* 36–45.

Jones, E. E. (1964). *Ingratiation.* New York: Appleton-Century-Crofts.

Jones, E. E., & Nisbett, R. E. (1976). The actor and the observer: Divergent perceptions of causality. In J. W. Thibaut, J. T. Spence, & R. C. Carson (Eds.), *Contemporary topics in social psychology* (pp. 37–52). Morristown, NJ: General Learning Press.

Jones, S. B., & Burgoon, M. (1975). Empirical investigations of language intensity: 2. The effects of irrelevant fear and language intensity on attitude change. *Human Communication Research, 1,* 248–251.

Kahneman, D., Knetsch, J. L., & Thaler, R. H. (1990). Experimental tests of the endowment effect and the Coase Theorem. *Journal of Political Economy, 98,* 1325–1348.

Kahneman, D., & Tversky, A. (1979). Prospect theory: An analysis of decisions under risk. *Econometrica, 47,* 263–291.

Kale, S. H., & Barnes, J. W. (1992). Understanding the domain of cross-national buyer-seller interactions. *Journal of International Business Studies, 23,* 101–132.

Kaplan, Robert. (1984, Spring). Trade routes: The manager's network of relationships. *Organizational Dynamics, 12,* 37–52.

Karrass, C. (1974). *Give and take.* New York: Thomas Y. Crowell.

Karrass, G. (1985). *Negotiate to close: How to make more successful deals.* New York: Simon & Schuster.

Kellerman, J. L., Lewis, J., & Laird, J. D. (1989). Looking and loving: The effects of mutual gaze on feelings of romantic love. *Journal of Research in Personality, 23,* 145–161.

Kelley, H. H. (1966). A classroom study of the dilemmas in interpersonal negotiation. In K. Archibald (Ed.), *Strategic interaction and conflict: Original papers and discussion* (pp. 49–73). Berkeley, CA: Institute of International Studies.

Kelley, H. H., & Thibaut, J. (1969). Group problem solving. In G. Lindzey & E. Aronson (Eds.), *Handbook of social psychology* (2nd ed.), (Vol. 4, pp. 1–101). Reading, MA: Addison-Wesley.

Keltner, D., & Robinson, R. J. (1993). Imagined ideological differences in conflict escalation and resolution. *The International Journal of Conflict Management, 4,* 249–262.

Kemp, K. E., & Smith, W. P. (1994). Information exchange, toughness, and integrative bargaining: The roles of explicit cues and perspective-taking. *International Journal of Conflict Management, 5,* 5–21.

Kennedy, G. (1985). *Doing business abroad.* New York: Simon & Schuster.

Kim, M. S., & Kitani, K. (1998). Conflict management styles of Asian- and Caucasion-Americans in romantic relationships in Hawaii. *Journal of Asian Pacific Communication, 8,* 51–68.

Kimmel, M. J., Pruitt, D. G., Magenau, J. M., Konar-Goldband, E., & Carnevale, P. J. D. (1980). Effects of trust aspiration and gender on negotiation tactics. *Journal of Personality and Social Psychology, 38,* 9–23.

Kipnis, D. (1976). *The powerholders.* Chicago: University of Chicago Press.

Kleinke, C. L. (1986). Gaze and eye contact: A research review. *Psychological Bulletin, 100,* 78–100.

Kleinke, C. L., & Pohlan, P. D. (1971). Effective and emotional responses as a function of other person's gaze and cooperativeness in two person games. *Journal of Personality and Social Psychology, 17,* 308–313.

Koehn, D. (1997). Business and game playing: The false analogy. *Journal of Business Ethics, 16,* 1447–1452.

Koh, T. T. B. (1996). American strengths and weaknesses. *Negotiation Journal, 12,* 313–317.

Kolb, D. (1983). *The mediators.* Cambridge, MA: MIT Press.

Kolb, D. (1985). *The mediators.* Cambridge, MA: MIT Press.

Kolb, D. (1995). The love for three oranges, or: What did we miss about Ms. Follett in the Library? *Negotiation Journal, 11,* 339–348.

Kolb, D. M., & Putnam, L. L. (1997). Through the looking glass: Negotiation theory refracted through the lens of gender. In S. Gleason (Ed.), *Frontiers in dispute resolution in labor relations and human resources* (pp. 231–257). East Lansing, MI: Michigan State University Press.

Komorita, S. S., & Brenner, A. R. (1968). Bargaining and concessions under bilateral monopoly. *Journal of Personality and Social Psychology, 9,* 15–20.

Komorita, S. S., & Mechling, J. (1967). Betrayal and reconciliation in a two person game. *Journal of Personality and Social Psychology, 6,* 349–353.

Kozan, M. K. (1997). Culture and conflict management: A theoretical framework. *International Journal of Conflict Management, 8*(4), 338–360.

Krackhart, D., & Hanson, J. R. (1993, July–August). Informal networks: The company behind the chart. *Harvard Business Review, 71,* 104–111.

Kramer, R. M., Pommerenke, P., & Newton, B. (1993). The social context of negotiation: Effects of trust, aspiration and gender on negotiation tactics. *Journal of Personality and Social Psychology, 38*(1), 9–22.

Kramer, R. M., Shah, P. P., & Woerner, S. L. (1995). Why ultimatums fail: Social identity and moralistic aggression in coercive bargaining. In R. M. Kramer & D. M. Messick (Eds.), *Negotiation as social process* (pp. 285–308). Thousand Oaks, CA: Sage.

Kremenyuk, V. A. (Ed.). (1991). *International negotiation: Analysis, approaches, issues.* San Francisco: Jossey-Bass.

Kristensen, H., & Garling, T. (1997). The effects of anchor points and reference points on negotiation process and outcome. *Organizational Behavior and Human Decision Processes, 71,* 85–94.

Kumar, R. (1997). The role of affect in negotiations: An integrative overview. *Journal of Applied Behavioral Science, 3*(1), 84–100.

Landon, E. L., Jr. (1997). For the most fitting deal, tailor negotiating strategy to each borrower. *Commercial Lending Review, 12,* 5–14.

Large, M. D. (1999). The effectiveness of gifts as unilateral initiatives in bargaining. *Sociological Perspectives, 42,* 525–542.

Lax, D., & Sebenius, J. (1986). *The manager as negotiator: Bargaining for cooperation and competitive gain.* New York: Free Press.

Le Poole, S. (1989). Negotiating with Clint Eastwood in Brussels. *Management Review, 78,* 58–60.

Leung, T., & Yeung, L. L. (1995). Negotiation in the People's Republic of China: Results of a survey of small businesses in Hong Kong. *Journal of Small Business Management, 33,* 70–77.

Levinson, J. C., Smith, M. S. A., & Wilson, O. R. (1999). *Guerilla negotiating.* New York: John Wiley.

Lewicki, R. J. (1983). Lying and deception: A behavioral model. In M. H. Bazerman & R. J. Lewicki (Eds.), *Negotiating in organizations* (pp. 68–90). Beverly Hills, CA: Sage.

Lewicki, R. J. (1992). Negotiating strategically. In A. Cohen (Ed.), *The portable MBA in management* (pp. 147–189). New York: John Wiley and Sons.

Lewicki, R. J., Gray, B., & Elliott, M. (2003). *Making sense of intractable environmental disputes.* Washington, DC: Island Press.

Lewicki, R. J., & Hiam, A. (1999). *The fast forward MBA in negotiation and dealmaking.* New York: John Wiley and Sons.

Lewicki, R. J., Hiam, A., & Olander, K. (1996). *Think before you speak: The complete guide to strategic negotiation.* New York: John Wiley and Sons.

Lewicki, R. J., McAllister, D., & Bies, R. H. (1998). Trust and distrust: New relationships and realities. *Academy of Management Review, 23*(3), 438–458.

Lewicki, R. J., & Robinson, R. (1998). A factor-analytic study of negotiator ethics. *Journal of Business Ethics, 18,* 211–228.

Lewicki, R. J., & Spencer, G. (1990, June). *Lies and dirty tricks.* Paper presented at the meeting of the International Association for Conflict Management, Vancouver, B. C., Canada.

Lewicki, R. J., & Spencer, G. (1991, August). *Ethical relativism and negotiating tactics: Factors affecting their perceived ethicality.* Paper presented at the meeting of the Academy of Management, Miami, FL.

Lewicki, R. J., & Stevenson, M. (1998). Trust development in negotiation: Proposed actions and a research agenda. *Journal of Business and Professional Ethics, 16*(1–3), 99–132.

Lewicki, R. J., Weiss, S., & Lewin, D. (1992). Models of conflict, negotiation and third-party intervention: A review and synthesis. *Journal of Organizational Behavior, 13,* 209–252.

Liebert, R. M., Smith, W. P., & Hill, J. H. (1968). The effects of information and magnitude of initial offer on interpersonal negotiation. *Journal of Experimental Social Psychology, 4,* 431–441.

Lim, R. G. (1997). Overconfidence in negotiation revisited. *The International Journal of Conflict Management, 8,* 52–70.

Lim, R. G., & Murnighan, J. K. (1994). Phases, deadlines, and the bargaining process. *Organizational Behavior and Human Decision Processes, 58,* 153–171.

Lituchy, T. R. (1997). Negotiations between Japanese and Americans: The effects of collectivism on integrative outcomes. *Canadian Journal of Administrative Sciences, 14,* 386–395.

Lukov, V. (1985). International negotiations of the 1980s: Features, problems and prospects. *Negotiation Journal, 1,* 139–148.

Mannix, E. A., Tinsley, C. H., & Bazerman, M. (1995). Negotiating over time: Impediments to integrative solutions. *Organizational Behavior and Human Decision Processes, 62,* 241–251.

Mautner-Markhof, F. (Ed.). (1989). *Processes of international negotiations.* Boulder, CO: Westview Press.

Mayer, B. (2000). *The dynamics of conflict resolution.* San Francisco: Jossey-Bass.

Mayer, J. D., Salovey, P., & Caruso, D. (2000). Emotional intelligence. In R. Sternberg (Ed.), *Handbook of intelligence* (pp. 396–420). Cambridge: Cambridge University Press.

Mayer, F. W. (1992). Managing domestic differences in international negotiations: The strategic use of internal side-payments. *International Organization, 46,* 793–818.

Mayfield, M., Mayfield, J., Martin, D., & Herbig, P. (1997). Time perspectives of the cross-cultural negotiations process. *American Business Review, 15,* 78–85.

McCornack, S. A., & Levine, T. R. (1990). When lies are uncovered: Emotional and relational outcomes of discovered deception. *Communication Monographs, 57,* 119–138.

McCroskey, J. C., Jensen, T., & Valencia, C. (1973, November). *Measurement of the credibility of mass media sources.* Paper presented at the Western Speech Communication Association, Albuquerque, NM.

McDonald, J. W. (1996). An American's view of a U. S. negotiating style. *International Negotiation, 1,* 323–326.

McGuire, W. J. (1964). Inducing resistance to persuasion: Some contemporary approaches. In L. Berkowitz (Ed.), *Advances in experimental social psychology* (Vol. 1, pp. 191–229). New York: Academic Press.

McGuire, W. J. (1973). Persuasion, resistance and attitude change. In I. S. Poole, F. W. Frey, W. Schramm, N. Maccoby, & E. B. Parker (Eds.), *Handbook of communication* (pp. 216–252). Skokie, IL: Rand McNally.

Michelini, R. L. (1971). Effects of prior interaction, contact, strategy, and expectation of meeting on gain behavior and sentiment. *Journal of Conflict Resolution, 15,* 97–103.

Michener, S. K., & Suchner, R. W. (1971). The tactical use of social power. In J. T. Tedeschi (Ed.), *The social influence process* (pp. 235–286). Chicago: AVC.

Milgram, S. (1974). *Obedience to authority: An experimental view.* New York: Harper & Row.

Miller, D. T., & Ross, M. (1975). Self-serving bias in the attribution of causality: Fact or fiction? *Psychological Bulletin, 82,* 213–225.

Miller, D. T., & Vidmar, N. (1981). The social psychology of punishment reactions. In M. J. Lerner (Ed.), *The justice motive in social behavior* (pp. 145–172). New York: Plenum Press.

Miller, S. K., & Burgoon, M. (1979). The relationship between violations of expectations and the induction of the resistance to persuasion. *Human Communication Research, 5,* 301–313.

Mintu-Wimsatt, A., & Gassenheimer, J. B. (2000). The moderating effects of cultural context in buyer-seller negotiation. *The Journal of Personal Selling and Sales Management, 1,* 1–9.

Mintzberg, H., & Quinn, J. B. (1991). *The strategy process: Concepts, contexts, cases* (2nd ed.). Englewood Cliffs, NJ: Prentice Hall.

Missner, M. (1980). *Ethics of the business system.* Sherman Oaks, CA: Alfred Publishing Company.

Miyahara, A., Kim, M. S., Shin, H. C., & Yoon, K. (1998). Conflict resolution styles among "collectivist" cultures: A comparison between Japanese and Koreans. *International Journal of Intercultural Relations, 22,* 505–525.

Morley, I., & Stephenson, G. (1977). *The social psychology of bargaining.* London: Allen and Unwin.

Nash, J. F. (1950). The bargaining problem. *Econometrica, 18,* 155–162.

Nash, L. L. (1990). *Good intentions aside: A manager's guide to resolving ethical problems.* Boston: Harvard Business School Press.

Natlandsmyr, J. H., & Rognes, J. (1995). Culture, behavior, and negotiation outcomes: A comparative and cross-cultural study of Mexican and Norwegian negotiators. *The International Journal of Conflict Management, 6,* 5–29.

Neale, M., & Bazerman, M. H. (1983). The role of perspective-taking ability in negotiating under different forms of arbitration. *Industrial and Labor Relations Review, 36,* 378–388.

Neale, M., & Bazerman, M. H. (1985). The effects of framing and negotiator overconfidence on bargaining behaviors and outcomes. *Academy of Management Journal, 28,* 34–49.

Neale, M., & Bazerman, M. H. (1991). *Cognition and rationality in negotiation.* New York: Free Press.

Neale, M., & Bazerman, M. H. (1992a). Negotiating rationally: The power and impact of the negotiator's frame. *Academy of Management Executive, 6*(3), 42–51.

Neale, M., Huber, V., & Northcraft, G. (1987). The framing of negotiations: Contextual vs. task frames. *Organizational Behavior and Human Decision Processes, 39,* 228–241.

Neale, M. A., & Bazerman, M. H. (1992b). Negotiator cognition and rationality: A behavioral decision theory perspective. *Organizational Behavior and Human Decision Processes, 51,* 157–175.

Neale, M. A., & Northcraft, G. B. (1986). Experts, amateurs, and refrigerators: Comparing expert and amateur negotiators in a novel task. *Organizational Behavior and Human Decision Processes, 38,* 305–317.

Neale, M. A., & Northcraft, G. B. (1991). Behavioral negotiation theory: A framework for conceptualizing dyadic bargaining. In L. Cummings & B. Staw (Eds.), *Research in organizational behavior* (Vol. 13, pp. 147–190). Greenwich, CT: JAI Press.

Neslin, S. A., & Greenhalgh, L. (1983). Nash's theory of cooperative games as a predictor of the outcomes of buyer-seller negotiations: An experiment in media purchasing. *Journal of Marketing Research, 20,* 368–379.

Nierenberg, G. (1976). *The complete negotiator.* New York: Nierenberg & Zeif Publishers.

Northcraft, G. B., & Neale, M. A. (1987). Experts, amateurs, and real estate: An anchoring and adjustment perspective on property pricing decisions. *Organizational Behavior and Human Decision Processes, 39,* 228–241.

Northrup, H. R. (1964). *Boulwarism.* Ann Arbor, MI: Bureau of Industrial Relations, University of Michigan.

O'Connor, K. M., & Arnold, J. A. (2001). Distributive spirals: Negotiation impasses and the moderating role of disputant self-efficacy. *Organizational Behavior and Human Decision Processes, 84,* 148–176.

Ogawa, N. (1999). The concept of facework: Its function in the Hawaii model of mediation. *Mediation Quarterly, 17,* 5–20.

Ohanyan, A. (1999). Negotiation culture in a post-Soviet context: An interdisciplinary perspective. *Mediation Quarterly, 17,* 83–104.

Ohbuchi, K., & Takahashi, Y. (1994). Cultural styles of conflict management in Japanese and Americans: Passivity, covertness, and effectiveness of strategies. *Journal of Applied Social Psychology, 24,* 1345–1366.

O'Keefe, D. J. (1990). *Persuasion: Theory and research.* Newbury Park, CA: Sage.

Olekalns, M., Smith, P. L., & Walsh, T. (1996). The process of negotiating: Strategy and timing as predictors of outcomes. *Organizational Behavior and Human Decision Processes, 68,* 68–77.

Oliver, R. L., Balakrishnan, P. V., & Barry, B. (1994). Outcome satisfaction in negotiation: A test of expectancy disconfirmation. *Organizational Behavior and Human Decision Processes, 60,* 252–275.

Osgood, C. E. (1962). *An alternative to war or surrender.* Urbana, IL: University of Illinois Press.

Oskamp, S. (1970). Effects of programmed initial strategies in a prisoner's dilemma game. *Psychometrics, 19,* 195–196.

Ostermeier, T. H. (1967). Effects of type and frequency of reference upon perceived source credibility and attitude change. *Speech Monographs, 34,* 137–144.

Parrott, W. (1994). Beyond hedonism: Motives for inhibiting good moods and for maintaining bad moods. In D. M. Wegner & J. W. Pennebaker (Eds.), *Handbook of mental control* (pp. 278–305). Englewood Cliffs, NJ: Prentice Hall.

Parrott, W. G. (2001). Emotions in social psychology: Volume overview. In W. G. Parrott (Ed.), *Emotions in social psychology* (pp. 1–19). Philadelphia: Psychology Press.

Patterson, J., & Kim, P. (1991). *The day America told the truth.* New York: Prentice Hall.

Pearson, V. S., & Stephan, W. G. (1998). Preferences for styles of negotiation: A comparison of Brazil and the U. S. *International Journal of Intercultural Relations, 22,* 67–83.

Petty, R. E. & Brock, T. C. (1981). Thought disruption and persuasion: Assessing the validity of attitude change experiments. In R. E. Petty, T. M. Ostrom, & T. C. Brook (Eds.), *Cognitive responses in persuasion* (pp. 55–79). Hillsdale, NJ: Lawrence Erlbaum.

Petty, R. E., & Cacioppo, J. T. (1986a). *Communication and persuasion: Central and peripheral routes to attitude change.* New York: Springer Verlag.

Petty, R. E., & Cacioppo, J. T. (1986b). The elaboration likelihood model of persuasion. In L. Berkowitz (Ed.), *Advances in experimental social psychology* (Vol. 19, pp. 123–205). New York: Academic Press.

Petty, R. E., & Cacioppo, J. T. (1990). Involvement and persuasion: Tradition versus integration. *Psychological Bulletin, 107,* 367–374.

Pfeffer, J. (1992). *Managing with power.* Boston: Harvard Business School Press.

Pfeffer, J., & Salancik, G. R. (1974). Organizational decision making as a political process: The case of a university budget. *Administrative Science Quarterly, 19,* 135–151.

Pfouts, R. W. (1994). Buying a pig when both buyer and seller are in a poke. *AEJ, 22,* 80–85.

Phatak, A. V., & Habib, M. H. (1996). The dynamics of international business negotiations. *Business Horizons, 39,* 30–38.

Pilisuk, N., & Skolnick, P. (1978). Inducing trust: A test of the Osgood proposal. *Journal of Personality and Social Psychology, 8,* 121–133.

Pinkley, R. L. (1992). Dimensions of conflict frame: Relation to disputant perceptions and expectations. *The International Journal of Conflict Management, 3,* 95–113.

Pinkley, R. L. (1995). Impact of knowledge regarding alternatives to settlement in dyadic negotiations: Whose knowledge counts? *Journal of Applied Psychology, 80,* 403–417.

Pinkley, R. L., Griffith, T. L., & Northcraft, G. B. (1995). "Fixed pie" a la mode: Information availability, information processing, and the negotiation of suboptimal agreements. *Organizational Behavior and Human Decision Processes, 62,* 101–112.

Pinkley, R. L., Neale, M. A., & Bennett, R. J. (1994). The impact of alternatives to settlement in dyadic negotiation. *Organizational Behavior and Human Decision Processes, 57,* 97–116.

Pinkley, R., & Northcraft, G. B. (1994). Cognitive interpretations of conflict: Implications for dispute processes and outcomes. *Academy of Management Journal, 37,* 193–205.

Provis, C. (1996). Interests vs. positions: A critique of the distinction. *Negotiation Journal, 12,* 305–323.

Pruitt, D. G. (1981). *Negotiation behavior.* New York: Academic Press.

Pruitt, D. G. (1983). Strategic choice in negotiation. *American Behavioral Scientist, 27,* 167–194.

Pruitt, D. G., & Carnevale, P. J. D. (1993). *Negotiation in social conflict.* Pacific Grove, CA: Brooks-Cole.

Pruitt, D. G., & Lewis, S. A. (1975). Development of integrative solutions in bilateral negotiation. *Journal of Personality and Social Psychology, 31,* 621–633.

Pruitt, D. G., & Rubin, J. Z. (1986). *Social conflict: Escalation, stalemate and settlement.* New York: Random House.

Pruitt, D. G., & Syna, H. (1985). Mismatching the opponent's offers in negotiation. *Journal of Experimental Social Psychology, 21,* 103–113.

Putnam, L. L. (1994). Productive conflict: Negotiation as implicit coordination. *The International Journal of Conflict Management, 5,* 284–298.

Putnam, L. L., & Geist, P. (1985). Argument in bargaining: An analysis of the reasoning process. *Southern Speech Communication Journal, 50,* 225–245.

Putnam, L. L., & Holmer, M. (1992). Framing, reframing, and issue development. In L. Putnam & M. Roloff (Eds.), *Communication and negotiation* (pp. 128–155). Newbury Park, CA: Sage.

Putnam, L. L., & Jones, T. S. (1982). Reciprocity in negotiations: An analysis of bargaining interaction. *Communication Monographs, 49,* 171–191.

Putnam, L. L., & Wilson, S. R. (1989). Argumentation and bargaining strategies as discriminators of integrative outcomes. In M. A. Rahim (Ed.), *Managing conflict: An interdisciplinary approach* (pp. 121–131). New York: Praeger.

Putnam, L., Wilson, S., & Turner, D. (1990). The evolution of policy arguments in teachers' negotiations. *Argumentation, 4,* 129–152.

Pye, L. W. (1992). *Chinese negotiating style.* New York: Quorum Books.

Quinn, J. B. (1991). Strategies for change. In H. Mintzberg & J. B. Quinn (Eds.), *The strategy process: Concepts, contexts, cases* (2nd ed., pp. 4–12). Englewood Cliffs, NJ: Prentice Hall.

Rahim, M. A. (1983). A measure of styles of handling interpersonal conflict. *Academy of Management Journal, 26,* 368–376.

Raiffa, H. (1982). *The art and science of negotiation.* Cambridge, MA: Belknap Press of Harvard University Press.

Rapoport, A. (1964). *Strategy and conscience.* New York: Harper & Row.

Rapoport, A., Erev, I., & Zwick, R. (1995). An experimental study of buyer-seller negotiation with one-sided incomplete information and time discounting. *Management Science, 41,* 377–394.

Raven, B. H., & Rubin, J. Z. (1973). *Social psychology: People in groups.* New York: John Wiley and Sons.

Reardon, K. K. (1981). *Persuasion theory and context.* Beverly Hills, CA: Sage.

Richardson, R. C. (1977). *Collective bargaining by objectives.* Englewood Cliffs, NJ: Prentice Hall.

Ritov, I. (1996). Anchoring in simulated competitive market negotiation. *Organizational Behavior and Human Decision Processes, 67,* 16–25.

Robinson, R. J. (1995). Defusing the exploding offer: The fairpoint gambit. *Negotiation Journal, 11,* 389–404.

Robinson, R., Lewicki, R. J., & Donahue, E. (2000). Extending and testing a five factor model of ethical and unethical bargaining tactics: The SINS scale. *Journal of Organizational Behavior, 21,* 649–664.

Rogers, C. R. (1957). *Active listening.* Chicago: University of Chicago Press.

Rogers, C. R. (1961). *On becoming a person: A therapist's view of psychotherapy.* Boston: Houghton Mifflin.

Rosnow, R. L., & Robinson, E. J. (1967). *Experiments in persuasion.* New York: Academic Press.

Ross, L., Green, D., & House, P. (1977). The false consensus phenomenon: An attributional bias in self-perception and social-perception processes. *Journal of Experimental Social Psychology, 13,* 279–301.

Ross, M. H. (2000). "Good-enough" isn't so bad: Thinking about success and failure in ethnic conflict management. *Peace and Conflict: Journal of Peace Psychology, 6,* 21–27.

Ross, W., & LaCroix, J. (1996). Multiple meanings of trust in negotiation theory and research: A literature review and integrative model. *International Journal of Conflict Management, 7,* 314–360.

Roth, A. E., Murnighan, J. K., & Schoumaker, F. (1988). The deadline effect in bargaining: Some empirical evidence. *American Economic Review, 78,* 806–823.

Roth, J., & Sheppard, B. H. (1995). Opening the black box of framing research: The relationship between frames, communication, and outcomes. *Academy of Management Proceedings.*

Rubin, J. Z., & Brown, B. R. (1975). *The social psychology of bargaining and negotiation.* New York: Academic Press.

Russo, J. E., & Schoemaker, P. J. H. (1989). *Decision traps: The ten barriers to brilliant decision making and how to overcome them.* New York: Simon & Schuster.

Salacuse, J. (1998). So, what's the deal anyway? Contracts and relationships as negotiating goals. *Negotiation Journal, 14*(1), pp. 5–12.

Salancik, G. R., & Pfeffer, J. (1977). Who gets power and how they hold on to it: A strategic-contingency model of power. *Organizational Dynamics, 5,* 3–21.

Savage, G. T., Blair, J. D., & Sorenson, R. L. (1989). Consider both relationships and substance when negotiating strategically. *Academy of Management Executive, 3*(1), 37–48.

Schatzski, M. (1981). *Negotiation: The art of getting what you want.* New York: Signet Books.

Schlenker, B. R., & Riess, M. (1979). Self-presentation of attitudes following commitment to proattitudinal behavior. *Journal of Human Communication Research, 5,* 325–334.

Schön, D. A., & M. Rein (1994). *Frame reflection: Toward the resolution of intractable policy controversies.* New York: Basic Books.

Schoppa, L. J. (1993). Two-level games and bargaining outcomes: Why gaiatsu succeeds in Japan in some cases but not in others. *International Organization, 47,* 353–386.

Schurr, P. H. (1987). Effects of gain and loss decision frames on risky purchase negotiations. *Journal of Applied Psychology, 72,* 351–358.

Schweitzer, M. E. (1997). *Omission, friendship and fraud: Lies about material facts in negotiation.* Unpublished manuscript.

Schweitzer, M., Brodt, S., & Croson, R. (working paper). *Visual access and context-dependent lies: The use of deception in videoconference and telephone mediated negotiations.* Wharton School OPIM Working Paper #99–07–02.

Schweitzer, M. E., & Croson, R. (2001). Curtailing deception: The impact of direct questions on lies and omissions. *International Journal of Conflict Management, 10*(3), 225–248.

Sebenius, J. K. (1992). Negotiation analysis: A characterization and review. *Management Science, 38,* 18–38.

Sebenius, J. K. (2002). The hidden challenge of cross-border negotiations. *Harvard Business Review, 80,* 76–85.

Selekman, B. M., Fuller, S. H., Kennedy, T., & Baitsel, J. M. (1964). *Problems in labor relations.* New York: McGraw-Hill.

Selekman, B. M., Selekman, S. K., & Fuller, S. H. (1958). *Problems in labor relations.* New York: McGraw-Hill.

Seligman, C., Bush, M., & Kirsch, K. (1976). Relationship between compliance in the foot in the door paradigm and size of first request. *Journal of Personality and Social Psychology, 33,* 517–520.

Sen, A. K. (1970). *Collective choice and individual values.* San Francisco: Holden-Day.

Sermat V. (1967). The effects of an initial cooperative or competitive treatment on a subject's response to conditional operation. *Behavioral Science, 12,* 301–313.

Sermat, V., & Gregovich, R. P. (1966). The effect of experimental manipulation on cooperative behavior in a checkers game. *Psychometric Science, 4,* 435–436.

Shapiro, D. L. (1991). The effects of explanations on negative reactions to deceit. *Administrative Science Quarterly, 36,* 614–630.

Shapiro, D. L., & Bies, R. J. (1994). Threats, bluffs and disclaimers in negotiation. *Organizational Behavior and Human Decision Processes, 60,* 14–35.

Shapiro, D. L., Sheppard, B. H., & Cheraskin, L. (1992). Business on a handshake. *Negotiation Journal, 8,* 365–377.

Shea, G. F. (1983). *Creative negotiating.* Boston: CBI Publishing Co.

Sheppard, B. H., Lewicki, R. J., & Minton, J. W. (1992). *Organizational justice: The search for fairness in the workplace.* New York: Lexington Books.

Sherif, M., Harvey, L., White, B., Hood, W., & Sherif, C. (1988). *The Robbers' Cave experiment: Intergroup conflict and cooperation.* Middletown, CT: Wesleyan University Press. (Original work published 1961.)

Short, J., Williams, E., & Christie, B. (1976). *The social psychology of telecommunications.* London: John Wiley.

Simons, T. (1993). Speech patterns and the concept of utility in cognitive maps: The case of integrative bargaining. *Academy of Management Journal, 36,* 139–156.

Sitkin, S. B., & Bies, R. J. (1993). Social accounts in conflict situations: Using explanations to manage conflict. *Human Relations, 46,* 349–370.

Smith, P. B., Dugan, S., Peterson, M. F., & Leung, K. (1998). Individualism/collectivism and the handling of disagreement: A 23 country study. *International Journal of Intercultural Relations, 22,* 351–367.

Solomon, L. (1960). The influence of some types of power relationships and game strategies upon the development of interpersonal trust. *Journal of Abnormal and Social Psychology, 61,* 223–230.

Solomon, M. (1990). *Working with difficult people.* Englewood Cliffs, NJ: Prentice Hall.

Solomon, R. H. (1987). China: Friendship and obligation in Chinese negotiating style. In H. Binnendijk (Ed.), *National negotiating styles* (pp. 1–16). Washington, DC: Foreign Service Institute.

Spector, B. I. (1995). Creativity heuristics for impasse resolution: Reframing intractable negotiations. *Annals of the American Academy of Political and Social Science, 542,* 81–99.

Stacks, D. W., & Burgoon, J. K. (1981). The role of non-verbal behaviors as distractors in resistance to persuasion in interpersonal contexts. *Central States Speech Journal, 32,* 61–80.

Staw, B. M. (1981). The escalation of commitment to a course of action. *Academy of Management Review, 6,* 577–587.

Stein, J. (1996). The art of real estate negotiations. *Real Estate Review, 25,* 48–53.

Stein, J. G. (1999). Problem solving as metaphor: Negotiation and identity conflict. *Peace and Conflict: Journal of Peace Psychology, 5,* 225–235.

Sternberg, R. (Ed.). (1988). *The nature of creativity.* New York: Cambridge University Press.

Stillenger, C., Epelbaum, M., Keltner, D., & Ross, L. (1990). *The "reactive devaluation" barrier to conflict resolution.* Working paper, Stanford University, Palo Alto, CA.

Stuhlmacher, A. F., Gillespie, T. L., & Champagne, M. V. (1998). The impact of time pressure in negotiation: A meta-analysis. *The International Journal of Conflict Management, 9*(2), 97–116.

Susskind, L., McKearnan, S., & Thomas-Larmer, J. (1999). *The consensus building handbook.* Thousand Oaks, CA: Sage Publications.

Swenson, R. A., Nash, D. L., & Roos, D. C. (1984). Source credibility and perceived expertness of testimony in a simulated child-custody case. *Professional Psychology, 15,* 891–898.

Swinth, R. L. (1967). Review of *A behavioral theory of labor negotiations. Contemporary Psychology, 12,* 183–184.

Tannenbaum, D., & Norris, E. (1966). Effects of combining congruity principle strategies for the reduction of persuasion. *Journal of Personality and Social Psychology, 3,* 233–238.

Tedeschi, J. T., Schlenker, B. R., & Bonoma, T. V. (1973). *Conflict, power and games: The experimental study of interpersonal relations.* Chicago: AVC.

Tenbrunsel, A. E. (1998). Misrepresentation and expectations of misrepresentation in an ethical dilemma: The role of incentives and temptation. *Academy of Management Journal, 4*(3), 330–339.

Tenbrunsel, A. E. (1999). Trust as an obstacle in environmental-economic disputes. *American Behavioral Scientist, 42,* 1350–1367.

Thomas, K. W. (1992). Conflict and negotiation processes in organizations. In M. D. Dunnette and L. H. Hough, *Handbook of industrial & organizational psychology* (2nd ed., Vol. 3, pp. 651–718). Palo Alto, CA: Consulting Psychologists Press.

Thomas, K. W., & Kilmann, R. H. (1974). *Thomas-Kilmann conflict mode survey.* Tuxedo, NY: Xicom.

Thompson, L. (1990a). An examination of naïve and experienced negotiators. *Journal of Personality and Social Psychology, 59,* 82–90.

Thompson, L. (1990b). Negotiation behavior and outcomes: Empirical evidence and theoretical issues. *Psychological Bulletin, 108,* 515–532.

Thompson, L. (1991). Information exchange in negotiation. *Journal of Experimental Social Psychology, 27,* 161–179.

Thompson, L. (1995). They saw a negotiation: Partnership and involvement. *Journal of Personality and Social Psychology, 68,* 839–853.

Thompson, L. (1998). *The mind and heart of the negotiator.* Upper Saddle River, NJ: Prentice Hall.

Thompson, L., & Hastie, R. (1990a). Social perception in negotiation. *Organizational Behavior and Human Decision Processes, 47,* 98–123.

Thompson, L., & Hastie, R. (1990b). Judgment tasks and biases in negotiation. In B. H. Sheppard, M. H. Bazerman, & R. J. Lewicki (Eds.), *Research on negotiation in organizations* (Vol. 2, pp. 31–54). Greenwich, CT: JAI Press.

Thompson, L., & Hrebec, D. (1996). Lose-lose agreements in interdependent decision making. *Psychological Bulletin, 120,* 396–409.

Thompson, L., & Loewenstein, G. (1992). Egocentric interpretations of fairness and interpersonal conflict. *Organizational Behavior and Human Decision Processes, 51,* 176–197.

Thompson, L., Valley, K. L., & Kramer, R. M. (1995). The bittersweet feeling of success: An examination of social perception in negotiation. *Journal of Experimental Social Psychology, 31,* 467–492.

Thompson, L. L., Nadler, J., & Kim, P. H. (1999). Some like it hot: The case for the emotional negotiator. In L. L. Thompson, J. M. Levine, & D. M. Messick (Eds.), *Shared cognition in organizations: The management of knowledge* (pp. 139–161). Mahwah, NJ: Erlbaum.

Ting-Toomey, S., & Kurogi, A. (1998). Facework competence in intercultural conflict: An updated face-negotiation theory. *International Journal of Intercultural Relations, 22,* 187–225.

Tinsley, C. H. (1998). Models of conflict resolution in Japanese, German, and American cultures. *Journal of Applied Psychology, 83,* 316–323.

Tinsley, C. H. (1997). Understanding conflict in a Chinese cultural context. In R. J. Bies, R. J. Lewicki, & B. H. Sheppard (Eds.), *Research on negotiation in organizations* (Vol. 6: 209–225). Greenwich, CT: JAI Press.

Triandis, H. C. (1982). Review of *Culture's consequences: International differences in work values. Human Organization, 41,* 86–90.

Tse, D. K., Francis, J., & Walls, J. (1994). Cultural differences in conducting intra- and inter-cultural negotiations: A Sino-Canadian comparison. *Journal of International Business Studies, 25,* 537–555.

Tung, R. L. (1991). Handshakes across the sea: Cross-cultural negotiating for business success. *Organizational Dynamics, 19,* Winter. 30–40.

Tutzauer, F. (1991). Bargaining outcome, bargaining process, and the role of communication. *Progress in Communication Science, 10,* 257–300.

Tutzauer, F. (1992). The communication of offers in dyadic bargaining. In L. Putnam & M. Roloff (Eds.), *Communication and negotiation* (pp. 67–82). Newbury Park, CA: Sage.

Tversky, A., & Kahneman, D. (1981). The framing of decisions and the psychology of choice. *Science, 211,* 453–458.

Ury, W. (1991). *Getting past no: Negotiating with difficult people.* New York: Bantam Books.

Ury, W. L., Brett, J. M., & Goldberg, S. B. (1988). *Getting disputes resolved.* San Francisco: Jossey-Bass.

Ury, W. L., Brett, J. M., & Goldberg, S. B. (1993). *Getting disputes resolved.* (2nd ed.). San Francisco: Jossey-Bass.

Valley, K. L., Moag, J., & Bazerman, M. H. (1998). A matter of trust: Effects of communication on the efficiency and distribution of outcomes. *Journal of Economic Behavior and Organization, 34,* 211–238.

van de Vliert, E. (1985). Escalative intervention in small group conflicts. *Journal of Applied Behavioral Science, 21,* 19–36.

Van Zandt, H. F. (1970 November–December). How to negotiate in Japan. *Harvard Business Review, 48*(6), 45–56.

Veitch, R., & Griffith, W. (1976). Good news–bad news: Affective and interpersonal affects. *Journal of Applied Social Psychology, 6,* 69–75.

Vroom, V. H., & Yetton, P. (1973). *Leadership and decision making.* Pittsburgh, PA: University of Pittsburgh Press.

Walcott, C., Hopmann, P. T., & King, T. D. (1977). The role of debate in negotiation. In D. Druckman (Ed.), *Negotiations: Social psychological perspectives* (pp. 193–211). Beverly Hills, CA: Sage.

Walton, R. (1987). *Managing conflict: Interpersonal dialogue and third-party roles* (2nd ed.). Reading, MA: Addison-Wesley.

Walton, R. E., & McKersie, R. B. (1965). *A behavioral theory of labor negotiations: An analysis of a social interaction system.* New York: McGraw-Hill.

Weingart, L. R., Hyder, E. B., & Prietula, M. J. (1996). Knowledge matters: The effect of tactical descriptions on negotiation behavior and outcome. *Journal of Personality and Social Psychology, 70,* 1205–1217.

Weingart, L. R., Prietula, M. J., Hyder, E. B., & Genovese, C. R. (1999). Knowledge and the sequential processes of negotiation: A Markov Chain analysis of response-in-kind. *Journal of Experimental Social Psychology, 35,* 366–393.

Weingart, L. R., Thompson, L. L., Bazerman, M. H., & Carroll, J. S. (1990). Tactical behaviors and negotiation outcomes. *The International Journal of Conflict Management, 1,* 7–31.

Weiss, S. E. (1994). Negotiating with "Romans": A range of culturally-responsive strategies. *Sloan Management Review, 35*(1), 51–61; (2), 1–16.

Weiss, S. E. (1996). International negotiations: Bricks, mortar, and prospects. In B. J. Punnett & O. Shenkar (Eds.), *Handbook for international management research* (pp. 209–265). Cambridge, MA: Blackwell.

Weiss, S. E. (1997). Explaining outcomes of negotiation: Toward a grounded model for negotiations between organizations. In R. J. Lewicki, R. J. Bies, & B. H. Sheppard (Eds.), *Research on negotiation in organizations* (Vol. 6, pp. 247–333). Greenwich, CT: JAI Press.

Weiss, S. E., & Stripp, W. (1985). *Negotiating with foreign business persons: An introduction for Americans with propositions on six cultures.* New York: New York University Graduate School of Business Administration, Working Paper 85–6.

Weldon, E., & Jehn, K. A. (1995). Examining cross-cultural differences in conflict management behavior: A strategy for future research. *The International Journal of Conflict Management, 6,* 387–403.

Werth, L. F., & Flannery, J. (1986). A phenomenological approach to human deception. In R. W. Mitchell & N. S. Thompson (Eds.), *Deception: Perspectives on human and nonhuman deceit* (pp. 293–311). Albany, NY: State University of New York Press.

Whiting, C. S. (1958). *Creative thinking.* New York: Reinhold.

Xing, F. (1995). The Chinese cultural system: Implications for cross-cultural management. *SAM Advanced Management Journal, 60,* 14–20.

Yan, A., & Gray, B. (1994). Bargaining power, management control, and performance in United States-China joint ventures: A comparative case study. *Academy of Management Journal, 37,* 1478–1517.

Yankelovich, D. (1982, August). Lying well is the best revenge. *Psychology Today, 71,* 5–6, 71.

Yook, E. L., & Albert, R. D. (1998). Perceptions of the appropriateness of negotiation in educational settings: A cross-cultural comparison among Koreans and Americans. *Communication Education, 47,* 18–29.

Yukl, G. (1974). Effects of the opponent's initial offer, concession magnitude, and concession frequency on bargaining behavior. *Journal of Personality & Social Psychology, 30,* 323–335.

Zartman, I. W. (1977). Negotiation as a joint decision making process. In I. Zartman (Ed.), *The negotiation process: Theories and applications* (pp. 67–86). Beverly Hills, CA: Sage.

Zartman, I. W. (1997). Conflict and order: Justice in negotiation. *International Political Science Review, 18,* 121–138.

Zartman, I. W., & Berman, M. (1982). *The practical negotiator.* New Haven: Yale University Press.

Index